2,200 Quotations
from the Writings
of Charles H. Spurgeon

Arranged Topically or Textually and
Indexed by Subject, Scripture, and People

COMPILED BY TOM CARTER

Foreword by Jay E. Adams

Baker Books

A Division of Baker Book House Co
Grand Rapids, Michigan 49516

Published by Baker Books
a division of Baker Book House Company
P.O. Box 6287, Grand Rapids, MI 49516-6287

Previously published under the title *Spurgeon at His Best*

Trade paperback edition published 1995

Printed in the United States of America

Library of Congress Cataloging-in-Publication Data

Spurgeon, C. H. (Charles Haddon), 1834–1892
    [Spurgeon at his best]
    2,200 quotations : from the writings of Charles H. Spurgeon : arranged topically or textually and indexed by subject, Scripture, and people / compiled by Tom Carter ; foreword by Jay E. Adams.
        p.   cm.
    Originally puublished : Spurgeon at his best. Grand Rapids, Mich. : Baker Book House, c1988.
    Includes indexes.
    ISBN 0-8010-5365-X (pbk.)
    1. Spurgeon, C. H. (Charles Haddon), 1834–1892—Quotations. 2. Theology—Quotations, maxims, etc. I. Carter, Tom, 1950–
BX6495.S7S68   1995
252'.061—dc20
                                      95-31421

2,200 Quotations

from the Writings
of Charles H. Spurgeon

Contents

Contents

Contents

Foreword

There is reason for all of us to rejoice over the results of Tom Carter's enthusiastic and untiring labor: We now have Spurgeon . . . at his best! Hardly any preacher can afford to be without this volume. It is invaluable in stirring thought and imagination, suggesting ways of presenting biblical truth, and providing material for quotation. Perhaps as important, the book can be read devotionally. The preacher who reads four or five quotations before turning to sermon preparation will find Spurgeon not only a stimulant to work but also a spiritual encouragement.

Spurgeon at His Best is the fruit of Tom Carter's work in the Doctor of Ministry program in preaching here at Westminster Theological Seminary in California. Although this volume was written primarily for preachers, I suspect there will be innumerable lay people who will find it useful and spiritually profitable. We are all better off now that we have easier access to the heart of Spurgeon, and we are all indebted to Tom for making this available. It is my privilege to commend this book to you.

Jay E. Adams
Director of Advanced Studies
Westminster Theological
Seminary in California
Escondido, California
1988

Introduction

"No ministerial success story is more fascinating than that of Charles Haddon Spurgeon." So say Clyde Fant, Jr. and William Pinson, Jr. in their 13-volume series, *20 Centuries of Great Preaching* (Waco, Tex.: Word Publishers, Vol. 6, p. 3). Here was a man who founded and oversaw an orphanage, a Christian magazine, and a pastor's college. But Spurgeon at his best was the preacher.

He was born in Kelvedon, Essex, England, on June 19, 1834, and lived fifty-seven years. By the time he was twenty-one, his sermons were appearing in annual volumes. The volumes were issued for sixty-three years, continuing twenty-six years after his death. In the first six years alone over six million copies of his books were sold. To this day Spurgeon remains history's most widely read preacher (apart from the biblical ones) and most prolific Christian author.

At the age of twenty-seven Spurgeon was preaching to crowds of 6,000 in London's Metropolitan Tabernacle, which his congregation had built to accommodate the ever-increasing crowds. Despite Spurgeon's lack of college education, in that same year over 200,000 copies of his sermon tracts were distributed at the universities of Oxford and Cambridge. The sermons were printed in more than twenty languages, including Russian, Chinese, Japanese, and Arabic. Some copies were also made in braille. American newspapers were printing his sermons in their entirety every week and calling him, "the greatest preacher of the age."

One Saturday night Spurgeon delivered an unprepared sermon in his sleep! His wife woke up, listened attentively, and gave him a full report in the morning. A few hours later he preached that very sermon to his congregation. It is found in *The New Park Street*

1

Pulpit (Pasadena, Tex.: Pilgrim Publications, Vol. 2, pp. 161–168).

Spurgeon's preaching was so popular that he occasionally begged the members of his congregation to stay away from church so that newcomers might hear him. The sermon given on the evening of August 10, 1879, reports that "the regular congregation unanimously left their seats to be occupied by strangers, who crowded the building to its utmost capacity" (*The Metropolitan Tabernacle Pulpit* [Pasadena, Tex.: Pilgrim Publications] Vol. 25, p. 457).

This giant of the pulpit turned down many invitations to preach in other countries, including the United States, Canada, and Australia, "because," he said, "I felt I did not have the Master's permission to leave my post."

Although physical discomfort caused by gout often led him to retreat to the south of France for several months a year, Spurgeon's congregation never grew impatient with him. He and they enjoyed a honeymoon period throughout his pastorate of nearly four decades!

Three days after his death, 60,000 mourners came to view his body as it lay in state in the Metropolitan Tabernacle. The funeral service itself had to be given four times to packed congregations. And several hundred thousand people lined the streets the entire five miles from the church to Norwood Cemetery, where Spurgeon was buried.

Why a Book of Quotations?

Spurgeon's 3,561 sermons make up the most exhaustive sermon series in history. They are bound in 63 volumes totaling about 20 million words and 38,000 pages. And all of it is worth reading! W. Y. Fullerton wrote that "the wise preacher or writer on religious subjects will do well if, after mapping out his own course, he sees 'what Spurgeon has to say about it'" (*Charles H. Spurgeon*, Moody Press, p. 175). But busy pastors and other interested people can seldom spare that kind of time. An attempt to discover what Spurgeon has to say about intercessory prayer or John 3:18, for example, because of time constraints, could be an exercise in frustration.

While this book does not inform the reader of every topic and text Spurgeon spoke on, it does attempt to quote him on a wide variety of subjects. Few people, if any, in the Christian church have been more quoted than Spurgeon. His words have a way of impressing themselves indelibly on the memory.

As a young student at Fuller Theological Seminary, I heard one of my professors, Ralph P. Martin, quote Spurgeon as saying, "Preaching that leaves out the cross is the laughingstock of hell." I found that sentence unforgettable, and I've used it as a plumbline to test my own preaching many times.

When Spurgeon's future wife first heard him preach, she wasn't very impressed. Susannah Thompson was distracted by the teenage preacher's badly trimmed hair and blue polka dot handkerchief. But she couldn't forget his description of the church as "living stones in the Heavenly Temple perfectly joined together with the vermilion cement of Christ's blood" (*Mrs. C. H. Spurgeon*, Pilgrim Publications, p. 10.).

As soon as I began reading Spurgeon's sermons, I almost automatically began quoting him, and I saw his words sink into my listener's hearts like David's stone into Goliath's forehead. My list of quotations quickly exceeded my ability to remember them, so I began to record them on index cards, assigning a heading to each one for easy reference. This is how the book developed.

Spurgeon's Sermon Content

Like the apostle Paul, C. H. Spurgeon preached the whole counsel of God. But in general, two ingredients dominated his sermon content.

The Bible

Spurgeon once challenged the students in his pastor's college to stay in God's Word until their blood became "bibline." He had a right to say that, because his sermons are thoroughly scriptural. Each one has a text, and the message is its exposition. Spurgeon had no doubts about the inspiration and authority of God's Word, as the quotations under **Bible, authority of** and **Bible, inspiration of** will show. He believed a preacher was to be God's mouthpiece, and so Spurgeon's goal was always to let Scripture speak for itself.

For Spurgeon, the Bible was no ancient museum; it was the living Word of God. So far from giving his listeners a guided tour through a dead book, Spurgeon made every part of Scripture speak personally to real people who sat in front of him. And happily, his sermons continue to confront the reader today!

Spurgeon's biblical preaching is doctrinal as well as expositional. His sermons are chockfull of the great themes of the Bible, most notably the doctrines of grace. Although this Prince of Preachers consistently had non-Christians flocking to hear him, he never shrank from proclaiming the themes of election, the sovereignty of God, the total depravity of man, the certainty of judgment, the terrors of hell, the deity of Christ, justification by faith, and atonement through the Savior's blood. He knew these were the truths that God honored for the salvation of souls.

Firmly believing that doctrinal

3

preaching doesn't have to be dry, Spurgeon prepared theological sermons which are at the same time inspirational, devotional, and practical; not ivory tower treatises, but personal messages from the living God through the living Word.

Jesus Christ

The Bible is the foundation of Spurgeon's sermons and the crucified Christ is the superstructure. No matter which text Spurgeon selected, he always made a beeline for the cross. Near the end of his ministry he said, "Oh, that my memorial might be, 'He preached Christ crucified'!"

Especially the entries listed under **Atonement, Blood, Cross, Jesus, Substitution, 1 Corinthians 1:23,** and **1 Corinthians 2:2** reveal what Spurgeon thought of his Lord. Jesus Christ is the melody line which his sermons follow.

Spurgeon recommended Christ to sinners and saints alike. No one had a problem the Master couldn't solve. And the supreme predicament of mankind, Spurgeon was convinced, was sin. Consequently, Spurgeon's greatest joy was to proclaim Christ as our substitute who paid the dreadful price of redemption for us with his blood. This concept, to Spurgeon, was the brain and spinal cord of Christianity, as well as the truth that shook the gates of hell.

Spurgeon's Preaching Style

Spurgeon's preaching style is like an autograph on all his sermons. Several elements are prominent.

Serious Spiritual Warfare

There was no more solemn place in the world than the pulpit for this great man of God. To him, preaching wasn't child's play; it was spiritual warfare against the powers of darkness. In every sermon Spurgeon stood toe to toe with the devil himself. Every convert was a jewel snatched from Satan's crown and presented to the Savior. On several occasions Spurgeon said that his knees knocked together when he mounted his pulpit. His listeners took him seriously because he took his calling seriously. The entries listed under **Pastor, responsibility of; Preacher, responsibility of;** and **Preaching** exemplify his sense of accountability as he gave himself to this most awesome task.

Evangelistic Zeal

The prince of preachers was always eager to win nonbelievers to his Lord. He never overlooked the lost in his messages. He warned them of the wrath of God, the punishment of hell, the terrors of damnation, and the dangers of unbelief. He spoke on these themes as a man who had tasted their realities, and no one dared to doubt him. He said that he didn't know of one sermon he had preached that didn't lead to conversions (see under **Preaching**) and that there was hardly a seat in his vast Tabernacle in which someone hadn't met Christ (see under **Salvation**). As Theodore Cuyler once put it, "Spurgeon sowed the gospel seed with one hand and reaped conversions with the other."

As a preacher Spurgeon was more an evangelist than a pastor. He viewed his task as one of snatching people as brands out of the fire. The entries under **Damnation, Evangelism, Hell,** and **Unbelief** especially reveal his heart on this subject.

Even when he preached to the saved, Spurgeon couldn't close without addressing the lost. He once spoke on Romans 8:31, "If God is for us, who is against us?" in which he proved from several points of view that God was the believer's advocate. But at the end of that sermon he posed the question to the nonbeliever, 'If God is *against* you, who can be *for* you?" It's typical of the way Spurgeon wouldn't allow himself to conclude a sermon without a loving yet solemn warning to the nonbeliever. The entry under **Romans 8:31** tells the reader how he put it on this occasion.

Compassion

Words like *Alas! Oh!* and *Ah!* frequently appear in these sermons. And they were no mere rhetorical devices. Such exclamations jumped straight out of Spurgeon's heart. It made the hair on the back of his neck stand on end to think that some of his hearers were perishing, and he frankly told them so. He threw dignity to the winds as he drenched his pulpit with tears and begged his listeners to be saved. On one occasion (see **Hebrews 10:31**) he lamented that his eyes could shed only tears and not blood in front of his listeners. Even in his printed sermons his impassioned pleas stir the reader's soul. One has to wonder how much of an impact his live preaching must have made on his congregation. The quotations under **Compassion, Damnation,** and **Lost** speak for themselves.

Conviction

When Spurgeon preached, hearts broke. Even the proud, the self-righteous, and hardened rebels couldn't resist coming to hear him preach. And then it wasn't long before many of them surrendered to his Lord.

One afternoon Spurgeon went to test the acoustics in the Crystal Palace, where he was to preach the next day. He thundered forth the words of John 1:29, "Behold the Lamb of God, which taketh away the sin of the world." Little did he realize that a custodian up in one of the balconies heard those words as a voice from heaven. He came under such conviction that he had to leave his work and get alone with God. After a brief season of spiritual struggling, he found peace and life by beholding the Lamb of God (*C. H. Spurgeon Autobiography*, The Banner of Truth Trust, Vol. 1, p. 534).

And now in print, Spurgeon still convicts the reader's heart. The quotations under **Conscience, Conviction,** and **Guilt** tell of his own sense of conviction before surrendering to Christ, as well as his power to bring others under the burden of sin.

Authority

There was no uncertain sound when Spurgeon spoke. He knew what he believed, and he preached it without apology. He was aware that others disagreed with him on points of doctrine. But still he never flinched.

He was an unashamed Calvinist who often spoke disparagingly of people who held to Arminian theology, as the quotations under **Arminianism** and **Calvinism** prove. But Spurgeon didn't follow Calvin blindly, either. He refused to accept the Reformer's teachings of infant baptism and God's election of the lost to damnation. But in the main, Spurgeon loved Calvin and his theology.

Spurgeon also knew how to love Arminians, despite his persuasion that their theology was faulty. One of his heroes was John Wesley, a leading proponent of Arminianism. Wesley's love for Christ and the lost bound him indissolubly with Spurgeon.

Boldness

Spurgeon possessed the boldness of John the Baptist. Unlike most preachers today, he normally used the second person pronoun rather than the first. Instead of saying, "In light of this truth, *we* need to repent," he'd say, " . . . *you* need to repent!" This wasn't arrogance on his part. It was merely a manifestation of Spurgeon's view of his craft, in which the preacher is called to be a spokesman *for* God *to* his people.

"Young man," he said one Sunday evening, pointing to the gallery, "the gloves you have in your pocket are not paid for." After the service the young man came and pleaded with him not to say anything more about it, and Spurgeon led him to Christ.

On another occasion Spurgeon accused his congregation of indifference toward Scripture. He said there was just enough dust on the cover of their Bibles to spell out "Damnation" with their fingers. This quote is found under **Bible, neglect of.**

After he spoke boldly against **Slavery** during the American Civil War, many newspapers there threatened to stop publishing his sermons. But Spurgeon refused to be intimidated. He said in a letter to a prominent American newspaper editor, "I believe slavery to be a crime of crimes, a soul-destroying sin, and an iniquity which cries aloud for vengeance. I would as soon think of receiving a murderer into church membership as a man-stealer."

Personal Application

This genius of the pulpit knew how to drive truth home to the listener's life. Whether he was preaching about a traitorous Judas, a self-righteous Pharisee, or a hard-hearted pharaoh, Spurgeon never settled for a mere study of their lives. He would typically ask, "Are *you* a Judas? Is there self-righteousness in *your* life? Have you been hardening *your* heart against the Lord God?" Or if he was preaching on faith, he'd ask, "In what are *you* trusting?"

Often Spurgeon's final point in his outline was the application of his text, and at times he announced at the beginning of his sermon that he was going to devote the entire message to personal lessons from a passage.

Simplicity

Spurgeon disdained the use of contrivance, artificiality, and formality in preaching. He avoided technical terms and always spoke in the language of the working man. Even children heard him gladly. He had a way of making profound truths simple. P. F. Barackman's description of the Gospel of John might be applied to a volume of Spurgeon's sermons: "It is a book in which a child can wade and an elephant can swim." The sermons at the same time strike readers with their profundity and kiss them with their simplicity.

Vivid Language

Though he spoke in simple terms, Spurgeon never droned. The quotations on the following pages illustrate his use of similes, metaphors, active verbs, hyperbole, and figures of speech. His creative imagination communicated a world of pictures to his listeners. His vivid language made his preaching unforgettable. The reader of his sermons can taste, smell, hear, see, and feel his captivating phrases. Jay Adams's book, *Sense Appeal in the Sermons of Charles Haddon Spurgeon* (Baker Book House), is an interesting study along this line.

Editorial Revisions

The most difficult decision concerning this anthology of quotations was whether or not I should edit Spurgeon's Victorian English. Far be it from me to tamper with this preacher's brilliance! Nor have I any intention of reinterpreting his ideas or paraphrasing his thoughts!

But neither do I wish to see newcomers to Spurgeon stumble over archaic words, such as *methinks, peradventure, vouchsafe,* and *fain*. And modern readers can get bogged down by his often lengthy sentences and paragraphs. Sadly, some people to whom I've recommended Spurgeon have given up in frustration before they've scarcely begun to read. And so I have decided to edit the quotations. Rest assured that the utmost care has been taken to allow the reader to hear Spurgeon's voice, not the editor's.

How to Use This Book

The first half of the book contains quotations listed by topics. Many of these contain cross references to related subjects.

A scriptural section of quotations follows the topical one. These quotations lend themselves more to specific Bible verses than to topics. In this part of the book you will learn what Spurgeon has to say about many different passages in the Bible.

Topical, scriptural, and name indexes will aid you in locating subjects, verses, and people easily.

A preacher who needs an illustration or quotation on the depravity of man, for example, will find Spurgeon's teaching on it under the heading, **Depravity.** There are also cross references to the related topics of **Calvinism; Carnality; Heart; Nature, human;** and **Sin;** all of which will provide additional insights into Spurgeon's view of depravity.

Or, a student wishing to write a paper on "Spurgeon's Prayer Life" will discover more than one-hundred treasures under **Prayer,** its thirteen subheadings, and the many cross references to **Prayer** and its subheadings.

This book may also be used for private devotional reading, study in doctrine and Scripture, inspiration for preaching, authoritative quotations for speeches, or to discover what Spurgeon believed about a particular subject or verse in the Bible.

The number at the end of the quotation indicates the source (e.g. 43.323) The number before the period refers to the volume number of Spurgeon's original sermon series. The number after the period gives the page number. In the example above, the quotation will be found in Volume 43, page 323.

There are sixty-three volumes of sermons, corresponding to the years 1855 through 1917, respectively. All the quotations in this book were collected from those volumes. Volumes 1 through 6 were published as the *New Park Street Pulpit,* named after Spurgeon's church at the time. Volumes 7 through 63 were published as the *Metropolitan Tabernacle Pulpit,* named after the 6,000-seat church that was built to accommodate the crowds that flocked to hear Spurgeon preach. It should be pointed out that the New Park Street Chapel and the Metropolitan Tabernacle were only different *buildings.* They belonged to the same congregation.

Volumes 1 through 37 contain the sermons published during Spurgeon's lifetime. Volumes 38 through 63 were issued after the preacher's death and contain sermons which until that time had not been published.

These are the sermon volumes and the year of their release.

Volume Number	Year Published	Volume Number	Year Published	Volume Number	Year Published
1	1855	22	1876	43	1897
2	1856	23	1877	44	1898
3	1857	24	1878	45	1899
4	1858	25	1879	46	1900
5	1859	26	1880	47	1901
6	1860	27	1881	48	1902
7	1861	28	1882	49	1903
8	1862	29	1883	50	1904
9	1863	30	1884	51	1905
10	1864	31	1885	52	1906
11	1865	32	1886	53	1907
12	1866	33	1887	54	1908
13	1867	34	1888	55	1909
14	1868	35	1889	56	1910
15	1869	36	1890	57	1911
16	1870	37	1891	58	1912
17	1871	38	1892	59	1913
18	1872	39	1893	60	1914
19	1873	40	1894	61	1915
20	1874	41	1895	62	1916
21	1875	42	1896	63	1917

These volumes were originally published by Passmore and Alabaster in London. Pilgrim Publications, Box 66, Pasadena, Texas 77501 has now reprinted them in their original form. The entire set is available through local Christian bookstores or directly from Pilgrim Publications.

On the following pages discover Spurgeon at his best, striking quotations of perhaps the finest preacher since apostolic times. I invite you to catch his spirit! Here are over 2,200 examples of his arresting statements, sermon illustrations, autobiographical material, personal anecdotes, humor, wisdom, beliefs, and scriptural insights. May you derive as much spiritual profit from studying them as I have from finding and compiling them.

Tom Carter
Dinuba, California

9

Quotations Arranged by Subject

Adultery   *See Fornication; Sex, abuse of*

Affliction   *See Suffering; Trials; Trouble*

[1] I bear my witness that the worst days I have ever had have turned out to be my best days. And when God has seemed most cruel to me, he has then been most kind. If there is anything in this world for which I would bless him more than for anything else, it is for pain and affliction. I am sure that in these things the richest, tenderest love has been manifested to me. Our Father's wagons rumble most heavily when they are bringing us the richest freight of the bullion of his grace. Love letters from heaven are often sent in black-edged envelopes. The cloud that is black with horror is big with mercy. Fear not the storm. It brings healing in its wings, and when Jesus is with you in the vessel, the tempest only hastens the ship to its desired haven.—27.373

[2] The affliction of today may have no reference to the circumstances of today, but to the circumstances of fifty years ahead. I do not know that that blade required the rain on such a day, but God was looking not to February as such, but to February in its relation to July, when the harvest should be reaped.—59.402

Age, old

[3] I remember the venerable Mr. Jay, when preaching, reaching out his hand to an old man who sat just as some of you are sitting there, and saying, "I wonder whether those gray hairs are a crown of glory or a fool's cap. They are one or the other." For a man to be unconverted at the age to which some of you have attained is indeed to have a fool's cap made of gray hairs. But if you have a heart consecrated to Christ, you have a crown of glory upon your brow.—3.428

Agnostic   *See Atheist; Doubt; Faith; Unbelief*

⁴ One walking with me observed, with some emphasis, "I do not believe as you do. I am an agnostic."

"Oh," I said to him, "that is a Greek word, is it not? The Latin word, I think, is *Ignoramus.*"

He did not like it at all. Yet I only translated his language from Greek to Latin. These are queer waters to get into, when all your philosophy brings you is the confession that you know nothing, and the stupidity which enables you to glory in your ignorance.—32.670

⁵ I could not bear to be an "ignoramus" or an "agnostic" about God! I must have a God! I cannot do without him.—38.242

Ambition

⁶ We do not serve our Master perfectly, but we would if we could. There are some of his commandments which we forget, but there are none which we would despise. We do, through infirmity, turn aside to crooked ways, but we find no comfort in them. Our meat and our drink is to do the will of him who sent us.—10.207

Angels

⁷ It is superstitious to worship angels; it is proper to love them. How free from envy the angels were! Christ did not come from heaven to save their peers when they fell. When Satan, the mighty angel, dragged with him a third part of the stars of heaven, Christ did not stoop from his throne to die for them. He left them to be reserved in chains and darkness until the last great day. Yet angels did not envy men. How free, too, they were from pride! They were not ashamed to come and tell the news of Christ's birth to humble shepherds. Mark how well they told the story, and you will love them.—4.25

Anger   *See Wrath, God's*

⁸ Anger is temporary insanity.—1.160

⁹ I have no more right as a Christian to allow a bad temper to dwell in me than I have to allow the devil himself to dwell there.—12.62

¹⁰ Oh, the hard, cruel thoughts which men have toward one another when they are angry! They kill and slay a thousand times over. These hasty sins are soon forgotten by us, but they are not forgotten by God.—12.544

¹¹ Do you ask, "How can a man master his temper?"

How can a man go to heaven if he does not? If the grace of God does not change us and help us to bridle that lion that is within us, what has it done for us? Only in salvation from sin is there salvation from wrath.—15.639

¹² Do not say, "I cannot help having a bad temper." Friend, you must help it. Pray to God to help you overcome it at once, for either you must kill it, or it will kill you. You cannot carry a bad temper into heaven.—35.562

¹³ One said in my hearing, as an excuse for a passionate speech, "I could not help it. If you tread on a worm, it will turn."
Is a worm to be the example for a saint?—37.102

¹⁴ I heard someone say that he was sorry he had lost his temper. I was uncommonly glad to hear that he had lost it, but I regretted that he found it again so soon.—41.212

¹⁵ When I hear of anybody losing his temper, I always pray that he may not find it again. Such tempers are best lost.—53.545

¹⁶ I believe that if you who are subject to a bad temper will lay this besetting sin before God in prayer and ask the Holy Spirit's help, you shall not only be able to curb it, but you will also acquire a sweeter and gentler spirit than some of those whose temperament is naturally even, with no propensity to fitful change or sudden storm. Do not tell me that there is anything in human nature too obdurate for the Lord to overcome, for there is not.—62.226

Anxiety   *See Worry*

Apologetics

¹⁷ I question whether the defenses of the gospel are not sheer impertinences. The gospel does not need defending. If Jesus Christ is not alive and cannot fight his own battles, then Christianity is in a bad state. But he is alive, and we have only to preach his gospel in all its naked simplicity, and the power that goes with it will be the evidence of its divinity.—19.214, 215

¹⁸ Suppose a number of persons were to take it into their heads that they had to defend a lion. There he is in the cage, and here come all the soldiers of the army to fight for him. Well, I should suggest to them that they should kindly stand back, open the door, and let the lion out! I believe that would be the best way of defending him. And the best "apology" for the gospel is to let the gospel out. Never mind defending Deuteronomy or the whole of the Pentateuch. Preach Jesus Christ and him crucified. The Lion of the tribe of Judah will soon drive away all his adversaries. This was how Christ's first disciples worked. They preached Jesus Christ wherever they went. They did not stop to apologize, but boldly bore their witness concerning him.—42.256

Apostasy   *See Backsliding*

¹⁹ If I must be lost, let it be any way rather than as an apostate. If there be any distinction among the damned, those have it who are wandering stars, for whom Jude (13) tells us, is "reserved the blackness of darkness for ever." Reserved! As if nobody else were qualified to occupy that place but themselves. They are to inhabit the darkest, hottest place, because they forsook the Lord. Let us then rather lose everything than lose Christ.—10.11

²⁰ I would choose to be cut limb from limb sooner than see those whom I have loved and honored fall from the faith. It is a bitter thing to us who are ministers of Christ, it is our curse and plague, it costs us sleepless nights and miserable days when we hear of those that did run well apparently who turn back to the world, who play the Judas.—12.595

²¹ There could not have been a Judas to betray Christ had he not been first distinguished as a disciple who ventured to kiss his Master. You must pick from among the apostles to find an apostate.—50.610

Arminianism   *See Calvinism*

²² I believe that very much of current Arminianism is simply ignorance of gospel doctrine. If people began to study their Bibles and to take the Word of God as they find it, they must inevitably, if believers, rise up to rejoice in the doctrines of grace.—11.29

²³ When a Calvinist says that all things happen according to the predestination of God, he speaks the truth, and I am willing to be called a Calvinist. But when an Arminian says that when a man sins, the sin is his own, and that if he continues in sin, and perishes, his eternal damnation will lie entirely at his own door, I believe that he also speaks the truth, though I am not willing to be called an Arminian. The fact is, there is some truth in both these systems of theology.—49.602, 603

Assurance   *See Doubt; Security*

²⁴ A person comes before the pastor and says, "I am so afraid I am not converted. I tremble lest I should not be a child of God." The pastor will put out his hands to him and say, "Dear brother, you are all right so long as you can doubt."

I hold that that is altogether wrong. Scripture never says, "He that doubteth shall be saved," but "He that believeth." It may be true that the man is in a good state. But his doubts are not good things, nor ought we to encourage him in his doubts. Our business is to encourage him out of his doubts.—3.132

²⁵ Assurance is a jewel for worth but not for rarity.—9.212

26 If you believe in Jesus Christ and are damned, I will be damned with you.—22.537

27 If any man is not sure that he is in Christ, he ought not to be easy one moment until he is sure. Dear friend, without the fullest confidence as to your saved condition, you have no right to be at ease, and I pray you may never be so. This is a matter too important to be left undecided.—24.206

28 We count it no presumption to say that we are saved, for the Word of God has told us so in those places where salvation is promised to faith in Christ. The presumption would lie in doubting the Word of God. But in simply believing what he says there is far greater humility than in questioning it.—27.196

29 The teachers of doubt are very doubtful teachers. A man must have something to hold to, or he will neither bless himself nor others.—29.57

30 Full assurance is not essential to salvation, but it is essential to satisfaction. May you get it—may you get it at once. May you never be satisfied to live without it.—34.266

31 If you do not know that you are saved, how dare you go to sleep tonight! How should a man dare to eat his meals and go about his business, yet say, "I do not know whether I am saved or not"? You may know it, and you ought to know it.—37.24

32 "But," says a friend, "if I believed that I was really saved, I should say, 'Now I may live as I like.' "
Ah, do you know how I would live if I could live as I liked? I would never sin again. If I could live as I liked, you should be able to call me a strait-laced old Puritan, with whom you could not find a fault. But if you, as an unconverted man, live as you like, I should not like to read the record of your life.—47.490

33 I heard of a man who I was told had walked in holiness for many years, yet he had never uttered an expression which could lead anyone to think that he really believed himself to be saved. As I listened to the story, I could not help asking, "How long has he lived in this state?"
"Forty years," was the answer.
"Well then," I replied, "he has been living for forty years in grievous sin, for there is no sin which so dishonors God as does the sin of unbelief."—54.40

34 We prize full assurance beyond all price. We count it to be a gem beyond all earthly values. But we think it is a distressing doctrine to some of the weak ones of the flock to say that full assurance is necessary to salvation. We believe it to be necessary to deep joy, necessary to edifica-

tion, necessary to usefulness, but necessary to salvation we do not believe it to be.—59.590

Atheist   *See Agnostic; Doubt; Unbelief*

35 There are no infidels anywhere but on earth. There are none in heaven, and there are none in hell. Atheism is a strange thing. Even the devils never fell into that vice, for "the devils also believe and tremble" (James 2:19). And there are some of the devil's children that have gone beyond their father in sin. But when God's foot crushes them, they will not be able to doubt his existence. When he tears them in pieces and there is none to deliver, then their empty logic and their bravadoes will be of no avail.—11.731

Atonement   *See Blood, Christ's; Cross; Death, Christ's; Substitution; Suffering, Jesus'*

36 The heart of Christ became like a reservoir in the midst of the mountains. All the tributary streams of iniquity, and every drop of the sins of his people, ran down and gathered into one vast lake, deep as hell and shoreless as eternity. All these met, as it were, in Christ's heart, and he endured them all.—5.271

37 Unbeliever, if God cannot and will not forgive the sins of penitent men without Christ taking their punishment, rest assured he will surely bring you to judgment. If, when Christ had imputed sin laid on him, God smote him, how will he smite you who are his enemy, and who have your own sins upon your head? God seemed at Calvary to take an oath and say, "By the blood of my Son I swear that sin must be punished!" If it is not punished in Christ for you, it will be punished in you for yourselves.—8.239

38 Atonement is the brain and spinal cord of Christianity. Take away the cleansing blood, and what is left to the guilty? Deny the substitutionary work of Jesus, and you have denied all that is precious in the New Testament. Never, never let us endure one wavering, doubtful thought about this all-important truth.—13.449

39 I believe that if I should preach to you the atonement of our Lord Jesus, and nothing else, twice every Sabbath day, my ministry would not be unprofitable. Perhaps it might be more profitable than it is.—18.73, 74

40 The great saving truth is the doctrine of atonement by substitution. Without it ministers will keep souls in bondage year after year, because they do not proclaim the finished redemption, nor let men know that sin was laid on Jesus that it might be forever removed from the believer.—20.642

41 To deny the great doctrine of atonement by the blood of Jesus

Christ is to hamstring the gospel, and to cut the throat of Christianity.—27.538

⁴² The heart of the gospel is redemption, and the essence of redemption is the substitutionary sacrifice of Christ. They who preach this truth preach the gospel, however else they may be mistaken. But they who preach not atonement, whatever else they declare, have missed the soul and substance of the divine message.—32.385

⁴³ I can truly declare among you that I do not preach this doctrine of vicarious sacrifice as one among many theories, but as the saving fact of my experience. I must preach this or nothing else.—33.569

⁴⁴ I do not think a man ought to hear a minister preach three sermons without learning the doctrine of atonement.—33.581

⁴⁵ If our Lord's bearing our sin for us is not the gospel, I have no gospel to preach. Brethren, I have befooled you these thirty-five years if this is not the gospel. I am a lost man, if this is not the gospel, for I have no hope beneath the canopy of heaven, neither in time nor in eternity, save only in this belief—that Jesus Christ, in my place, bore both my punishment and sin.—35.92

⁴⁶ The marvel of heaven and earth, of time and eternity, is the atoning death of Jesus Christ. This is the mystery that brings more glory to God than all creation.—35.467

⁴⁷ If you do not believe in the power of the atoning blood, never go and see believers die, for you will find that they trust in nothing else. A dying Christ is the last resort of the believer.—37.43

⁴⁸ The chief aim of the enemy's assaults is to get rid of Christ, to get rid of the atonement, to get rid of his suffering in the place of men. Some say they can embrace the rest of the gospel. But what "rest" is there? What is there left? A bloodless, Christless gospel is fit neither for the land nor for the dunghill. It neither honors God nor converts men.—40.315

⁴⁹ If the atoning sufferings of Christ are left out of a ministry, that ministry is worthless. "The blood is the life thereof" (Lev. 17:14) is as true about sermons as it is about animals and sacrifices. A bloodless gospel, a gospel without the atonement, is a gospel of devils.—45.89

⁵⁰ May this house be utterly consumed with fire before the day should come when here there should be given an uncertain sound about the atonement. This is not merely *a* doctrine of the church. It is *the* doctrine of the church. Leave this out, and you have no truth, no Savior, no church. As Luther said of the

doctrine of justification by faith, that it was the article of a standing or falling church, so we affirm of the atonement, the substitutionary sacrifice of Christ for the sins of men.—61.455

Atonement, definite   *See Atonement, limited*

Atonement, limited   *See Calvinism*

[51] I would rather believe a limited atonement that is efficacious for all men for whom it was intended, than a universal atonement that is not efficacious for anybody, except the will of men be joined with it.—4.70

[52] If it were Christ's intention to save all men, how deplorably has he been disappointed!—4.316

[53] Some insist that Christ died for everybody. Why, then, are not all men saved? Because all men will not believe? That is to say that believing is necessary in order to make the blood of Christ efficacious for redemption. We hold that to be a great lie.

We believe the very contrary, that faith does not give efficacy to the blood, but is only the proof that the blood has redeemed that man. We hold that Christ only redeemed those men who will ultimately attain unto eternal life. We do not believe that he redeemed the damned. We do not believe that he poured out his life blood for souls already in hell. We never can imagine that Christ suffered in the stead of all men, and that afterwards these same men have to suffer for themselves, that in fact Christ pays their debts, and then God makes them pay their debts over again. We think that the doctrine that men by their wills give efficacy to the blood of Christ is derogatory to the Lord Jesus. We rather hold that he laid down his life for his sheep, and that this secured the salvation of every one of them. We believe this because "of him, and through him, and to him, are all things" (Rom. 11:36).—10.309

[54] Some say that all men are Christ's by purchase. But, beloved, you and I do not believe in a sham redemption which does not redeem. We do not believe in a universal redemption which extends even to those who were in hell before the Savior died, and which includes the fallen angels as well as unrepentant men. We believe in an effectual redemption, and can never agree with those who would teach us that Christ's blood was shed in vain.—48.303

[55] A redemption which pays a price, but does not ensure that which is purchased—a redemption which calls Christ a substitute for the sinner, but yet which allows the person to suffer—is altogether unworthy of our apprehensions of Almighty God. It offers no homage to his wisdom, and does despite to his covenant

faithfulness. We could not and would not receive such a travesty of divine truth as that would be. There is no ground for any comfort whatever in it.—49.39

Backsliding   *See Apostasy*

⁵⁶ Christian, what do you have to do with sin? Has it not cost you enough already? What, man! Have you forgotten the times of your conviction? If you have, *I have not!* Burnt child, will you play with the fire? What! When you have already been rent in pieces by the lion, will you step a second time into his den? Have you not had enough of the old serpent? Did he not poison all your veins once?—7.67

⁵⁷ So mature a servant of the devil as Judas is not purchased all at once. It takes time to educate a man for the scorner's seat. If you begin to slip on the side of a mountain of ice, the first slip may not hurt if you can stop and slide no further. But alas, you cannot so regulate sin! When your feet begin to slide, the rate of the descent increases, and the difficulty of arresting this motion is incessantly becoming greater. It is dangerous to backslide in any degree, for we know not to what it may lead.—16.150

⁵⁸ The falls are mostly of middle-aged or elderly people. We have hardly in Scripture an instance of any young professor that turned aside. The reason is, I think, because when we are weak, then are we strong; and when we conceive ourselves to be strong, we become weak.—20.525

⁵⁹ The Christian life is very much like climbing a hill of ice. You cannot slide up. You have to cut every step with an ice ax. Only with incessant labor in cutting and chipping can you make any progress. If you want to know how to backslide, leave off going forward. Cease going upward and you will go downward of necessity. You can never stand still.—21.292

⁶⁰ Remember that if you are a child of God, you will never be happy in sin. You are spoiled for the world, the flesh, and the devil. When you were regenerated there was put into you a vital principle, which can never be content to dwell in the dead world. You will have to come back, if indeed you belong to the family.—32.671, 672

Baptism   *See Ordinance*

⁶¹ I should think it a high sin and treason against heaven, if, believing that baptism signifies immersion only, I should pretend to administer it by sprinkling. Or, believing that baptism pertains to believers only, I should consider myself a criminal in the sight of God if I should give it to any but those who believe.—4.170

⁶² We think it to be a sweet sign of a humble and broken heart

when the child of God is willing to obey a command which is not essential to his salvation. It is no mean sign of grace when the young convert yields himself to be baptized.—9.690

63 A man who knows that he is saved by believing in Christ does not, when he is baptized, lift his baptism into a saving ordinance. In fact, he is the very best protester against that mistake, because he holds that he has no right to be baptized until he is saved.—10.326

Note: This quotation comes from CHS's most widely read sermon, Baptismal Regeneration, *which sold over 250,000 copies in tract form. The debate over the place of baptism in salvation was one of the two biggest controversies of his life, along with the Downgrade Controversy.*

64 Do not imagine that immersion in water can wash away sin. But do remember that if the Lord puts this outward profession side by side with the washing away of sins, it is no trifling matter.—31.251

65 Someone says, "I can be saved without being baptized."

So you will do nothing that Christ commands, if you can be saved without doing it? You are hardly worth saving at all! A man whose one idea of religion is that he will do what is essential to his own salvation, only cares to save his own skin. Clearly, you are no servant of Christ's. Baptism, if not essential to your salvation, is essential to your obedience to Christ.—39.607, 608

66 There is a distinct blessing in the observance of the ordinance. It was so in my case. Up to that time I was afraid to confess Christ. But after I was publicly baptized into his death, I lost all fear of man, and I have never been ashamed to own my Lord from that day to this. That coming out boldly for Christ was like crossing the Rubicon or burning the boats. No retreat was possible after that, nor have I ever wanted to go back to the world from which I then came out.—47.268

67 Nothing is more plainly taught in the New Testament than that it is the duty of every believer in Christ to be baptized.—54.68

68 I once met a man who had been 40 years a Christian and believed it to be his duty to be baptized. But when I spoke to him about it, he said, "He that believeth shall not make haste" (Isa. 28:16).

I quoted to him another passage: "I made haste, and delayed not to keep thy commandments" (Ps. 119:60), and showed him what the meaning of his misapplied passage was.—56.333

69 I think I could as soon doubt that the deity of Christ is declared

as doubt that the baptism of believers is enjoined, for the one thing appears to me to be as plainly revealed in Scripture as the other.—62.489

Baptism, infant   *See Children, dedication of*

70 When Jesus said, "Suffer the little children to come unto me" (Mark 10:14), they did come to him. But I do not find that he baptized or sprinkled them at all. He gave them his blessing and they went away. I am sure he did not baptize them, for it is expressly said, "Jesus Christ baptized not, but his disciples" (John 4:2).

I am informed, however, that the reason why children are baptized is that we are told in the Bible that Abraham's children were circumcised. But why were they circumcised? Because they were Israelites. I would not hesitate to baptize any Christian, though he be a babe in Christ, as soon as he knows the Lord Jesus.—5.111

71 As long as you give baptism to an unregenerate child, people will imagine that it must do the child good. They will ask, "If it does not do the child any good, why is it baptized?" The statement that it puts children into the covenant, or renders them members of the visible church, is only a veiled form of the fundamental error of Baptismal Regeneration. If you keep up the ordinance, you will always have men superstitiously believing that some good comes to the babe thereby. And what is that but Popery?—19.556

72 I am amazed that an unconscious babe should be made the partaker of an ordinance which, according to the plain teaching of the Scriptures, requires the conscious and complete heart-trust of the recipient. Very few, if any, would argue that infants ought to receive the Lord's Supper. But there is no more scriptural warrant for bringing them to the one ordinance than there is for bringing them to the other.—47.351

Bible   *See Gospel; Preaching, expository; Revelation, modern*

73 Martin Luther said, "I have covenanted with my Lord that he should not send me visions or dreams or even angels. I am content with this gift of the Scriptures, which teaches and supplies all that is necessary, both for this life and that which is to come."—10.536

74 The words of Scripture thrill my soul as nothing else ever can. They bear me aloft or dash me down. They tear me in pieces or build me up. The words of God have more power over me than ever David's fingers had over his harp strings. Is it not so with you?—24.487

75 If you wish to know God, you must know his Word. If you wish

to perceive his power, you must see how he works by his Word. If you wish to know his purpose before it comes to pass, you can only discover it by his Word.—27.377

76 I hold one single sentence out of God's Word to be of more certainty and of more power than all the discoveries of all the learned men of all the ages.—30.680

77 I would rather speak five words out of this book than 50,000 words of the philosophers. If we want revivals, we must revive our reverence for the Word of God. If we want conversions, we must put more of God's Word into our sermons.—38.114

78 God's Word is like the wheat in the hand of the mummy, of which you have often heard. It had lain there for thousands of years, but men took it out of the hand and sowed it, and the bearded wheat, which has now become so common in our land, sprang up. So you take a divine promise, spoken thousands of years ago, and lo, it is fulfilled to you! It becomes as true to you as if God had spoken it for the first time this very day, and you were the person to whom it was addressed.—39.74

79 Be walking Bibles.—43.507

80 Remember that our Bible is a blood-stained book. The blood of martyrs is on the Bible, the blood of translators and confessors. The doctrines which we preach to you are doctrines that have been baptized in blood—swords have been drawn to slay the confessors of them. And there is not a truth which has not been sealed by them at the stake or the block, where they have been slain by hundreds.—54.248, 249

81 If the whole of us went to prison and to death for the preservation of a single sentence of Scripture, we should be fully satisfied in making such a sacrifice.—57.208

82 Precious book! I would say of you what David said of Goliath's sword: "There is none like that; give it me" (1 Sam. 21:9). You are marrow and fatness, honey and wine. Yes, manna of angels and water from the Rock, Christ Jesus. Of all soul medicines you are the most potent. Of all mental dainties you are the sweetest. And of all spiritual food you are the most sustaining.—58.242

Bible, authority of

83 Never be afraid of your Bibles. If there is a text of Scripture you dare not meet, humble yourself till you can. If your creed and Scripture do not agree, cut your creed to pieces, but make it agree with this book. If there be anything in the church to which you belong which is contrary to the inspired Word, leave that church.—20.335

[84] Have you never noticed that some people who are ill and are ordered to take pills are foolish enough to chew them? That is a very nauseous thing to do, though I have done it myself. The right way to take medicine of such a kind is to swallow it at once. In the same way there are some things in the Word of God which are undoubtedly true which must be swallowed at once by an effort of faith, and must not be chewed by perpetual questioning. Let the difficult doctrines go down whole into your very soul by a grand exercise of confidence in God.—26.51

Bible, criticism of

[85] He that reads his Bible to find fault with it will soon discover that the Bible finds fault with him.—36.88

Bible, defense of   *See Apologetics*

Bible, difficulties in

[86] I view the difficulties of Holy Scripture as so many prayer stools upon which I kneel and worship the glorious Lord. What we cannot comprehend by our understandings we apprehend by our affections. Awe of God's Word is a main element in that love of God's law which brings great peace.—34.40

Bible, inspiration of

[87] Let those give up the inspiration of the Bible who can afford to do so, but you and I cannot. Let those cast away the sure promise of God who have got something else to comfort them, who can go to their philosophy or turn to their self-conceit. But as for you and for me, it is a desperate matter for us if this book be not true. And therefore let us be ready to defend it at all hazards, and if need be to die for it. Oh, brethren, it were better to die, that book being true, than to live, that book being false.—12.278

[88] If we are left in doubt as to which part is inspired and which is not, we are as badly off as if we had no Bible at all. I hold no theory of inspiration; I accept the inspiration of the Scriptures as a fact.—34.152

[89] If I did not believe in the infallibility of this book, I would rather be without it. If I am to judge the book, it is no judge of me. If I am to sift it, and lay *this* aside and only accept *that*, according to my own judgment, then I have no guidance whatever, unless I have conceit enough to trust my own heart. The new theory denies infallibility to the words of God, but practically imputes it to the judgments of men. At least, this is all the infallibility which they can get at. I protest that I will rather risk my soul with a guide inspired from heaven, than with the differing leaders who arise from the earth at the call of "modern thought."—35.257

90 The Bible must have been written by our Creator, for nobody but the Lord who created men could know so much about them. This volume reveals the secrets of all hearts. It unveils our private thoughts.—35.494

91 If I did not believe in the infallibility of Scripture—the absolute infallibility of it from cover to cover, I would never enter this pulpit again!—36.9

92 Everything in the railway service depends upon the accuracy of the signals. When these are wrong, life will be sacrificed. On the road to heaven we need unerring signals, or the catastrophes will be far more terrible. It is difficult enough to set myself right and carefully drive the train of conduct. But if, in addition to this, I am to set the Bible right, and thus manage the signals along the permanent way, I am in an evil plight indeed.—36.167

93 We will not have it that God, in his holy book, makes mistakes about matters of history or of science, any more than he does upon the great truths of salvation. If the Lord be God, he must be infallible. And if he can be described as in error in the little respects of human history and science, he cannot be trusted in the greater matters.—37.159, 160

94 Men talk of "the mistakes of Scripture." I thank God that I have never met with any. Mistakes of translation there may be, for translators are men. But mistakes of the original word there never can be, for the God who spoke it is infallible, and so is every word he speaks, and in that confidence we find delightful rest.—39.195, 196

95 I am prepared to believe whatever it says, and to take it believing it to be the Word of God. For if it is not all true, it is not worth one solitary penny to me.—39.475

96 We believe in plenary, verbal inspiration, with all its difficulties, for there are not half as many difficulties in that doctrine as there are in any other kind of inspiration that men may imagine.—45.21

97 The Bible is a harbor where I can drop down my anchor, feeling certain that it will hold. Here is a place where I can find sure footing; and, by the grace of God, from this confidence I shall never be moved.—45.39

98 Scripture never errs.—54.206

99 We must settle in our minds that the Word of God must certainly be true, absolutely infallible, and beyond all question.—55.242

100 There are many who refuse to believe in the verbal inspiration of the Scriptures. But I fail to see how the sense of Scripture can be inspired if the words in which that sense is expressed are not also inspired. I believe that the

very words, in the original Hebrew and Greek, were revealed from heaven; and notwithstanding every objection that can be brought from any quarter, I have never been able to get away from the firm belief that, if I give up my Master's words, I give up his thoughts also.—57.187

Bible, interpretation of

[101] I have always found that the meaning of a text can be better learned by prayer than by any other way. Of course, we must consult lexicons and commentaries to see the literal meaning of the words and their relation to one another. But when we have done all that, we shall still find that our greatest help will come from prayer.—56.5

Bible, neglect of   See Bible, reading of

[102] There is dust enough on some of your Bibles to write "damnation" with your fingers.—1.112

[103] Perhaps there is no book more neglected in these days than the Bible. I believe there are more moldy Bibles in this world than there are of any sort of neglected books. We have no book that is so much bought, and then so speedily laid aside and so little used, as the Bible.—2.273

[104] If you find a professing Christian indifferent to his Bible, you may be sure that the very dust upon its cover will rise up in judgment against him.—46.280

[105] I am inclined to think that although there may be more Bibles in England than any other book, there is less of Bible reading than anything else in literature.—60.147

Bible, reading of   See Bible, neglect of

[106] When you shall come before him, he shall say, "Did you read my Bible?"

"No."

"I wrote you a letter of mercy. Did you read it?"

"No."

"Rebel! I sent you a letter inviting you to me. Did you ever read it?"

"Lord, I never broke the seal. I kept it shut up."

"Wretch," says God, "then you deserve hell."

Oh, let it not be so with you! Be Bible readers; be Bible searchers.—1.112, 113

[107] Bible study is the metal that makes a Christian. This is the strong meat on which holy men are nourished. This is that which makes the bone and sinew of men who keep God's way in defiance of every adversary.—26.155

[108] Some people like to read so many chapters every day. I would not dissuade them from the practice, but I would rather lay my soul asoak in half a dozen verses

all day than rinse my hand in several chapters. Oh, to be bathed in a text of Scripture, and to let it be sucked up into your very soul, till it saturates your heart! Set your heart upon God's Word! Let your whole nature be plunged into it as cloth into a dye!—27.42

109 If my sermons kept people from reading the Bible for themselves, I would like to see the whole stock in a blaze and burned to ashes. But if they serve as fingers pointing to the Scriptures and saying, "Read this and this and this," then I am thankful to have printed them.—57.500

Bible, truth of   *See Truth*

110 Go to Christ with prayer yourself, go to God with repentance yourself, and see whether he does not pardon you and bless you and change you and make a new creature of you. And when he has done that, believe me, you will never again doubt whether the Bible is true, for when it shall have saved you from your fears, rescued you from your sins, and brought you into life and light and liberty, you will be absolutely certain that it is true, because you have tried and tested it yourself.—41.173

Blood, Christ's   *See Atonement; Cross; Death, Christ's; Substitution*

111 There may be some sins of which a man cannot speak, but there is no sin which the blood of Christ cannot wash away.—4.470

112 See how red is your guilt, mark the scarlet stain. If you were to wash your soul in the Atlantic Ocean, you might incarnadine every wave that washes all its shores, and yet the crimson spots of your transgression would still remain. But plunge into the "fountain filled with blood, drawn from Immanuel's veins," and in an instant you are whiter than snow. Every speck, spot, and stain of sin is gone, and gone forever.—47.321

113 There are some preachers who cannot or do not preach about the blood of Jesus Christ, and I have one thing to say to you concerning them: *Never go to hear them! Never listen to them!* A ministry that has not the blood in it is lifeless, and a dead ministry is no good to anybody.—54.405

114 I hope that there is never a Sunday but what I teach this one doctrine. And until this tongue is silent in the grave, I shall know no other gospel than just this: Trust Christ, and you shall live. The bloody sacrifice of Calvary is the only hope of sinners.—58.127

Calling, effectual   *See Calling, God's; Grace, irresistible*

Calling, God's

115 The general call of the gospel is like the common "cluck" of the

hen which she is always giving when her chickens are around her. But if there is any danger impending, then she gives a very peculiar call, quite different from the ordinary one, and the little chicks come running as fast as they can, and hide for safety under her wings. That is the call we want, God's peculiar and effectual call to his own.—43.339

Calvinism *See Arminianism; Atonement, limited; Depravity; Election; Election, unconditional; Grace, irresistible; Perseverance; Predestination; Sovereignty*

116 Calvinism is the gospel.—1.50

117 I do not ask whether you believe Calvinism. It is possible you may not. But I believe you will before you enter heaven. I am persuaded that as God may have washed your hearts, he will wash your brains before you enter heaven.—1.92

118 I love the pure doctrine of unadulterated Calvinism. But if that be wrong—if there be anything in it which is false—I for one say, "Let that perish too, and let Christ's name last forever. Jesus! Jesus! Jesus! Crown him Lord of all!"—1.212

119 George Whitefield said, "We are all born Arminians." It is grace that turns us into Calvinists.—2.124

120 "Calvinism" did not spring from Calvin. We believe that it sprang from the great Founder of all truth.—7.298

121 There are certain doctrines called Calvinistic, which I think commend themselves to the minds of all thoughtful persons for this reason mainly—they ascribe to God everything.—10.308

122 John Calvin propounded truth more clearly than any other man who ever breathed, knew more of Scripture, and explained it more clearly.—10.310

123 If you ask me, "Do you hold the doctrinal views which were held by John Calvin?" I reply, "I do in the main hold them, and rejoice to avow it." But far be it from me even to imagine that Zion contains none within her walls but Calvinistic Christians, or that there are none saved who do not hold our views.—10.699
Note: CHS did not accept everything Calvin taught, as is clear from the above quotation. Most notably he did not agree with infant baptism and predestination to hell. When he spoke of Calvinism as the essence of the gospel, he had the five points of Calvinism in mind: total depravity, unconditional election, limited atonement, irresistible grace, and the perseverance of the saints. All these topics are included in this anthology.

27

[124] Rest assured that the doctrines commonly called Calvinistic are the only doctrines that can shut the mouths of devils and fill the mouths of saints in the day of famine and in the time of extremity.—11.57

[125] I am not a Calvinist by choice, but because I cannot help it.—18.692

[126] I believe nothing merely because Calvin taught it, but because I have found his teaching in the Word of God.—44.402

[127] We hold and assert again and again that the truth which Calvin preached was the very truth which the apostle Paul had long before written in his inspired epistles, and which is most clearly revealed in the discourses of our blessed Lord himself.—47.398

[128] I will defy any man who has had a deep experience of his own odious depravity to believe any other doctrines but those which are commonly called Calvinism.—49.257

[129] When my spirit gets depressed, nothing will sustain it but the good old-fashioned Calvinistic doctrine.—58.380

[130] I was reading the other day a book containing the life of a very excellent Methodist minister, and I was greatly amused to find in his diary an allusion to myself. He says, "Went to hear Mr. Spurgeon. He is a rank Calvinist, but a good man." I was pleased to find that I was a good man, and I was equally pleased to find that I was a rank Calvinist. I believe that he is one, too, now that he has gone to heaven. There may be Arminians on earth, but they are not after they get there.—60.201, 202

Carnality   *See Depravity; Heart; Nature, human; Pleasure; Sin*

[131] Inbred corruption is the worst corruption. "Lord," said Augustine, "deliver me from my worst enemy, that wicked man—myself."—10.409

[132] I have heard of hungry travelers who were lost in the wilderness and came upon a bag which they hoped might yield them a supply of food. They eagerly opened the bag, but it contained nothing but pearls, which they poured out contemptuously upon the desert sand. Even so, when a man is hungering and thirsting after things of this life, and all his thoughts are taken up with carnal appetites, he will reject as worthless the priceless promises of God.—29.661

[133] I daresay the devil finds himself at home in hades. But if he could be converted into a seraph, he would not stop in hell for an hour. He would never want to go there again for pleasure. Of that I am certain. And when a man who professes to be converted says that he goes into the world and into sin for pleasure, it

is as if an angel went to hell for enjoyment.—44.251

Catechism   *See Children, teaching of; Teaching*

[134] I am more and more persuaded that the study of a good scriptural catechism is of infinite value to our children. Even if the youngsters do not understand all the questions and answers in the Westminster Assembly's catechism, yet it will be of infinite service when the time of understanding comes to have known those very excellent, wise, and judicious definitions of the things of God. I think we must use the method of catechising. It will be a blessing to them in life and death, in time and eternity, the best of blessings God himself can give.—10.215

Catholicism   *See Church, denominations of; Jesus, deity of; Mass; Pope; Purgatory; Saint*

[135] I question if hell can find a more fitting instrument within its infernal lake than the Church of Rome is for the cause of mischief.—11.510

[136] I do not think I should care to go on worshiping a Madonna even if she did wink. One cannot make much out of a wink. We want something more than that from the object of our adoration.—40.505

Chastisement   *See Discipline, God's*

Childlikeness

[137] Some man says, "Why should I believe? The Sunday school child reads his Bible and says it is true. Am I, a man of intellect, to sit side by side with him? I would rather be a lost man than a saved child." Like Satan, he declares it would be better to rule in hell than serve in heaven, and he goes away an unbeliever, because to believe is too humbling.—2.413

Children, death of   *See Children, salvation of; Death*

[138] We are convinced that all of our race who die in infancy partake in the redemption wrought out by our Lord Jesus. Whatever some may think, we believe that the whole spirit and tone of the Word of God, as well as the nature of God himself, lead us to believe that all who leave this world as babes are saved.—24.583

Children, dedication of   *See Baptism, infant*

[139] I hope many of us, as soon as our children saw the light, if not before, presented them to God with this anxious prayer, that they might sooner die than live to disgrace God. We only desired children that we might in them live another life of service to God. And when we looked into their young faces, we never asked wealth for them, nor fame, nor anything else. Only that they

might be dear to God, and that their names might be written in the Lamb's Book of Life.—10.417

Children, rebellious

140 To bury a child is a great grief. But to have that child live and sin against you is ten times worse.—12.69

Children, salvation of   *See Children, death of; Children, teaching of; Salvation*

141 Children need to be saved and may be saved. The conversion of a child involves the same work of divine grace and results in the same blessed consequences as the conversion of the adult. But there is this additional matter for joy, that a great preventive work is done when the young are converted. Conversion saves a child from a multitude of sins. If God's mercy shall bless your teaching to a little prattler, how happy that boy's life will be compared with what it might have been if it had grown up in folly, sin, and shame, and only been converted after many days! It is the highest wisdom to pray for our children that while they are young their hearts may be given to the Savior.—19.585, 586

142 Those children who are of sufficient years to sin and be saved by faith have to listen to the gospel and receive it by faith. And they can do this, God the Holy Spirit helping them. There is no doubt about it, because great numbers have done it. I will not say at what age children are first capable of receiving the knowledge of Christ, but it is much earlier than some fancy.—24.583

Children, teaching of   *See Catechism; Children, salvation of; Parents; Teaching*

143 I am afraid that many Sunday school addresses have no gospel in them. I do not see why the same gospel should not be preached to children as to grown-up people. I think it should. To stand up in a Sunday school and say, "Now be good boys and girls and God will love you" is telling lies.—11.426

144 O dear mothers, you have a very sacred trust reposed in you by God! If God spares you, you may live to hear that pretty boy speak to thousands, and you will have the sweet reflection in your heart that the quiet teachings of the nursery led the man to love his God and serve him.—31.580

145 I heard of a man who said that he did not like to prejudice his boy, so he would not say anything to him about religion. The devil, however, was quite willing to prejudice the lad, so very early in life he learned to swear, although his father had a foolish and wicked objection to teaching him to pray. If ever you feel it incumbent upon you not to prejudice a piece of ground by sowing good seed in it, you may rest assured that the

weeds will not imitate your impartiality. Where the plow does not go and the seed is not sown, the weeds are sure to multiply. And if children are left untrained, all sorts of evil will spring up in their hearts and lives.—47.278

146 I was pleased, in reading the life of John Wesley's mother, to notice how she set apart Monday to speak to one of her daughters; Tuesday to speak to another; Wednesday to speak, as she says, "to Jack," meaning John; and Thursday to speak to Charles; so that they each had a day. And there was an hour each day given to speak to each child about the affairs of the soul. That is the way to win children for God.—61.562

Christ   *See Jesus*

Christian   *See Saint*

147 The distinguishing mark of a Christian is his confidence in the love of Christ, and the yielding of his affections to Christ in return.—13.277

148 If I had to die like a dog, and there were no hereafter, I would still choose to be a Christian, for of all lives that can be lived, there is none that can compare with this.—23.348

149 A true Christian would rather go without a meal than without a sermon. He would sooner miss a meal than lose his daily portion of Scripture or his daily resort to the house of prayer.—47.244

Christmas   *See Incarnation; Mass*

150 He that is God this day was once an infant, so that if my cares are little, trivial, and comparatively infantile, I may go to him.—12.716

151 We do not believe in the present ecclesiastical arrangement called Christmas. First, because we do not believe in the mass at all, but abhor it. And second, because we find no scriptural warrant for observing any day as the birthday of the Savior. Consequently, its observance is a superstition.—17.697

Church   *See Fellowship; Perfection*

152 The treasury of the church is the liberality of God. The power of the church is the omnipotence of Jehovah. The persuasions of the church are the irresistible influences of the Holy Ghost. The destiny of the church is an ultimate conquest over all the sons of men.—14.324

153 I have heard of some who stay away because the church is not perfect. Are you perfect? Why, if the church were perfect, we should not endure *you* in it! I have no doubt that you will find the church quite as perfect as you are. There are others who keep aloof from the people of God because they feel they are not perfect themselves. My dear friend, if you

were perfect we should not want you, because you would be the only perfect member among us.—17.478

154 If I had never joined a church till I had found one that was perfect, I should never have joined one at all. And the moment I did join it, if I had found one, I should have spoiled it, for it would not have been a perfect church after I had become a member of it. Still, imperfect as it is, it is the dearest place on earth to us.—37.633

155 Never think of the church of God as if she were in danger. If you do, you will be like Uzza. You will put forth your hand to steady the ark and provoke the Lord to anger against you. If it were in danger, you could not deliver it. If Christ cannot take care of his church without you, you cannot do it. Be still, and know that he is God.—60.634

Church, Catholic   *See Catholicism*

Church, denominations of   *See Catholicism; Mormon, Book of; Unity*

156 There never ought to have been any denominations at all, for according to Scripture, every church is independent of every other. There ought to have been as many separate churches as there were separate opinions. But denominations, which are the gathering up of those churches, ought not to have existed at all.

They do a world of mischief.—3.335

157 It is not likely we should all see eye to eye. You cannot make a dozen watches all tick to the same time, much less make a dozen men all think the same thoughts. But still, if we should all bow our thoughts to that one written Word, and would own no authority but the Bible, the church could not be divided. It could not be cut in pieces as she now is. We come together when we come to the Word of God.—6.167

158 A plague upon denominationalism! There should be but one denomination. We should be denominated by the name of Christ, as the wife is named by her husband's name. As long as the church of Christ has to say, "My right arm is Episcopalian, my left arm is Wesleyan, my right foot is Baptist, and my left foot is Presbyterian," she is not ready for the marriage. She will be ready when she has washed out these stains, when all her members have "one Lord, one faith, one baptism" (Eph. 4:5).—35.406, 407

159 I recollect my mother saying to me, "I prayed that you might be a Christian, but I never prayed that you might be a Baptist." But nevertheless, I became a Baptist, for as I reminded her, the Lord was able to do for her exceeding abundantly above what she asked

or thought (Eph. 3:20). And he did it.—51.439

Church, disdain of

160 It may appear a trifle to make a saint the target of ridicule, but his Father in heaven does not think so. I know this, that many patient men will bear a great deal, but if you strike their children, their blood is up, and they will not have it. A father will not stand by to see his child abused, and the great Father above is as tender and fond as any other father. You have seen among birds and beasts that they will put forth all their strength for their young. A hen, naturally very timid, will fight for her little chicks with all the courage of a lion. Some of the smallest and least powerful animals become perfectly terrible when they are taking care of their offspring. And do you think that the everlasting God will bear to see his children maligned, slandered, and abused, for their following of him?—31.232

Church, membership in

161 If it is right for one Christian not to confess Christ and join a church, it must be allowable for others to do the same. Where would churches be, where would the continuance of gospel ordinances be, and who would be bound to be a preacher if no one is even bound to make an open profession?—34.221

162 Some people say, "We belong to such-and-such a church, but we don't approve of its teaching or its practice."

What! You belong to it, yet you do not approve of its principles? Out of your own mouth you are condemned. If I unite with a church whose creed I do not believe, I am guilty of my own share in all the error that is there. It is no use for me to say, "I am trying to undo the mischief." I have no business to be there.—53.427

163 I well remember how I joined the church after my conversion. I forced myself into it by telling the minister, who was lax and slow, after I had called four or five times and could not see him, that I had done my duty. And if he did not see me, I would call a church meeting myself and tell them I believed in Christ, and ask them if they would have me.—60.294, 295

164 I know there are some who say, "Well, I have given myself to the Lord, but I do not intend to give myself to any church."

Now, why not?

"Because I can be a Christian without it."

Are you quite clear about that? You can be as good a Christian by disobedience to your Lord's commands as by being obedient? There is a brick. What is it made for? To help build a house. It is of no use for that brick to tell you

33

that it is just as good a brick while it is kicking about on the ground as it would be in the house. It is a good-for-nothing brick. So you rolling-stone Christians, I do not believe that you are answering your purpose. You are living contrary to the life which Christ would have you live, and you are much to blame for the injury you do.—60.295, 296

Church, purpose of   *See Purpose*

165 A church that does not exist to reclaim heathenism, to fight evil, to destroy error, to put down falsehood, a church that does not exist to take the side of the poor, to denounce injustice and to hold up righteousness, is a church that has no right to be. Not for yourself, O church, do you exist, any more than Christ existed for himself.—15.597

Church Growth   *See Church Planting*

166 My good ministering brother, have you got an empty church? Do you want to fill it? I will give you a good receipt, and if you will follow it, you will in all probability have your chapel full to the doors.

Burn all your manuscripts. That is number one. Give up your notes. That is number two. Read your Bible and preach it as you find it in the simplicity of its language. Begin to tell the people what you have felt in your own heart, and beg the Holy Spirit to make your heart as hot as a furnace for zeal. Then go out and talk to the people. Speak to them like their brother. Be a man among men. Tell them what you have felt and what you know, and tell it heartily with a good, bold face. And my dear friend, I do not care who you are, you will get a congregation.

But if you say, "Now, to get a congregation, I must buy an organ," that will not serve you a bit.

"But we must have a good choir."

I would not care to have a congregation that comes through a good choir.

"No," says another, "but I must alter my style of preaching."

My dear friend, it is not the style of preaching. It is the style of feeling.—3.262

Church Planting   *See Church Growth*

167 It is with cheerfulness that we dismiss our twelves, our twenties, our fifties, to form other churches. We encourage our members to leave us to found other churches. We even seek to persuade them to do it. We ask them to scatter throughout the land, to become the goodly seed which God shall bless. I believe that so long as we do this, we shall prosper. I have marked other churches that have adopted the other way, and they have not succeeded.—11.238

Commitment   *See   Discipleship;
Lordship*

168 I have now concentrated all my prayers into one, and that one prayer is this, that I may die to self, and live wholly to him.— 2.380

169 Suppose a house is attacked by seven thieves. The good man of the house has arms within, and he manages to kill six of the thieves. But if one survives, and he permits him to range his house, he may still be robbed, perhaps still be slain.

And if I have had seven evil vices, and if by the grace of God six of these have been driven out, if I yet indulge and pamper one that remains, I am still a lost man.—6.182, 183

170 I wish that saints would cling to Christ half as earnestly as sinners cling to the devil. If we were as willing to suffer for God as some are to suffer for their lusts, what perseverance and zeal would be seen on all sides!— 12.500

171 I am afraid for you who go ankle-deep into religion and never venture further. I am afraid that you might return to the shore. But as for you who plunge into the center of the stream and find waters to swim in, I have no fears. You shall be carried onward by a current ever increasing in strength, till in the ocean of eternal love you shall lose

yourselves in heaven above.— 27.580

172 Be dogmatically true, obstinately holy, immovably honest, desperately kind, fixedly upright.—59.558, 559

Compassion   *See Evangelism; Indifference; Love; Sympathy*

173 There was once in a village a man who was a confirmed infidel. In spite of all the efforts of the minister and many Christian people, he had resisted all attempts, and appeared to be more and more confirmed in his sin. Finally, the people held a prayer meeting especially to intercede for his soul. Afterward God put it into the heart of one of the elders of the church to spend a night in prayer on behalf of the poor infidel. In the morning the elder rose from his knees and traveled to the man's smithy. He meant to say a great deal to him, but all he could say was, "O sir! I am deeply concerned for your salvation. I have been wrestling with God all night for your salvation." He could say no more, his heart was too full. He then went away.

Down went the blacksmith's hammer, and he went immediately to see his wife. She said, "What is the matter with you?"

"Matter enough," said the man, "I have been attacked with a new argument this time. The elder has been here, and he said, 'I am concerned about your salvation.'

Why, if he is concerned about my salvation, it is a strange thing that I am not concerned about it."

The man's heart was captured. He went to the elder's house. When he arrived, the elder was in his parlor, still in prayer, and they knelt down together. God gave him a contrite spirit and a broken heart, and brought that poor sinner to the feet of the Savior.—1.343

174 O Lord, let thy servant confess that he feels that his prayers are not as earnest as they should be for his people's souls, that he does not preach so frequently as he ought with that fire, that energy, that true love to men's souls. But, O Lord, damn not the hearers for the preacher's sin. Oh, destroy not the flock for the shepherd's iniquity. Have mercy on them, good Lord, have mercy on them! There are some of them, Father, that will not have mercy on themselves.—2.43

175 My eye runs down with grief when I think of some of you who listen to my voice year after year, and yet do not hear. You hear *me,* but not *my Master.* Alas! How many have been the arrows out of God's bow which I have shot at you? Have they not been wasted? They have rattled upon your armor, but they have not pierced your hearts. I can say solemnly I have sometimes stood in this pulpit and have labored with your souls to the best of my power, and

I have felt that I would have cheerfully resigned all I had on earth if I might but have brought you to Christ. Oh, I must have you saved! I must have you lay hold on eternal life! I must see you look to Jesus!—10.480

176 Ah, souls, if you are lost, it is not for lack of praying for. It is not for lack of weeping over. It is not for lack of faithful gospel preaching.—12.455, 456

177 I cannot bear the thought that any of you should ever be bound in bundles to be burned. What, will any of you ever be lost, and be borne into the flame which never can be quenched? It must not be. Turn, turn! Why will you die?—12.467

178 The man who cannot weep cannot preach. At least, if he never feels tears within, even if they do not show themselves without, he can scarcely be the man to handle such themes as those which God has committed to his people's charge.—15.233

179 I lay last night by the hour on my bed awake, tossing with a burden on my heart, and I tell you that the only burden I had was your soul. I cannot endure it, man, that you should be cast into the "lake that burneth with fire and brimstone" (Rev. 21:8).—16.95

180 O my hearers, do not kill me by destroying your own souls!—31.362

36

181 I think the preacher should feel a burning desire for his hearers' conversion, and even an intense anguish of heart for the immediate salvation of those to whom he speaks. To this I have attained. I long for your salvation most vehemently. I would say anything, and say it any way, if I could but win you to immediate faith in the Lord Jesus. The desire is so strong upon me that should I not succeed on this occasion, I will try again. And if, unhappily, I should fail again, I will continue at the work as long as you live and I am able to reach you. I will go before God in secret, lay your case before him, and beg him to interpose. We cannot let you be damned! It is dreadful. We cannot stand by and see you lost!—33.369

182 I am certain that to preach the wrath of God with a hard heart, a cold lip, a tearless eye, and an unfeeling spirit is to harden men, not benefit them.—33.700

183 I sometimes start in my sleep at the thought of one of my hearers being in hell. Ah, if you do not care about your own souls, we at least will care about them for you.—39.405

184 Love your fellowmen, and cry about them if you cannot bring them to Christ. If you cannot save them, you can weep over them. If you cannot give them a drop of cold water in hell, you can give them your heart's tears while they are still in this body.—59.514

Complacency   *See Indifference*

Complaining   *See Murmuring*

Compromise

185 If I thought I could save every soul in this place by making the slightest compromise with my conscience, I dare not in the sight of the living God do it. Consequences and usefulness are nothing to us. Duty and right—these are to be our guides.—20.56

186 I would not utter what I believed to be a falsehood concerning the Lord, even though the evil one offered me the bait of saving all mankind thereby.—30.447

187 Though the heavens should fall through our doing right, we are not to sin in order to keep them up.—49.571

Condemnation   *See Damnation; Hell; Lost; Punishment; Wrath, God's*

188 My mother said to me once, after she had long prayed for me and had come to the conviction that I was hopeless, "My son, if at the last great day you are condemned, remember that your mother will say 'Amen' to your condemnation." That stung me to the quick.—5.447

189 Will you do me a favor? I asked it once, and it was blessed to

the conversion of several. Will you take a little time alone this evening, and after you have weighed your own condition before the Lord, write down one of two words? If you feel that you are not a believer, write down *Condemned.* And if you are a believer in Jesus and put your trust in him alone, write down *Forgiven.* Do it, even if you have to write down the word *Condemned.*

We received into church fellowship a young man who said, "Sir, I wrote down the word *Condemned,* and I looked at it. There it was. I had written it myself—*Condemned.*" As he looked, the tears began to flow and the heart began to break. And before long he fled to Christ, put the paper in the fire, and wrote down *Forgiven.* This young man was about the sixth who had been brought to the Lord in the same way. So I ask you to try it. Remember, you are either one or the other—condemned or forgiven. Do not stand between the two. Let it be decided. And remember, if you are condemned today, yet you are not in hell. There is still hope!—9.360

190 You are losers in this world if you love not God. You are losers of peace and comfort and strength and hope even now. But what will be your loss hereafter, with no wing to cover you when the destroying angel is abroad, no feathers beneath which you may hide when the dread thunderbolts of justice shall be launched, one after another, from God's right hand? You have no shelter, and consequently no safety.—40.475

Confession   *See Conviction; Guilt; Repentance; Sin*

191 Imagine that some creditor has a debtor who owes him a thousand pounds. He calls him and says, "I demand my money."

"But," says the other, "I owe you nothing."

That man will be arrested and thrown into prison. However, the creditor says, "I wish to deal mercifully with you. Make a frank confession, and I will forgive you all the debt."

"Well," says the man, "I do acknowledge that I owe you 200 pounds."

"No," says he, "that will not do."

"Well, sir, I confess I owe you 500 pounds," and by degrees he comes to confess that he owes the thousand. Is there any merit in that confession? No, but yet you could see that no creditor would think of forgiving a debt which was not acknowledged. It is the least you can do to acknowledge your sin. And though there be no merit in the confession, yet, true to his promise, God will give you pardon through Christ.—6.47

192 It is easy to commit sin, but hard to confess it. Man will

transgress without a tempter. But even when urged by the most earnest pleader, he will not acknowledge his guilt.—8.121

193 "Savior" is the harp, but "sinner" is the finger that must touch the strings and bring forth the melody.—22.713

194 You have heard the story of the English king who was angry with the burgesses of Calais, and declared that he would hang six of them. They came to him with ropes about their necks, submitting to their doom. That is the way I came to Jesus. I accepted my punishment, pleaded guilty, and begged for pardon. Put your rope upon your neck, confess that you deserve to die, and come to Jesus.—32.306

195 Sin confessed with tears, sin which causes the very heart to bleed—killing sin, damning sin—this is the kind of sin for which Jesus died. Sham sinners may be content with a sham Savior, but our Lord Jesus is the real Savior, who did really die, and died for real sin. Oh, how this ought to comfort you who are sadly bearing the pressing burden of an abominable life! You, too, who are crushed into the mire of despondency beneath the load of your guilt!—32.544

196 It does not spoil your happiness to confess your sin. The unhappiness is in not making the confession.—46.427

197 We do admit that we make mistakes, though we set them down to weakness rather than willfulness. We apologize for our infirmities, and rather excuse than accuse our own hearts.—49.195

198 People make a general confession such as, "I am a great sinner," who would still resist any special charge brought home to their consciences, however true. Say to such a person, "You are a cheater," and he replies, "No, I am not a cheater!"
"What are you, then? A liar?"
"Oh, no!"
"Are you a Sabbath breaker?"
"No, nothing of the kind."
And so when you come to sift it, you find them sheltering themselves under the general term *sinner*, not to make confession, but to evade it.—53.420

Conscience   *See Conviction; Guilt; Sin*

199 Conscience may tell me that something is wrong, but how wrong it is conscience itself does not know. Did any man's conscience, unenlightened by the Spirit, ever tell him that his sins deserved damnation? Did it ever lead any man to feel an abhorrence of sin as sin? Did conscience ever bring a man to such self-renunciation that he totally abhorred himself and all his works and came to Christ?—4.140

200 A man sees his enemy before him. By the light of his candle, he marks the insidious approach. His enemy is seeking his life. The man puts out the candle and then exclaims, "I am now quite at peace."

That is what you do. Conscience is the candle of the Lord. It shows you your enemy. You try to put it out by saying, "Peace, peace! Put the enemy out!"

God give you grace to thrust *sin* out!—6.120

201 Conscience is like a magnetic needle, which, if once turned aside from its pole, will never cease trembling. You can never make it still until it is permitted to return to its proper place.—11.366

202 I recollect the time when I thought that if I had to live on bread and water all my life and be chained in a dungeon, I would cheerfully submit to that if I might but get rid of my sins. When sin haunted and burdened my spirit, I am sure I would have counted the martyr's death preferable to a life under the lash of a guilty conscience.—12.275

203 O believe me, guilt upon the conscience is worse than the body on the rack. Even the flames of the stake may be cheerfully endured, but the burnings of a conscience tormented by God are beyond all measure unendurable.—15.159, 160

204 This side of hell, what can be worse than the tortures of an awakened conscience?—19.153

205 He was a fool who killed the watchdog because it alarmed him when thieves were breaking into his house. If conscience upbraids you, feel its upbraiding and heed its rebuke. It is your best friend.— 22.68

206 Give me into the power of a roaring lion, but never let me come under the power of an awakened, guilty conscience. Shut me up in a dark dungeon, among all manner of loathsome creatures—snakes and reptiles of all kinds—but, oh, give me not over to my own thoughts when I am consciously guilty before God!— 37.303

207 Fire such as martyrs felt at the stake were but a plaything compared with the flames of a burning conscience. Thunderbolts and tornadoes are nothing in force compared with the charges of a guilty conscience.—38.41

208 When a swarm of bees gets about a man, they are above, beneath, around, everywhere stinging, every one stinging, until he seems to be stung in every part of his body. So, when conscience wakes up the whole hive of our sins, we find ourselves compassed about with innumerable evils: sins at the board and sins on the bed, sins at the task and sins in the pew, sins in the street and sins in

the shop, sins on the land and sins at sea, sins of body, soul, and spirit, sins of eye, of lip, of hand, of foot, sins everywhere. It is a horrible discovery when it seems to a man as if sin had become as omnipresent with him as God is.—40.135

209 The conscience of man, when he is really quickened and awakened by the Holy Spirit, speaks the truth. It rings the great alarm bell. And if he turns over in his bed, that great alarm bell rings out again and again, "The wrath to come! The wrath to come! The wrath to come!"—41.39

210 Nothing can be more horrible, out of hell, than to have an awakened conscience but not a reconciled God—to see sin, yet not see the Savior—to behold the deadly disease in all its loathsomeness, but not trust the good Physician, and so to have no hope of ever being healed of our malady.—54.398

211 I would bear any affliction rather than be burdened with a guilty conscience.—56.595

212 It is a blessed thing to have a conscience that will shiver when the very ghost of a sin goes by—a conscience that is not like our great steamships at sea that do not yield to every wave, but, like a cork on the water, goes up and down with every ripple, sensitive in a moment to the very approach of sin. May God the Holy Spirit make us so! This sensitiveness the Christian endeavors to have, for he knows that if he has it not, he will never be purified from his sin.—57.55, 56

213 There are thousands of people in this country who would be greatly troubled in their minds if they did not go to church twice on Sundays. And they get comfort in this because their conscience is dead. If their conscience were really awakened, they would understand that there is no connection between conscience and outward forms.—61.173

Contentment   *See Satisfaction*

214 No man ever need fear offering a reward of a thousand pounds to a contented man, for if anyone came to claim the reward, he would prove his discontent.—1.88

215 I have heard of some good old woman in a cottage, who had nothing but a piece of bread and a little water. Lifting up her hands, she said as a blessing, "What! All this, and Christ too?"—1.89

216 You say, "If I had a little more, I should be very satisfied." You make a mistake. If you are not content with what you have, you would not be satisfied if it were doubled.—5.154

217 A man's contentment is in his mind, not in the extent of his possessions. Alexander the Great, with all the world at his feet, cries for another world to conquer.—6.272

Conversion *See Evangelism; Forgiveness; Regeneration*

[218] Conversion is of absolute importance. It is the hinge of the gospel. It is the point upon which most Christians are agreed. It is a subject which lies at the very basis of salvation.—3.185

[219] It is a physical impossibility that a swine should ever deliver a lecture on astronomy. Every man will clearly perceive that it must be impossible that a snail should build a city. And there is just as much impossibility that a sinner, unmended, should enjoy heaven.—3.188

[220] "I can't understand," a bird said to a fish, "how it is that you always live in the cold element. I could not live there. It must be a great self-denial to you not to fly up to the trees."

"Ah," said the fish, "it is no self-denial to me to live here. It is my element. I never aspire to fly, for it would not suit me. If I were taken out of my element, I should die unless I was restored to it very soon, and the sooner the better."

So the believer feels that God is his native element.—8.327

[221] In all true conversions there are points of essential agreement. There must be in all a penitent confession of sin and a looking to Jesus for the forgiveness of it. And there must also be a real change of heart such as shall affect the entire life. And where these essential points are not to be found, there is no genuine conversion.—20.398

[222] Mr. Rowland Hill was met one evening by a drunken man, who staggered up to him and said, "Hallo, Mr. Hill, I am one of your converts!"

"Ah," said Mr. Rowland Hill, "very likely, but you are none of God's converts, or else you would not be drunk."

Now, our converts, if they be *our* converts, will be very poor productions. If one man can convert you, another man can unconvert you.—25.174

[223] Conversion is the standing miracle of the church.—34.93

[224] Do you not remember your birthday?

"No, sir, I do not."

Suppose I were to tell her she was not alive because she did not know her birthday—I should be very foolish. And if you say to yourself, "You were never born again because you do not know when the event happened," you will be very foolish, too. If you can say, "One thing I know, whereas I was blind, now I see," be satisfied and grateful, even though you cannot tell when the great miracle was wrought.—38.566

[225] We are not what we ought to be, we are not what we want to be, we are not what we shall be. But we are something very differ-

ent from what we used to be.—43.45

226 I have sometimes likened an unconverted man to a wild giraffe in an African forest. Christ's gospel, like a mighty lion, leaps upon him from the thicket, fastens its powerful fangs in his flesh, and begins to tear away his very life. He strives and struggles, dashes here and there, and tries to rid himself of the awful load that he bears upon his back. But all his efforts are in vain. The poor giraffe in the grip of the lion is distracted, and the man under conviction of sin cannot imagine what is to become of him. He thinks that he is lost and that he must feel the full force of divine wrath against sin.

Yet this is the way of mercy; it is thus that men are saved. Down falls the man at last, and then he, who seemed to be his enemy, stoops down and nobly gives back the life that appeared to have gone from him. Or rather, gives him an infinitely nobler life, and so the forgiven sinner lives forever. Oh, that the power of the gospel may thus be exerted upon some wild, untameable spirit that may be here just now!—53.235

Conviction   *See Confession; Conscience; Guilt; Repentance; Sin*

227 There was nothing in the whole Garden of Eden that could give Adam a moment's delight, because he was under a sense of sin. And so it will be with you. If you could be put in paradise, you would not be the happier. Now that God has convinced you of sin, there's only one cure for you, and that one cure you must have. You may ramble the world round and you will never find another. You may try your best with all the pleasures and mercies of this life, but you would be in torment, even though you could be taken to heaven, unless this one remedy should appease your aching heart.—6.216, 217

228 It is as when a housewife cleans her chamber. She looks, and there is no dust; the air is clear, and all her furniture is shining brightly. But there is a chink in the window shutter, a ray of light creeps in, and you see the dust dancing up and down, thousands of grains, in the sunbeam. It is all over the room the same, but she can see it only where the sunbeam comes. It is just so with us. God sends a ray of divine light into the heart, and then we see how vile and full of iniquity it is.—6.400, 401

229 A sermon often does a man most good when it makes him most angry. Those people who walk down the aisles and say, "I will never hear that man again," very often have an arrow rankling in their breast.—9.350

230 Oh, what wretchedness was mine before I laid hold on Christ!

43

There are some who feel not so acutely the agony of conflict with sin, but it was my lot to feel a horror of great darkness, verging upon despair, so that had I not soon found a Savior, my soul had chosen strangling rather than life. Believe me, there is no pain so bitter as the pain of sin, and no curse so heavy as the curse which comes from the black lips of our own iniquities. And yet I would to God that some of you felt it now that you might not feel it hereafter. I would that this whip would fall upon your backs, that you might be flogged out of your self-righteousness and made to fly to Jesus Christ and find a shelter there.—11.136

231 If we begin to preach to sinners that they must have a certain sense of conviction, such teaching would turn the sinner away from Christ to himself. The man begins at once to say, "Have I a broken heart? Do I feel the burden of sin?" This is only another form of looking to self. Man must not look to himself to find reasons for God's grace. The remedy does not lie in the seat of the disease; it lies in the Physician's hand. Come to Jesus just as you are, and do not wait for a preparation made out of your own miseries.—33.114, 115

232 I remember the time when I dared not go to sleep, for fear I might wake up in hell.—34.390

233 A naked sin stripped of all excuse and set in the light of truth is a worse sight than to see the devil himself.—37.224

234 There was a time when no poor wretch on earth was more sunken in despair than I was. I knew that, though but young, I had broken God's righteous law and had grievously sinned against him. And, under a sense of my guilt, I went about burdened day after day. If I slept, I dreamed of an angry God, and thought that he would cast me forever into hell. When I attended to my daily calling, the dreadful thought of my sin haunted and followed me wherever I went. If anyone said to me then, "Sin is a fiction," I could not have laughed him to scorn, for I was in no laughing humor. But I could have sat down and wept to think that anyone should fancy that this grim reality was but a matter of foolish fear.—44.292, 293

235 There is no trouble like genuine conviction of sin. Racks, scorpions, death—these are troubles to be laughed at, as compared with the weight of guilt pressing on the conscience, the sight of an angry God, and the fear of the wrath to come.—45.514

236 John Bunyan, in his *Grace Abounding*, says there were times when his sins seemed so great, and his horror of them so terrible, that he felt he must go to Christ.

Says he, "Though I sometimes used to think of Christ as one who stood with a pike in his hand to push me back, yet my terrible necessity sometimes came upon me with such force that I would gladly have run even upon the very pike than endure my sin."—50.366

237 What memories that expression awakens in some of us—"conviction of sin!" Why, it was to some of us a very martyrdom. I think it would have been less painful to have been burned alive at the stake than to have passed through those horrors and depressions of spirit which some of us passed through while we were seeking pardon, but in the wrong way.—53.137, 138

238 I felt my soul plowed as though the law, with its ten great black horses, was dragging the plow up and down my soul, breaking, crushing, furrowing my heart, and all for sin. Let me tell you, though we read of the cruelties of the Inquisition and the sufferings which the martyrs have borne from cruel men, no racks, firepans, or other instruments of torture can make a man so wretched as his own conscience when he is stretched upon its rack.—53.605, 606

239 My heart was fallow and covered with weeds, but on a certain day the great Farmer came and began to plow my soul.

Ten black horses were his team, and it was a sharp plowshare that he used, and the plowers made deep furrows. The Ten Commandments were those black horses, and the justice of God, like a plowshare, tore my spirit. I was condemned, undone, destroyed, lost, helpless, hopeless. I thought hell was before me.

But after the plowing came the sowing. God who plowed the heart in mercy made it conscious that it needed the gospel, and then the gospel seed was joyfully received.—58.388, 389

240 I do remember well when my sins compassed me about like bees, and I thought it was all over with me, and I must be destroyed by them. It was at that moment when Jesus revealed himself to me. Had he waited a little longer, I had died of despair.—60.622

Courage   *See Fear*

241 Alexander, when they said that the Persians were as the sands on the seashore, replied, "One butcher is not afraid of a whole flock of sheep." So let it be with us. Let us feel that we are men of another mold than to be afraid, that believing in God, we do not know how to spell "cowardice."—12.358

Covenant   *See Grace; Law; Works*

242 We were all lost through a covenant. God made a covenant of works with Adam: "This do,

and you shall live. Abstain from eating of the forbidden tree, and you and those whom you represent shall live in my favor." Adam broke the condition of the agreement, and there and then you and I fell down and perished by the fatal act of our first parent.

The Lord has now arranged a new covenant of a different character. It is made with Christ Jesus, the second Adam, and with all whom he represents. It is on this wise: "You, Jesus, shall keep the law, and you shall also suffer a penalty for all the breaches of my law by all who are in you. If you do this, all those who are in you shall live eternally."—14.544

243 What a Magna Charta is this! The old covenant says, "Keep the law and live." The new covenant is, "You shall live, and I will lead you to keep my law, for I will write it on your heart."—33.379

244 The man who can fully understand the word *covenant* is a theologian. That is the key of all theology—the covenant of works by which we fell, and the covenant of grace by which we stand, Christ fulfilling the covenant for us as our surety and representative, fulfilling it by the shedding of his blood, so leaving for us a covenant wholly fulfilled on our side, which is Christ's side, and only to be fulfilled now by God.—46.608

Covetousness   *See Greed*

Creation   *See Evolution*

Criticism   *See Judgment*

Cross   *See Atonement; Blood, Christ's; Death, Christ's; Substitution*

245 Calvary preaching, Calvary theology, Calvary books, Calvary sermons! These are the things we want. And in proportion as we have Calvary exalted and Christ magnified, the gospel is preached.—1.263

246 No scene in sacred history ever gladdens the soul like the scene on Calvary. Nowhere does the soul find such consolation as on that very spot where misery reigned, where woe triumphed, where agony reached its climax.—3.153

247 Oh, down, down, down with everything else, but up, up, up with the cross of Christ! Down with your baptism and your masses and your sacraments! Down with your priestcraft and your rituals and your liturgies! Down with your fine music and your pomp and your robes and your garments and all your ceremonials. But up, up, up with the doctrine of the naked cross and the expiring Savior!—14.464

248 When I see a cross embossed on Bibles, wrought out in jewelry or fashioned gold, I cannot but think how contradictory it all seems. The cross, a thing of

shame, the instrument of our Lord's execution by those who abhorred him, and yet worn as an ornament! Surely men might as well wear at their belts the dagger with which their friend was stabbed! Why do not ladies wear a gibbet from their necks? For what more or less is a cross? Such was not the cross which Paul gloried in; he would have despised such idolatry. He gloried in the gospel, which is a spiritual cross.—14.519

249 The most terrible warning to impenitent men in all the world is the death of Christ. For if God spared not his own Son, on whom was only laid *imputed* sin, will he spare sinners whose sins are their own?—22.599

250 The crucifixion of Christ was the crowning sin of our race. In his death we shall find all the sins of mankind uniting in foul conspiracy. Envy and pride and hate are there, with covetousness, falsehood, and blasphemy, eager to rush on to cruelty, revenge, and murder. As all the rivers run into the sea, and as all the clouds empty themselves upon the earth, so did all the crimes of man gather to the slaying of the Son of God. It seemed as if hell held an assembly, and all the various forms of sin came flocking to the rendezvous. Army upon army, they hastened to the battle. As the vultures hasten to the body, so came the flocks of sins to make the Lord their prey.—28.133

251 All historians must confess that the turning point of the race is the cross of Christ. It would be impossible to fix any other hinge of history. From that moment the power of evil received its mortal wound. It dies hard, but from that hour it was doomed.—29.124

252 Crucifixion was a death worthy to have been invented by devils. The pain which it involved was immeasurable. I will not torture you by describing it. I know dear hearts that cannot read of it without tears and without lying awake for nights afterward.—32.222

253 Nothing provokes the devil like the cross.—32.224

254 I wish that our ministry—that mine especially—might be tied and tethered to the cross. I would have no other subject to set before you but Jesus only.—33.25

255 Leave out the cross, and you have killed the religion of Jesus. Atonement by the blood of Jesus is not an arm of Christian truth; it is the heart of it.—33.375

256 Christ's five wounds kill my suspicions and fears. A crucified Savior is the life of faith and the death of unbelief. Can you view the flowing of the Savior's precious blood upon the tree of doom and not trust him? What more can he do to prove his sincerity than

to die for us? His life is the mirror of love, but in his death the sun shines on it with a blaze of glory.—33.465

257 We took our sins and drove them like nails through his hands and feet. We lifted him high up on the cross of our transgressions, and then we pierced his heart through with the spear of our unbelief.—42.615

258 On whatever subjects I may be called to preach, I feel it to be a duty which I dare not neglect to be continually going back to the doctrine of the cross—the fundamental truth of justification by faith which is in Christ Jesus. This topic is essential to the life of the soul.—45.277

Damnation *See Condemnation; Hell; Lost; Punishment; Wrath, God's*

259 To lose the sight of Christ, the company of Christ, to lose the beholding of his glories, this must be the greatest part of the damnation of the lost.—4.192

260 It seems as if every hair on my head must stand on end to think of any hearer of mine being damned.—5.21

261 He who can make jokes with regard to his end will find that if he should die jesting, it will be no joke to be damned.—6.143

262 Never let us speak of the doom of the wicked harshly, flippantly, or without holy grief. The loss of heaven and the endurance of hell must always be themes for tears. That men should live without Christ is grief enough. But that they should die without Christ is an overwhelming horror, which should grind our hearts to powder before God and make us fall on our faces and cry, "O God, have mercy upon them and save them, for thy grace and love's sake!" The deepest tenderness, it may be, some of us have yet to learn.—26.666, 667

263 We hold tenaciously that salvation is all of grace, but we also believe with equal firmness that the ruin of man is entirely the result of his own sin. It is the will of God that saves; it is the will of man that damns.—40.470

264 You will find all true theology summed up in these two short sentences: Salvation is all of the grace of God. Damnation is all of the will of man.—41.209

Death *See Children, death of; Martyrdom; Punishment, capital; Time*

265 Suppose you are a gardener employed by another. It is not your garden, but you are called upon to tend it. You come one morning into the garden, and you find that the best rose has been taken away. You are angry. You go to your fellow servants and charge them with having taken the rose. They declare that they had nothing to do with it, and one says, "I saw the master walking

here this morning; I think he took it." Is the gardener angry then? No, at once he says, "I am happy that my rose should have been so fair as to attract the attention of the master. It is his own. He has taken it, let him do what seems good."

It is even so with your friends. They wither not by chance. The grave is not filled by accident. Men die according to God's will. Your child is gone, but the Master took it. Your husband is gone, your wife is buried—the Master took them. Thank him that he let you have the pleasure of caring for them and tending them while they were here. And thank him that as he gave, he himself has taken away.—4.183, 184

266 Let us learn to hold loosely our dearest friends. Let us love them, but let us always learn to love them as dying things.—7.10

267 It is remarkable that the Holy Spirit has given us very few deathbed scenes in the book of God. We have very few in the Old Testament, fewer still in the New. And I take it that the reason may be, because the Holy Ghost would have us take more account of how we live than how we die, for life is the main business. He who learns to die daily while he lives will find it no difficulty to breathe out his soul for the last time into the hands of his faithful Creator.—13.662

268 The young *may* die; the old *must.*—13.718

269 Depend upon it, there is no pain in dying. The pain is in living.—17.419

270 We admit that we shall die, but not so soon as to make it a pressing matter. We imagine that we are not within measurable distance of the tomb. Even the oldest man gives himself a little longer lease, and when he has passed his eighty years, we have seen him hugging life with as much tenacity as if he had just commenced it. Brethren, in this we are not wise. Death will not spare us because we avoid him.—30.182

271 Men have been helped to live by remembering that they must die.—30.183

272 St. Augustine used to say he did not know whether to call it a dying life or a living death.—30.185

273 It is said that the ostrich buries its head in the sand and fancies itself secure when it can no longer see the hunter. I can hardly imagine that even a bird can be quite so foolish, and I beg you, do not enact such madness. If I do not think of death, yet death will think of me. If I will not go to death by meditation, death will come to me.—32.531

Death, Christian *See Death, fear of; Death, preparation for; Martyrdom*

274 A good Welsh lady, when she lay dying, was visited by her minister. He said to her, "Sister, are you sinking?" She answered him not a word, but looked at him with incredulous eye. He repeated the question, "Sister, are you sinking?"

At last, rising a little in the bed, she said, "Sinking! Sinking! Did you ever know a sinner to sink through a rock? If I had been standing on the sand, I might sink. But thank God, I am on the rock of ages, and there is no sinking there!"—1.66

275 A saint was once dying, and another who sat by him said, "Farewell, brother, I shall never see you again in the land of the living."

"Oh," said the dying man, "I shall see you again in the land of the living, where I am going. This is the land of the dying."—5.9

276 We are speeding onward through our brief life like an arrow shot from a bow, and we feel that we shall not drop down at the end of our flight into the dreariness of annihilation. We shall find a heavenly target far across the flood of death. The force which impels us onward is too mighty to be restrained by death.—5.393

277 At Stratford-on-Bow, in the days of Queen Mary, there was once a stake erected for the burning of two martyrs, one of them a lame man and the other a blind man. Just when the fire was lit, the lame man hurled away his staff and said to the blind man, "Courage, brother, this fire will cure us both!"

So can the righteous say of the grave, "Courage, the grave will cure us all; we shall leave our infirmities behind us." What patience this should give us to endure all our trials, for they are not of long duration.—6.163

278 A child once found a bird's nest in which were eggs, which he looked upon as a great treasure. He left them, and when a week had passed, went back again. He returned to his mother grieving, "I had some beautiful eggs in this nest, and now they are destroyed. Nothing is left but a few pieces of broken shell."

But the mother said, "Child, here is no destruction. There were little birds within those eggs, and they have flown away, and are singing now among the branches of the trees. The eggs are not wasted, but have answered their purpose. It is better far as it is."

So, when we look at our departed ones, we are apt to say, "Is this all you have left us, ruthless spoiler?"

But faith whispers, "No, the shell is broken, but among the birds of paradise, you shall find the spirits of your beloved ones singing. Their true manhood is not here, but has ascended to its Father God."

It is not a loss to die, it is a lasting, perpetual gain.—18.100, 101

279 When Richard Baxter lay dying, and his friends came to see him, almost the last word he said was in answer to the question, "Dear Mr. Baxter, how are you?"

"Almost well," said he, and it is so. Death cures; it is the best medicine, for they who die are not only almost well, but healed forever.—18.101

280 A lady once asked Mr. Wesley, "Suppose that you knew you were to die at 12 o'clock tomorrow night. How would you spend the intervening time?"

"Why, just as I intend to spend it now," he replied. "I should preach this evening at Gloucester, and again at five tomorrow morning. After that I should ride to Tewkesbury, preach in the afternoon, and meet the society in the evening. I should then repair to friend Martin's house, who expects to entertain me. I should converse and pray with the family as usual, retire to my room at 10 o'clock, commend myself to my heavenly Father, lie down to rest, and wake up in glory."—32.538

281 The very happiest persons I have ever met with have been departing believers. The only people for whom I have felt any envy have been dying members of this very church, whose hands I have grasped in their passing away. Almost without exception I have seen in them holy delight and triumph. And in the exceptions to this exceeding joy I have seen deep peace, exhibited in a calm and deliberate readiness to enter into the presence of their God.— 34.165

282 "What!" cries one, "Is there not a terrible amount of pain connected with death?"

I answer, No. It is life that has the pain; death is the finis of all pain. You blame death for the disease of which he is the cure.— 34.467

283 It is a grand thing to see a man dying full of life. The river of his mortal life comes to an end, but only by widening into the ocean of the glory life above. God makes his dying people to be like the sun, which never seems so large as when it sets. All the glories of midday are eclipsed by the marvels of sunset.—34.544

284 It is the very joy of this earthly life to think that it will come to an end.—43.492

285 The best moment of a Christian's life is his last one, because it is the one that is nearest heaven. And then it is that he begins to strike the keynote of the song which he shall sing to all eternity.—58.600

Death, Christ's   *See Atonement; Blood, Christ's; Cross; Gospel; Substitution*

286 Nothing puts life into men like a dying Savior.—31.202

287 All other topics in Holy Scripture are important, and none of them are to be cast into the shade. But the death of the Son of God is the central sun of all these minor luminaries. It is the great Alpha and Omega. It is not only eminent, it is preeminent with us.—53.50

288 If there is anything in all the world that ought to interest a man, it is the death of Christ.—59.302

Death, fear of   *See Death, Christian; Fear*

289 Fear to die? Thank God, I do not. The cholera may come again next summer—I pray it may not. But if it does, it matters not to me. I will toil and visit the sick by night and by day until I drop. And if it takes me, sudden death is sudden glory.—1.66

290 I should like you to be able to think of death. He that is afraid of solemn things has probably solemn reason to be afraid of them.—31.629

291 Never fear dying, beloved. Dying is the last, but the least matter that a Christian has to be anxious about. Fear living—that is a hard battle to fight, a stern discipline to endure, a rough voyage to undergo.—62.188, 189

Death, influence of

292 History tells us of Peter Waldo of Lyons, who was sitting at a banquet as thoughtless and careless as any of the revelers. Suddenly one at the table bowed his head and died. Waldo was startled into thought and went home to seek his God. He searched the Scriptures and became the second founder of the Waldenesian Church.—30.182

Death, preparation for

293 To be prepared to die is to be prepared to live. To be ready for eternity is in the best sense to be ready for time. Who is so fit to live on earth as the man who is fit to live in heaven? Who has brightness of the eye? Is it not the man who has looked within the gate of pearl and seen his place prepared among the blessed? Who has lightness of heart? Is it not the man who has unloaded his sin and has found mercy through the blood of Christ? Who can go to his bed and sleep in peace and wake with joy? Who but the man that is reconciled to God by the death of his Son? Who has the best of this world as well as the world to come? Is it not he to whom death has now become a changed thing?—23.512

Death, suddenness of

294 Life will fall before a touch, a breath. Justinian, an emperor of Rome, died by going into a room which had been newly painted. Adrian, a pope, was strangled by a fly. A consul struck his foot against his own threshold, and his foot mortified, so that he died thereby.—30.184

295 I remember standing in the pulpit one sultry summer afternoon, preaching the joys of heaven, and there was one woman's eye that especially caught mine. I knew not why it was, but it seemed to fascinate me. And as I spoke of heaven, she seemed to drink in every word, and her eyes flashed back again the thoughts I uttered. She seemed to lead me on to speak more and more of the streets of gold and the gates of pearl, till suddenly her eyes appeared to me to be too fixed. At last it struck me that, while I had been talking of heaven, she had gone there!

I paused and asked if someone in the pew would kindly see whether the friend sitting there was not dead, and in a moment her husband said, "She is dead, sir." I had known her long as a consistent Christian, and as I stood there, I half wished that I could have changed places with her. There was not a sigh nor a tear. She seemed to drink in the thoughts of heaven, and then immediately go and enjoy it.—53.139

Death, time of

296 All fruits do not get ripe and mellow at the same season. So with Christians. They are at a full age when God chooses to take them home. They are at full age if they die at 21; they are not more than full age if they live to be 90.—1.328

Death Sentence   *See Punishment, capital*

Depravity   *See Calvinism; Carnality; Heart; Nature, human; Sin*

297 Our prayers have stains in them, our faith is mixed with unbelief, our repentance is not so tender as it should be, our communion is distant and interrupted. We cannot pray without sinning, and there is filth even in our tears.—11.135

298 In the best prayer that was ever offered by the holiest man that ever lived, there was enough sin to render it a polluted thing, if the Lord had looked upon it by itself. The sins of our holy things are alone enough to condemn us.—18.278

299 As the salt flavors every drop in the Atlantic, so does sin affect every atom of our nature. It is so sadly there, so abundantly there, that if you cannot detect it, you are deceived.—21.365

300 No man living has ever exaggerated his own sin or thought too basely of himself. There does not live beneath the canopies of heaven any man whose sense of sin is as deep as the sin really is.—22.221

301 There is no beast in wolf or lion or serpent that is so brutish as the beast in man. According to the Levitical law, he that touched a dead animal was unclean till evening, but he who touched a dead man was unclean seven days. For man is a seven times more polluting creature than any of the beasts of the field when his animal nature rules him.—25.373

302 A very hell of corruption lies within the best saint.—28.33

303 When young folks tell me how terribly wicked they are, and therefore they are afraid that they cannot be saved, I sometimes reply, "Yes, but you are much worse than you think you are." They look so astonished, for they hoped to be comforted, and they are plunged into a deeper ditch. I tell them that the Lord Jesus came to save the weak and worthless. We lay the ax to the tree of self that men may fly to the tree of life.—28.293

304 Objection is sometimes made to the doctrine of total depravity. If men turn away from God in anger, I can understand it. If men turn aside from God in justice, I can understand it. But when they so hate God that they will not even have his salvation, when they refuse pardon through the precious blood of Christ, when they will sooner be damned than reconciled to God, this shows that their heart is desperately wicked. The cross rejected is the clearest proof of the heart depraved.—34.257

305 The treatment of our Lord Jesus Christ by men is the clearest proof of total depravity. Those must be stony hearts indeed which can laugh at a dying Savior and mock even his faith in God!—34.337

306 Hell itself does not contain greater monsters of iniquity than you and I might become. Within the magazine of our hearts there is powder enough to destroy us in an instant, if omnipotent grace did not prevent.—35.412

307 If you do not believe in human depravity, accept a pastorate in this wicked London, and if you are true to your commission, you will doubt no more!—37.43

308 All manner of evils and sins multiply in the heart like fishes in the sea.—37.297

309 Our very prayers need to be prayed over; our tears need to be wept over; our repentance has something in it that needs to be repented of; and our spiritual life itself often has much of death about it. Sin penetrates our holy things.—44.134

310 I truly believe that if the devil were to be converted and become a holy angel again, it would not be more wonderful than the conversion of some who are now present.—44.354

311 You may walk over a grassy hill and think yourself perfectly secure. Yet underneath there may be a slumbering volcano, liable to break out at any moment. By the Word of God we are faithfully warned that there is a sink of iniquity within our soul—a black and foul spring—a foul generator of everything that is evil in the very fountain of our nature.— 48.182

312 Nothing that I know of so clearly proves that man's heart is absolutely estranged from all that is good as that man rejects the gospel of grace, refuses divine mercy, and tramples underfoot the very blood of the Son of God.—48.529

313 There is enough of the fire of hell in you who are the most like Christ to set all hell alight again if the infernal fires were ever put out.—51.174

314 I can well remember, when I was under deep conviction of sin, wishing that I had been a frog or a toad rather than a human being, because I felt myself to be so foul in the sight of God.—53.596

315 The depravity of mankind is a miracle of sin. It is as great a miracle, from one point of view, as the grace of God is from another. Jesus Christ neglected! Eternal love slighted! Infinite mercy disregarded!—54.165

316 A good brother said to me the other day, concerning a certain boy, that he was afraid we should never do much with him because he was of very corrupt origin.
I said, "So were you."
"Ah!" he replied, "I do not quite mean it that way."
"No," I said, "but I do."— 54.235, 236

Depression *See Despair; Disappointment; Discouragement*

317 I, of all men, am perhaps the subject of the deepest depression at times. Yet there lives not a person who can say more truthfully than I, "My soul doth magnify the Lord, and my spirit hath rejoiced in God my Savior" (Luke 1:46, 47).—10.352

318 I am the subject of depression so fearful that I hope none of you ever get to such extremes of wretchedness as I go to. But I always get back again by this—I know that I trust Christ. I have no reliance but in him, and if he falls, I shall fall with him. But if he does not, I shall not. Because he lives, I shall live also, and I spring to my legs again and fight with my depressions of spirit and get the victory through it. And so may

you do, and so you *must*, for there is no other way of escaping from it.—12.298

319 Although my joy is greater than most men, my depression is such as few can have an idea of. This week has been in some respects the crowning week of my life, but it closed with a horror of great darkness, of which I will say no more than this: I bless God that at my worst, underneath me I found the everlasting arms.—14.188

320 I often feel very grateful to God that I have undergone fearful depression. I know the borders of despair and the horrible brink of that gulf of darkness into which my feet have almost gone. But hundreds of times I have been able to give a helpful grip to brethren and sisters who have come into that same condition, which grip I could never have given if I had not known their deep despondency. So I believe that the darkest and most dreadful experience of a child of God will help him to be a fisher of men if he will but follow Christ.—32.344

321 When I am seeing troubled people, I enter into one sorrowful case after another till I am more sad than any of them. I try as far as I can to have fellowship with the case of each one, in order to be able to speak a word of comfort to him; and I can say from personal experience that I know of nothing that wears the soul down so fast as the outflow of sincere sympathy with the sorrowing, desponding, depressed ones. I have sometimes been the means in God's hand of helping a man who suffered with a desponding spirit. But the help I have rendered has cost me dearly. Hours after, I have been myself depressed, and I have felt an inability to shake it off.—36.37

322 I know, perhaps as well as anyone, what depression means, and what it is to feel myself sinking lower and lower. Yet at the worst, when I reach the lowest depths, I have an inward peace which no pain or depression can in the least disturb. Trusting in Jesus Christ my Savior, there is still a blessed quietness in the deep caverns of my soul, though upon the surface, a rough tempest may be raging, and there may be little apparent calm.—47.483

323 I find myself frequently depressed—perhaps more so than any other person here. And I find no better cure for that depression than to trust in the Lord with all my heart, and seek to realize afresh the power of the peace-speaking blood of Jesus, and his infinite love in dying upon the cross to put away all my transgressions.—56.595

Despair *See Conviction; Depression; Disappointment; Discouragement*

324 A Christian's despair makes him pray; it is a despair of self. A worldling's despair makes him rave against God and give up prayer.—17.209

325 I have never heard yet of anybody who derived any good from despair. Let me correct myself, there is a kind of despair which is the work of the Spirit of God; I wish that you all felt it—a despair of self-salvation, a despair of washing away your own sin.—40.446

326 With heights of joy in serving my Master I am happily familiar. But into the very depths of despair—such an inward sinking as I cannot describe—I have likewise sunk. Yet I do know that my Redeemer lives, that the battle is sure, that the victory is safe.—62.187

Devil

327 There is something very comforting in the thought that the devil is an adversary (1 Peter 5:8). I would sooner have him for an adversary than a friend. O my soul, it were dread work with you if Satan were a friend of yours, for then with him you must forever dwell in darkness, shut out from the friendship of God. But to have Satan for an adversary is a comfortable omen, for it looks as if God were our friend, and so far let us be comforted in this matter.—11.53

328 He can make men dance upon the brink of hell as though they were on the verge of heaven.—11.75

329 He is more cunning than the wisest: How soon he entangled Solomon! He is stronger than the strongest: How fatally he overthrew Samson! Yes, and men after God's own heart, like David, have been led into most grievous sins by his seductions.—36.520

330 A great many of the devil's servants are so disrespectful to their lord that they even deny his existence. And the devil himself is so self-denying that he denies his own existence.—44.123

331 There is a minister now preaching the gospel, and God is greatly blessing him, who says he owes his earnestness to a remark I made in a certain college that I visited. I was asked on the spur of the moment to speak a word to the students, and I said, "Well, brethren, I have nothing to say to you except this—Whenever you see the devil, have a shot at him."

The young man told me that he recollected that sentence, and it had often been of service to him. So I say it again to every Christian here—Whenever you see the devil, have a shot at him. If you see sin, rebuke it. If you see doubt, try to remove it. If you see darkness, bring the light to bear upon it.—45.185

332 Martin Luther used to say, "I often laugh at Satan, and there is nothing that makes him so angry as when I attack him to his face, and tell him that through God I am more than a match for him."—49.142

333 Troubled ones, I urge you to resolve that if you cannot have comfort from God, at any rate you will not have it from the devil. Determine that if you cannot do business with heaven, you will not trade with hell, and say that you would rather live in a dungeon with God than dwell in tents of ease with Satan. If your life must always be one of sorrow, be content that it shall be so if the Lord wills it.—53.86

Devotions   *See Prayer, family*

Disappointment   *See Depression; Despair; Discouragement*

334 I read of a Christian who said, "I used to have many disappointments, until I changed one letter of the word and chopped it in two, so that instead of 'disappointments,' I read it, 'his appointments.' "

That was a wonderful change, for "disappointments" break your heart, but "his appointments" you accept cheerfully.—41.321

Discipleship   *See Commitment; Lordship*

335 If persecution should arise, you should be willing to part with all that you possess—with your liberty, with your life itself, for Christ—or you cannot be his disciple.—58.618

Discipline, God's   *See Punishment; Wrath, God's*

336 God's people can never by any possibility be punished for their sins. God has punished them already in the person of Christ, their substitute. But yet, while the Christian cannot be condemned, he can be chastised. Punishment is laid on a man in anger; God strikes him in wrath. But when he afflicts his child, chastisement is applied in love. The rod has been baptized in deep affection before it is laid on the believer's back.—1.363

337 Whenever God uses a rod to his children, he always burns it as soon as he has done with it. He does not put it up by the looking glass, but he destroys it, for he hates the sight of it. Thus he used Sennacherib as a rod, but he broke him in pieces. He used Babylon for the same purpose, and then blotted it out of existence. He employed Assyria also, but he destroyed her power. The rod reminds him of his children's cries, and he cannot endure it.—20.261

338 A dog will follow a man as long as he throws him a bone, but that is a man's own dog which will follow him when he strikes him with the whip and will even fawn upon him when he speaks roughly to him. Such Christians ought we to be who will keep close to God when he is robed in thunder.—25.654

339 This is one of the sure marks of the children of God—they kiss the rod. And the more the Lord chastens them, the more they cling to him.—26.530

340 I owe everything to the furnace and the hammer. I have made no progress in heavenly learning except when I have been whipped by the great Schoolmaster. The best piece of furniture in my house has been the cross. My greatest enricher has been personal pain, and for that I desire to thank God.—32.683

341 The hardest blow that God ever laid upon his child was inflicted by the hand of love.—33.306

342 You have never seen the great Artist's masterpiece. You have seen the rough marble, you have marked the chippings that fall on the ground, you have felt the edge of his chisel, you know the weight of his hammer. But, oh, could you see that glorious image as it will be when he has put the finishing stroke to it, you would then understand the chisel and the hammer and the Worker better than you now do!—33.307

343 No honey was sweeter than that which dropped from the end of Jonathan's rod (1 Sam. 14:27). But that is nothing to the sweetness of the consolation which comes through Jehovah's rod. Our brightest joys are the birth of our bitterest griefs. When the woman has her travail pangs, joy comes to the house because the child is born; and sorrow is to us also often the moment of the birth of our graces.—38.4

344 I have never learned anything from God except by the rod.—40.386

Discouragement   *See Depression; Despair; Disappointment*

345 If the excuse for fainting be that the work is toilsome, that it is too much a drag upon you, why did you begin it? You ought to have known this at the first. You should have counted the cost. But let me add, the work was not toilsome when your heart was loving, neither would it now be so hard if your soul were right with God.—18.498

Dishonesty   *See Lying*

Division   *See Unity*

346 Satan always hates Christian fellowship; it is his policy to keep Christians apart. Anything which can divide saints from one another he delights in. He attaches

far more importance to godly intercourse than we do. Since union is strength, he does his best to promote separation.—11.602

Doctrine   *See Catechism; Teaching*

Doubt   *See Agnostic; Assurance; Atheist; Faith; Unbelief*

347 "Doubts and fears," said an old preacher, "are like the toothache; nothing more painful, but never fatal."—3.330

348 There is only one creature that God has made that ever doubts him. The sparrows doubt not. They sweetly sing at night as they go to their roosts, though they know not where tomorrow's meal shall be found. The very cattle trust him, and even in days of drought, you have seen them when they pant for thirst, how they expect the water. The angels never doubt him, nor the devils. Devils believe and tremble (James 2:19). But it was left for man, the most favored of all creatures, to mistrust his God.—7.122,123

349 My peculiar temptation has been constant unbelief. I know that God's promise is true. Yet does this temptation incessantly assail me—"Doubt him; distrust him; he will leave you yet." I can assure you when that temptation is aided by a nervous state of mind, it is very hard to stand day by day and say, "No, I cannot doubt my God."—7.573

350 Some of us who have preached the Word for years, and have been the means of working faith in others and of establishing them in the knowledge of the fundamental doctrines of the Bible, have nevertheless been the subjects of the most fearful and violent doubts as to the truth of the very gospel we have preached.—11.290

351 I suppose no man is a firm believer who has not once been a doubter.—17.55

352 It seems to me that doubt is worse than trial. I had sooner suffer any affliction than be left to question the gospel or my own interest in it.—29.79

353 It is an inconsistent thing for a believing man to doubt his God. If you believe, why doubt? If faith, why *little* faith? If you doubt, why believe? Oil and water will not mix. Oh, how should faith and unbelief unite?—31.467

354 I have heard much about "honest doubt," but I honestly believe that much of doubt is the most dishonest thing out of perdition. Take heed that you be not hardened by the deceitfulness of this sin; it will ruin you if you indulge in it. "Believe and live" is the gospel. "Doubt and die" is the alternative.—35.321

355 Some of you are always fashioning fresh nets of doubt for your own entanglement. You invent

snares for your own feet and are greedy to lay more of them. You are mariners who seek the rocks, soldiers who court the point of the bayonet. It is an unprofitable business. Practically, morally, mentally, spiritually, doubting is an evil trade. You are like a smith, wearing out his arm in making chains with which to bind himself. Doubt is sterile, a desert without water. Doubt discovers difficulties which it never solves; it creates hesitancy, despondency, despair. Its progress is the decay of comfort, the death of peace. "Believe!" is the word which speaks life into a man, but doubt nails down his coffin.—35.455

356 "Well," says one, "I quarrel with the Bible."

Do you? The only real argument against the Bible is an unholy life. When a man argues against the Word of God, follow him home, and see if you cannot discover the reason of his enmity to the Word of the Lord. It lies in some form of sin.—35.618

357 I have looked down the list of crimes, and though there are some that are truly abominable, yet I have not seen anything so vile as the sin of a man who doubts the love and power of Christ, who died that men might live. This is the masterpiece of hell's temptation.—37.510

358 Salvation is by faith. Damnation comes by doubt.—38.93

359 The first time I can recommend any sinner to doubt the Savior is when he finds a fellow sinner who has been to Jesus, has rested in him, and yet has perished. The other reason is this. Try him yourself, and if he rejects you, then you shall have cause for doubting.—57.204

360 There are many who cannot believe in Jesus because they have a besetting sin that they cannot give up. There is the bottom of most men's doubts. They would not doubt if they did not sin. If they could have their sins and be believers, they would be believers fast enough. But there is that company that must be given up, that company which, instead of sanctifying the soul, depraves it.— 61.280, 281

Dreams   See Revelation, modern

Drunkenness

361 My soul might be perpetually dropping showers of tears, if it might know the doom and destruction brought on by that one demon, and by that one demon only! Though I am no total abstainer, I hate drunkenness as much as any man breathing, and have been the means of bringing many poor creatures to relinquish this bestial indulgence. We believe drunkenness to be an awful crime and a horrid sin. We stand prepared to go to war with it. How many thousands are murdered

every year by that accursed devil of drunkenness!—3.344

362 You condemn the Jews for choosing Barabbas; where will you find a counselor to plead for you when you choose drunkenness? If it was sinful for them to choose a murderer, what must it be for you to choose this cursed vice, which murders its hundreds of thousands?—28.138

363 If there are any here who require a homily upon drunkenness, they have only to let conscience speak, and it will tell them how base a sin it is. Perhaps of all the sins that are rife today, drunkenness brings the most present misery upon mankind. Other sins may seem to go deeper into the soul, but for creating widespread suffering, suffering brought upon the innocent wife and child, this vice raises its head above all others.—35.578

364 Drunkenness is the devil's back door to hell and everything that is hellish. For he that once gives away his brains to drink is ready to be caught by Satan for anything.—46.64

365 I do not believe that the devil himself is ever guilty of anything like that. I never hear even him charged with being drunk.—57.30

Election   *See Calvinism; Predestination; Sovereignty; Will, free*

366 If left to ourselves, the road to hell would be as naturally our choice as for a piece of inanimate matter to roll downwards, instead of assisting itself upwards.—1.254

367 You must first deny the authenticity and full inspiration of the Holy Scripture before you can legitimately and truly deny election.—3.130

368 If God requires of the sinner, dead in sin, that he should take the first step, then he requires just that which renders salvation as impossible under the gospel as it was under the law, since man is as unable to believe as he is to obey.—3.195

369 Your damnation is your own election, not God's.—5.119

370 I believe the man who is not willing to submit to the electing love and sovereign grace of God has great reason to question whether he is a Christian at all, for the spirit that kicks against that is the spirit of the unhumbled, unrenewed heart.—5.424

371 I have never preached this doctrine without seeing conversions, and I believe I never shall.—10.84

372 Who is to have authority in the matter of gracious adoption? The children of wrath? Surely not; and yet all men are such! No, it stands to reason, to common sense, that none but the parent can have the discretion to adopt.—10.488

373 Is your heart resting upon Jesus Christ? Does it meditate upon divine things? Is your heart a humble heart? Are you constrained to ascribe all to sovereign grace? Do you desire holiness? Do you find your pleasure in it? Does your heart ascribe praises to God? Is it a grateful heart? And is it a heart that is wholly fixed upon God, desiring never to go astray? If it be, then you have the marks of election.—11.381

374 It always seems inexplicable to me that those who claim free will so very boldly for man should not also allow some free will to God. Why should not Jesus Christ have the right to choose his own bride?—13.412

375 I can never cease to wonder that God has elected me.—14.350

376 From the Word of God I gather that damnation is all of man, from top to bottom, and salvation is all of grace, from first to last. He that perishes chooses to perish; but he that is saved is saved because God has chosen to save him.—34.538

377 A controversialist once said, "If I thought God had a chosen people, I should not preach." That is the very reason why I do preach. What would make him inactive is the mainspring of my earnestness. If the Lord had not a people to be saved, I should have little to cheer me in my ministry.—36.551

378 I believe that God will save his own elect. And I also believe that if I do not preach the gospel, the blood of men will be laid at my door.—39.170

379 Whatever may be said about the doctrine of election, it is written in the Word of God as with an iron pen, and there is no getting rid of it. To me, it is one of the sweetest and most blessed truths in the whole of revelation, and those who are afraid of it are so because they do not understand it. If they could but know that the Lord had chosen them, it would make their hearts dance for joy.—39.374, 375

380 I believe in divine election, because somebody must have the supreme will in this matter, and man's will must not occupy the throne, but the will of God.—48.294

381 Our Savior has bidden us to preach the gospel to every creature (Mark 16:15). He has not said, "Preach it only to the elect," and though that might seem to be the most logical thing for us to do, yet since he has not been pleased to stamp the elect in their foreheads or put any distinctive mark upon them, it would be an impossible task for us to perform. When we preach the gospel to every creature, the gospel makes its own division, and Christ's sheep hear his voice, and follow him.—51.262

382 I am quite certain that God has an elect people, for he tells me so in his word. And I am equally certain that everyone who comes to Christ shall be saved, for that also is his own declaration in the Scriptures. When people ask me how I reconcile these two truths, I usually say that there is no need to reconcile them, for they have never yet quarreled with one another.—56.631

383 I have sometimes felt that, had God not redeemed my soul, I must reverence him for redeeming others. Had I never tasted of his love at all myself, yet the story of his love to his enemies is such that I could fall down and worship him.—62.446

Election, disbelief in   See Election, justification of

384 Can you, O rejector, cast election out of the Bible? Would you be like the woman at the feet of Solomon, and have the child rent in halves, that you might have your half (1 Kings 3:26)? Is it not here in Scripture?—1.315, 316

385 It has been said that the doctrine of election leads to carelessness and to hard-heartedness in sin. What truth has not been perverted? You may teach rightly that God is long-suffering, and that at the eleventh hour he still invites a sinner to himself. But has not that very fact helped to lull sinners to sleep? There is no passage in Scripture which may

not be the means of a man's destruction, if he wills to make it so.—6.302

386 Rebellion against divine election is often founded on the idea that the sinner has a sort of right to be saved, and this is to deny the full desert of sin.—24.302

Election, justification of   See Election, disbelief in

387 Some say, "It is unfair for God to choose some and leave others."

Now, I will ask you one question: Is there any of you here who wishes to be holy, who wishes to be regenerate, to leave off sin and walk in holiness?

"Yes, there is," says someone. "I do!"

Then God has elected you.

But another says, "No, I don't want to be holy; I don't want to give up my lusts and my vices."

Why should you grumble, then, that God has not elected you? For if you were elected, you would not like it, according to your own confession.—1.316

388 Our opponents put the case thus: Suppose a father should condemn some of his children to extreme misery, and make others supremely happy, out of his own arbitrary will! Would it be just? Would it not be brutal and detestable?

My answer is, of course it would. It would be execrable in the highest degree. But the case stated is not at all the one under consideration, but one as opposite from it as light from darkness. Sinful man is not now in the position of a well-deserving or innocent child.

We will suppose another case far nearer the mark. A number of criminals, guilty of the most aggravated and detestable crimes, are righteously condemned to die, and die they must, unless the king shall give them a free pardon. If for good and sufficient reasons, known only to himself, the king chooses to forgive a certain number and to leave the rest for execution, is there anything cruel or unrighteous here? And so may we well ask, "Is there unrighteousness with God? God forbid!"—10.77

Election, preaching on   See Preaching

389 Some of you have never preached on election since you were ordained. "These things," you say, "are offensive." And so you would rather offend God than offend man.

But you reply, "These things will not be practical." I do think that the climax of all man's blasphemy is centered in that utterance. Tell me that God put a thing in the Bible that I am not to preach! You are finding fault with my God.

But you say, "It will be dangerous." What! God's truth dangerous? I should not like to stand in your shoes when you have to face your Maker on the day of judgment after such an utterance as that.—3.432

390 God gave me this great book to preach from, and if he has put anything in it you think is not fit, go and complain to him, not to me. I am simply his servant, and if his errand that I am to tell is objectionable, I cannot help it. Let me tell you, the reason why many of our churches are declining is just because this doctrine has not been preached.—4.340

391 "But some truths ought to be kept back from the people," you will say, "lest they should make an ill use thereof."

That is Popish doctrine. It was upon that very theory that the priests kept back the Bible from the people. They did not give it to them lest they should misuse it. Besides all this, remember that men do read the Scriptures and think about these doctrines and often make mistakes about them. Who then, shall set them right if we who preach the Word hold our tongues about the matter?—51.49

Election, unconditional   See Calvinism; Election

392 "But," say others, "God elected them on the foresight of their faith."

Now, God gives faith, therefore he could not have elected them on account of faith which he foresaw.—1.317

393 Should any here, supposing themselves to be the children of God, imagine that there is some reason in them why they should have been chosen, let them know that as yet they are in the dark concerning the first principles of grace, and have not yet learned the gospel.—3.146

394 How is it that some of us are converted, while our companions in sin are left to persevere in their godless career? Was there anything good in us that moved the heart of God to save us? God forbid that we should indulge the blasphemous thought!—6.34

395 If I were to plead that the rose bud were the author of the root, I might indeed be laughed at. That which is the effect cannot be the cause. But what original good is there in any man? If God chose us for anything good in ourselves, we must all be left unchosen. Have we not all an evil heart of unbelief? Have we not all departed from his ways?—6.135

396 An old woman told John Newton she was sure that God chose her before she was born, for he never would have chosen her afterwards, and I think there is some truth in that remark.—43.416

Envy   *See Greed*

397 Does the dove grieve because the raven can gloat itself on carrion? No, for it lives on other food. Will the eagle envy the wren his tiny nest? Oh, no! So the Christian will mount aloft as the eagle, saying, "I look upon the low places of this earth with contempt; I envy not your greatness, I desire not your fame, I ask not for wealth, I beg not for power. My portion is the Lord."—1.190

Eternal Security   *See Security*

Eternity   *See Heaven; Hell; Time*

398 Eternity, eternity, mountain without a summit! Up its sides you must climb, O sinner, and find it an ever-burning volcano.—8.514

399 If at this instant you were to leave your body, where would your soul be? You may know very readily. Where does it delight to be now? Your delight prophesies your destiny. What you have chosen here shall be your portion hereafter. If you loved sin, you shall be steeped up to the throat in it, and it shall burn around you like liquid fire. But if your delights have been with your God, you shall dwell with him.—23.514, 515

400 That only is worth my having which I can have forever. That only is worth my grasping which death cannot tear out of my hand.—29.509

401 Heaven and hell are not places far away. You may be in heaven before the clock ticks

again, it is so near. Oh, that we, instead of trifling about such things because they seem so far away, would solemnly realize them, since they are so very near! This very day, before the sun goes down, some hearer now sitting in this place may see the realities of heaven or hell.—35.191

Evangelism   *See Compassion; Conversion; Preaching; Salvation*

402 If I had worlds to buy one of your souls, I would readily give them, if I might but bring one of you to Christ.—2.424

403 To be laughed at is no great hardship to me. I can delight in scoffs and jeers. Caricatures, lampoons, and slanders are my glory. But that you should turn from your own mercy, this is my sorrow. Spit on me, but, oh, repent! Laugh at me, but, oh, believe in my Master! Make my body as the dirt of the streets, but damn not your own souls!—4.56

404 If then, you will be damned, let me have this one thing as a consolation for your misery, that you are not damned for the lack of calling after; you are not lost for the lack of weeping after, and not lost for the lack of praying after.—4.304

405 The saving of souls, if a man has once gained love to perishing sinners and his blessed Master, will be an all-absorbing passion to him. It will so carry him away, that he will almost forget himself in the saving of others. He will be like the brave fireman, who cares not for the scorch or the heat, so that he may rescue the poor creature on whom true humanity has set his heart.—5.474, 475

406 If sinners will be damned, at least let them leap to hell over our bodies. And if they will perish, let them perish with our arms about their knees, imploring them to stay. If hell must be filled, at least let it be filled in the teeth of our exertions, and let not one go there unwarned and unprayed for.—7.11

407 The fact is, brethren, we *must* have conversion work here. We cannot go on as some churches do without converts. We cannot, we will not, we must not, we dare not. Souls must be converted here, and if there be not many born to Christ, may the Lord grant to me that I may sleep in the tomb and be heard of no more. Better indeed for us to die than to live, if souls be not saved.—7.221

408 I would freely give my eyes if you might but see Christ, and I would willingly give my hands if you might but lay hold on him.—10.584

409 To be a soul winner is the happiest thing in this world. And with every soul you bring to Jesus Christ, you seem to get a new heaven here upon earth.—11.431

410 You cannot stop their dying, but, oh, that God might help you to stop their being damned! You cannot stop the breath from going out of their bodies, but, oh, if the gospel could but stop their souls from going down to destruction!—12.466

411 I would be willing to die if I could but be honored by the Holy Spirit to win this mass of souls to God.—13.204

412 If we had to preach to thousands year after year, and never rescued but one soul, that one soul would be full reward for all our labor, for a soul is of countless price.—13.692

413 It is a very solemn delusion when ministers think they are prospering, and yet do not hear of conversions.—14.378

414 He succeeds best who expects conversion every time he preaches.—15.32

415 If I never won souls, I would sigh till I did. I would break my heart over them if I could not break their hearts. Though I can understand the possibility of an earnest sower never reaping, I cannot understand the possibility of an earnest sower being content not to reap. I cannot comprehend any one of you Christian people trying to win souls and not having results, and being satisfied without results.—15.237

416 If the preacher himself were dead, if his interment in the grave could bring you to the Savior, it were a cheap price to pay.—16.299

417 If a change of messengers will win you, much as I love the task of speaking in my Master's name, I would gladly die now, that some other preacher might occupy this platform, if thereby you might be saved.—17.94

418 If any minister can be satisfied without conversions, he shall have not conversions.—17.495

419 It were worthwhile to preach every Sabbath for a million years, if but one soul were brought in at last.—17.691

420 The Holy Spirit will move them by first moving *you*. If you can rest without their being saved, *they* will rest, too. But if you are filled with an agony for them, if you cannot bear that they should be lost, you will soon find that they are uneasy, too. I hope you will get into such a state that you will dream about your child or your hearer perishing for lack of Christ, and start up at once and begin to cry, "O God, give me converts, or I die." Then you will have converts.—22.143, 144

421 I would sooner bring one sinner to Jesus Christ than unpick all the mysteries of the divine

Word, for salvation is the thing we are to live for.—22.263

422 If a man could tell me that he stopped Niagara at a word, I would not envy him his power if God will only allow me to stop a sinner in his mad career of sin. If a creature could put his finger on Vesuvius and quench its flame, I would not at all regret that I had no such power if I might but be the means of staying a blasphemer and teaching him to pray. This spiritual power is the greatest power imaginable, and the most to be desired.—24.643

423 I count nothing to be worthy of your pastor's life and soul and energy but the winning of you to Christ. Nothing but your salvation can ever make me feel that my heart's desire is granted.—25.677

424 I would sooner preach the dullest sermon that was ever preached than preach the most brilliant that was ever spoken, if I could by that poor sermon lead you quite away from myself to seek the Lord Jesus Christ. That is the one thing I care about.—29.7

425 Have you no wish for others to be saved? Then you are not saved yourself. Be sure of that.—34.222

426 If there existed only one man or woman who did not love the Savior, and if that person lived among the wilds of Siberia, and if it were necessary that all the millions of believers on the face of the earth should journey there, and every one of them plead with him to come to Jesus before he could be converted, it would be well worth all the zeal, labor, and expense. One soul would repay the travail in birth of myriads of zealous Christians.—34.610, 611

427 My main business is the saving of souls. This one thing I do.—36.277

428 If no soul gets saved by this discourse, I cannot carry on my business. "Oh, well," says one, "a man may preach very faithfully, and yet he may have no souls saved."

Yes, a fisherman may fish and never catch any fish, but he is not much of a fisherman. And so, if there were no souls saved, perhaps I might find some way of satisfying my conscience, but it is unknown to me as yet. If my hearers are not converted, I have lost my time; I have lost the exercise of brain and heart. I feel as if I had lost my hope and lost my life, unless I find for my Lord some of his blood-bought ones, and I must find some of them by this sermon.—37.593

429 Preaching the gospel is to us a matter of life and death; we throw our whole soul into it. We live and are happy if you believe in Jesus and are saved. But we are

almost ready to die if you refuse the gospel of Christ.—43.249

430 I would willingly lay down my very life if I could bring all in this tabernacle to the Lord Jesus Christ.—49.310

431 My anxious desire is that every time I preach, I may clear myself of the blood of all men; that if I step from this platform to my coffin, I may have told out all I knew of the way of salvation.—50.286

432 Do you want arguments for soul winning? Look up to heaven, and ask yourself how sinners can ever reach those harps of gold and learn that everlasting song, unless they have someone to tell them of Jesus, who is "mighty to save." But the best argument of all is to be found in the wounds of Jesus. You want to honor him, you desire to put many crowns upon his head, and this you can best do by winning souls for him. These are the spoils that he covets, these are the trophies for which he fights, these are the jewels that shall be his best adornment.—57.333

433 I do not envy Gabriel his crown when God gives me souls. I have thought that I would rather be here to talk with you and point you to my Master's cross than be up there and cast my crown at his feet. For surely there can be no joy in heaven greater than the joy of doing the Master's will in winning souls for him.—59.140

434 Oh, if it were possible, I would gladly translate you all to heaven at once—from the tabernacle to the temple, from this place where we sing his praises at his footstool to the place where we will sing them to his face more sweetly and more loudly. Not one of you, oh, not one of you would we have absent.—60.201

435 Gladly would I meet a martyr's death, if you would be persuaded thereby to come to Christ for life.—62.58

Evolution   *See Science*

436 I wish that Darwin's theory might be carried out in us as Christians, until, as he talks of an oyster developing into an Archbishop of Canterbury, we who at our conversion were little better than the oyster, should go on developing in spiritual things, until we should know what John meant, who said, "It doth not yet appear what we shall be, but we know that, when he shall appear, we shall be like him; for we shall see him as he is" (1 John 3:2).—51.130

Example   *See Parents, example of*

437 It is an awful fact that there may be souls in hell whom you have sent there! It was a wise penitential prayer of a converted man who had exercised influence for evil—"Lord, forgive me my

other men's sins." When you lead others to sin, their sins are to a large extent your sins.—31.235

438 Oh, that we might all repent of other people's sins! Did you ever repent of them?

"I have had enough to do to repent of my own sins," says one.

But these sins of which I am speaking *are* your own, as well as other people's, if you have led others into the way of committing the sin.—41.89

Faith   *See Doubt; Feelings; Indecision; Prayer, of faith; Trust; Unbelief; Works*

439 The pith, the essence of faith, lies in this—a casting oneself on the promise.—3.3

440 Some years ago two men were in a boat and found themselves unable to manage the stupendous falls of Niagara. Persons on the shore saw them but were unable to do much for their rescue. At last, however, one man was saved by floating a rope to him, which he grasped. The same instant the rope came into his hand, a log floated by the other man. Instead of seizing the rope, he laid hold on the log. It was a fatal mistake. The one was drawn to shore because he had a connection with the people on the land, while the other, clinging to the log, was borne irresistibly along, and was never heard of afterwards.

Do you not see here a practical illustration? Faith is connection with Christ. Christ is on the shore, so to speak, holding the rope of faith, and if we lay hold of it with the hand of our confidence, he pulls us to shore. But our good works, having no connection with Christ, are drifted along down the gulf of despair. Grapple them as tightly as we may, even with hooks of steel, they cannot avail us in the least degree.—3.5, 6

441 Remember, he that believes shall be saved, be his sins ever so many. And he that believes not must perish, be his sins ever so few.—3.176

442 To trust a doctor to cure you when you believe you are getting better is very easy. But to trust your physician when you feel as if the sentence of death were in your body, to bear up when the disease is rising into the very skin and when the ulcer is gathering its venom—to believe even then in the efficacy of the medicine—that is faith.—7.107

443 If God gives you the power to believe that any soul will be saved, it will be saved; there is no doubt about that.—10.35

444 There is not an angel before the throne who can believe such great things of God as you can. An angel has no sin. He cannot, therefore, believe that Jesus can put away his sin. But you can.—13.72

445 Never think for a moment that strong faith in the Lord is necessarily pride. It is the reverse. It is one of the worst forms of pride to question the promise of God.—14.151

446 A real faith is to the believer like the hair of Samson, in which his great strength lies. It is his Moses' rod, dividing seas of difficulty, his Elijah's chariot, in which he mounts about the earth.—14.319

447 There is no sin that shall damn the man who believes, and nothing can save the man who will not believe.—17.539

448 Do I hear it said, "Love Jesus, dear children"? That is not the gospel. It is "Trust him. Believe." Not love, but faith is the saving grace.—20.563

449 You believe in God for your soul. Believe in him about your property. Believe in God about your sick wife or your dying child. Believe in God about your losses and bad debts and declining business.—21.149

450 The believer knows that his faith is not a weed indigenous to the soil of his heart, but a rare plant, an exotic which has been planted there by divine wisdom. And he knows that if the Lord does not nourish it, his faith will die like a withered flower. He knows that his faith is a perpetual miracle, for it is begotten, sustained, and preserved by a power not less mighty than that which raised our Lord Jesus from the dead.—23.201

451 Why is faith so essential? It is because of its receptive power. A purse will not make a man rich, and yet without some place for his money, how could a man acquire wealth? Faith of itself could not contribute a penny to salvation, but it is the purse which holds a precious Christ within itself. It holds all the treasures of divine love.

If a man is thirsty, a rope and a bucket are not in themselves of much use to him. But yet if there is a well near at hand, the very thing that is needed is a bucket and a rope, by means of which a man may draw water out of the wells of salvation, and drink to his heart's content.—23.293

452 Faith is a secondary thing compared to Christ. We must have faith to be as the finger with which we touch the hem of the Master's garment, but the finger does not work the cure. Shall I refuse to touch because I have not washed my finger clean, or it has no gold ring on it? To attach so much importance to the finger as to refuse to touch Christ's garment with it would be insanity. Do not mind your finger; touch the garment's hem! Get to Christ somehow, anyhow, for if you get to him you shall live. It is not the greatness nor the perfection of

your faith, it is *his* greatness and *his* perfection which is to be depended on.—29.560

453 Faith is the queen bee. You may get temperance, love, hope, and all those other bees into the hive, but the main thing is to get simple faith in Christ, and all the rest will come after it. Get the queen bee of faith, and all the other virtues will attend her.—31.310

454 Faith is so contrary to nature, that its existence in the heart is like a spark burning in the sea. Faith is so much attacked in this evil day that it is like a candle kept alight in a cyclone.—33.494

455 Faith is the linen which binds the plaster of Christ's reconciliation to the sore of our sin. The linen does not heal; that is the work of the ointment. So faith does not heal; that is the work of the atonement of Christ.—33.714

456 It is easy enough to believe in a mere priestly absolution if you have enough credulity, but we need more than this. It is very easy to believe in baptismal regeneration, but what is the good of it? What practical result does it produce? A child remains the same after he has been baptismally regenerated as he was before, and he grows up to prove it. To believe that the Lord Jesus Christ can make us love the good things we once despised, and shun those evil things in which we once took

pleasure—this is to believe in him.—34.92

457 Faith is the surest of all sin-killers.—34.393

458 Faith is the soul's eye by which it sees the Lord. Faith is the soul's ear by which we hear what God will speak. Faith is the spiritual hand which touches and grasps the things not seen as yet. Faith is the spiritual nostril which perceives the precious perfume of our Lord's garments. Faith also is the soul's taste by which we perceive the sweetness of our Lord, and enjoy it for ourselves.—36.558

459 I would recommend you either believe God up to the hilt, or else not to believe at all. Believe this book of God, every letter of it, or else reject it. There is no logical standing place between the two. Be satisfied with nothing less than a faith that swims in the deeps of divine revelation; a faith that paddles about the edge of the water is poor faith at best. It is little better than a dry-land faith, and is not good for much.—38.35

460 Faith is hard because it is easy. It is difficult because there is no difficulty in it. And it seems obscure simply because it is so clear.—41.101

461 Nothing will bring you near to God but believing, and nothing can shut you out from God but your unbelief. Only trust him;

that is the whole of the matter.—44.33, 34

462 You may be an eyewitness and yet perish, as Judas did. You may be an eyewitness and yet be as lost as Pilate was. You may be an eyewitness and still hate Christ, as Caiaphas did. But if you become a faith-witness, then shall you be included among those of whom it is written, "They shall look upon me whom they have pierced, and they shall mourn for him, as one mourneth for his only son" (Zech. 12:10). Such a faith-view begets repentance and hope and love, and brings salvation to every soul that has it.—45.89

463 The moment I am unbelieving, I am unhappy. It is not a vain thing for me to believe in Christ. It is my life, it is my strength, it is my joy. I am a lost man, and it were better for me that I had never been born, unless I have the privilege of believing.—45.211

464 If all my senses were to contradict God, I would deny every one of them and sooner believe myself to be out of my right mind than believe that God could lie. And I desire to feel that in every emotion of my spirit, every throb of my heart, every thought of my brain, and everything that is contrary to the plainly revealed truth of God, I will count myself a fool and a madman, and I will reckon God to be wise and true.—47.161

465 There is no saint here who can out-believe God. God never out-promised himself yet.—49.501

466 It is said that if we were to fold our arms and lie motionless on the water, we should not sink. To believe is to float upon the streams of grace.—57.288

467 Speaking of faith, a poor countryman said, "The old enemy has been troubling me very much lately, but I told him that he must not say anything to me about my sins. He must go to my Master, for I had transferred the whole concern to him, bad debts and all." That is believing in Jesus.—57.288

468 I have heard of a captain who had a little son, and this little boy was fond of climbing. One day he climbed to the masthead, and the father saw that if the boy attempted to return, he would be dashed to pieces. He therefore shouted to him not to look down, but to drop into the sea. The poor boy kept fast hold of the mast, but the father said it was his only chance of safety, and he shouted once more, "Boy, the next time the ship lurches, drop, or I will shoot you."

The boy is gone; he drops into the sea and is saved. Had he not dropped, he must have perished.

This is just your condition. So long as you cling to works and ceremonies, you are in the utmost peril. But when you give yourselves up entirely to the mercy of Christ, you are safe. Try it, sinner! Try it, that is all.—61.80, 81

Faith, dead

469 If you believe that repentance and faith bring salvation, why have you not repented and believed? If you believe that there is a God who hears prayer, why do you not pray? If you know that you must be born again, how is it you are content without the new birth?—33.364

Faith, little

470 Is it not a wonderful thing that Christ Jesus should ever enter into a man? Yes, but I will tell you something more wonderful, and that is that he should enter in by so narrow an opening as our little faith. There is the sun; I do not know how many thousands of times the sun is bigger than the earth, and yet the sun can come into a little room. And what is more, the sun can get in through a chink. So Christ can come in through a little faith, a mere chink of confidence.—29.272

471 Strong faith, like Mary, sits still in the house. Little faith is feverish after immediate joy. Little faith wants to be in heaven tomorrow. Little faith would convert the world before the sun went down, and she grows faint because her zeal has not fulfilled her wish. Little faith must pluck the promises while they are green. She is not content to wait till they become ripe and mellow.—31.459

Faith, object of   See Jesus

472 A man may say, "I have faith." But another question arises: What have you faith in?

"Well, I have faith in what I have felt."

Then get rid of it, for what you have felt is not an object of faith, nor to be trusted in at all.

"I have faith," says another, "in the doctrines which I have been taught."

I am glad you believe them, but remember, doctrines are not the Savior. A creed cannot save. What is the object of faith, then? It is a person, a living, divine, appointed person. And who is that person? He is none other than Jesus.—20.328

473 The eye cannot see itself. Did you ever see your own eye? In a mirror you may have done so, but that was only a reflection of it. And you may, in like manner, see the evidence of your faith, but you cannot look at the faith itself. Faith looks away from itself to the object of faith, even to Christ.—45.520

Faithfulness

474 I know of nothing which I would choose to have as the subject of my ambition for life than to be kept faithful to my God till death, still to be a soul winner,

still to be a true herald of the cross, and testify the name of Jesus to the last hour. It is only such who in the ministry shall be saved.—10.87

475 Remember John Bunyan when he refused to give up preaching. They put him in prison and said to him, "Mr. Bunyan, you can come out of prison whenever you will promise to cease preaching the gospel."

He said, "If you let me out of prison today, I will preach again tomorrow, by the grace of God."

"Well," said they, "then you must go back to prison," and he answered, "I will go back and stay there if need be till the moss grows on my eyelids, but I will never deny my Master."—42.452

Family *See Father; Mother; Parents; Parents, example of; Prayer, family*

Father *See Mother; Parents; Parents, example of; Prayer, family*

476 You act not the part of a true father unless you see to your son—whether he be in church membership or not—that on the slightest inconsistency he receives a gentle word of rebuke from you.—11.166

477 It was a great joy to me when my sons were born, but it was an infinitely surpassing joy as they told me that they had sought and found the Savior. To pray with them, to point them yet more fully to Christ, to hear the story of their spiritual troubles, and to help them out of their spiritual difficulties was an intense satisfaction to my soul.—46.293

Fear *See Courage; Death, fear of; Fear, of the Lord*

478 There is nothing in the Bible to make any man fear who puts his trust in Jesus. Nothing in the Bible, did I say? There is nothing in heaven, nothing on earth, nothing in hell, that need make you fear who trust in Jesus. The past you need not fear, for it is forgiven you. The present you need not fear; it is provided for. The future you need not fear; it is secured by the living power of Jesus.—15.189, 190

479 Fear came into man's heart with sin. Adam was never afraid of his God till he had broken his commands.—16.267

480 There is the natural fear which the creature has of its Creator, because of its own insignificance and its Maker's greatness. From that we shall never be altogether delivered. With holy awe we shall bow before the divine majesty, even when we come to be perfect in glory.

Second, there is a carnal fear, that is, the fear of man. May God deliver us from it! May we never cease from duty because we dread the eye of man! Who are you that should be afraid of a man that shall die? From this cowardice God's Spirit delivers believers.

The next fear is a servile fear—the fear of a slave toward its master, lest he should be beaten when he has offended. That is a fear which should rightly dwell in every unregenerate heart. Until the slave is turned into a child, he ought to feel that fear which is suitable to his position. By means of this fear the awakened soul is driven and drawn to Christ, and learns the perfect love which casts out fear.

If servile fear be not cast out, it leads to a fourth fear, namely, a diabolical fear. We read of the devils, that they "believe and tremble" (James 2:19). This is the fear of the malefactor toward the executioner.

But fifth, there is a filial fear which is never cast out of the mind. This is to be cultivated. This is "the fear of the Lord" which is "the beginning of wisdom" (Prov. 9:10).—30.18

481 A dear brother reminded us that we may tremble on the rock, but the Rock never trembled under us. Another reminded me of a remark I made some time ago: "What time I am afraid, I will trust in thee" (Ps. 56:3). "Well," I said, "that is going to heaven third-class, but the better way is to go to heaven first-class: 'I will trust, and not be afraid' (Isa. 12:2), letting no fear come in at all, but depending entirely on what God has declared in his Word."—48.406

482 You have heard that story of the woman on board ship, who was much disturbed in a storm, while her husband, the captain, was calm and restful. She asked him why he was so placid when she was so distressed. He did not answer in words, but he took down his sword and held it to her breast. She smiled. He said, "Why are you not afraid? This is a sharp sword with which I could slay you in a minute."

"Ah," she replied, "but I am not afraid of a sword when it is my husband who wields it."

"So" said he, "neither am I afraid of a storm when it is my Father who sends it and manages it."—49.485

Fear, of the Lord   *See Fear*

483 One said to me this week, "I am afraid to come to God, for I believe I am only driven to him by the vile motive of fear."

"Ah," I replied, "it was the devil who told you that, because in Hebrews 11 we read that 'Noah, being moved with fear, built an ark for the saving of his house' " (v. 7). Fear is a very proper motive for a guilty man to feel. Where else can such poor sinners as we are begin, except with selfish fear? As to its being vile to fear, it would be viler still to defy your God. You ought not to say "It is too vile a motive." Why, what but a vile motive can be expected from such a vile wretch as you?—30.492

484 I would rather go to heaven doubting all the way, than be lost through self-confidence. There is a

holy fear which must not be banished from the church of God. There is a sacred anxiety which puts us to the question, and examines us whether we be in the faith, and it is not to be disdained.—42.532

Feelings   *See Faith*

485 Experience is like a sundial. When I wish to know the time of day with my spirit, I look upon it. But then there must be the sun shining, or else I cannot tell by my sundial what and where I am. If a cloud passes before the face of the sun, my dial is of little service to me. But then my faith comes out in all its excellency, for my faith pierces the cloud, and reads the state of my soul—not by the shade on the dial, but by the position of the sun in the heavens themselves. Faith is a greater and grander thing than all experience; less fickle, more stable. It is the root of grace, and feelings are but the flowers, the germs, the buds.—6.238

486 How many there are among God's people who say, "I know that Christ died for sinners, but I don't get any comfort from it, because I do not feel as if I were saved."

That is self-righteousness in a very deceitful shape. You will not be saved by feeling that Christ died for you, but by his dying for you. If there be a lifeboat, and some poor man is ready to drown, and some strong hand rescues him, when he comes to himself he realizes he is in the boat. But it is not the realizing that he is in the boat that saves him. It is the lifeboat. So it is that Christ saves the sinner, not the sinner's feelings.—7.46

487 Men are not only to come *with* broken hearts, but *for* broken hearts. If they cannot feel their need, they should come to Jesus to be helped to feel their need.—14.474

488 A man said to me the other day, "Sir, I despair of myself."

"Give me your hand," I said, "you are on the right road. But I want you to go a little further. I want you to feel that you are too great a fool even to despair of yourself."

When you cry, "I cannot feel my own folly as I should," then I think your folly will be ended. I like to hear a man cry, "I feel unhappy because I cannot feel. I am grieved to think that I cannot grieve. I am in agony because I cannot get into an agony." You are getting right, my brother. You are the sort of man that God will bless. Now, look away from yourself, agony and all, and just trust in Jesus Christ, who is able to save to the uttermost them that come unto God by him. Own your blindness, and you shall find the light come streaming into your eyes.—30.490

489 There is nothing so deluding as feelings. Christians cannot live by feelings. Let me further tell you that these feelings are the work of Satan, for they are not right feelings. What right have you to set up your feelings against the word of Christ?—49.351

490 There once came into this place a young man, who is now a minister of the gospel, and he has told us how he became converted to God. He sat over the gallery yonder in great distress of mind, because he could not feel his sins enough. On that particular occasion I said, "There is over in the gallery yonder a young man who feels that he is too great a sinner to be saved; therefore he does not believe in Jesus."

"Ah," my friend said, "I thought to myself, 'I wish I was like that young man, I should like to feel the greatness of my sin.' "

But then in my sermon I went on to say, "There is another young man in that gallery who would give his eyes to feel as the other one feels. They are a pair of fools: the one for believing that he is too great a sinner for an omnipotent Savior to forgive, and the other for imagining that Christ wants his strength of feeling to fit him for salvation, as if Jesus could not save him just as he is."—57.201

491 The young Christian will say, "I believe that I am saved, because I am so happy." He is no more correct than the old Christian would be if he should say, "I believe that I am saved, because I am unhappy."—59.423

Fellowship   *See Church*

492 Some Christians try to go to heaven alone, in solitude. But believers are not compared to bears or lions or other animals that wander alone. Those who belong to Christ are sheep in this respect, that they love to get together. Sheep go in flocks, and so do God's people.—30.597

Follow   *See Obedience*

493 The proud flesh wants to serve Christ by striking out new paths. Proud man has a desire to preach new doctrine, to set up a new church, to be an original thinker, to judge and consider and do anything but obey. This is no service to Christ. He that would serve Christ must follow him. He must be content to tread only in the old footsteps, and go only where Christ has led the way. It is not for you and me to be originals; we must be humble copies of Christ.—8.438

Forgiveness   *See Christian; Conversion; Grace; Joy; Justification; Salvation*

494 I will tell you why you think forgiveness too good to be true. It is because you measure God's corn by your own bushel. Remember that his ways are not your ways, nor his thoughts your thoughts. Why, you think that if any man

had offended you, you could not have forgiven him. But God is not a man; he can forgive where you cannot. And where you would take your brother by the throat, God would forgive him seventy times seven.—4.158

495 There is as much joy in the heart of God when he forgives, as there is in the heart of the sinner when he is forgiven. God is as blessed in giving as we are in receiving.—6.77

496 I have heard of a man who was so constantly in debt and continually being arrested by the police, that once, when going by a fence, having caught his sleeve on one of the rails, he turned around and said, "I don't owe you anything, sir." He thought it was a sheriff. And so it is with unforgiven sinners. Wherever they are, they think they are going to be arrested. They can enjoy nothing.—6.79

497 You are nothing better than deceitful hypocrites if you harbor in your minds a single unforgiving thought. There are some sins which may be in the heart, and yet you may be saved. But you cannot be saved unless you are forgiving. If we do not choose to forgive, we choose to be damned.—13.718

498 I was years and years upon the brink of hell—I mean in my own feeling. I was unhappy, I was desponding, I was despairing. I dreamed of hell. My life was full of sorrow and wretchedness, believing that I was lost. But, oh, the blessed gospel of the God of grace came to me, and with it a sovereign word, "Deliver him!" And I who was but a minute before as wretched as a soul could be, could have danced for the very merriment of heart. And as the snow fell on my road home from the little house of prayer, I thought every snowflake talked with me and told of the pardon I had found, for I was white as the driven snow through the grace of God.—15.693

499 I did really think when God forgave me that I was the most extraordinary instance of his sovereign love that ever lived, and that I should be bound in heaven itself to tell to others how God's infinite mercy had pardoned in my case the biggest sinner that ever was forgiven.—19.156

500 I believe that as often as I transgress, God is more ready to forgive me than I am ready to offend.—22.573

501 You can be forgiven all your sin in half the tick of the clock, and pass from death to life more swiftly that I can utter the words.—27.384

502 You cannot sin so much as God can forgive. If it comes to a pitched battle between sin and grace, you shall not be so bad as God shall be good. I will prove it to you. You can only sin as a man, but God can forgive as a God. You sin as a finite creature, but the Lord forgives as the infinite Creator.—28.344

503 To be forgiven is such sweetness that honey is tasteless in comparison with it. But yet there is one thing sweeter still, and that is to forgive. As it is more blessed to give than to receive, so to forgive rises a stage higher in experience than to be forgiven. To be forgiven is the root; to forgive is the flower.—31.287, 288

504 However great your sin at present is, do not make it more by insinuating that he cannot forgive you. For of all sins this must be the most cruel, to think that he is unable to forgive. This stabs at Christ's Saviorship, which is his very heart.—39.581

505 Do you find it difficult to forgive one who has wronged you? Then you will find it difficult to get to heaven.—43.42

506 As long as you are forgiven, what does anything else matter? Go to a man condemned to die, and take him a free pardon. Do you think he will begin murmuring because some little thing is not just as he would like it? Oh, no! He will say, "It is enough for me that my life is spared."—53.572, 573

Forgiveness, self

507 No man sins more unreservedly than he who sins in despera-tion, believing that there is no pardon for him from God.—30.446

Fornication   *See Sex, abuse of*

508 All sorts of hearers come to this place, and they will be the first to say, "The preacher should not mention such a subject as fornication."

My answer to that remark is, "Then you should not commit such iniquity, and give me reason to speak of it."—46.62

Gambling

509 I believe that every form of gambling, though it may take a business shape, tends more or less to harden the heart. As for the naked form of play, which risks on the roll of a ball, it is murder to all the finer feelings of the heart. Nobody but gamblers could have cast the dice, all blood-bespattered, at the foot of the cross of our Redeemer. Gambling brings men into a state of heart worse than almost any other form of sin. Can the gambler pray? Can he meditate? Can he commune with the Lord Jesus? Can he be without anxiety? Where can be his trust? Where his faith in God? When he has practically committed his fortunes to the devil, how can he confide in his God?—28.667

510 I dare to say that there is no sin that does more swiftly send men down to hell than gambling.—43.462

511 When a man takes to the gaming table, it seems as if his whole soul ran out at the sluice, and his entire life is just nothing to him. Wife, children, substance—all must go at the throw of the dice or be staked at the running of a horse.—43.597

512 The soldiers at the foot of the cross threw dice for my Savior's garments. And I have never heard the rattling of dice but I have conjured up the dreadful scene of Christ on his cross, and gamblers at the foot of it, with their dice bespattered with his blood. I do not hesitate to say that of all sins, there is none that more surely damns men, and, worse than that, makes them the devil's helpers to damn others, than gambling.—45.319

Giving   *See Money; Stewardship; Tithing*

513 The Egyptian hieroglyph for charity is very suggestive. It is a naked child giving honey to a bee which has lost its wings. Notice, it is a child: We should give in meekness. It is a naked child: We should give from pure motives, and not for show.—8.634

514 Many people will always be poor because they never give to the cause of God.—31.84

515 We have known warm-spirited brethren and sisters give grandly, under a certain impulse, what they never thought of giving when they entered into the assembly. I shall not blame them; rather do I commend them for obeying gracious impulses. But it is not the best way of doing service to our Master. Passion seldom gives so acceptably as principle. Mary did not perform a thoughtless action under a tempestuous force of unusual zeal. No, "she kept this" (John 12:7).—31.199

516 We want personal consecration. I have heard that word pronounced *purse and all* consecration, a most excellent pronunciation. He who loves Jesus consecrates to him all that he has, and feels it a delight that he may lay anything at the feet of him who laid down his life for us.—54.476

517 God has a way of giving by the cartloads to those who give away by shovelfuls.—56.451

518 I do not believe in a perfect sanctification which allows a man to lay up so much treasure on earth, while so many works for the Lord Jesus need his help. Systematic hoarding of wealth, to my mind, does not indicate a perfect character.—61.498

Giving, sacrificial

519 A man boasted that religion had been to him a very cheap thing, costing him only a few cents a year. A good man said to him, "The Lord have mercy on your little stingy soul." If a man has no more religion than that, if

he has not a religion that will make him generous, he has no religion at all.—1.183

520 A merchant in America had devoted a large part of his money for the maintenance of the cause of Christ, and one said to him, "What a sacrifice you make every year."

Said he, "Not so. I have a clerk. Suppose I give that clerk 50 pounds to pay a schoolmaster, and when he goes to the schoolmaster, he should say, 'Here is your salary, what a sacrifice it is to me to give you that!'

" 'Why,' the schoolmaster would say, 'Sir, it is not yours; it is no sacrifice at all to you.' "

So said this good man, "I gave up all when I came to God. I became his steward, and no longer head of the firm. I made God the head of the firm. And now when I distribute my wealth, I only distribute it as his trustee, and it is no sacrifice at all."

If we talk of sacrifices, we make a mistake.—3.126

Glory, God's

521 "To whom be glory forever" (2 Tim. 4:18). This should be the single desire of the Christian. I take it that he should not have twenty wishes, but only one. He may desire to see his family brought up well, but only that "to God may be glory forever." He may wish for prosperity in business, but only so far as it may help

him to promote this: "to whom be glory forever." He may desire to attain more gifts and more graces, but it should only be that "to him may be glory forever." This one thing I know, Christian: You are not acting as you ought to do when you are moved by any other motive than the one motive of your Lord's glory.—10.310

522 Oh, this is our exultation, this is our joy, our triumph, our blessedness. If we can but promote his glory, the place where we can best promote it shall be our heaven. The sickbed, the hospital, or the poorhouse shall be our heaven, if we can there best serve the Lord Jesus Christ, who is the King of Glory.—13.275

523 If I might have but one prayer, it would be, "O God, glorify thyself in thine own church, and in the salvation of men!"—37.575

Gluttony   *See Drunkenness*

524 I believe that gluttony is as much a sin in the sight of God as drunkenness.—59.134,135

God   *See Holy Spirit; Jesus; Jesus, deity of; Trinity*

God, presence of   *See Omnipresence*

525 There is no place so well-adapted for the discovery of sin and recovery from its power and guilt as the immediate presence of God. Get into God's arms, and you will see how to hit at sin. You

will gather strength to give the final blow which shall lay the monster in the dust. Job never knew how to get rid of sin half so well as he did when his eye of faith rested on God, and he abhorred himself, and repented in dust and ashes (Job 42:5, 6).—11.216

526 Where we cannot enjoy God's company, we will not go. Our motto is, "With God, anywhere. Without God, nowhere."—37.2

527 Your elbow touches the next person in your seat, but that person is not so near to you as God is.—55.449

God, resisting

528 Who shall stand against the Almighty God? As well might the fly hope to quench the sun when he has already burned up his wings in a candle! As well might you seek to dry up the Atlantic, or bid Niagara leap up the rock instead of down! As well might you hope to stop the moon in its course, or to pluck the stars from their places, as think to stand against God!—16.532

Gospel   See Bible; Death, Christ's; Law; Legalism; Truth; Works

529 I do not believe there is a single honest man living who, having once heard the gospel simply preached, does not in his conscience believe it to be true. I am persuaded that light will pene-

trate. There is such force, such energy in Christ, it must and will pierce through some crevice and convince at least a natural conscience. But this is the very reason why men oppose it. They do not want it to be true.—7.372

530 Never lose heart in the power of the gospel. Do not believe that there exists any man, much less any race of men, for whom the gospel is not fitted.—10.147

531 The hearing of the gospel involves the hearer in responsibility. It is a great privilege to hear the gospel. You may smile and think there is nothing very great in it. The damned in hell know. Oh, what would they give if they could hear the gospel now? If they could come back and entertain but the shadow of a hope that they might yet escape from the wrath to come? The saved in heaven estimate this privilege at a high rate, for, having obtained salvation through the preaching of this gospel, they can never cease to bless their God for calling them by his word of truth. O that *you* knew it! On your dying beds the listening to a gospel sermon will seem another thing than it seems now.—10.552

532 If God does not save men by truth, he certainly will not save them by lies. And if the old gospel is not competent to work a re-

vival, then we will do without the revival.—20.213

533 Whitefield and Wesley might preach the gospel better than I do, but they could not preach a better gospel.—28.339

534 Let this be to you the mark of true gospel preaching—where Christ is everything, and the creature is nothing; where it is salvation all of grace, through the work of the Holy Spirit applying to the soul the precious blood of Jesus.—42.586

535 Oh, if the damned in hell could come to earth, they would let you know what solemn work it is to hear the gospel. Think not that you can hear the gospel without having your salvation or damnation affected thereby.—44.467

536 You, dear friends, are deriving from every gospel sermon that you hear either life unto life, or else death unto death. If you get no good from it, you will assuredly get harm. An unbelieving hearing of the gospel is a multiplication of curses to your soul—another sermon for which you have to give account, another rejected exhortation recorded against you, another earnest invitation which you have refused, and for which you will be held responsible.—46.270

537 It is a wonderful thing, I have often thought, that any man should be able, day after day and week after week, to attract thousands of people to hear him talk. I do not believe any man could do it with any other subject except the gospel.—47.195

538 Do you know, my dear unsaved hearer, what God's estimate of the gospel is? Do you not know that it has been the chief subject of his thoughts and acts from all eternity? He looks on it as the grandest of all his works. You cannot imagine that he has sent this gospel into the world to be a football for you to play with—that you may give it a kick, as Felix did when he said to Paul, "Go thy way for this time; when I have a convenient season, I will call for thee" (Acts 24:25). You surely cannot believe that God sent his gospel into the world for you to make a toy of it, and to say, as Agrippa said to Paul, "Almost thou persuadest me to be a Christian" (Acts 26:28), and then put away all thought of it out of your souls. You cannot even speak of it irreverently without committing a great sin.—48.536

539 Avoid a sugared gospel as you would shun sugar of lead. Seek that gospel which rips up and tears and cuts and wounds and hacks and even kills, for that is the gospel that makes alive again. And when you have found it, give good heed to it. Let it enter into your inmost being. As the

rain soaks into the ground, so pray the Lord to let his gospel soak into your soul.—48.538

540 I always feel that I have not done my duty as a preacher of the gospel if I go out of this pulpit without having clearly set before sinners the way of salvation. I sometimes think that you have so often and so long heard me tell this story that you will get weary of it, but I cannot help it if you do. I had better weary you than be false to my charge.—49.559

541 For me there is no joy in life and no hope in death except in that gospel which I have continually expounded here.—51.3

542 "Possession is nine points of the law," and it is all ten points of the gospel. So long as you have Christ, there is no need to ask how you got him.—53.6, 7

543 On Christ, and what he has done, my soul hangs for time and eternity. And if your soul also hangs there, it will be saved as surely as mine shall be. And if you are lost trusting in Christ, I will be lost with you and will go to hell with you. I must do so, for I have nothing else to rely upon but the fact that Jesus Christ, the Son of God, lived, died, was buried, rose again, went to heaven, and still lives and pleads for sinners at the right hand of God.—53.569

86

Gospel, defense of *See Apologetics*

Gossip *See Slander*

544 Most persons who have secrets told them are like the lady of whom it is said she never told her secrets except to two sorts of persons—those that asked her, and those that did not.—1.351

Grace *See Covenant; Forgiveness; Justice; Law; Legalism; Mercy; Works*

545 When we pass a prostitute in the street, we say, "Oh, poor creature! I pity you. I have not a harsh word for you, for I had been as you are, had not God preserved me."—5.300, 301

546 If heaven were by merit, it would never be heaven to me, for if I were in it I should say, "I am sure I am here by mistake; I am sure this is not my place; I have no claim to it." But if it be of grace and not of works, then we may walk into heaven with boldness.—6.354

547 Observe the rain which drops from heaven. It falls on the desert as well as on the fertile field. It drops on the rock that will refuse its fertilizing moisture as well as on the soil that opens its gaping mouth to drink it in with gratitude. It falls on the streets of the city, where it is not required, and where men will even curse it for coming, and it falls not more freely where the sweet flowers have been panting for it and the withering leaves have been rustling forth their prayers. Such is the grace of God. It does not visit us because we ask for it, much less because we deserve it, but as God wills it.—9.171

548 It is an amazing thing—we may have been the instrument of sending others down to the pit, yet we may by grace, amazing grace, be delivered ourselves from the horrible doom of sinners.—12.102

549 Suppose that God saved men on account of their merits. Where would you drunkards be? Where would you swearers be? You who have been unclean and unchaste, and you whose hearts have cursed God, and who even now do not love him, where would you be? But when it is all of grace, then all your past life, however black and filthy it may be, need not keep you from coming to Jesus.—12.431, 432

550 We are accustomed not only to say "grace," but "free grace." It has been remarked that this is a tautology. So it is, but it is a blessed one, for it makes the meaning doubly clear and leaves no room for mistake. We feel no compunction in ringing such a silver bell twice over—grace, free grace. Lest any should imagine that grace can be otherwise than free, we shall continue to say not only grace, but free grace, so long as we preach.—26.122

551 I hear someone murmur, "God will not give grace to men who do not repent."

God gives men grace to repent, and no man ever repents till grace first is given him to lead him to repentance.

"But God will not give his grace to those who won't believe," says another.

I reply, God gives grace to men by which they are moved to believe. It is through the grace of God that they are brought to faith in Christ.—27.183

552 I sometimes think if men did but understand grace they would be sure to accept the Lord Jesus. I heard of a minister in Edinburgh who went to visit one of his poor people. He heard that she was in deep poverty, and therefore he went to take her help. When he came to her house, he could not make anybody hear, though he knocked loud and long. Seeing her sometime after, he said, "Janet, I knocked at your door with help for you, but you did not hear me."

"What time did you come, sir?" said she.

"It was about 12 o'clock."

"Oh," she said, "I did hear you, but I thought it was the man calling for the rent."

Just so. Men do hear the calls of Christ, but they are willfully deaf, because they think he wants them to do something. But he does not want anything of you; he wants you to receive what he has already done. He comes laden with mercy, with his hands full of blessing, and he knocks at your door. You have only to open it and he will enter in, and salvation will enter with him.—30.414

553 If the people do not like the doctrine of grace, give them all the more of it.—37.49

554 An old friend said to me yesterday, "Nothing will do for you and me but grace."

I said to him, "Yes, and that won't do unless it is the grace of God." It must be God's own grace, or else we never can be saved.—41.379

555 You might as soon yoke a gnat with an archangel as think of your going in to help Christ save you. To join a filthy rag from off a dunghill with the golden garments of a king or a queen cannot be permitted. Christ will be everything, or else he will be nothing. You must be saved wholly by mercy, or else not at all. There must not be even a trace of the fingers of self-righteousness on the acts and documents of divine grace.—43.453

556 If sin will be the ruin of men—and surely it will—yet our Lord Jesus Christ knows how to take the ruined sinners and build them up to be temples for his indwelling. Christ will take the very castaways of the devil and use them for himself. He delights to stoop over the dunghill and pick up a broken vessel that is thrown away, and make it into a vessel fit for the Master's use.—44.177

557 I do not wonder that John Bradford said, as he saw men taken to be hanged at Tyburn, "There goes John Bradford, but for the grace of God." There is powder enough in all our hearts to blow our character to pieces if God does not keep the devil's sparks away, or quench them in a mighty stream of grace before they can do us mischief.—54.16

558 Sin comes up like Noah's flood, but grace rides over the tops of the mountains like the ark. Sin, like Sennacherib, pours forth its troops to swallow up the land; grace, like the angel of the Lord, goes through the camp of Sennacherib and lays sin dead.—61.232

Grace, irresistible   *See Calvinism; Will, free*

559 What is there to be said to you sinners about this power of the Spirit? Why, to me, there is some hope for you. I cannot save you; I cannot get at you. I make you cry sometimes—you wipe your eyes, and it is all over. But this power can save you. It is able to break your heart, though it is an iron one. It is able to make your eyes run with tears, though they have been like rocks before.—1.236

560 I believe that Christ came into the world not to put men into

a *salvable* state, but into a *saved* state. Not to put them where they could save themselves, but to do the work in them and for them, from first to last. If I did not believe that there was might going forth with the Word of Jesus which makes men willing, and which turns them from the error of their ways by the mighty, overwhelming, constraining force of a divine influence, I should cease to glory in the cross of Christ.—3.34

561 I take it that the highest proof of Christ's power is not that he offers salvation, not that he bids you take it if you will, but that when you reject it, when you hate it, when you despise it, he has a power whereby he can change your mind, make you think differently from your former thoughts, and turn you from the error of your ways.—3.35

562 If God should please, the Holy Spirit could at this moment make every one of you fall on your knees, confess your sins, and turn to God. He is an Almighty Spirit, able to do wonders.—3.38

563 I must confess I never would have been saved if I could have helped it. As long as I could, I rebelled and revolted and struggled against God. When he would have me pray, I would not pray. When he would have me listen to the sound of the ministry, I would not. And when I heard, and the

tear rolled down my cheek, I wiped it away and defied him to melt my heart. Then he gave me the effectual blow of grace, and there was no resisting that irresistible effort. It conquered my depraved will and made me bow myself before the sceptre of his grace.

And so it is in every case. Man revolts against his Savior, but where God determines to save, save he will. God never was thwarted yet in any one of his purposes. Man does resist with all his might, but all the might of man, tremendous though it be for sin, is not equal to the majestic might of the Most High.—4.383

564 Man by nature is as a wild horse dashing to the precipice. If he be restrained in his course and turned away from danger, it is because he has a mighty Rider, and one that knows how to pull the bit and guide him as he pleases. And though he kick and plunge and long to turn away, his Rider can pull him up on his very haunches, turn him around, and make him go as he wills. In this matter is it true that all the bringing home of the gospel to the soul of man is of God.—6.256

565 Oh, what a joy it is to think that it does not rest with man whether he should belong to Christ or not. If the Father has ordained him to be Christ's, then Christ's that man shall be. Rampart yourselves about with preju-

dices, but Christ shall scale your ramparts. Pile up your walls, bring up the big stones of your iniquity, but Christ shall yet take your citadel and make you a captive. Plunge into the mire if you will, but that strong arm can bring you out and wash you clean. There is not strength enough in sin to overcome his grace.—6.289

566 Erskine, in speaking of his own conversion, says he ran to Christ "with full consent against his will," by which he meant it was against his old will, against his will as it was till Christ came. But when Christ came, then he came to Christ with full consent, and was willing to be saved—as pleased to receive Christ as if grace had not constrained him.—8.189

567 A man is not saved against his will, but he is made willing by the operation of the Holy Ghost. A mighty grace which he does not wish to resist enters into the man, disarms him, makes a new creature of him, and he is saved.—10.309

568 *Difficulty* is not a word to be found in the dictionary of heaven. Nothing can be impossible with God. The swearing reprobate, whose mouth is blackened with profanity, whose heart is a very hell, and his life like the reeking flames of the bottomless pit—such a man, if the Lord but looks on him and makes bare his

arm of irresistible grace, shall yet praise God and bless his name and live to his honor. Do not limit the Holy One of Israel. Persecuting Saul became loving Paul, and why should not that person be saved for whom you have been praying until now, but of whose case you almost despair?—12.32

569 "You deny, then," says one, "the free will of man?"

Who says that? I never denied it. On the contrary, I insist on it more than most men. There is no opposition between the doctrine of irresistible grace and the free agency of man.

"How," say you, "if man be thus irresistibly carried as by storm, can he be free?"

Think, man, and answer for yourself. Were you never overcome in argument? Did you never resist an argument for a time, till at last another reason was given, and then another, and you could not but yield to the overwhelming arguments? Did you then prove that you had no reason of your own? No, it proved you had a reason.—14.365

570 I do not come into this pulpit hoping that perhaps somebody will of his own free will return to Christ. My hope lies in another quarter. I hope that my Master will lay hold of some of them and say, "You are mine, and you shall be mine. I claim you for myself." My hope arises from the freeness of grace, and not from the freedom

90

of the will. A poor haul of fish will any gospel fisherman make if he takes none but those who are eager to leap into the net. Oh, for five minutes of the great Shepherd's handiwork!—29.188, 189

571 Man is perfectly free, and God violates not the human will. Yet he is as much able to rule perfectly free agents as he is to control the atoms of inert matter. It is omnipotence which compels yonder starry orbs to obey the laws which God has made and to travel in their appointed courses. But to my mind it is even more marvelous omnipotence which leaves men free agents and controls not their will, but yet sweetly triumphs over them.—47.421

572 Sometimes the more unlikely ones are the first to be converted. You probably remember the story of the man who went to hear George Whitefield preach, who had filled his pocket with stones to throw at God's servant. But as he preached the gospel, the man dropped one stone after another, until all the stones were gone. And better still, God had taken the stony heart out of his flesh and given him a heart of flesh.—48.471

573 In one sense, no man comes to God with compulsion; and in another sense, no man comes without compulsion. You see two boxes opened. There are two ways of opening them. You see one box wrenched. Who opened it? A thief. God never opens men's hearts in that way.

You see another box open—no sign of damage, no sign of any particular labor. Who opened it? The person who had the key—the owner. Hearts belong to God, and he has the keys and opens them—sweetly opens them.—61.28

Greed *See Envy*

574 There is nothing in this world but lives by giving, except a covetous man, and such a man is a piece of grit in the machinery. He is out of gear with the universe.—14.571

575 Where will you find an instance of a single saint in Scripture that ever fell into covetousness? Into all other sins have they fallen, but into this one, I do not remember that one child of God mentioned in Scripture ever descended.—15.20

576 Greed's near relations are the Screws, the Skinflints, and the Graballs. But he will not own them, but always mentions his great-uncle, Squire Prudence, and his mother's brother, Professor Economy, of the University of Accumulation.—32.39

577 A Roman Catholic priest, who had heard the confessions of some two thousand persons, said he had heard men confess heinous iniquities of every kind,

even murder and adultery, but he had never heard any man confess covetousness.—62.535

Grief   *See Suffering*

578 Our joy is like the wave as it dashes on the shore—it throws us on the earth. But our sorrows are like that receding wave which sucks us back again into the great depth of godhead. We would have been stranded and left high and dry on the shore if it had not been for that receding wave, that ebbing of our prosperity, which carried us back to our Father and our God again.—5.470

579 Tacitus tells us that an amber ring was thought to be of no value among the Romans till the emperor took to wearing one, and then immediately an amber ring was held in high esteem. Bereavements might be looked on as very sad things, but when we recollect that Jesus wept over his friend Lazarus, they are choice jewels and special favors from God. Christ wore this ring. Then I must not blush to wear it.—10.199

580 Our sorrows are all, like ourselves, mortal. There are no immortal sorrows for immortal souls. They come, but blessed be God, they also go. Like birds of the air, they fly over our heads. But they cannot make their abode in our souls. We suffer today, but we shall rejoice tomorrow.—52.183

581 The Quaker was right who, when he saw a lady fretting on the sofa some year or so after her husband was dead, still harboring grief without a token of resignation, said to her, "Madam, I see you have not forgiven God yet." Sometimes grief is not a sacred feeling, but only a murmur of rebellion against the Most High.—54.523

Growth, spiritual

582 "Alas," says one, "I do not feel as I once did."

Well, dear friend, it may be that you make some mistake in reference to your own experience. When the passion of love was first lighted in your breast, there was, as it were, a blaze of the match, the paper, and the wood, although the coals had not yet ignited. Yours was then the flush of joy, but not the vehement heat. Now your heart is all on fire like a solid ruby. There is much more heat, though there is less blaze.—8.341

583 Many Christians appear to think that if they are just believers, it is enough. We do not in business think it enough if we barely escape bankruptcy. A man does not say, if his dear child has been ill in bed for years, that it is quite enough so long as the child is alive. We do not think of our own bodies, that so long as we can breathe, it is enough.—16.452

584 When the great bridge across the Niagara was made, the diffi-

culty was to pass the first rope across the broad stream. I have read that it was accomplished by flying a kite, and allowing it to fall on the opposite bank. The kite carried across a piece of string, then to the string was tied a line, and to the line a rope, and to the rope a stronger rope, and before long the Niagara was spanned and the bridge was finished. Even thus by degrees God works.—16.712

Guidance   *See Revelation, modern; Will, God's*

Guilt   *See Confession; Conviction; Motive; Sin*

585 A railroad worker neglected to turn a switch, but by the care of another no accident occurred. Is he to be excused? Another man was equally negligent, certainly not more so. But in his case the natural result followed. There was a collision, and many lives were lost. This last man was blamed most deservedly, but yet the former offender was equally guilty. If we do wrong and no harm comes of it, we are not thereby justified. If we did evil and good came of it, the evil would be just as evil. It is not the result of the action, but the action itself which God weighs.—29.461

586 I must confess that I never realize Christ's preciousness so much as when I feel myself still to be, apart from him, an undeserving, hell-deserving sinner.—55.583

Habit

587 One of these days you may be unable to get rid of those habits which you are now forming. At first the net of habit is made of cobweb; you can soon break it through. Before long it is made of twine. Soon it will be made of rope. And last of all it will be strong as steel, and then you will be fatally ensnared.—56.189

Healing   *See Miracles, Jesus'; Prayer, answered; Sickness*

588 In our prayers for the lives of beloved children of God we must not forget that there is one prayer which may be crossing ours. For Jesus prays, "Father, I will that they also, whom thou has given me, be with me where I am, that they may behold my glory" (John 17:24). We pray that they may remain with us, but when we recognize that Jesus wants them above, what can we do but admit his larger claim and say, "Not as I will, but as thou wilt"?—26.75

589 I hope there are none here who claim a right to healing. For if so, the Lord will not listen to them.—27.343

590 In every healing of which we are the subjects we have a pledge of the resurrection. Every time a man who is near the gates of death rises up again he enjoys a kind of rehearsal of that grand rising when from beds of dust and silent clay the perfect saints

shall rise at the trump of the archangel and the voice of God. We ought to gather from our restorations from serious and perilous sickness a proof that the God who brings us back from the gates of the grave can also bring us back from the grave itself whenever it shall be his time to do so.—28.332

Heart *See Depravity; Motive; Sin, hardening effects of*

591 Whence come our carnality, covetousness, pride, sloth, and unbelief? Are they not all to be traced to the corruption of our hearts? When the hands of a clock move in an irregular manner, and when the bell strikes the wrong hour, be assured there is something wrong within. Oh, how needful that the mainspring of our motives be in proper order, and the wheels in a right condition.—4.117

592 Many a man has died from internal bleeding, and yet there has been no wound whatever to be seen by the eye. You may go to hell as well dressed in the garnishings of morality as in the rags of immorality. Unless the very center of your soul and the core of your being be made obedient to the living God, he will not accept you, for he looks not only to your outward condition, but to your heart's secret loyalty or treachery toward himself.—13.55

593 The heart is very much like Africa, a region unexplored.—27.345

Heart, hardness of *See Indifference; Sin, hardening effects of*

594 I remember a story of one, who remarked to a minister what a wonderful thing it was to see so many people weeping. "No," said he, "I will tell you something more amazing still, that so many will forget all they wept about when they get outside the door."—4.239

595 There is no heart so hard but what God's hammer can dash it in pieces.—12.82

596 Nothing good can come out of a stony heart; it is barren as a rock. To be unfeeling is to be unfruitful. Prayer without desire, praise without emotion, preaching without earnestness—what are all these? Like the marble images of life, they are cold and dead. Insensibility is a deadly sign. Frequently it is the next stage to destruction. Pharaoh's hard heart was a prophecy that his pride would meet a terrible overthrow. The hammer of vengeance is not far off when the heart becomes harder than an adamant stone.—33.517

597 A hard-hearted Christian—is not that a complete contradiction? Must not our hearts have been broken before we could

ourselves be penitent? And he who bound them up and healed them did not harden them with his gentle touch. I reckon that he gave them an additional tenderness by the very act of binding them up with his own dear pierced hands.—43.374

Heaven   *See Eternity; Hell; Session, Jesus'*

598 I believe there will be more in heaven than in hell. If you ask me why I think so, I answer, because Christ in everything is to have the preeminence (Col. 1:18), and I cannot conceive how he could have the preeminence if there are to be more in the dominions of Satan than in paradise.

Moreover, it is said there is to be a multitude that no man can number in heaven (Rev. 7:9). I have never read that there is to be a multitude that no man can number in hell.

I rejoice to know that the souls of all infants, as soon as they die, speed their way to paradise. Think what a multitude there is of them! And then there are the just and the redeemed of all nations up till now. And there are better times coming, when the religion of Christ shall be universal. And in the thousand years of the great millennial state there will be enough saved to make up all the deficiencies of the thousands of years that have gone before.—3.28

599 Some of you could not be happy if you were allowed to enter heaven. Shall I tell you why? It is a land of spirit, and you have neglected your spirit. Some of you even deny that you have a spirit.—13.224

600 I bear my testimony that there is no joy to be found in all this world like that of sweet communion with Christ. I would barter all else there is of heaven for that. Indeed, that is heaven. As for the harps of gold and the streets like clear glass and the songs of seraphs and the shouts of the redeemed, one could very well give all these up, counting them as a drop in a bucket, if we might forever live in fellowship and communion with Jesus.—14.247

601 Whoever may have invented the doctrine of degrees in heaven I do not know, but I believe there is as much foundation for it in Scripture as there is for the doctrine of purgatory, and no more. All the saints shall see their Master's face.—14.442

602 Oh, to think of heaven without Christ! It is the same thing as thinking of hell. Heaven without Christ! It is day without the sun, existing without life, feasting without food, seeing without light. It involves a contradiction in terms. Heaven without Christ! Absurd. It is the sea without water, the earth without its fields, the heavens without their stars. There cannot

be a heaven without Christ. He is the sum total of bliss, the fountain from which heaven flows, the element of which heaven is composed. Christ is heaven and heaven is Christ.—19.570, 571

603 Someone said to a Christian man, "What is your age?" and he replied, "I am on the right side of 70."

They found out he was 75, and they said, "You told us you were on the right side of 70."

"So I am," he answered. "That is the right side, for it's the side nearest heaven, my blessed home."

Why should not all Christians think so?—26.700, 701

604 The true Christian life, when we live near to God, is the rough draft of the life of full communion above.—30.506

605 If there were no hell, the loss of heaven would be hell.—41.418

606 Above, beneath, around, within, without, everywhere it is heaven. I breathe heaven, I drink heaven, I feel heaven, I think heaven. Everything is heaven. Oh, "what must it be to be there?" To be there is to be with Christ.—44.261

607 You remember the story of the three wonders in heaven. The first wonder was that we should see so many there we did not expect to see. The second was that we should miss so many we did expect to see there. But the third wonder would be the greatest wonder of all—to see ourselves there.—48.44

608 There is a crown there which nobody's head but yours can ever wear. There is a seat in which none but yourself can sit. There is a harp that will be silent till your fingers strike its strings. There is a robe, made for you, which no one else can wear. They are wanting you up there.

"Oh," say you, "they are so happy, so perfect, that they surely do not want me."

But they do. "They without us should not be made perfect" (Heb. 11:40). Jesus Christ has not all the jewels of his crown yet, and he will have a perfect crown. So they are waiting and watching for you.—50.34, 35

609 I suspect that every saved soul in heaven is a great wonder, and that heaven is a vast museum of wonders of grace and mercy, a palace of miracles, in which everything will surprise everyone who gets there.—50.213

610 I must frankly confess that of all my expectations of heaven, I will cheerfully renounce ten thousand things if I can but know that I shall have perfect holiness. If I may become like Jesus Christ— pure and perfect—I cannot understand how any other joy can be denied me. If we shall have that,

surely we shall have everything.—57.50

Heaven, recognition in

611 I have heard of a good woman, who asked her husband when she was dying, "Do you think you will know me when you and I get to heaven?"

"Shall I know you?" he said. "Why, I have always known you while I have been here, and do you think I shall be a greater fool when I get to heaven?"—1.302

612 I believe that heaven is a fellowship of the saints, and that we shall know one another there.—1.302

613 I reckon on meeting David, whose psalms have so often cheered my soul. I long to meet with Martin Luther and Calvin, and to have the power of seeing such men as Whitefield and Wesley, and walking and talking with them in the golden streets. Yes, heaven would scarcely be so full of charms in the prospect if there were not the full conviction in our minds that we should know the saints.—62.403

Hell   *See Condemnation; Damnation; Eternity; Heaven; Judgment; Lost; Punishment; Wrath, God's*

614 If there be one thing in hell worse than another, it will be seeing the saints in heaven. Oh, to think of seeing my mother in heaven while I am cast out! Husband, there is your wife in heaven, and you are among the damned. And do you see your father? Your child is before the throne, and you—accursed of God and of man—are in hell. Oh, the hell of hells will be to see our friends in heaven, and ourselves lost.—1.24

615 The hell of hells will be the thought that it is *forever.* You will look up on the throne of God, and it shall be written, "Forever!" When the damned jingle the burning irons of their torments, they shall say, "Forever!" When they howl, echo cries, "Forever!"—1.124

616 I can conceive of no one entering hell with a worse grace than the man who goes there with drops of his mother's tears on his head, and with his father's prayers following him at his heels.—1.306

617 The soul sees written over its head, "You are damned forever." It hears howlings that are to be perpetual; it sees flames which are unquenchable; it knows pains that are unmitigated.—1.397

618 Do not begin telling me that there is a metaphorical fire in hell. Who worries about that? If a man were to threaten to give me a metaphorical blow on the head, I should worry very little about it. He would be welcome to give me as many as he pleased. And what do the wicked say? "We do not worry about metaphorical fires."

But they are real, sir, yes, as real as yourself.—2.104

619 Your heart beating with a high fever; your pulse rattling at an enormous rate in agony; your limbs cracking like the martyrs in the fire, and yet unburned; yourself put in a vessel of hot oil, pained, yet coming out undestroyed; all your veins becoming a road for the hot feet of pain to travel on; every nerve a string on which the devil shall ever play his diabolical tune of Hell's Unutterable Lament; your soul forever and ever aching, and your body palpitating in unison with your soul. Fictions, sir? They are no fictions, but as God lives, solid, stern truth. If God be true, and this Bible be true, what I have said is the truth, and you will find it one day to be so.—2.105

620 As every man who is going to be hung finds fault with the gallows, so do many men find fault with hell because they fear they are in danger of it.—2.260

621 Who can tell the hideous shriek of a lost soul? It cannot reach heaven. But if it could, it might well be dreamed that it would suspend the melodies of angels, might make even God's redeemed weep, if they could hear the wailings of a damned soul.—3.316

622 You may laugh yourself into hell, but you cannot laugh yourself out of it.—6.88

623 If hell be a fiction, say so, and honestly play the infidel. But if it be real, and you believe it, wake up. You that believe so, leave no stone unturned, no means untried by which through the power of the Holy Spirit sinners may be saved.—10.676

624 Think lightly of hell, and you will think lightly of the cross. Think little of the sufferings of lost souls, and you will soon think little of the Savior who delivers you from them.—12.174

625 I greatly fear that the denial of the eternity of future punishment is one wave of an incoming sea of infidelity.—16.691

626 If we could hear the wailings of the pit for a moment, we should earnestly entreat that we might never hear them again.—17.78

627 It is shocking to reflect that a change in the weather has more effect on some men's lives than the dread alternative of heaven or hell.—22.136

628 None used stronger or more alarming language than our dear Redeemer concerning the future of ungodly men. He knew nothing of that pretended sympathy which will rather let men perish than warn them against perishing. Such tenderness is merely selfishness excusing itself from a distasteful duty.—32.433

⁶²⁹ Some say, "I could not rest comfortably if I believed the orthodox doctrine about the ruin of men."

Most true. But what right have we to rest comfortably?—35.104

⁶³⁰ He who does not believe that God will cast unbelievers into hell will not be sure that he will take believers into heaven.—36.303

⁶³¹ You are hanging over the mouth of hell by a single thread, and that thread is breaking. Only a gasp for breath, only a stopping of the heart for a single moment, and you will be in an eternal world, without God, without hope, without forgiveness. Oh, can you face it?—37.527

⁶³² When men talk of a little hell, it is because they think they have only a little sin, and they believe in a little Savior. But when you get a great sense of sin, you want a great Savior, and feel that if you do not have him, you will fall into a great destruction, and suffer a great punishment at the hands of the great God.—38.512

⁶³³ What woe it would be to be only an hour in hell! Oh, how you would wish then that you had sought the Savior! But alas, there is no such thing as an hour in hell. Once lost, you are lost forever! Therefore, seek the Lord now.—47.574

⁶³⁴ Some have staggered over the doctrine of eternal punishment, because they could not see how that could be consistent with God's goodness. I have only one question to ask concerning that: Does God reveal it in the Scriptures? Then I believe it, and leave to him the vindication of his own consistency. If we do not see it to be so, it will be nonetheless so because we are blind.—49.609

Hell, preaching about   See Preaching

⁶³⁵ There are some ministers who never mention anything about hell. I heard of a minister who once said to his congregation, "If you do not love the Lord Jesus Christ, you will be sent to that place which it is not polite to mention." He ought not to have been allowed to preach again, I am sure, for he could not use plain words.—1.306

Holiness   See Holy Spirit; Righteousness

⁶³⁶ There is nothing which my heart desires more than to see you, the members of this church, distinguished for holiness. It is the Christian's crown and glory. An unholy church! It is of no use to the world and of no esteem among men. Oh, it is an abomination, hell's laughter, heaven's abhorrence. And the larger the church, the more influential, the worse nuisance does it become when it becomes unholy. The

worst evils which have ever come upon the world have been brought upon her by an unholy church.—10.60

637 While the Christian religion is an internal thing, there is no religion in the world which shows itself so much externally.—14.534

638 In proportion as a church is holy, in that proportion will its testimony for Christ be powerful.—15.92

639 In holiness God is more clearly seen than in anything else, save in the person of Christ Jesus the Lord, of whose life such holiness is but a repetition.—15.366

640 I believe the holier a man becomes, the more he mourns over the unholiness which remains in him.—16.221

641 Holiness is better than morality. It goes beyond it. Holiness affects the heart. Holiness respects the motive. Holiness regards the whole nature of man. A moral man does not do wrong in act; a holy man hates the thought of doing wrong. A moral man does not swear, but a holy man adores. A moral man would not commit outward sin; a holy man would not commit inward sin. And if committed, he would pour forth floods of tears.—16.392

642 There can be no such thing as perfect happiness till there is perfect holiness.—24.642, 643

643 I should like to coin my heart to pass it round to you in living medallions, bearing each one this inscription—*for Jesus' sake be holy.* Unless you are a holy people, it were better for me that I had never been born.—30.368

644 A faith which works not for purification will work for putrefaction. Unless our faith makes us pine after holiness, it is no better than the faith of devils, and perhaps it is not even so good as that. A holy man is the workmanship of the Holy Spirit.—30.388

645 We say of a river that it runs to the south, although there may be eddies along the banks which run in an opposite direction to the main stream. Still, these are inconsiderable matters. The main stream of the Thames is running constantly toward the sea, and we speak not untruthfully when we say that it is so. And the main stream and set of the current of the life of a child of God runs toward that which is right and true and holy, both toward God and man. If it is not so with you, you do not know the Lord. You need to be born again.—30.462

646 The raw material of a devil is an angel bereft of holiness. You cannot make a Judas except out of an apostle. The eminently good in outward form, when without inward life, decays into the foulest thing under heaven.—35.302

647 To me the greatest privilege in all the world would be perfect holiness. If I had my choice of all the blessings I can conceive of, I would choose perfect conformity to the Lord Jesus, or, in one word, holiness.—36.350

648 Of all the griefs the church ever feels, the keenest is when those who once stood in her midst dishonor the name of Christ by unholy living.—43.427

649 Did you ever see a bush burn, and yet not be consumed? Did you ever see a spark float in the sea, and yet not be quenched? Many persons here are, to themselves, just such wonders. They are living godly lives in the midst of temptation, holy in the midst of impurity, serving God in spite of all opposition. They are strange things!—45.139

650 If your religion does not make you holy, it will damn you. It is simply painted pageantry to go to hell in.—46.225

651 Though you have struggled in vain against your evil habits, though you have wrestled with them sternly, and resolved, and re-resolved, only to be defeated by your giant sins and your terrible passions, there is One who can conquer all your sins for you. There is One who is stronger than Hercules, who can strangle the hydra of your lust, kill the lion of your passions, and cleanse the Augean stable of your evil nature

by turning the great rivers of blood and water of his atoning sacrifice right through your soul. He can make and keep you pure within. Oh, look to him!—55.420

652 I would sooner be holy than happy if the two things could be divorced. Were it possible for a man always to sorrow and yet to be pure, I would choose the sorrow if I might win the purity, for to be free from the power of sin, to be made to love holiness, is true happiness.—58.521

Holy Spirit   *See Holiness; Trinity; Unction*

653 In ancient history there is a story of a valiant captain whose sword was dreaded by his enemies. His monarch once demanded of him that he should send this potent sword to him to be examined. The monarch took the sword, quietly criticized it, and sent it back with this message—"I see nothing wonderful in the sword; I cannot understand why any man should be afraid of it."

The captain sent back a message of this kind—"Your Majesty has been pleased to examine the sword, but I did not send the arm that wielded it. If you had examined that, you would have understood the mystery."

And now we look at men and see what they have done, and we say, "I cannot understand this; how was it done?" Why, we are only seeing a sword. If we could see the heart of infinite love that guided that man in his onward course, we should not wonder that he, as God's sword, gained the victory.—3.394

654 If you could pray the best prayer in the world without the Holy Spirit, God would have nothing to do with it. But if your prayer be broken and lame and limping, if the Spirit made it, God will look upon it and say, as he did upon the works of creation, "It is very good."—5.216

655 If there were only one prayer which I might pray before I died, it should be this: "Lord, send thy church men filled with the Holy Ghost and with fire."—10.337

656 Commentators are good in their way, but give me the teaching of the Holy Ghost. He makes the passage clear. How often we have found our utter inability to understand some part of divine truth. We asked some of God's people, and they helped us a little. But after all, we were not satisfied till we took it to the throne of heavenly grace and implored the teachings of the blessed Spirit. Then how sweetly it was opened to us; we could eat of it spiritually. It was no longer husk and shell, hard to be understood. It was as bread to us, and we could eat to the full.—11.286

657 I dread beyond all things the Spirit's withdrawal. Death has

not half the terror of that thought. I would sooner die a thousand times than lose the helpful presence of the Holy Ghost.—16.559

658 Without the Spirit of God we can do nothing. We are as ships without wind or chariots without steeds. Like branches without sap, we are withered. Like coals without fire, we are useless. As an offering without the sacrificial flame, we are unaccepted.—20.16

659 Prayer without the Spirit is as a bird without wings or an arrow without a bow. As well hope to see a dead man sit up in his coffin and plead a case in a court of law as hope to see a man prevail in prayer who is a stranger to the Holy Ghost. You will leave your prayer closet unrefreshed if you have been in it without the Spirit. Even the desire to pray is not with us unless the Holy Ghost has wrought it in the soul.—30.389

660 It were better to speak six words in the power of the Holy Ghost than to preach seventy years of sermons without the Spirit.—32.487

661 All the hope of our ministry lies in the Spirit of God operating on the spirits of men.—34.260

662 Unless the Holy Ghost blesses the Word, we who preach the gospel are of all men most miserable, for we have attempted a task that is impossible. We have

entered on a sphere where nothing but the supernatural will ever avail. If the Holy Spirit does not renew the hearts of our hearers, we cannot do it. If the Holy Ghost does not regenerate them, we cannot. If he does not send the truth home into their souls, we might as well speak into the ear of a corpse.—42.236

663 A very ugly word—*ghost*. A better translation of the original Greek word would be "Spirit." "Holy Spirit," and I sometimes wish that we always called him by that name. It is far more expressive. The word *ghost* bears such a strange and weird meaning now, that it were better in this connection entirely to abandon it.—59.442

Homosexuality   *See Sex, abuse of*

664 This once brought hell out of heaven on Sodom.—11.525

Honesty   *See Lying; Sincerity; Slander; Truth*

665 "We must live, you know," said a money-loving shopkeeper, as his excuse for doing what he could not otherwise defend.

"Yes, but we must die," was the reply, "and therefore we must do no such thing."—14.101

Hope

666 Christ always preached doctrine that was hopeful. While he denounced self-righteousness, he would turn round and say, "I

came not to call the righteous, but sinners to repentance" (Luke 5:32). If he ever had a frown on his brow, it was for the hypocrite and the proud man. But he had tears for sinners and loving invitations for penitent ones.—60.282

Humility   *See Meekness; Pride*

667 It is not humility to underrate yourself. Humility is to think of yourself as God thinks of you. It is to feel that if we have talents, God has given them to us. And let it be seen that, like freight in a vessel, they tend to sink us low. The more we have, the lower we ought to lie.—2.350

668 Very likely the most humble man in the world won't bend to anybody. Cringing men that bow before everybody are truly proud men. But humble men are those who think themselves so little, they do not think it worthwhile to stoop to serve themselves. Shadrach, Meshach, and Abednego were humble men, for they did not think their lives were worth enough to save them by a sin. Daniel was a humble man; he did not think his place, his station, his whole self worth enough to save them by leaving off prayer. Humility is a thing which must be genuine; the imitation of it is the nearest thing in the world to pride.—2.351

669 I imagine there may be some of you ready to say, "Sir, I am

nothing." Then I shall reply, "You are a young Christian."

There will be others of you who will say, "Sir, I am less than nothing." And I shall say, "You are an old Christian," for the older Christians get, the less they become in their own esteem.—4.364

670 If you and I empty ourselves, depend on it, God will fill us. Divine grace seeks out and fills a vacuum. Make a vacuum by humility, and God will fill that vacuum by his love.—13.249

671 I know of no consideration which tends more to humble us than the great mercy of God. Like Peter's boat, which floated high in the water when there was nothing in it, but when it was filled with fish it began to sink, our minds are humbled by a sense of undeserved love.—13.551

672 Our Lord never crushed a soul yet that lay prostrate at his feet, and never will.—20.475

673 The way to heaven is downhill, not uphill.—22.10

674 I believe every Christian man has a choice between being humble and being humbled.—30.533

675 If I knew that I must die in a ditch and be forgotten or slandered and abhorred by men, I would yet rejoice and cry "Hosanna" at the prospect of my Lord's sure victory.—32.610

676 The best definition of humility I ever heard was this—to think rightly of ourselves.—57.320

677 In a company where certain people were displaying their spiritual attainments, it was noticed that one devout person remained silent, and a talkative man turned to him and asked, "Have you no sanctification?" He replied, "I never had any to boast of, and I hope I never shall have." The more high in grace, the more low in self-esteem.—59.125

678 When you are half an inch above the ground, you are that half-inch too high. Your place is to be nothing.—63.143, 144

Hypocrite
See Self-righteousness; Sincerity

679 Because there is one hypocrite, men set down all the rest the same. I heard one man say that he did not believe there was a true Christian living, because he had found so many hypocrites. I reminded him that there could be no hypocrites if there were no genuine Christians. No one would try to forge bank notes if there were no genuine ones.—1.171

680 A mere profession is but painted pageantry to go to hell in. It is like the plumes on the hearse and the trappings on black horses which drag men to their graves, the funeral array of dead souls.—3.75

681 If I knew that I must be damned, one of my prayers should be, "Lord, let me not be damned with hypocrites," for surely to be damned with them is to be damned twice over.—3.410

682 Your Maker says, "Thou shalt love me with all thine heart." It is of no use for you to point your finger across the street at a minister whose life is inconsistent or at a deacon who is unholy or a member of the church who does not live up to his profession. When your Maker speaks to you, he appeals to you personally. And if you should tell him, "My Lord, I will not love thee, because there are hypocrites," would not your own conscience condemn you of the absurdity of your reasoning? Ought not your better judgment to whisper, "Inasmuch as so many are hypocrites, take heed that you are not. And if there be so many pretenders who injure the Lord's cause by their lying and pretensions, so much the more reason why you should have the real thing, and help to make the church sound and honest"?—3.439

683 Of all things in the world that stink in the nostrils of men, hypocrisy is the worst.—5.411

684 Read the letter of Jude, and you will find that there are some for whom are *reserved* "the blackness of darkness forever" (verse 13). That is your case, and this will be the aggravation of it: You sat at the Master's table, and you must now drink the cup of fire. You preached in Christ's courts, but you must now give forth a dolorous sermon concerning your own apostasy. You sang God's praises once; you must now howl out the *miserére* of the damned. You had a glimpse of heaven; you shall now have a dread insight into hell. You talked about eternal life; you shall now feel eternal death.—11.82

685 They believe the doctrine of election, but they have not the faith of God's elect. They swear by final perseverance, but persevere in unbelief. They confess all the five points of Calvinism, but they have not come to the one most needful point of looking unto Jesus, that they may be saved.—17.531

686 Surely I had better give up the preaching of the gospel when you give up the living of the gospel. My task, in itself difficult, is rendered absolutely impossible if, while I preach one thing, you live another.—30.13

687 It is a terribly easy matter to be a minister of the gospel and a vile hypocrite at the same time.—52.483

688 An unholy professor outside the church may batter against the walls with small effect, but inside he would be like the concealed soldiers in the wooden horse, who opened the gates of Troy to the

besiegers. It was only an apostle who could be such a "son of perdition" as Judas was (John 17:12). So beware, you who profess to be followers of Christ! You have great capacities for usefulness. But your position gives you immense capacities for doing damage to the cause of Christ.—53.305

689 The more a church flourishes, the more, I believe, do hypocrites get in, just as you see many a noxious creeping thing come and get into a garden after a shower of rain. The very things that make glad the flowers bring out these noxious things. And so hypocrites get in and steal much of the church's sap away.—60.416

690 There never was a good thing in the world but what people did make shams of it. It is because the world knows that faith in God makes men happier and nobler that men make pretense of having what they have not.—61.284

Idleness

691 The most likely man to go to hell is the man who has nothing to do on earth. Idle people tempt the devil to tempt them.—11.201

Idolatry

692 You may depend on it that the belief that this building or any other building is a house of God, a place peculiarly suitable for worship, is idolatry. You are giving to bricks and mortar some little of the honor which is due only to Christ as an altar. If you suppose that there is any more acceptableness to God in a church or a cathedral than in any public hall or in the open air, you have made a material building into an altar. You have set up an Antichrist, and you have robbed the Lord Jesus.—14.525, 526

693 Children are often idols, and in such cases their too ardent lovers are idolaters. We might as well make a god of clay and worship it, as worship our fellow creatures, for what are they but clay?—26.76

Inability   See Calvinism

694 I have myself been in such a condition that if heaven could have been purchased by a single prayer, I should have been damned, for I could no more pray than I could fly.—1.290, 291

695 Says one, "I cannot come to God."

Your powerlessness to come lies in the fact that you have no will to come. If you were willing, you would lack no power. You cannot come, because you are so wedded to your lusts, so fond of your sin. That very inability of yours is your crime, your guilt. Your inability lies not in your physical nature, but in your depraved moral nature.—6.137

696 I remember an anecdote of Dr. Gill which hits this nail on

the head. A man came to him and said, "Dr. Gill, you have been preaching the doctrine of human inability. I don't believe you. I believe that man can repent and believe, and is not without spiritual power."

"Well," said the doctor, "have you repented and believed?"

"No," said the other.

"Very well, then," said he, "you deserve double damnation."—8.355, 356

697 This inability is our own sin. This is laid at our door, not as an excuse for our sinfulness, but as a frightful aggravation of our guilt, that we have become so bad that we cannot make ourselves good, that our nature is now so desperately evil, that iniquity has become our nature, so that it is as natural for us to sin as for water to descend or sparks to fly upward.—8.495

698 There lies a woman who has fainted. You tell her to open her eyes, move her limbs, to recover. Yes, but she cannot do any one of these things. In one sense she can. The faculties are there. But they are all in a dormant state, and so utterly powerless, that all the woman is conscious of is her inability. Such is the state of the sinner when under a sense of guilt.—9.439

699 You tell me that you cannot pray, but Jesus healed one possessed of a dumb devil. You feel hardened and insensible, but he cast out a deaf devil. You tell me you cannot believe. Neither could that man with the withered arm stretch it out, but he did do it when Jesus bade him. You tell me you are dead in sin, but Jesus made even the dead live.—15.502

700 God helps those who cannot help themselves.—33.630

701 What a dreadful inability sin brings with it! That simple command of the gospel, "Believe," the sinner cannot obey in himself. He can no more repent and believe without the Holy Spirit's aid than he can create a world.—49.280

702 All the "cannots" in the Bible about spiritual inability are tantamount to "will nots." When you say, "I cannot repent," you mean, "I will not."—61.595

Incarnation *See Christmas*

703 Infinite, and an infant. Eternal, and yet born of a woman. Almighty, and yet hanging on a woman's breast. Supporting a universe, and yet needing to be carried in a mother's arms. King of angels, and yet the reputed son of Joseph. Heir of all things, and yet the carpenter's despised son.—4.396

704 He that made man was made man.—32.600

Indecision *See Faith*

705 I am always fearful about those who are so near salvation and yet not decided. The raw

material for a devil is an angel. The raw material for the son of perdition was an apostle. And the raw material for the most horrible of apostates is one who is almost a saint.—32.623

706 There was a man who was almost saved in a fire, but he was burned. There was another who was almost healed of a disease, but he died. There was one who was almost reprieved, but he was hanged. And there are many in hell who were almost saved.—41.206

Indifference   *See Compassion; Heart, hardness of*

707 Once if you thought of a man's being damned, you would weep your very soul out in tears. But now you could sit at the very brink of hell and hear its wailings unmoved.—2.82

708 Who can shut his eyes to the sad fact that in days of revival there are some who are unblessed? I am anxious about you who are like Gideon's fleece—dry when the floor is wet (Judg. 6:39, 40)! You remain in a barren spot of ground when all the earth is filled with fertility!—6.332

709 Do you not find, my brethren, that almost unconsciously to yourselves a spirit of indifference steals over you? You do not give up private prayer, but it becomes a mere mechanical operation. You do not forsake the assem-

bling of yourselves together, but still your bodily presence is all that is given, and you derive no refreshment from the unspiritual exercise. Have you not sat at the Lord's table spiritually asleep?—14.62

710 If you can, without emotion, think of a soul being damned, I fear that it will be your own lot. If you can look on the ignorant and the perverse and the rebellious, and think of their destruction with complacency, you are no child of God. Your Savior wept over Jerusalem. Have you no tears? Then you are not a member of the family of which he is the head.—19.489

711 To be on the high road to hell, and yet to be trifling with eternal things; to be on the brink of perdition, and yet to be jesting at religion; to be nearing the everlasting burnings, and yet to be treading the blood of Christ beneath your feet; oh, this is mad work!—48.152

712 Trifle not with God, who can cast you into hell forever. Trifle not with Christ, whose hands and feet were nailed to the accursed tree for sinners such as you. Trifle not with his precious blood, for that is your only hope of redemption. Trifle not with the Holy Spirit, for if he should leave you to perish, your case would be hopeless. Trifle not with the gospel; what would the lost in hell not

give to hear another proclamation of mercy! The devil does not trifle; he is very earnestly seeking your destruction. God and Christ and the Holy Spirit are not trifling with you, and we are not trifling with you.—53.405

713 What a hopeful sign it would be even if people were excited against religion! Really, I would sooner that they intelligently hated it than that they were stolidly indifferent to it. A man who has enough thought about him to oppose the truth of God is a more hopeful subject than the man who does not think at all. We cannot do anything with logs. But we feel that we could brace up our nerves to the charge amidst men possessed with devils while we have the gospel to cast the devils out.—54.146

Inspiration   *See Bible, inspiration of*

Intercession   *See Prayer, intercessory*

Irresistible grace   *See Grace, irresistible*

Jesus   *See Faith, object of; Lordship; Redeemer; Trinity*

714 I would propose that the subject of the ministry of this house, as long as this platform shall stand, shall be the person of Jesus Christ. I am never ashamed to avow myself a Calvinist, but if I am asked to say what is my creed, I think I must reply, "It is Jesus Christ." The body of divinity to which I would pin and bind myself forever, God helping me, is Christ Jesus, who is the sum and substance of the gospel, who is himself all theology, the incarnation of every precious truth, the all-glorious personal embodiment of the way, the truth, and the life.—7.169

Note: These words were spoken on March 25, 1861, in the first sermon delivered in the newly constructed Metropolitan Tabernacle. Compare CHS's last words from the Tabernacle more than 30 years later, found under this same topic, from source 37.324.

715 What the sun is to the day, what the moon is to the night, what the dew is to the flower, such is Jesus Christ to us. What bread is to the hungry, clothes to the naked, the shadow of a great rock to the traveler in a weary land, such is Jesus Christ to us. What the husband is to his spouse, what the head is to the body, such is Jesus Christ to us.—9.627

716 As the river seeks the sea, so Jesus, I seek thee! O let me find thee and melt my life into thine forever!—11.125

717 Bleeding and dying that we might neither bleed nor die, descending that we might ascend, and wrapped in swaddling bands that we might be unwrapped of the grave clothes of corruption.—11.710

718 There are three stages of the human soul in connection with Christ. The first is "without Christ" (John 15:5). This is the state of nature. The next is "in Christ" (2 Cor. 5:17). This is the state of grace. The third is "with Christ" (Phil. 1:23). That is the state of glory.—15.397

719 God is more glorified in the person of his Son than he would have been by an unfallen world.—17.124

720 The less you make of Christ, the less gospel you have to trust in. If you get rid of Christ from your creed, you have at the same time destroyed all its good news. The more gospel we would preach, the more of Christ we must proclaim.—35.174

721 Beware of studying doctrine, precept, or experiences apart from the Lord Jesus, who is the soul of all. Doctrine without Christ will be nothing better than his empty tomb. Doctrine with Christ is a glorious high throne, with the King sitting on it.—35.206

722 I sometimes wonder that you do not get tired of my preaching, because I do nothing but hammer away on this one nail. With me it is, year after year, "None but Jesus! None but Jesus!" Oh, you great saints, if you have outgrown the need of a sinner's trust in the Lord Jesus, you have outgrown your sins, but you have also outgrown your grace, and your saintship has ruined you!—37.311

723 He is the most magnanimous of captains. If there is anything gracious, generous, kind and tender, lavish, and superabundant in love, you always find it in him. These forty years and more have I served him, and I have nothing but love for him. His service is life, peace, joy. Oh, that you would enter it at once! God help you to enlist under the banner of Jesus even this day!—37.324

Note: These are CHS's last words from the pulpit of the Metropolitan Tabernacle, spoken on June 7, 1891. Compare his first words from the Tabernacle more than thirty years earlier, found under this same topic, from the source 7.169.

724 I do not believe that I have a wish in all the world except to know more of my Master, and to win more souls for him.—40.619, 620

725 If there did lie between my soul and Christ seven hells, I would swim through them that I might get to him.—42.431

726 There never was a sinner half as big as Christ is as a Savior. Come and measure the sinner from head to foot and all around. Make him out to be an elephantine sinner, yet there is room for him in the ark, Christ Jesus. There is room in the heart of Jesus for the vilest of the vile. Oh, that

you would turn your eyes to him, pray to him from your very heart, and trust in him with your whole soul!—45.419

⁷²⁷ This is the very essence of true religion—personally living with a personal Savior, personally trusting a personal Redeemer, personally crying out to a personal Intercessor, and receiving personal answers from a Person who loves us, and who manifests himself to us.—47.136

⁷²⁸ I have often tried to imagine what the first five minutes with Jesus Christ in heaven will be. But I have in vain sought to picture the novelty and freshness of that wondrous time when the soul, filled with amazement, will exclaim, "The half has never been told me." The Queen of Sheba was astonished when she saw all the glory of King Solomon. But he was a mere nobody compared with our Lord Jesus Christ. Oh! What will it be to see him?—47.261

⁷²⁹ Are you satisfied with Christ? If you are not, you have not really got him. If you have got him, he is everything to you.—47.492

⁷³⁰ I would sooner lie on a bed and ache in every limb, with the death sweat standing on my brow, by the month and year persecuted, despised, and forsaken, poor and naked, with the dogs to lick my sores and the devils to tempt my soul, and have Christ for my friend, than I would sit in the palaces of wicked kings with all their wealth and luxury and pampering and sin.—51.239

⁷³¹ It would be worthwhile to die a thousand painful deaths in order to get one brief glimpse of Christ as he is.—52.441

⁷³² If you cannot say, "Jesus is precious to me," I do not care to what church you belong or what creed you are ready to die for. You do not know the truth of God unless the person of Christ is dear to you.—52.561

⁷³³ Out of all our Savior's names, there is not one which rings with such sweet music as this blessed name, "Jesus." I suppose the reason of this is that it answers to our own name, the name of sinner.—54.350

⁷³⁴ I cannot describe all that Christ is to us, for what is he *not* to us? He is the sun of our day; he is the star of our night; he is our life; he is our life's life; he is our heaven on earth, and he shall be our heaven in heaven.—56.320

Jesus, birth of   *See Christmas; Incarnation*

Jesus, death of   *See Death, Christ's*

Jesus, deity of   *See Lordship*

⁷³⁵ Who less than God could have carried your sins and mine and cast them all away? Who less

than God could have interposed to deliver us from the jaws of hell's lions, and bring us up from the pit, having found a ransom? On whom less than God could we rely on to keep us from the innumerable temptations that beset us? How can Christ be less than God, when he says, "Lo, I am with you always, unto the end of the world" (Matt. 28:20)? How could he be omnipresent if he were not God? How could he hear our prayers, the prayers of millions scattered through the leagues of earth, and attend to them all, and give acceptance to all, if he were not infinite in understanding and infinite in merit?—7.379

736 It is not possible that the man who denies the deity of Christ can be a Christian. He deliberately refuses the only way of escape from the wrath to come. I can understand a man getting to heaven as a Roman Catholic, notwithstanding all his errors, because he believes in the divinity of Christ and relies on the expiatory sacrifice of his death. But I cannot understand, nor do I believe, that any man will ever enter those pearly gates who, in doubting or discrediting the deity of our blessed Lord and Savior, Jesus Christ, renounces the sheet anchor of our most holy faith and dares to face his maker without a counselor, without an advocate, without a plea for mercy! It is time we said so, and spoke out

plainly. This is no theme for trifling.—19.104

737 Depend on it, my hearer, you never will go to heaven unless you are prepared to worship Jesus Christ as God.—21.177

738 If Christ was not God, we are not Christians. We are deceived dupes; we are idolaters, as bad as the heathen whom we now pity. It is making a man into a God if Christ be not God.—46.142

739 I never wonder, when persons once doubt the deity of Christ, if they go to great lengths in slandering his character. I heard the other day something said with regard to our Savior's birth which it is not right for any man to repeat. Yet I said when I heard it, "Yes, and it must be so if he was not really God."—54.183

Jesus, love for   *See Love, for Christ*

Jesus, name of   *See Prayer*

740 If we forget this in our prayers, we have lost the muscle and sinew from the arm of prayer, we have snapped the spinal column by which the manhood of prayer is sustained erect, we have pulled down about our own ears the whole temple of supplication, as Samson did the house of the Philistines. "For Christ's sake." This is the one unbuttressed pillar on which all prayer must lean. Take this away, and it comes

down with a crash. Let this stand, and prayer stands like a heaven-reaching minaret holding communion with the skies.—11.85, 86

Jesus, nature of

741 He is not humanity deified. He is not Godhead humanized. He is God. He is man. He is all that God is, and all that man is as God created him.—30.28

Jesus, paintings of

742 You never saw a picture of *his* face which satisfied you, and you never will. You shall go all over the continent, and see some of the marvelous productions of the masters put up as altar pieces, and you will say when you see them, "That is not like Jesus Christ." They can paint Judas. There are some fine heads of Peter, sweet guesses at John. They can paint Mary Magdalene if you will, but never Jesus Christ. They can never paint him. No artist that ever lived can catch his expression of countenance, much less put it on canvas.—9.369

Jesus, preaching about   See Preaching

743 If you leave out Christ, you have left the sun out of the day and the moon out of the night. You have left the waters out of the sea and the floods out of the river. You have left the harvest out of the year, the soul out of the body, you have left joy out of heaven, you have robbed *all* of its

all. There is no gospel worth thinking of, much less worth proclaiming, if Jesus be forgotten. We must have Jesus as Alpha and Omega in all our ministries.—9.720

744 I would never preach a sermon—the Lord forgive me if I do—which is not full to overflowing with my Master. I know one who said I was always on the old string, and he would come and hear me no more. But if I preached a sermon without Christ in it, he would come. Ah, he will never come while this tongue moves, for a sermon without Christ in it—a Christless sermon! A brook without water, a cloud without rain, a well which mocks the traveler, a tree twice dead, a sky without a sun, a night without a star. It were a realm of death, a place of mourning for angels and laughter for devils. O Christian, we must have Christ!—10.139

745 The preaching of Christ is the whip that flogs the devil. The preaching of Christ is the thunderbolt, the sound of which makes all hell shake.—12.130

746 The most prominent agency in the church of God is the preaching of Christ. This is the trumpet of heaven and the battering ram of hell.—18.718

747 A sermon without Christ as its beginning, middle, and end is a mistake in conception and a crime in execution.—27.598

⁷⁴⁸ I remember once feeling many questions as to whether I was a child of God or not. I went into a little chapel, and I heard a good man preach. I made my handkerchief sodden with my tears as I heard him talk about Christ and the precious blood. When I was preaching the same things to others, I was wondering whether this truth was mine. But while I was hearing for myself, I knew it was mine, for my very soul lived on it.

I went to that good man and thanked him for the sermon. He asked me who I was. When I told him, he turned all manner of colors. "Why," he said, "that was your own sermon."

I said, "Yes, I knew it was, and it was good of the Lord to feed me with food that I had prepared for others."—32.10

⁷⁴⁹ Leave Christ out of your preaching, and you have taken the milk from the children. You have taken the strong meat from the men. But if your object as a teacher or preacher is to glorify Christ and to lead men to love him and trust him, that is the very work on which the heart of God himself is set. The Lord and you are pulling together, and God the Holy Ghost can set his seal to a work like that.—41.187

⁷⁵⁰ I have heard of ministers who can preach a sermon without mentioning the name of Jesus from beginning to end. If you ever hear such a sermon as that, mind that you never hear another from that man. Let those go and hear him who do not value their immortal souls, but dear friends, your soul and mine are too precious to be placed at the mercy of such a preacher. Paul's harp had only one string, but he brought such music out of it as never came from any other. He found such infinite variety in Christ that he never exhausted his theme. With him it was Christ first, Christ last, Christ midst, Christ everywhere. He could never have his pen in his hand without writing something in praise of his glorious Lord and Savior.—49.613

⁷⁵¹ If I had only one more sermon to preach before I died, it would be about my Lord Jesus Christ. And I think that when we get to the end of our ministry, one of our regrets will be that we did not preach more of him. I am sure no minister will ever repent of having preached him too much.—54.149

⁷⁵² I have no belief in the preaching of Christ unsuccessfully. I think a dear brother may preach the gospel for years and see no conversions, and perhaps there may be none just then. But they will come.—60.596

Joy   *See Forgiveness; Pleasure*

⁷⁵³ Why should Christians be such a happy people? It is good for

our God; it gives him honor among men when we are glad. It is good for us; it makes us strong. "The joy of the Lord is your strength" (Neh. 8:10). It is good for the ungodly; when they see Christians glad, they long to be believers themselves. It is good for our fellow Christians; it comforts them and tends to cheer them.—8.333

754 I would sooner possess the joy of Christ five minutes than I would revel in the mirth of fools for half a century. There is more bliss in the tear of repentance than in the worldling's joys.—29.67

755 The greatest joy of a Christian is to give joy to Christ.—42.356

756 I thought I could have leaped from earth to heaven at one spring when I first saw my sins drowned in the Redeemer's blood.—45.475

757 It is an unfortunate thing for the Christian to become melancholy. If there is any man in the world that has a right to have a bright, clear face and a flashing eye, it is the man whose sins are forgiven him, who is saved with God's salvation.—62.126

Judgment   *See Hell; Wrath, God's*

758 Sinners are not, as a general rule, punished here. Their sentence is reserved until the day of judgment. Some people regard every accident as a judgment, but we do not agree with them at all, else should we have frequently to condemn the innocent. This is not the time of judgment. Judgment is yet to come.—54.554

Justice   *See Grace; Mercy*

759 I used to think that if I could see the lost in hell, surely I must weep for them. But there is no such sentiment as that known in heaven. The believer there shall be satisfied with all God's will. Even their loss has been their own fault. If my parents could see me in hell, they would not have a tear to shed for me, though they were in heaven, for they would say, "It is justice, thou great God."—1.194

760 A good old saint who lately lay dying told her pastor that she was resting on the *justice* of God. The good man thought that she had chosen a strange point of the divine character to rest on, but she explained, "I rest in his justice to my great Substitute, that he would not let him die for me in vain."—24.715

761 Had it been possible for God to set aside the claims of his justice and simply to forgive without making satisfaction to his law, we should have felt our standing to be questionable. Unjustly saved? Poor position for one who has a conscience.—36.545

762 If we had lain in hell forever, yet divine justice would not have been fully justified, for after thou-

sands of years of suffering there would remain still an eternity of debt due to God's justice. If God had annihilated all the sinners that ever lived, at one stroke, he would not have so honored his justice as he did when he took sin and laid it on his Son, and his Son bore divine wrath which was due to that sin. For now there has been rendered unto divine justice a full equivalent, a complete recompense for all the dishonor which it suffered.—63.112

Justification   *See Forgiveness; Salvation*

763 It is admitted by all evangelical Christians that the standing or falling in the church is that of justification by faith.—12.279

764 I said that clothed in the righteousness of Christ, we are accepted as if we had never sinned. I correct myself—had we never sinned, we could only have stood in the righteousness of man. But this day by faith we stand in the righteousness of God himself. The doings and the dying of our Lord Jesus Christ make up for us a wedding dress more glorious than human merit could have spun, even if unfallen Adam had been the spinner.—21.210

765 Any church which puts in the place of justification by faith in Christ another method of salvation is a harlot church.—35.398

766 I can sympathize with Luther when he said, "I have preached justification by faith so often, and I feel sometimes that you are so slow to receive it, that I could almost take the Bible and bang it about your heads."—38.272

767 The doctrine of justification by faith through the substitutionary sacrifice of Christ is very much to my ministry what bread and salt are to the table. As often as the table is set, there are those necessary things. This is the very salt of the gospel. It is impossible to bring it forward too often. It is the soul-saving doctrine. It is the foundation doctrine of the gospel of Jesus Christ.—61.565

Knowledge   *See Omniscience; Wisdom*

768 Many of the fears of Christians would be driven away if they knew more. Ignorance is not bliss in Christianity, but misery. And knowledge sanctified and attended by the presence of the Holy Spirit is as wings by which we may rise out of the mists and darkness into the light of full assurance. The knowledge of Christ is the most excellent of sciences. Seek to be masters of it, and you are on the road to full assurance.—16.9

769 Some aspire to know that others may know that they know. To be reputed wise is the heaven of most mortals. Learn to know that

you may make other people know. This is not the avarice but the commerce of knowledge. Acquire knowledge that you may distribute it.—36.641

770 "Ignorance is the mother of devotion," according to the Church of Rome. "Ignorance is the mother of error," according to the Word of God. What we want our fellowmen to possess is spiritual knowledge. Especially do we desire that they may have knowledge with regard to God's righteousness, for men do not know what that righteousness is which God requires.—37.387

771 The knowledge of God is the great hope of sinners. Oh, if you knew him better, you would fly to him! If you understood how gracious he is, you would seek him. If you could have any idea of his holiness, you would loathe your self-righteousness. If you knew anything of his power, you would not venture to contend with him. If you knew anything of his grace, you would not hesitate to yield yourself to him.—37.566

Knowledge, spiritual gift of

772 I remember quite well, and the subject of the story is most probably present, that a very singular conversion was wrought at the New Park Street Chapel. A man who had been accustomed to go to a bar for gin saw a crowd round the door of the chapel. He looked in and forced his way to the top of the gallery stairs. Just then I looked in the direction in which he stood. I remarked that there might be a man in the gallery who had come in with no good motive, for even then he had a gin bottle in his pocket. The singularity of the expression struck the man, and being startled because the preacher so exactly described him, he listened attentively to the warnings which followed. The Word reached his heart, the grace of God met him, he became converted, and he is walking humbly in the fear of God.—54.28, 29

773 An aged minister came into my vestry and said, "I have got this letter which I should like you to see." Before I read it, he explained to me that he had a son who had made a profession of religion but had gone aside from it, and it had broken his heart. The letter was from his son, and it said, "I went to hear Mr. Spurgeon, and I have not the slightest doubt that it has had an influence on my whole life. The text was, 'He is as a root out of a dry ground.' What surprised me most was that out of five or six thousand, he fastened his eyes on me, though I was in the farthest gallery"—(the young man's name was Thomas)—"and suddenly he shouted out these words, 'There's a wild, daredevil, Tom. God means to save him, and he will be

a comfort to his father in his old age.' "

The old gentleman took off his glasses when he got to that and said, "And so he is."—55.429

Law   *See Covenant; Gospel; Grace; Legalism; Works*

774 There is no point on which men make greater mistakes than on the relation which exists between the law and the gospel. Some men put the law instead of the gospel; others put the gospel instead of the law. A certain class maintains that the law and the gospel are mixed, and that partly by observance of the law, and partly by God's grace men are saved. These men understand not the truth and are false teachers.—1.285

775 To convince and condemn is all the law can do.—9.529

776 I do not believe that any man can preach the gospel who does not preach the law. The law is the needle, and you cannot draw the silken thread of the gospel through a man's heart unless you first send the needle of the law to make way for it. If men do not understand the law, they will not feel that they are sinners. And if they are not consciously sinners, they will never value the sin offering. There is no healing a man till the law has wounded him, no making him alive till the law has slain him.—32.27

Law, purpose of

777 Imagine a case. Some young men are about to go to sea, where I foresee they will meet with a storm. Suppose you put me in a position where I may cause a tempest before the other shall arise. By the time the natural storm comes on, those young men will be a long way out at sea, and they will be wrecked and ruined before they can put back and be safe. But what do I? When they are just in the mouth of the river, I send a storm, putting them in the greatest danger, and hastening them ashore, so that they are saved.

Thus did God. He sends a law which shows them the roughness of the journey. The tempest of law compels them to put back to the harbor of free grace and saves them from a most terrible destruction. The law never came to save men. It came on purpose to make the evidence complete that salvation by works is impossible, and thus to drive the elect of God to rely wholly on the finished salvation of the gospel.—1.287

778 The heart is like a dark cellar, full of lizards, cockroaches, beetles, and all kinds of reptiles and insects, which in the dark we see not. But the law takes down the shutters and lets in the light, and we see the evil.—1.289

779 The law stirs the mud at the bottom of the pool and proves

how foul the waters are. The law compels the man to see that sin dwells in him, and that it is a powerful tyrant over his nature. All this is with a view to his cure. God be thanked when the law so works as to take off the sinner from all confidence in himself! To make the leper confess that he is incurable is going a great way toward compelling him to go to that divine Savior, who alone is able to heal him. This is the whole end of the law toward men whom God will save.—34.135

Layman   *See Ministry, lay*

Laziness   *See Idleness*

Legalism   *See Gospel; Grace; Law; Works*

780 The poor sinner trying to be saved by law is like a blind horse going round and round a mill, and never getting a step further, but only being whipped continually. The faster he goes, the more work he does, the more he is tired. The better legalist a man is, the more he may rest assured of his own final rejection and eternal portion with Pharisees. — 2.123

781 Many preachers have had to confess the uselessness of mere moral preaching. There is no instance, I believe, on record, where the mere preaching of the law made a man love God, or where the heart ever was, or ever could be, renewed by inculcating good works. As well hope to make

a black man white by pelting him with snowballs.—12.523

782 It would appear that God does not know the best way of saving men, and men are so wise that they amend his methods! Is not this a refinement of blasphemy? It is a hideous farce to see a rebellious sinner suddenly become jealous about good works and greatly concerned for public morality. Does it not make laughter in hell to see licentious men censuring the pure gospel of the Lord Jesus and finding fault with free forgiveness because it might make men less mindful of purity? It makes one sick to see the hypocrisy of legalists.—29.86

Limited Atonement   *See Atonement, limited*

Lord's Day   *See Sabbath*

783 I believe that Sunday should be spent in recreation. You are dreadfully shocked, and well you may be. But what do I mean by "recreation"? It means creating us new. Oh, that everybody who talks about spending Sunday in recreation would come to be re-created, regenerated, renewed, refreshed, revived, and made to rejoice in God.—27.474

784 One man traveling on the road saw a poor man in distress, and having but seven shillings, the generous person gave the poor man six. But when the wretch had scrambled to his feet, he followed

his benefactor to knock him down and steal the seventh shilling from him. How many do this! The Sabbath is their day for sport, for amusement, for anything but the service of God. They rob God of his day, though it be but one in seven. This is base unthankfulness.—38.245, 246

785 The change which our Lord has made in the Sabbath is indicative of the change which he has made in our life. The law says, "Work six days and then observe the seventh as the Sabbath." But under the gospel the arrangement is, "Rest on the first day before you have done a stroke of work. Just as the week begins, take your rest, and after that, in the strength derived from it, and from the grateful motives which arise out of that one blessed day of rest, give to the Lord the six days of the week." There is a change from law to gospel indicated in that very change. So let it be with you.—49.243

786 "Sunday is our best day for business," says somebody.

Well then, so much more opportunity is there for you to make a greater sacrifice to prove your love to Jesus. — 51.363

787 The Christian will lose the Sunday trade, even if thereby he should lose half his living, rather than break God's command.—61.497

Lordship *See Commitment; Jesus; Jesus, deity of*

788 Verily I say unto you, you cannot have Christ for your Savior unless you also have him as your Lord.—47.570

789 I cannot conceive it possible for anyone truly to receive Christ as Savior and yet not to receive him as Lord. A man who is really saved by grace does not need to be told that he is under solemn obligations to serve Christ. The new life within him tells him that. Instead of regarding it as a burden, he gladly surrenders himself—body, soul, and spirit—to the Lord who has redeemed him, reckoning this to be his reasonable service.—56.617

Lord's Supper *See Ordinance*

790 Shame on the Christian church that she should put it off to once a month and mar the first day of the week by depriving it of its glory in the meeting together for fellowship and breaking of bread and showing forth the death of Christ till he comes. They who once know the sweetness of each Lord's day celebrating his supper, will not be content, I am sure, to put it off to less frequent seasons. Beloved, when the Holy Ghost is with us, ordinances are wells to the Christian, wells of rich comfort and of near communion.—13.423

791 I do not know how I could bring my soul as a child of God to refuse any man communion at my Master's table, who believed that Jesus is the Christ.—17.144

792 After our Lord's death was over, the blood of animals was not the type, but the blood of the grape. That which was terrible in prospect is joyous in remembrance. That which was blood in the shedding is wine in the receiving. It came from him with a wound, but it comes to us with a blessing.—33.377

793 You are taught by this institution that the very best way in which you can remember Christ is by receiving him. You are not asked to bring bread with you. It is here. You are not asked to bring a cup with you. It is already provided. What have you to do? Nothing but to eat and to drink. You have to be receivers, and nothing more. Well now, whenever you want to remember your Lord and Master, you need not say, "I must do something for him." No, no, let him do something for you.—34.453

794 I love to come every Lord's day to the communion table. I should be very sorry to come only once a month. I need to be reminded, forcibly reminded, of my dear Lord and Master very often.—39.220

795 The Lord's Supper. There is no teaching anywhere like it. I have been in the habit of coming to the Lord's table every first day of the week now for many years. Has it lost its freshness? Oh, dear no!—44.537

796 Never mind that bread and wine, unless you can use them as folks often use their spectacles. What do they use them for? To look at? No, to look *through* them. So, use the bread and wine as a pair of spectacles. Look through them, and do not be satisfied until you can say, "Yes, yes, I can see the Lamb of God, which taketh away the sin of the world."—45.525

797 I think the moments we are nearest to heaven are those we spend at the Lord's table.—54.332

Lost   *See Condemnation; Damnation; Hell; Wrath, God's*

798 It is a very remarkable fact that no inspired preacher of whom we have any record ever uttered such terrible words concerning the destiny of the lost as our Lord Jesus Christ.—12.172

799 If you do get lost, some of you will have to wade through your mother's tears and leap over your father's prayers and your minister's entreaties. You will have to force a passage through the warnings of godly people and the examples of pious relatives. Why this effort to destroy your own souls?—26.441

800 I do not know if there is a more dreadful word in the English language than that word *lost*.—58.67

801 We are lost willfully and willingly; lost perversely and utterly; but still lost of our own accord, which is the worst kind of being lost. We are lost to God, who has lost our heart's love, confidence, and obedience; lost to the church, which we cannot serve; lost to truth, which we will not see; lost to right, whose cause we do not uphold; lost to heaven, into whose sacred precincts we can never come; lost, so lost that unless almighty mercy shall intervene, we shall be cast into the pit that is bottomless to sink forever. Lost! Lost! Lost! Better a whole world on fire than a soul lost! Better every star quenched and the skies a wreck than a single soul to be lost!—58.317

Love   *See Compassion*

802 He who does not love sinners cannot pray aright for them. When we love sinners, then prayer is fervent. And when we love Jesus, then will the prayer be earnest. Love is the flaming torch to kindle the pile of our devotions.—12.597

803 A man will love a dog or a bird sooner than be loveless. Captives have been known to fall in love with rats, and even spiders on the wall have been the objects of their affection. A little flower that could not speak has been the prisoner's beloved friend. We must have something to love. Oh, and what wealth of love Jesus brings into the heart when he enters it!—16.281

804 It is reported that Mr. Whitefield was one day asked by a partisan, "Do you think that we, when we get to heaven, shall see John Wesley there?"

"No," said George Whitefield, "I do not think we shall." The questioner was very delighted with that answer, but Mr. Whitefield added, "I believe that Mr. John Wesley will have a place so near the throne of God, and that such poor creatures as you and I will be so far off, as to be hardly able to see him."

As I read such remarks, I have said to myself, "By this I know that he must be a Christian," for I saw that he loved his brother Wesley even while he so earnestly differed from him on certain points of doctrine.—51.249

Love, Christ's   *See Love, God's*

805 I would rather have one mouthful of Christ's love and a sip of his fellowship than a whole world full of carnal delights. What is the chaff to the wheat? What is the sparkling paste to the true diamond? What is a dream to the glorious reality? What is time's mirth in its best trim compared to our Lord Jesus in his most despised estate? — 10.135

806 It is when you get to doubt the love of God that you grow

hard and cold. But when you are fired with the love of a dying Savior who gave himself for you, you feel as if you loved every beggar in the street, and you long to bring every harlot to Christ's dear feet. You cannot help it. If Christ baptizes your heart into his love, you will be covered with it and filled with it.—29.118

807 If there is one subject more than another upon which I wish ever to speak, it is the love of Christ. But if there is one which quite baffles me and makes me go back from this platform utterly ashamed of my poor feeble words, it is this subject. This love of Christ is the most amazing thing under heaven, if not in heaven itself.—42.505

808 In math, if you divide an infinite number by any number, no matter how large, you still have an infinite quotient. So Jesus' love, being infinite, even though it is divided up for every person on earth, is still infinitely poured out on each one of us!— 55.315

Love, for Christ

809 If there were a stake and burning faggots, I might flinch from the fire. But so mighty is divine love that it would doubtless drive me to the flames sooner than let me leave Jesus.—10.136

810 I had rather be blind and deaf and dumb, and lose my taste and smell, than not love Christ. To be unable to appreciate him is the worst of disabilities, the most serious of calamities. It is not the loss of a single spiritual faculty, but it proves the death of the soul.—21.554

811 No joy on earth is equal to the bliss of being all taken up with love to Christ. If I had my choice of all the lives that I could live, I certainly would not choose to be an emperor, nor to be a millionaire, nor to be a philosopher, for power and wealth and knowledge bring with them sorrow. But I would choose to have nothing to do but to love my Lord Jesus—nothing, I mean, but to do all things for his sake, and out of love to him.—32.587, 588

812 We love our dear ones on earth, but we love Jesus better than all of them put together. We could not live without him.— 36.53

813 Look through all the pages of history, and put to the noblest men and women this question, "Who loves Christ?" At once, up from dark dungeons and cruel racks there rises the confessors' cry, "We love him!" And from the fiery stake, where they clapped their hands as they were being burned to death, the same answer comes, "We love him!" If you could walk through the miles of catacombs at Rome, and if the

holy dead, whose dust lies there, could suddenly wake up, they would all shout, "We love him!" Happy are they who enlist in such an army as this, which has emblazoned on its banners this grand declaration, "We love him!"—47.268

814 There is a fleet lying in the river, richly laden, but it cannot come up, because the river is blocked up with ice. So I see my Master's love lying out far down the river, and it would gladly come to my poor soul to enrich me and make me holy and heavenly, but the coldness of my heart, like ice, blocks up the channel, and I get not what I might obtain. Come, heavenly love, and melt the ice. Flow, streams of grace, and dissolve every barrier. Come, Jesus, come into my heart, and let thy treasures be mine forevermore!—53.513

815 If you make doctrine the main thing, you are very likely to grow narrow-minded. If you make your own experience the main thing, you will become gloomy and critical of others. If you make ordinances the main thing, you will be apt to grow merely formal. But you can never make too much of the living Christ Jesus. Remember that all things else are for his sake. Doctrines and ordinances are the planets, but Christ is the sun. Get to love *him* best of all. —54.472

816 I cannot bear it that we should love Jesus little. It seems to me horrible. Not to have your heart all on fire for Christ—this is execrable! Let us love him to the utmost. Let us ask him to give us larger hearts, and to fire them with the flame that is in his own, that we may love him to the utmost possibilities of affection.—58.221

Love, God's   *See Love, Christ's*

817 A man breaks a leg, and the surgeon sets the bone. That is kindness. But suppose the man's mother should set the bone. Oh, how she would do it with lovingkindness! That is how God has dealt with us. Oh, how tenderly!—27.480

818 If a man could know that he was loved by all his fellowmen, if he could have it for certain that he was loved by all the angels, yet these were but so many drops, and all put together could not compare with the main ocean contained in the fact that "God loved us."—29.114

819 Oh, to be beloved of God! Had you the hatred of all mankind, this honey would turn their gall into sweetness.—63.195

Lying   *See Honesty; Slander*

820 Show me a man who is habitually or frequently a liar, and you show me a man who will have his portion in the lake that burns with fire and brimstone. I do not care to which denomina-

tion of Christians he may belong. I am sure he is none of Christ's. And it is very sad to know that there are some in all fellowships who have this great and grievous fault, that you cannot trust them in what they say. God deliver us from that.—11.403

821 I have seen almost all sorts of people converted—great blasphemers, pleasure-seekers, thieves, drunkards, unchaste persons, and hardened reprobates. But rarely have I seen a man converted who has been a thorough-paced liar. The heart which is crammed with craft and treachery seems as if it had passed out of the reach of grace.—27.113, 114

Martyrdom   See Death; Death, Christian; Persecution; Suffering

822 Where is the zeal which counted not its life dear so that it might win Christ? I believe that the killing of a few of our ministers would have prospered Christianity. I would count my own blood most profitably shed in so holy a struggle.—2.180

823 Look at old Ignatius. He is brought into the Roman circus, and after facing the taunts of the emperor and the jeers of the multitude, the lions are let loose on him. He thrusts his arm into a lion's mouth, poor aged man as he is, and when the bones are cracking, he says, "Now I begin to be a Christian."—6.481

Mass   See Catholicism; Christmas; Pope; Purgatory

824 The mass is a mass of abominations, a mass of hell's own concocting, a crying insult against the Lord of glory. It is not to be spoken of in any terms but those of horror and detestation. Whenever I think of another sacrifice for sin being offered, by whomever it may be presented, I can only regard it as an infamous insult to the perfection of the Savior's work.—12.561

Maturity   See Growth, spiritual

Meditation

825 To believe a thing is to see the cool crystal water sparkling in the cup. But to meditate on it is to drink of it. Reading gathers the clusters; contemplation squeezes forth their generous juice.—17.400

826 I would earnestly persuade everyone here who is not saved to get an hour alone somehow. Make up your mind to do so. Shut yourself up, and give an hour to solemn, earnest thought and consideration of your condition before God. I am persuaded it would end well, and we should have before long to bless God for the happy result of that hour.—26.396

827 I would to God that after every sermon all my hearers, young and old, had a quarter of an hour alone! A night of wakeful

thought over it would be better still.—37.28

Meekness *See Humility*

828 There are mentioned in Scripture three men whose faces shone. The first was Moses, the man who was very meek (Num. 12:3), and it is recorded that his face shone so that he had to put a veil over it (Exod. 34:30, 33). God had beautified that meek man.

Another of the meek ones was Stephen, whose dying prayer for his murderers proves how meek and forgiving he was (Acts 7:60). It is written of him that when he was accused before the council, they "saw his face as it had been the face of an angel" (Acts 6:15).

And the third, not only did his face shine, but his whole person shone, and his garments were whiter than any fuller could make them (Mark 9:3). That was our blessed Lord, who could truly say, "I am meek and lowly in heart" (Matt. 11:29). See then, how God puts the beauty of his own brightness on meek men.—43.126

Mercy *See Grace; Justice*

829 God's mercy is so great that you may sooner drain the sea of its water, or deprive the sun of its light, or make space too narrow, than diminish the great mercy of God.—9.441

830 The Lord's mercy is a sea which cannot be filled, though mountains of sin be cast into its midst. It is like Noah's flood, which covers all and drowns even the mountaintops of heaven-defying sins.—18.436

831 When you go to God, ask for mercy, not for justice. A mother went to the Emperor Napoleon to ask for mercy for her son. He had committed some breach of the French law, and the emperor replied, "Madam, this is the second time the boy has offended. Justice requires that he should die."

She answered, "I did not come to ask for justice. I beg for mercy."

He answered, "He does not deserve mercy."

"Sire," she said, "it would not be mercy if he deserved it. I ask for mercy."

When she put it that way, the emperor replied, "Well then, I will have mercy."—28.698

832 Do not dream of asking for justice, for justice will be your ruin. But get hold of this word, "Lord, I ask for mercy." And if something whispers, "Why, you have been a hardened sinner," say "Lord, it is true. But I ask for mercy."

"But you have been a backslider."

Reply, "Lord, that I have, but I ask for mercy on that account."

"But you have resisted and rejected grace."

"Lord, that is true. But I shall want all the more mercy because of that."

"But there is nothing in you to argue for forgiveness."

Say, "Lord, I know there is not, and that is why I ask for mercy."—28.698

Mind   *See Thoughts*

Minister   *See Pastor; Preacher*

Ministry   *See Preaching; Service*

833 Everything is a trifle to a man who is a Christian except the glorifying of Christ. If a man who lives for Jesus and preaches the gospel could suddenly be transformed into the Emperor of Germany, it would be a frightful comedown for him.—20.166

834 If you plan to be lazy, there are plenty of avocations in which you will not be wanted. But above all, you are not wanted in the Christian ministry. The man who finds the ministry an easy life will also find that it will bring a hard death.—59.189

Ministry, call to   *See Ordination; Pastor; Preacher*

835 He that should take on himself to be a policeman and go and do the work of arresting others, without having received a commission, must be in danger of being taken up himself for being a deceiver. And if I had not been called to the ministry, I had better leave it alone, lest I go without God's commission.—3.319

836 I always say to young fellows who consult me about the ministry, "Don't be a minister if you can help it," because if the man can help it, God never called him. But if he cannot help it, and he must preach or die, then he is the man. — 19.465

837 He that can toy with his ministry and count it to be like a trade, or like any other profession, was never called of God. But he that has a charge pressing on his heart, and a woe ringing in his ear, and preaches as though he heard the cries of hell behind him, and saw his God looking down on him—oh, how that man entreats the Lord that his hearers may not hear in vain!—60.189

Ministry, lay

838 How pleased I was when I was seeing applicants who wished to join the church, to see that God is blessing many of you in the conversion of souls. One or two of the number were converted under my ministry out of some fifteen or sixteen. The most of them were under your ministries.—27.400

Miracles, Jesus'

839 All our Lord's miracles were intended to be parables. They were intended to instruct as well as to impress. They are sermons to the eye, just as his spoken discourses were sermons to the ear.—34.26

Missions   *See Evangelism*

⁸⁴⁰ If there be any one point in which the Christian church ought to keep its fervor at a white heat, it is concerning missions. If there be anything about which we cannot tolerate lukewarmness, it is in the matter of sending the gospel to a dying world.—14.220

⁸⁴¹ There is a prayer I mean to continue to offer until it is answered, that God would pour out on this church a missionary spirit.—17.240

⁸⁴² We tell our young men in the college that they must prove that they have *not* to go, or else their duty is clear. All other things being equal, ministers should take it for granted that it is their duty to invade new territory unless they can prove to the contrary.—23.336

⁸⁴³ You will never make a missionary of the person who does no good at home. He that will not serve the Lord in the Sunday school at home, will not win children to Christ in China.—34.522

⁸⁴⁴ I remember one who spoke on the missionary question one day saying, "The great question is not, 'Will not the heathen be saved if we do not send them the gospel?' but 'Are we saved our-selves if we do not send them the gospel?' "—51.30

⁸⁴⁵ Every Christian is either a missionary or an impostor.—54.476

Money   *See Giving; Prosperity; Stewardship; Tithing; Wealth*

⁸⁴⁶ One said to a minister who preached a sermon, after which there was to be a collection, "You should preach to our hearts, and then you would get some money."
The minister replied, "Yes, I think that is very likely, for that is where you keep your money."—38.135

⁸⁴⁷ I have heard of the stewardess of an American vessel, who, when the ship was sinking, saw heaps of gold coin scattered upon the cabin floor by those who had thrown it there in the confusion of their escape. She gathered up large quantities of it, wrapped it round her waist, and leaped into the water. She sank like a millstone, as though she had studiously prepared herself for destruction.—52.329

Mormon, Book of

⁸⁴⁸ One of the most modern pretenders to inspiration is the Book of Mormon. I could not blame you should you laugh outright while I read aloud a page from that farrago.—37.45

Mother   *See Father; Parents; Parents, example of; Prayer; Prayer, family*

849 If a mother's prayers do not bring us to Christ, they are like drops of oil dropped into the flames of hell that will make them burn more fiercely on the soul forever and ever. Take heed of rushing to perdition over your mother's prayers.—3.103

850 I cannot tell you how much I owe to the solemn words of my good mother. While we were yet little children, we sat round the table and read verse by verse, and she explained the Scripture to us. Then came the time of pleading. Then came mother's prayer. I remember on one occasion her praying thus: "Now, Lord, if my children go on in their sins, it will not be from ignorance that they perish. And my soul must bear a swift witness against them at the day of judgment if they lay not hold of Christ." That thought of a mother's bearing swift witness against me pierced my conscience and stirred my heart. This pleading with them for God and with God for them is the true way to bring children to Christ. — 10.418

Motive   *See Guilt; Heart*

851 If you should fire at a man, and the bullet were unexpectedly turned aside, you would be as truly guilty as if your victim had died. Human law might not call you a murderer, because human law is obliged very much to judge a sin by the effect. But the Lord looks at the heart and weighs the motive, the desire, and the design.—12.543

Murder   *See Suicide*

852 Murder is hate ripened into deed.—32.257

Murmuring   *See Quarreling*

853 The very word *murmur*, how simple it is, made up to two infantile sounds—*mur mur*. No sense in it, no wit in it, no thought in it. It is the cry rather of a brute than of a man. Murmur— just a double groan.—17.233

854 Ten minutes' praying is better than a year's murmuring.—37.284

855 As long as a man is alive and out of hell, he cannot have any cause to complain.—51.365

Music   *See Church Growth; Praise; Worship*

856 If I might choose my vocation on earth, I think I would choose above all things to write hymns and psalms, such as the Lord's people might sing when they praise him. And my highest wish would be to be one of heaven's poets, to write psalms for the spirits before the throne, and compose celestial sonnets for the blood-bought ones who praise him day and night. Oh, to praise the Lord!—12.188

857 I am afraid that where organs, choirs, and singing men and

women are left to do the praise of the congregation, men's minds are more occupied with the due performance of the music than with the Lord, who alone is to be praised. God's house is meant to be sacred unto himself, but too often it is made an opera house, and Christians form an audience, not an adoring assembly. We come not together to amuse ourselves, to display our powers of melody, or our aptness in creating harmony. We come to pay our adoration at the footstool of the great King, to whom alone be glory forever and ever.—17.663

858 There is no more of music to God's ear in any service than there is of heart love and holy devotion.—19.590

859 Singing should be congregational, but it should never be performed for the credit of the congregation. "Such remarkable singing! The place is quite renowned for its musical performances!" This is a poor achievement. Our singing should be such that God hears it with pleasure—singing in which there is not so much art as heart, not so much of musical sound as of spiritual emotion.—27.483, 484

860 To my mind, there is no teaching that is likely to be more useful than that which is accompanied by the right kind of singing.—46.283

861 I hardly like to hear the high praises of God sung to the tune of a comic song or of a dance. There is a certain congruity about things that must be observed, and some good music may have associated with it such queer ideas that we had better let it alone till those associations have died out, lest, while we are uttering holy words, some people may be reminded by the tune of unholy things.—51.305, 306

862 It is always a token of revival of religion, it is said, when there is a revival of psalmody. Whitefield and John Wesley would never have done the great work they did if it had not been for Charles Wesley's poetry, and for the singing of such men as Toplady, Scott, and Newton. When your heart is full of Christ, you will want to sing. — 53.509, 510

863 Do we sing as much as the birds do? Yet what have birds to sing about, compared with us? Do we sing as much as the angels do? Yet they were never redeemed by the blood of Christ. Birds of the air, shall you excel me? Angels, shall you exceed me? You have done so, but I intend to emulate you, and day by day, and night by night, pour forth my soul in sacred song.—61.436

Nature, human   See Carnality; Depravity; Heart; Pride; Sin; Will, free

864 A man by nature has his heart where his feet ought to be.

His heart is set on the earth, whereas he ought to be treading it beneath his feet. And the stranger mystery still, his heels are where his heart should be. He is kicking against the God of heaven when he ought to be setting his affections on things above.—6.44

865 Man is a reeking mass of corruption. His whole soul is by nature so debased and depraved, that no description which can be given of him even by inspired tongues can fully tell how base and vile a thing he is.—6.104

866 The best of men are still men at their best.—12.251

867 It is a most solemn fact that human nature can scarcely bear a long continuance of peace and health. It is almost necessary that we should be every now and then salted with affliction, lest we putrefy with sin.—12.452

868 We never pray a prayer but what we would wish to have it forgiven as well as answered. Our faith is frequently so weak that we scarce know whether to call it faith or unbelief. As for ourselves, we are a mass of flaws and infirmities.—16.668

869 You might as well rake hell over to find heaven in it, as look into your own carnal nature to find consolation.—19.210

870 The saints are sinners still. Our best tears need to be wept over, the strongest faith is mixed with unbelief, our most flaming love is cold compared with what Jesus deserves, and our intensest zeal still lacks the full fervor which the bleeding wounds and pierced heart of the crucified might claim at our hands. Our best things need a sin offering, or they would condemn us.—20.375, 376

871 Look at fallen human nature. Whitefield used to say that it was half beast and half devil. I question whether both beast and devil are not slandered by being compared with man when he is left to himself.—22.298

872 There is no doctrine more true to experience than this, that corruption remains even in the hearts of the regenerate, and that when we would do good evil is present with us.—24.436

873 Sin bribes the judgment, intoxicates the will, and perverts the memory. Like a sea which comes up and floods a continent, penetrating every valley, deluging every plain, and invading every mountain, so has sin penetrated our entire nature.—27.26

874 We are often like a glass of water which has been standing still for hours and looks very clear and bright. But there is a sediment, and a little stir soon discovers it and clouds the crystal. That sediment is the old nature.—27.640

875 We glide from one sin to another, even as a waterfall descends from rock to rock. As weeds multiply in the soil, so do sins spring up in our hearts. Like the pendulum, we swing to the right hand and then to the left. We err first in one way and then in another. We are ever inclined to evil.—29.165

876 All the fire which the devil can bring from hell could do us little harm if we had not so much fuel in our nature. It is the powder in the magazine of the old man which is our perpetual danger.—30.289

877 There is nothing that the worst of men have done which the best of men could not do if they were left by the grace of God.—39.89

878 I must confess that I have a daily fighting of my better self against the old self, the newborn nature against the old nature, which will, if it can, still keep its hold upon me.—39.111

879 I question the Christianity of that man who doubts whether there are in his soul the remains of such corruption as drown the ungodly in perdition, or whether, though a quickened child of God, he has another law in his members warring against the law of his mind.—49.198

880 The sin which Christ came to heal is not something on the skin, or a mere matter of custom or habit. The venom of sin is in the very fountain of our being; it has poisoned our heart. It is in the very marrow of our bones and is as natural to us as anything that belongs to us. You might even tear the man in pieces, but you could not tear his sin from him.—49.278

881 You have heard of the women who were ordered to fill a large vessel with water, and were told to bring the water in buckets that were full of holes. This is just your toil. You have to fill the tremendous ocean of the law, and your buckets are full of holes. Your nature, mend it as you may and repair it as you will, is still full of holes. Your pretended goodness will ooze out drop by drop, and your labors shall be like water spilled on the ground, which cannot be gathered up.—51.269

882 Good men usually fail just where they think they are strongest, and where they really are strongest. Noah was a preacher of righteousness, yet did he fail in righteousness when his sons saw him in a state of drunkenness. Moses was exceeding meek, yet did he lose his temper and say, "Hear now, ye rebels; must we fetch you water out of this rock?" (Num. 20:10). Look too, at Job, one who excelled in patience, yet he failed in patience.

And you and I will find that the devil will carry our hearts by storm, not where we think the walls are weak, but just where the flag waves defiantly over the strongest and loftiest part of our bastion. For Satan delights to pull down our lofty things of which we are proud, just as God loves to pull down the lofty things of sin.—52.339, 340

883 Even you who are favored by divine grace to enter into rich fellowship with Christ are no better naturally than the lost spirits in hell. There was no difference at the birth, and no intrinsic essential difference of moral constitution between Peter and Judas, between Paul and Demas, between the brightest apostle and the bloodiest persecutor. We have grown in grace; had we been left to ourselves, we would have rotted in sin.—59.147

Obedience   See Follow

884 It is a very shocking thing, but I have known the case of a man—I hope a Christian man—knowing such-and-such a thing to be right, yet not attending to it, but saying that he was praying about it. He wanted it to be "brought home" to his conscience, so he said. All I can say about such conduct is that it is a kind of rebellion against God, a shameful piece of hypocrisy, pretending to honor God in one duty while you know that you are neglecting another. — 49.471

Omnipresence   See God, presence of

885 God is everywhere. His circumference is nowhere, but his center is everywhere.—33.400

886 I heard the story of a man, a blasphemer, profane, an atheist, who was converted singularly by a sinful action of his. He had written on a piece of paper, "God is nowhere," and ordered his child to read it, for he would make him an atheist too. The child spelled it, "God is n-o-w h-e-r-e—God is now here." It was a truth instead of a lie, and the arrow pierced the man's own heart.—62.65

Omniscience   See Knowledge

887 Suppose for a moment that Jehovah could not see the works and know the thoughts of man. Would you then become more careless concerning him than you are now? I think not. In nine cases out of ten, and perhaps in a far larger and sadder proportion, the doctrine of divine omniscience, although it is believed, has no practical effect on our lives at all. The mass of mankind forget God.—4.97

888 I have known a man who was once stopped from an act of sin by there being a cat in the room. He could not bear even the eyes of that poor creature to see him. Swearer! Could you swear if you could see God's eye looking at you? Thief! Drunkard! Harlot! Could you indulge in your sins if

you saw his eyes on you? Oh, I think they would startle you, and bid you pause, before you did in God's own sight rebel against his law.—4.104

889 When a great Grecian artist was fashioning an image for the temple, he was diligently carving the back part of the goddess. One said to him, "You need not finish that part of the statue, because it is to be built into the wall."

He replied, "The gods can see in the wall."

He had a right idea of what is due to God. That part of my religion which no man can see should be as perfect as if it were to be observed by all.—29.58

890 I have sometimes stood in a picture gallery, and there has been a painting of some old warrior, and he has looked straight at me. If I have gone to the other end of the room, he has still looked at me. Wherever you are in the room, a well-painted portrait will be looking at you. Such is God. Wherever you are, the eye of God will be on you—as much on you as if there were not another person in the whole world.—54.496

Ordinance   See Baptism; Lord's Supper

891 If your heart be not right with God, you shall perish with the sacramental bread in your mouth, and go from the baptismal waters to the fires of hell. Beware

134

of the peace which is drawn from the stagnant pool of superstition. It will carry death into your soul.—36.426

Ordination   See Ministry, call to

892 There is a great deal of fuss made nowadays about "ordaining" a minister. I was never "ordained" by mortal men, for I did not believe in having their empty hands laid on my head. I believe that every true Christian is ordained of God to his particular work, and in the strength of that divine ordination, let him not bother his head about merely human forms and ceremonies, but just keep to his proper work.—49.213

Pain   See Affliction; Sickness; Suffering; Trials

893 I can truly say of everything I have ever tasted in this world of God's mercy—and my path has been remarkably strewn with divine lovingkindness—I feel more grateful to God for the bodily pain I have suffered, and for all the trials I have endured of different sorts, than I do for anything else except the gift of his dear Son. I am sure I have derived more real benefit, permanent strength, growth in grace, and every precious thing from the furnace of affliction than I have ever derived from prosperity.—16.381, 382

894 "Oh," said a worldling to me when I was in great pain and weakness of body, "is this the way God treats his children? Then I am glad I am not one."

How my heart burned within me, and my eyes flashed, as I said that I would take an eternity of such pain as I endured sooner than stand in the place of the man who preferred ease to God. I felt it would be hell to me to have a doubt of my adoption, and whatever pain I might suffer was a trifle so long as I knew that the Lord was my God.—36.609

Parents *See Children, teaching of; Father; Mother; Parents, example of; Prayer, family*

895 I pray you so live, that when you stand over your child's dead body, you may never hear a voice coming up from that clay, "Father, your negligence was my destruction. Mother, your prayerlessness was the instrument of my damnation."—7.11

896 When I see so many children of Christians turn out worse than others, when I find some of the sons of ministers among the ringleaders in sin, what can I do but pray that I may sooner die than have such a curse fall on myself? If any of us have neglected home duties, let us beware lest we have the blood of our children laid at our door.—12.547

897 Parents who teach their children to sing the silly, frivolous, and perhaps licentious songs are sacrificing them to Moloch. Shame is it when from a father's lips the boy hears the first oath and learns the alphabet of blasphemy.—14.628

898 You cannot control your children, you say. Then the Lord have mercy on you! It is your business to do it, and you must do it, or else you will soon find they will control you. No one knows what judgment will come from God upon those who allow sin in children to go unrebuked.—19.102, 103

899 O fathers and mothers, the ruin of your children or their salvation, will, under God, very much depend on you.—21.303

900 The greatest desire of my heart for my sons was that they might become the servants of God. I never wished for them that they might be great or rich, but, oh, if they would but give their young hearts to Jesus! This I prayed for most heartily. It was one of the happiest nights of my life when I baptized them on profession of their faith. And now, while I am speaking to you, one is preaching in New Zealand, and another at Greenwich. And my heart is glad that the gospel which the father preaches, the sons are preaching too.—29.506, 507

Note: Thomas Spurgeon was the son preaching in New Zealand, and Charles in Greenwich.

They were twins. Thomas became the pastor of the Metropolitan Tabernacle for fourteen fruitful years after CHS's death. During that time 2,200 people were received into the membership of the Tabernacle.

901 Has anybody made you a minister, and you are not trying to save your own children? I tell you, sir, I do not believe that God made you a minister, for if he had, he would have begun with making you a minister to your own family.—32.699

Parents, example of   *See Example; Father; Mother; Parents*

902 It is a blessed thing for some of us that we can look back on a father's example and a mother's example with nothing but unalloyed gratitude to God for both. But there are others among you who, in looking back, must say, "I thank God I was delivered from the evil influence to which I was subjected as a child." Do not let your child ever have to say that of you, but ask for grace that in your own house you may walk with a perfect heart.—21.238

903 I was cradled in the home of piety, nurtured with the tenderest care, taught the gospel from my youth up, with the holiest example of my parents, the best possible checks all around to prevent me running into sin.—55.352

Pastor   *See Ministry, call to; Preacher; Preaching*

904 This I know, that no Christian minister will ever be able to enter into the trials and experiences of God's people, unless he has stood foot to foot with the arch fiend and wrestled with the prince of hell.—11.293

905 The true shepherd spirit is an amalgam of many precious graces. He is hot with zeal, but he is not fiery with passion. He is gentle, and yet he rules his class. He is loving, but he does not wink at sin. He has power over the lambs, but he is not domineering or sharp. He has cheerfulness, but not levity; freedom, but not license; solemnity, but not gloom.—28.573

906 Somebody once said that it proved the divinity of our holy religion that it survived ministers, and there is a good deal of truth in that remark. How I have wondered that this congregation has survived me.—34.376

907 I know of no life that has more trouble in it, I know of no occupation that brings more awful despondency of spirit on a man's mind than my ministry brings on me.—50.368

Pastor, responsibility of   *See Preacher, responsibility of*

908 There have been times when I have wished to imitate Jonah and take ship and flee away from the work which God has thrust on me,

for I am conscious that I have not served him as I ought. When I have preached most earnestly, I go to my chamber and repent that I have preached in so heartless a manner. When I have wept over your souls, when I have agonized in prayer, I have yet been conscious that I have not wrestled with God as I ought to have wrestled, and that I have not felt for your souls as I ought to feel. The errors which a man may commit in the ministry are incalculable.—6.103

909 I remember the dream of a minister. He thought he was in hell, and being there, he was dreadfully distressed, and cried out, "Is this the place where I am to be forever? I am a minister."

A grim voice replied, "No, it is lower down for unfaithful ministers, much lower down than this."

And then he awoke. Ah, and if we do not agonize till souls are brought to Christ, we shall have to agonize to all eternity.—22.536

910 "I have only one hundred people to preach to," said a country pastor to me. And I replied, "If you give a good account of those hundred, you have quite enough to do."—37.411

Patience *See Patience, God's*

911 The anvil is struck by the hammer, and the anvil never strikes in return. Yet the anvil wears the hammer out. Patience baffles fury and vanquishes malice. The nonresistance principle involves a resistance which is irresistible.—25.546

Patience, God's *See Patience*

912 There is no greater proof of the omnipotence of God than his longsuffering, for it shows the greatest possible power for God to be able to control himself, to be able to keep in an anger which naturally must boil, and restrain a fury which else must burn.—8.477

913 What do you think? Shall God be always provoked? Shall mercy be preached to you forever in vain? Shall Christ be presented and always rejected, and will you continue to be his enemies, and shall he never proclaim war against your souls? It is a marvel, it is a wonder that these God-provoking sins have so long been borne with, and that you are not yet cut down.—11.526

914 We have heard in these days a blasphemer stand on a public platform and say, "There is no God, and if there is a God," taking out his watch, "let him strike me dead in five minutes." When he still found himself alive, he argued that there was no God. The fact was, God was much too great to be put out of patience by such an insignificant wretch as he.—15.213

Peace *See Contentment; Satisfaction*

915 Look upward, and you will perceive no seat of fiery wrath to

shoot devouring flame. Look downward, and you discover no hell, for there is no condemnation to them that are in Christ Jesus. Look back, and sin is blotted out. Look around, and all things work together for good to them that love God. Look beyond, and glory shines through the veil of the future, like the sun through a morning's mist. Look outward, and the stones of the field and the beasts of the field are at peace with us. Look inward, and the peace of God, which passes all understanding, keeps our hearts and minds by Christ Jesus.—31.27

916 A martyr was fastened to the stake, and the sheriff who was to execute him expressed his sorrow that he should persevere in his opinions and compel him to set fire to the pile. The martyr answered, "Come and lay your hand on my heart, and see if it does not beat quietly." His request was complied with, and he was found to be quite calm. "Now," said he, "lay your hand on your own heart, and see if you are not more troubled than I am. Then go your way, and instead of pitying me, pity yourself."—36.165

Perfection   *See Church*

917 "Oh," says one, "I will join the church when I can find a perfect one."

Then you will never join any.

"But," you say, "perhaps I may."

Well, but it will cease to be perfect as soon as it receives you into its membership.—46.299

918 Some brethren and sisters believe themselves to be perfect. But if you watch those in whom sin is said to be dead, you will find that if it is dead, it is not buried, and that it smells remarkably like other dead things which ought to be buried. It is, possibly, worse than when it was alive, for it has become alive again, in an even worse sense, with a double putridity.—50.577

919 I remember hearing a man say that he had lived for six years without having sinned in either thought, word, or deed. I apprehend that he committed a sin then, if he never had done so before, in uttering such a proud, boastful speech. It seemed to me that if he had known anything about his own heart, he would not have dared to speak so confidently.—57.176

Persecution   *See Martyrdom; Suffering; Trials*

920 Never did the church so much prosper and so truly thrive as when she was baptized in blood. The ship of the church never sails so gloriously along as when the bloody spray of her martyrs falls on her deck. We must suffer and we must die, if we

are ever to conquer this world for Christ.—6.154

921 The doctrine that Christ Jesus came into the world to save sinners is no more to be wounded by the sword of persecution than is the ocean to be scarred by the keels of navies.—12.268

Perseverance   *See Calvinism; Security*

922 I think few doctrines more vital than that of the perseverance of the saints, for if ever one child of God did perish, or if I knew it were possible that one could, I should conclude at once that I must, and I suppose each of you would do the same. And then where is the joy and happiness of the gospel?—1.201

923 If anybody could possibly convince me that final perseverance is not a truth of the Bible, I should never preach again, for I feel I should have nothing worth preaching.—3.436

924 That doctrine of the final perseverance of the saints is, I believe, as thoroughly bound up with the standing or falling of the gospel as is the article of justification by faith. Give that up, and I see no gospel left.—6.12

925 If I did not believe the doctrine of the final perseverance of the saints, I think I should be of all men the most miserable, because I should lack any ground for comfort.—13.107

926 I have often said that if any man could convince me that Scripture did not teach the perseverance of believers, I would at once reject Scripture altogether as teaching nothing at all, as being an incomprehensible book, of which a plain man could make neither head nor tail, for this seems to be of all doctrines the one that lies most evidently upon the surface.—15.294

927 If there is one doctrine I have preached more than another, it is the doctrine of the perseverance of the saints even to the end.—18.337

928 I protest that if you take final perseverance from me, you have robbed the Bible of one of its crowning attractions.—27.79

929 We never preach the saving power of temporary, unpractical, unsanctifying faith. If a man says, "I believe in Christ, and therefore I shall be saved," his faith will have to be tested by his life. If, sometime after, he has no faith in Christ, that faith which he claimed to have is proved to be good for nothing. The faith of God's elect is an abiding faith. "Now abideth faith, hope, charity, these three" (1 Cor. 13:13). Thus true faith is classed among the abiding things; it is undying, unquenchable. If you truly believe in Jesus, it is for life.—37.114

930 If you take away from me the doctrine of the final perseverance of the saints, I have not anything left that is worth keeping. I should not care about the gospel if that essential feature of it were gone. That truth seems to me to be the very soul of it.—45.173

931 I think that the doctrine of the final perseverance of the saints is one of those that are most plainly taught in the Scriptures. Those who oppose it have an irresistible array of passages of Scripture to contend with. They have, indeed, when they attack this truth, to leap into a lion's den.—49.41

932 The doctrine of final perseverance of believers seems to me to be written as with a beam of sunlight throughout the whole of Scripture. If that is not true, there is nothing at all in the Bible that is true. It is impossible to understand the Bible at all if it is not so.—51.454

933 If there is anything taught in Scripture for certain, it is the doctrine of the final perseverance of the saints. I am as sure that doctrine is as plainly taught as the doctrine of the deity of Christ.—63.57

Pleasure   *See Carnality; Joy*

934 Amusement should be used to do us good "like a medicine." It must never be used as the food of the man.—34.476

935 "Well, Jack," said one who met a man who had lately joined the church, "I hear you have given up all your pleasures."

"No, no," said Jack, "the fact lies the other way. I have just found all my pleasures, and I have only given up my follies."—37.64

Politics

936 I often hear it said, "Do not bring religion into politics." This is precisely where it ought to be brought! I would have the Cabinet and Members of Parliament do the work of the nation as before the Lord, and I would have the nation, either in making war or peace, consider the matter by the light of righteousness. We have had enough of clever men without conscience. Now let us see what honest, God-fearing men will do.—27.225

937 Do you know any Christian man who goes into politics who is the better for it? If I find such a man, I will have him stuffed if I can, for I have never seen such a specimen yet. I will not say, "Do not attend to politics," but I do say, "Do not let them stain you."—39.295

Pope   *See Catholicism; Mass; Purgatory*

938 Of all the dreams that ever deluded men, and probably of all blasphemies that ever were uttered, there has never been one which is more absurd and which

is more fruitful in all manner of mischief than the idea that the Bishop of Rome can be the head of the church of Jesus Christ. No, these popes die, and how could the church live if its head were dead? The true Head ever lives, and the church ever lives in him.—14.621

939 Christ did not redeem his church with his blood that the pope might come in and steal away the glory. He never came from heaven to earth, and poured out his very heart that he might purchase his people, that a poor sinner, a mere man, should be set upon high to be admired by all the nations, and to call himself God's representative on earth. Christ has always been the Head of the church.—60.592

Poverty   *See Wealth*

Praise   *See Music; Prayer; Thanksgiving; Worship*

940 I feel like that good old saint, who said that if she got to heaven, Jesus Christ should never hear the last of it. Truly he never shall!—11.336

941 Preaching is sowing, prayer is watering, but praise is the harvest.—17.717

942 Prayer is the stalk of the wheat, but praise is the ear of the wheat. It is the harvest itself. When God is praised, we have come to the ultimatum. This is the thing for which all other things are designed.—26.28

943 Praise is the rehearsal of our eternal song. By grace we learn to sing, and in glory we continue to sing. What will some of you do when you get to heaven, if you go on grumbling all the way? Do not hope to get to heaven in that style. But now begin to bless the name of the Lord.—36.12

944 Two Welshmen were going out to preach, and they parted at the crossroads. One of them said to his friend, "Brother Jones, may you get the light of his countenance in your preaching today!"

"I hope so, brother," he answered, "but if I do not get the light of his countenance, I will speak well of him behind his back!"

Just so! When we see his face, we realize what a blessed Christ he is. But if we do not see his face, we are not going to find fault with him.—41.316

945 It is a good thing to praise Christ in the presence of his friends. It is sometimes a better thing to extol him in the presence of his enemies. It is a great thing to praise Jesus Christ by day, but there is no music sweeter than the nightingale's, and she praises God by night. It is well to praise the Lord for his mercy when you are in health, but make sure that you do it when you are sick, for then your praise is more likely to

be genuine. When you are deep down in sorrow, do not rob God of the gratitude that is due to him. Never stint him of his revenue of praise whatever else goes short.—42.453

946 If I did not praise and bless Christ my Lord, I should deserve to have my tongue torn out by its roots from my mouth. If I did not bless and magnify his name, I should deserve that every stone I tread on in the streets should rise up to curse my ingratitude, for I am a drowned debtor to the mercy of God—over head and ears—to infinite love and boundless compassion I am a debtor. Are you not the same? Then I charge you by the love of Christ, awake, awake your hearts now to magnify his glorious name.—61.441

Prayer   *See Bible, interpretation of; Jesus, name of; Mother; Praise; Worship*

947 If any of you should ask me for an epitome of the Christian religion, I should say it is in that one word—*prayer.*—1.122

948 All our perils are nothing, so long as we have prayer.—1.204

949 Even as the moon influences the tides of the sea, even so does prayer—which is the reflection of the sunlight of heaven, and is God's moon in the sky—influence the tides of godliness.—3.251

950 My own soul's conviction is that prayer is the grandest power in the entire universe, that it has a more omnipotent force than electricity, attraction, gravitation, or any other of those other secret forces which men have called by name, but which they do not understand.—6.336

951 Oh, without prayer what are the church's agencies, but the stretching out of a dead man's arm, or the lifting up of the lid of a blind man's eye? Only when the Holy Spirit comes is there any life and force and power.—8.465

952 If there be anything I know, anything that I am quite assured of beyond all question, it is that praying breath is never spent in vain.—11.150

953 Remember that prayer is your best means of study.—11.152

954 There is no secret of my heart which I would not pour into his ear. There is no wish that might be deemed foolish or ambitious by others, which I would not communicate to him. For surely if "the secret of the Lord is with them that fear him" (Ps. 25:14), the secrets of them that fear him ought to be, and must be, with their Lord.—11.210

955 Prayer may be salted with confession or perfumed with thanksgiving; it may be sung to music or wept out with groanings. As many as are the flowers of summer, so many are the varieties of prayer.—12.614

956 You can draw near to God even though you cannot say a word. A prayer may be crystallized in a tear. A tear is enough water to float a desire to God.—15.382

957 If ten thousand saints were burned tomorrow, their dying prayers would make the church rise like a phoenix from her ashes.—17.201

958 Never account prayer second to preaching. No doubt prayer in the Christian church is as precious as the utterance of the gospel. To speak to God for men is a part of the Christian priesthood that should never be despised.—17.293

959 Do not reckon you have prayed unless you have pleaded, for pleading is the very marrow of prayer.—17.606

960 I usually feel more dissatisfied with my prayers than with anything else I do.—17.681

961 The Christian should work as if all depended on him, and pray as if it all depended on God.—17.689

962 Praying is a saving of time. You remember Luther's remark, "I have so much to do today that I shall never get through it with less than three hours' prayer."—18.140

963 No man can do me a truer kindness in this world than to pray for me.—18.255

964 The more we pray, the more we shall want to pray. The more we pray, the more we can pray. The more we pray, the more we shall pray. He who prays little will pray less, but he who prays much will pray more. And he who prays more, will desire to pray more abundantly.—18.288

965 It is a good rule never to look into the face of man in the morning till you have looked into the face of God.—19.597

966 My heart has no deeper conviction than this, that prayer is the most efficient spiritual agency in the universe, next to the Holy Ghost.—19.603

967 Only that prayer which comes from our heart can get to God's heart.—20.65

968 I believe that when we cannot pray, it is time that we prayed more than ever. And if you answer, "But how can that be?" I would say, pray to pray. Pray for prayer. Pray for the spirit of supplication. Do not be content to say, "I would pray if I could." No, but if you cannot pray, pray till you can.—24.258

969 I could as soon think of living without eating or living without breathing, as living without prayer.—25.47

970 When a poor man was breaking granite by the roadside, he was down on his knees while he gave his blows. A minister passing by said, "Your work is just like mine. You have to break stones, and so do I."

"Yes," said the man, "and if you manage to break stony hearts, you will have to do it as I do, down on your knees."

The man was right. The gospel hammer soon splits flinty hearts when a man knows how to pray.—25.682

971 The sinew of the minister's strength under God is the supplication of his church. We can do anything and everything if we have a praying people around us. But when our dear friends and fellow helpers cease to pray, the Holy Ghost hastens to depart, and "Ichabod" is written on the place of assembly.—25.695

972 We heard of a certain clergyman, who was said to have given forth "the finest prayer ever offered to a Boston audience." Just so! The Boston audience received the prayer, and there it ended. The tail feathers of pride should be pulled out of our prayers, for they need only the wing feathers of faith. The peacock feathers of poetical expression are out of place before the throne of God.—26.224

973 Every prayer is an inverted promise. That is to say, God promises us such a blessing, and therefore we pray for it. If God teaches us to pray for any good thing, we may gather by implication the assurance that he means to give it.—28.241

974 It is the usual rule with God to make us pray before he gives the blessing.—29.305

975 Prayer is the autograph of the Holy Ghost upon the renewed heart.—31.505

976 It is easier to attend a thousand masses or to go to church every day in the week, than to offer one true prayer.—31.511

977 No prayer will ever prevail with God more surely than a liquid petition, which, being distilled from the heart, trickles from the eye and waters the cheek. Then is God won when he hears the voice of your weeping.—35.343

978 Prayer is the thermometer of grace.—37.95

979 To me it is a boundless solace that I live in the prayers of thousands. We can do better without the voice that preaches than without the heart that prays. The petitions of our bedridden sisters are the wealth of the church.—37.320

980 I would rather be Master of the Art of Prayer than M.A. of both universities (Oxford and Cambridge). He who knows how

to pray has his hand on the leverage which moves the universe.—37.328

981 The best prayers have usually been the shortest. An arrow may easily be too long, and prayers should be like arrows shot from the bow of faith. If they are short, it does not matter so long as they are sharp and sent on their way with a good pull of the bowstring.—40.362

982 In prayer the heart of man empties itself before God, and then Christ empties his heart out to supply the needs of his poor believing child. In prayer we confess to Christ our deficiencies, and he reveals to us his fulness. We tell him our sorrows, he tells us his joys. We tell him our sins, he shows to us his righteousness. We tell him the dangers that lie before us, he tells us of the shield of omnipotence with which he can and will guard us. Prayer talks with God; it walks with him. And he who is much in prayer will hold very much fellowship with Jesus Christ.—44.255

983 The best style of prayer is that which cannot be called anything else but a cry.—47.247

984 A man scarcely needs to be reminded that he must breathe. It is essential to his very life that he should breathe. And it is essential to our spiritual life that we should pray. I never thought it necessary to prepare a discourse to exhort

you to eat, neither ought it to be necessary to exhort Christians to pray. It should be to you an instinct of your new nature, as natural to your spiritual being as a good appetite is to a man in health. There should be a holy hunger and thirst to pray. And the soul never prays so well as when it is reminded, not by the hour of the day or night, but by its real needs, and when it resorts to its place of private prayer, not because it thinks it ought, but because it feels that it must, and shall, and will go there, and is delighted at the privilege of having communion with its God.—48.486

985 If any man thinks that his prayers have any merit in them, every prayer that he presents is an insult to the Lord Jesus Christ. If you think that your prayers help to put away sin, you make an antichrist of your prayers, and the more you pile them up, the more you multiply your sin.—49.473, 474

986 I cannot help praying. If I were not allowed to utter a word all day long, that would not affect my praying. If I could not have five minutes that I might spend in prayer by myself, I should pray all the same. Minute by minute, moment by moment, somehow or other, my heart must commune with my God. Prayer has become as essential to me as the heaving

of my lungs and the beating of my pulse.—49.476

987 God the Holy Ghost writes our prayers, God the Son presents our prayers, and God the Father accepts our prayers. And with the whole Trinity to help us in it, what cannot prayer perform?—54.342, 343

988 I always feel that there is something wrong if I go without prayer for even half an hour in the day.—56.98

989 How often have I said, "All our strength lies in prayer!"—61.527

990 You see the men in the belfry sometimes down below with the ropes. They pull them, and if you have no ears, that is all you know about it. But the bells are ringing up there. They are talking and discoursing sweet music up aloft in the tower. And our prayers do, as it were, ring the bells of heaven. They are sweet music in God's ear.—63.22

Prayer, answered   *See Healing; Prayer, power of*

991 Watch for answers to your prayers. When you mail a letter to a friend, requesting a favor, you watch for an answer. When you pray to God for a favor, you do not expect him to hear you, some of you. If the Lord were to hear some of your prayers, you would be surprised. Sometimes when I have met with a special answer to

prayer and have told it, some have said, "Is it not wonderful?" No, not at all! It would be wonderful if it were not so!—7.54

992 I am persuaded we only want more prayer, and there is no limit to the blessing. You may Christianize the world, if you but know how to pray. Prayer can get anything of God, prayer can get everything. God denies nothing to the man who knows how to ask. The Lord never shuts his storehouse till you shut your mouth. God will never stop his arm till you stop your tongue.—10.340

993 When God does not answer his children according to the letter, he does so according to the spirit. If you ask for silver, will you be angry if he gives you gold? If you seek bodily health, should you complain if instead he makes your sickness turn to the healing of spiritual maladies? Is it not better to have the cross sanctified than to have the cross removed? Was not the apostle more enriched when God allowed him still to endure the thorn in the flesh, and yet said to him, "My grace is sufficient for thee" (2 Cor. 12:9)?—11.299

994 I should find it difficult to discover a season in which I have cried unto God and not received deliverance during the whole run and tenor of my life. In hundreds of instances I have had as distinct answers to prayer as if God had

thrust his right hand through the blue sky and given right into my lap the bounty which I had sought from him.—11.448

995 If you cannot find that God has promised a blessing, you have no right to ask for it, and no reason to expect it. There is no use in asking money from a banker without a check. Christians take their arrows from God's quiver and shoot them with this on their lips: "Do as thou hast said. Remember thy word unto thy servant upon which thou hast caused me to hope." True prayers are like those carrier pigeons which find their way so well. They cannot fail to go to heaven, for it is from heaven that they came. They are only going home.—20.514, 515

996 There was a very large sum of money to be paid for the building of the orphanage, and I was up with certain friends at Regent's Park, dining at the house of one of our brethren. I there mentioned that I was short two thousand pounds to meet an account which would very soon be due, but that I was sure God would graciously give it, for it was *his* work, and he would supply its need in answer to prayer. We were discussing as to whether it was not rather bold to speak too positively about answers to a prayer of such a kind, and while we were still discoursing there came a telegram from

the Tabernacle to me, saying, "A person unknown has called and left 2,000 pounds in bank notes for the orphanage." I read the telegram to the friends assembled, and their gratitude and astonishment abounded.—25.142

997 I have seen enough in my own lifetime to fill a volume concerning the goodness of the Lord in answer to his children's prayers.—28.670

998 I cannot imagine any one of you tantalizing your child by exciting in him a desire that you do not intend to gratify. It were a very ungenerous thing to offer alms to the poor, and then when they hold out their hand for it, to mock their poverty with a denial. It were a cruel addition to the miseries of the sick if they were taken to the hospital and there left to die untended and uncared for. Where God leads you to pray, he means you to receive.—30.539, 540

999 What, give us the new birth, and then not hear us? Did he bless us when we did not seek him, and will he not hear us when we do seek him? What, look after us when we were like stray sheep, deaf to all his calls; seek after us till he restored us, and then not hear us when we become the sheep of his pasture? Impossible!—31.43

1000 It is neither desirable nor possible that all things should be left to our choice. So much do I feel this, that if my Lord should say to me, "From this hour I will always answer your prayer just as you pray it," the first petition I would offer would be, "Lord, do nothing of the sort." That would be putting the responsibility of my life on myself, instead of allowing it to remain on God.—31.45

1001 I am constantly witnessing the most unmistakable instances of answers to prayer. My whole life is made up of them. To me they are so familiar as to cease to excite my surprise, but to many they would seem marvelous, no doubt. Why, I could no more doubt the efficacy of prayer than I could disbelieve in the law of gravitation. The one is as much a fact as the other, constantly verified every day of my life.—37.137, 138

1002 Not long ago a woman came to see me about joining the church. She was in great trouble, for her husband had gone away, under rather sad circumstances, to Australia, and she could not hear any news of him. I said to her, "Well, let us pray for him." When I had prayed for his conversion, I prayed that he might come back to his wife, and I said to her, "Your husband will come back to you. I am persuaded that God has heard my prayer. So when he returns, bring him to see me in this room."

In a little over twelve months that woman was in my vestry *with her husband.* I had forgotten the circumstances till she recalled them to me. About the time of our prayer, God had met with him on the sea, while he was reading one of my sermons. He was brought to the feet of Jesus, he came back, joined this church, and is with us this day in answer to that prayer.

"Oh," says someone, "that is merely a coincidence."

Well, that woman did not think so, nor did her husband, nor do I. You may call it a coincidence if you like, but I call it an answer to prayer. And as long as I get such coincidences, I shall be perfectly satisfied to go on praying!—44.293, 294

1003 I saw the other day in a newspaper a sketch concerning myself, in which the author offers me one rather pointed rebuke. I was preaching at the time in a tent, and only part of the people were covered. It began to rain just before prayer, and one petition was, "O Lord, be pleased to grant us favorable weather for this service, and command the clouds that they rain no more on this assembly!"

Now he thought this preposterous. He admits that it did not rain a drop after it. Still, of course, he did not infer that God heard and answered the prayer. If I had asked for a rain of grace, it would have been quite credible that God would send that. But when I ask him not to send a temporal rain, that is fanaticism. I bless God, however, that I fully believe the absurdity, preposterous as it may appear. I know that God hears prayer in temporal things.—51.333

1004 I can never forget a certain illness, when I had been racked with pain and brought very low with heaviness of spirit. I felt driven almost to despair one night, until I laid hold of God in an agony of prayer and pleaded with him something like this: "If my child were in such anguish as I am in, I would listen to him and relieve him if I could. Thou art my Father, and I am thy child. Then wilt thou not treat me like a child?"

Almost at the very moment when I presented that plea before God, my pain ceased, and I fell into a sweet slumber, from which I woke up with "Abba! Father!" on my lip and in my heart.—52.126

Prayer, ejaculatory

1005 I have not preached this morning half as much as I have prayed. For every word that I have spoken, I have prayed two words silently to God.—34.528

1006 I consider ejaculatory prayer to be the very best form of prayer.—43.604

Note: Ejaculatory prayer is that which ascends to God abruptly and briefly, such as Peter's prayer in Matthew 14:30. CHS once preached an extraordinary sermon entitled EJACULATORY PRAYER, found in 23.709-720. It is also found in CHS's 12 Sermons on Prayer, pp. 81–91, published by Baker Book House.

Prayer, of faith   See Faith

1007 When I was conversing lately with our dear friend, George Muller, he frequently astonished me with the way in which he mentioned that he had for so many months and years asked for such and such a mercy, and praised the Lord for it, as though he had actually obtained it. Even in praying for the conversion of a person, as soon as he had begun to intercede, he began also to praise God for the conversion of that person. I think he told us he had in one instance already prayed for thirty years and the work was not yet done, yet all the while he had gone on thanking God, because he knew the prayer would be answered.—25.222

1008 We have this morning been praying for the conversion of many. We expect our prayers to be heard. The question is not, "Will there be any converted under this sermon?" but "Who will it be?"—35.421

1009 Mr. Muller supports 300 orphan children on no resources but his own faith and prayer. When he needs anything, he calls them together, offers supplication to

God, and asks that necessaries may be supplied. When I saw what a great work he had done by his faith, and began to remark upon it, he said, "Oh, it is only a little thing that I have done. Faith could do far more than that. If it were God's will that I should feed the universe on prayer and faith, I could do it. I believe God has made me to be here to be to the world a proof that he hears and answers prayer."—46.100, 101

1010 Unbelieving prayers! Shall I call them prayers? Prayers without faith! They are birds without wings, ships without sails, beasts without legs. Prayers that have no faith in Christ are prayers without the blood on them. They are deeds without the signature, without the seal, without the stamp. They are impotent, illegal documents.—59.118

Prayer, family   *See Father; Mother*

1011 How can a man be a believer in Jesus Christ, and yet have a cold and hard heart in the things of the kingdom toward his children? I have heard of ministers who have despised family prayer, who have laughed at family godliness and thought nothing of it. I cannot understand how the men can know as much as they do about the gospel, and yet have so little of the spirit of it.—3.348

1012 I remember in the hour of overwhelming anguish, when I feared that my beloved wife was about to be taken from me, how I was comforted by the loving prayers of my two dear sons. We had communion not only in our grief, but also in our confidence in the living God.—34.29

1013 When my father was absent preaching the gospel, my mother always filled his place at the family altar. And in my own family, if I have been absent, and my dear wife has been ill, my sons, while yet boys, would not hesitate to read the Scriptures and pray. We could not have a house without prayer. That would be heathenish or atheistical.—43.501

1014 I know that the words of my father with me alone, when he prayed for me and bade me to pray for myself—not to use any form of prayer, but to pray just as I felt, and to ask from God what I felt that I really wanted—left an impression on my mind that will never be erased.—53.263

1015 I cannot make out how you Christians live who have not family prayer in your houses. You will find that where sons and daughters have turned out a curse to their parents, and those parents have been Christians, it might have been set down to this, that while the parents have been Christians, they were not Christians at home. They had not family prayer. They never reared a family altar. I believe nine out of ten such cases can be explained that way.—54.333

1016 I am sure we cannot expect our children to grow up a godly seed if there is no family prayer.—61.526

Prayer, fervent   *See Prayer, importunate; Zeal*

1017 It is the burning lava of the soul that has a furnace within—a very volcano of grief and sorrow—it is that burning lava of prayer that finds its way to God. No prayer ever reaches God's heart which does not come from our hearts.—5.333

1018 We must get rid of the icicles that hang about our lips. We must ask the Lord to thaw the ice caves of our soul and to make our hearts like a furnace of fire heated seven times hotter. If our hearts do not burn within us, we may well question whether Jesus is with us. Those who are neither cold nor hot he has threatened to spew out of his mouth (Rev. 3:16). How can we expect his favor if we fall into a condition so obnoxious to him?—13.79, 80

1019 The Lord does not play at promising. Jesus did not sport at confirming the word by his blood, and we must not make a jest of prayer by going about it in a listless, unexpecting spirit.—17.607

1020 He who prays without fervency does not pray at all. We cannot commune with God, who is a consuming fire (Heb. 12:29), if there is no fire in our prayers.—28.547

1021 I know of no better thermometer to your spiritual temperature than this, the measure of the intensity of your prayer.—41.518

Prayer, importunate   *See Prayer, fervent; Zeal*

1022 A mother has been anxious for her children's conversion. At last she says, "These many years have I sought God for this one blessing; I will seek no longer. I will pray another month, and then if he hears me not, I think I can never pray again."

Mother, retract the words. Blot out such a thought from your soul, for in this you are limiting the Holy One of Israel. He is trying your faith. Persevere, persevere while life lasts, and if your prayers be not answered in your lifetime, perhaps from the windows of heaven you shall look down and see the blessing of your prayers descend on the head of your child.—5.379, 380

1023 If you are sure it is a right thing for which you are asking, plead now, plead at noon, plead at night, plead on. With cries and tears spread out your case. Order your arguments. Back up your pleas with reasons. Urge the precious blood of Jesus. Set the wounds of Christ before the Father's eyes. Bring out the atoning sacrifice. Point to Calvary. Enlist the crowned Prince, the Priest who stands at the right hand of God. And resolve in your very soul that if souls be not saved, if your family be not blessed, if your own zeal be not revived, yet you will die with the plea on your lips, and with the importunate wish on your spirits.—15.108

1024 The Lord give me a dozen importunate pleaders and lovers of souls, and by his grace we will shake all London from end-to-end yet.—17.498, 499

1025 Some mercies are not given to us except in answer to importunate prayer. There are blessings which, like ripe fruit, drop into your hand the moment you touch the bough. But there are others which require you to shake the tree again and again, until you make it rock with the vehemence of your exercise, for only then will the fruit fall down.—21.437

Prayer, intercessory

1026 I commend intercessory prayer, because it opens man's soul, gives a healthy play to his sympathies, constrains him to feel that he is not everybody, and that this wide world was not, after all, made that he might be its petty lord. It does him good to make him know that the cross was not uplifted alone for him, for its far-reaching arms were meant to drop with benedictions on millions of the human race.—7.451

1027 What wonders it has wrought! Intercessory prayer has stayed plagues (Exod. 7–11). Intercessory prayer has healed diseases. We know it did in the early church. It has restored withered limbs. Intercessory prayer has raised the dead (1 Kings 17). As to how many souls intercessory prayer has instrumentally saved, recording angel, you can tell! Eternity, you shall reveal! There is nothing which intercessory prayer cannot do.—7.453

1028 Let me have your prayers, and I can do anything! Let me be without my people's prayers, and I can do nothing.—11.236

1029 Do you say you have nothing to pray for? What, no children unconverted, no friends unsaved, no neighbors who are still in darkness? What! Live in London and not pray for sinners?—12.623

1030 Perhaps you hear a sinner swear. What does that say to you, but "Pray for that sinner"? All the sins we see other men commit ought to be so many jogs to our memory to pray for the coming of Christ and the salvation of souls.—13.478

1031 Until the gate of hell is shut upon a man we must not cease to pray for him. And if we see him hugging the very doorposts of damnation, we must go to the mercy seat and beseech the arm of grace to pluck him from his dangerous position. While there is life there is hope, and although the soul is almost smothered with despair, we must not despair for it, but rather arouse ourselves to awaken the almighty arm.—14.53

1032 Earnest intercession will be sure to bring love with it. I do not believe you can hate a man for whom you habitually pray. If you dislike any brother Christian, pray for him doubly, not only for his sake, but for your own, that you may be cured of prejudice and saved from all unkind feeling.—18.258

1033 Those who are short of breath in soul winning will never be successful. If they are not saved after twenty years of prayer, follow them up to the gates of hell! If they once pass those gates, your prayers are unallowable and unavailing, but to the very verge of the infernal pit follow them with your prayers. If they will not hear you speak, they cannot prevent your praying. Do they jest at your exhortations? They cannot disturb you at your prayers. Are they far away so that you cannot reach them? Your prayers can reach them. Have they declared that they will never listen to you again, nor see your face? Never mind, God has a voice which they must hear. Speak to him, and he will make them feel. Though they now treat you despitefully, rendering evil for your good, follow them with your prayers. Never let them perish for lack of your supplications.—18.263, 264

1034 Those who were in Christ before me prayed for me; should I not pray for others? The treasury of the church's prayers has been expended on us in bringing us to Christ's feet. Let us now contribute to the common stock, casting in our prayers for the conversion of others.—22.406, 407

1035 What can we do without your prayers? They link us with the omnipotence of God. Like the lightning rod, they pierce the clouds and bring down the mighty and mysterious power from on high.—23.445

1036 God will bless Elijah and send rain on Israel, but Elijah must pray for it. If the chosen nation is to prosper, Samuel must plead for it. If the Jews are to be delivered, Daniel must intercede. God will bless Paul, and the nations shall be converted through him, but Paul must pray. Pray he did without ceasing; his epistles show that he expected nothing except by asking for it.—28.548

1037 There are some I know who cannot get down to hell, though they seem to try to do so, for whichever way they move, there is somebody or other praying for them. And they are conscious that at this very moment they are the subject of some loved one's

153

prayer. Surely God has an eye of love on those whom he has encompassed with his own dear servants who day and night are praying for them.—43.414

1038 It has been truly said that if you have a very hard thing, you can cut it with something harder. And if any heart is especially hard, God can use the hard, strong, persistent vehemence of other mighty, passionate souls to pray the blessing of eternal life into that stubborn, rebellious heart.—47.285

Prayer, neglect of *See Bible, neglect of*

1039 Live and die without prayer, and you will pray long enough when you get to hell.—1.7

1040 Could you read the story of Abraham's interceding for Sodom and say that you have interceded for London like that? Can you read of Jacob at the brook Jabbok and say that you ever spent an hour, much less a night, in wrestling with the angel? The prayerlessness of this age is one of its worst signs.—13.127

1041 Neglect of private prayer is the locust which devours the strength of the church.—17.157

1042 A prayerless church member is a hindrance. He is in the body like a rotting bone or a decayed tooth. Before long, since he does not contribute to the benefit of his brethren, he will become a danger and a sorrow to them.—18.255

Prayer, posture in

1043 He that is never on his knees on earth shall never stand upon his feet in heaven.—6.251

Prayer, power of *See Prayer, answered*

1044 Luther, when Melancthon was dying, went to his deathbed and said, "Melancthon, you shall not die!"

"Oh," said Melancthon, "I must die! It is a world of toil and trouble."

"Melancthon," said he, "I have need of you, and God's cause has need of you, and as my name is Luther, you shall not die!"

The physician said he would. Well, down went Luther on his knees, and began to tug at death. "Drop him," said Luther, "drop him, I want him!"

"No," said death, "he is my prey, I will take him!"

"Down with him," said Luther, "down with him, death, or I will wrestle with you!" And he seemed to take hold of the grim monster and hurl him to the ground. And he came off victorious up from the very shades of death. He had delivered Melancthon from death by prayer!—3.13

1045 You can be omnipotent if you know how to pray, omnipotent in all things which glorify God.—17.611

¹⁰⁴⁶ There is no force in nature that is equal to the power of prayer. The law of gravitation holds the planets in their orbits, and links the sun to all the spheres that circle round him. But prayer has now made gravitation itself cease to exert its energy: "Sun, stand thou still upon Gibeon," said Joshua, who had first spoken to the Lord about the matter (Josh. 10:12).—55.258, 259

Prayer, public

¹⁰⁴⁷ When you pray in public, as a rule, the shorter the better.—15.106

Prayer, specific

¹⁰⁴⁸ There is a general kind of praying which fails for lack of precision. It is as if a regiment of soldiers should all fire off their guns anywhere. Possibly somebody would be killed, but the majority of the enemy would be missed.—32.116

Prayer Meeting

¹⁰⁴⁹ The condition of the church may be very accurately gauged by its prayer meetings. So is the prayer meeting a grace-ometer, and from it we may judge of the amount of divine working among a people. If God be near a church, it must pray. And if he be not there, one of the first tokens of his absence will be slothfulness in prayer.—19.218

¹⁰⁵⁰ Prayer is the breath of faith. Prayer meetings are the lungs of the church.—29.143

Preacher   *See Ministry, call to; Pastor; Preaching*

¹⁰⁵¹ May I beg you carefully to judge every preacher, not by his gifts, not by his elocutionary powers, not by his status in society, not by the respectability of his congregation, not by the prettiness of his church, but by this—does he preach the word of truth, the gospel of your salvation? If he does, your sitting under his ministry may prove to you the means of begetting faith in you. But if he does not, you cannot expect God's blessing.—10.552

¹⁰⁵² The true ambassador for Christ feels that he himself stands before God and has to deal with souls in God's stead as God's servant, and stands in a solemn place—a place in which unfaithfulness is inhumanity to man as well as treason to God.—16.529

¹⁰⁵³ We have grown professional in our service, and now we preach like automatons, wound up for a sermon, to run down when the discourse is over. And we have little more care for the souls of men than if they were so much dirt.—17.524

¹⁰⁵⁴ An idler has no right in the pulpit. He is an instrument of Satan in damning the souls of men. The ministry demands brain

labor. The preacher must throw his thought into his teaching, and read and study to keep his mind in good trim. Above all, he must put heart work into his preaching. He must feel what he preaches. It must never be with him an easy thing to deliver a sermon. He must feel as if he could preach his very life away before the sermon is done.—19.462

1055 The private Christian will have some persecution, but the minister must expect far more. His words will be misrepresented and tortured into I know not what of evil, and his actions will be the theme of slander and falsehood. If he shall speak straight out and boldly, fearless of man, and only fearful lest he should grieve his God, he will stir the kennels of hell, and make all the hounds of Satan howl at his heels.—19.605

Preacher, responsibility of *See* *Pastor, responsibility of*

1056 I have come forth Sunday mornings with the burden of the Lord on my heart, till I have been bowed down with the weight. And there is not a Sunday night, and has not been for many a day, when I do not come on this platform in such a state, both of body and soul, that I pity a dog who has to suffer what I have, under the terror and the weight of the awful responsibility of having to preach to such a crowd as this. If you perish, it is not because I

have not warned you, it is not because I have shunned to use plain language. I have come down on your consciences as with a sledge hammer. I have sought to dash at your hearts, that you might turn unto the Lord my God. Woe, then, to those that are at ease under a faithful, laborious, and earnest ministry!—7.557, 558

1057 Sometimes when I have gone down out of the pulpit, and somebody has said, "There are six or seven thousand people without excuse because they have heard the gospel," I have said, "Yes, it is so."

But I have thought, "Have I preached it as earnestly as I ought?" And many a time it has made me toss on my bed to think of the responsibility of this mass of human beings, and the twenty thousand or more who regularly read the sermons as they come from the press. Who is sufficient for these things? Truly a saved minister will be an everlasting wonder!—12.551

1058 I have preached the gospel now these thirty years and more, and some of you will scarcely believe it, but before I come to address the congregation in this Tabernacle, I tremble like an aspen leaf. And often, in coming down to this pulpit, have I felt my knees knock together—not that I am afraid of any one of my hearers, but I am thinking of that account which I must render to

God, whether I speak his Word faithfully or not. On this service may hang the eternal destinies of many. O God, grant that we may all realize that this is a matter of the most solemn concern.—44.296

1059 My deacons know well enough how, when I first preached in Exeter Hall, there was scarcely ever an occasion in which they left me alone for ten minutes before the service, but they would find me in a most fearful state of sickness, produced by that tremendous thought of my solemn responsibility. I am compelled to put my responsibilities where I put my sins, on the back of the Lord Jesus Christ.—48.619

1060 I dare not play with you, sinner. I dare not tell you sin is a trifle. I dare not tell you that the world to come is a matter of no great account. I dare not come and tell you that you need not be in earnest. I shall have to answer for it to my Master.—61.621

Preaching *See Election, preaching on; Evangelism; Jesus, preaching about; Ministry; Preacher*

1061 My motto is, "I yield to none." I preach what I like, when I like, and as I like.—1.90, 91

1062 When I pass a day without preaching my Master's name I feel that I have not done what I ought to have done, and I do not rest satisfied till I am within the four boards of a pulpit again.—1.223

1063 Men do not hear the truth as they used to. The organ is the only thing in the building which gives forth a certain sound.—3.44

1064 I am often charged with preaching doctrines that may do a great deal of hurt. I have my witnesses here present to prove that the things which I have preached *have* done a great deal of hurt, but they have not done hurt either to morality or to God's church. The hurt has been on the side of Satan.—4.141

1065 I have not softened down the Bible to suit the carnal tastes of men. I have said "damn" where God said "damn." I have not sweetened it into "condemn."—4.237

1066 You might as well expect to raise the dead by whispering in their ears, as hope to save souls by preaching to them, if it were not for the agency of the Spirit.—5.211

1067 Oh, what would the damned in hell give for a sermon, could they but listen once more! They would consent, if it were possible, to bear ten thousand years of hell's torments, if they might but once more have the Word presented to them! If I had a congregation such as that would be, of men who have tasted the wrath of God, of men who know what an awful thing it

157

is to fall into the hands of an angry God, how would they lean forward to catch every word.—6.488

1068 It will be our dull sermons that will haunt us on our dying beds, our tearless preaching, our long studyings, when we might have preached better had we come away and preached without them, our huntings after popularity, instead of saying to the people, "You are dying, escape for your life, and fly to Christ," preaching to them in red-hot, simple words the wrath to come, and the love of Christ.—7.13

1069 We are told men ought not to preach without preparation. Granted. But, we add, men ought not to *hear* without preparation. Which, do you think, needs the most preparation, the sower or the ground? I would have the sower come with clean hands, but I would have the ground well-plowed and harrowed, well-turned over, and the clods broken before the seed comes in. It seems to me that there is more preparation needed by the ground than by the sower, more by the hearer than by the preacher.—7.582, 583

1070 Preach the gospel, the gates of hell shake. Preach the gospel, prodigals return. Preach the gospel to every creature, it is the Master's mandate and the Master's power to everyone who believes.—10.23

1071 I am fearful that even preaching against sin may have an injurious effect on the preacher. I frankly confess that there is a tendency with those of us who have to speak on these themes to treat them professionally, rather than to make application of them to ourselves. And thus we lose our dread of evil in some degree, just as young doctors soon lose their tender nervousness in the dissecting room.—11.159

1072 That is the worst kind of preaching anywhere, preaching before people. Preaching right *at* people is the only preaching worth hearing and worth uttering.— 12.634

1073 I do not know of any sermon preached here without conversions.—14.130

1074 It is a long time since I preached a sermon that I was satisfied with. I scarcely recollect ever having done so.—14.176

1075 The best sermons are the sermons which are fullest of Christ. A sermon without Christ, it is an awful, a horrible thing. It is an empty well; it is a cloud without rain; it is a tree twice dead, plucked up by the roots. It is an abominable thing to give men stones for bread and scorpions for eggs, yet they do so who preach not Jesus. A sermon without Christ! As well talk of a loaf of bread without any flour in it. How can it feed the soul? Men die and perish because Christ is not there, and yet his glorious gospel is the easiest thing to preach, and the sweetest thing to preach. There is most variety in it, there is more attractiveness in it than in all the world besides.—14.467

1076 No man who preaches the gospel without zeal is sent of God to preach at all.—15.75

1077 Let us stand to our preaching like soldiers to their guns. The pulpit is the Thermopylae of Christendom where our foes shall receive a check, the field of Waterloo on which they shall sustain a defeat. Let us preach, and preach evermore.—16.254

1078 I like the idea of pouring our sermons out of our own hearts. They must come from our hearts, or they will not go to our hearers' hearts.—17.112

1079 Ministers who do not aim to cut deep are not worth their salt. God never sent the man who never troubles men's consciences.—19.464

1080 Take it as a rule that the truth of God prayed over, spoken in the fear of the Lord, with the Holy Spirit dwelling in the man who speaks it, will produce the effect which is natural to it. We know that our labor is not in vain in the Lord. I do not come into this pulpit myself with any fear that I shall preach in vain. It does not occur to me that such a thing can happen.—23.633

1081 We cannot play at preaching. We preach for eternity.—23.698

1082 Preaching is often too much like a fiddler's playing. People come to see how it is done, and then they pass round the question, "What do you think of him?" Now, I do not care two straws what you think of me. But I do care a whole world what you think of Christ and of yourselves and of your future state.—25.192

1083 The sermon which does not lead to Christ, or of which Jesus Christ is not the top and the bottom, is a sort of sermon that will make the devils in hell laugh, but might make the angels of God weep.—25.634

1084 I have so seldom the privilege of hearing a sermon that, when I do, it occasions an intense delight which I can scarcely describe, and then I draw nearer to God than in any other exercise.—28.357

1085 A sermon wept over is more acceptable with God than one gloried over.—32.35

1086 When that which comes of his sowing is unfruitful, the sower's work is wasted; he has spent his strength for nought. Preaching is the idlest of occupations if the Word be not adapted to enter the heart and produce good results. O my hearers, if you are not converted, I waste time and energy in standing here!—34.469

1087 Many people, when they hear a sermon, say, "How did you enjoy it?" If you always enjoy sermons, the minister is not a good steward. He is not acting wisely who deals out nothing but sweets. God's people need that the Word should at times be medicine to them.—35.417

1088 You cannot preach conviction of sin unless you have suffered it. You cannot preach repentance unless you have practiced it. You cannot preach faith unless you have exercised it. True preaching is artesian; it wells up from the great depths of the soul. If Christ has not made a well within us, there will be no outflow from us.—35.615

1089 A minister flings his soul away if he spends his energies in the attempt to please his congregation. It may not be well that some of you should be pleased. I have never yet heard of a salmon that liked the hook which had taken sure hold of it, nor do men admire sermons which enter their souls.—36.152

1090 I do not suppose that any of you women can sew without needles. Yet your object is not simply to get the needle into the stuff, is it? No, you want to get in a bit of thread. Try whether you can sew with a piece of thread alone. You cannot. You must put

in the needle first. And he who would do any work for God must have a sharp needle, as he deals plainly with the sin of man, and he must then draw after it the silken thread of the gospel of Christ.—38.571

1091 Life, death, hell, and worlds unknown may hang on the preaching and hearing of a sermon.—39.170

1092 It is hard to go to heaven from such a place as that which I occupy! Your eyes sometimes startle me in my dreams. I think sometimes, "What shall I do in eternity if six thousand pairs of eyes are forever seeming to stick, like daggers, into my heart?" Oh, but it will not be so!—39.429

1093 There is no worship of God that is better than the hearing of a sermon. I venture to say that if a sermon be well-heard, it puts faith in exercise as you believe it, it puts love in exercise as you enjoy it, it puts gratitude in exercise as you think of all the blessings that God has given you. If the sermon be what it should be, it stirs all the coals of fire in your spirit, and makes them burn with a brighter flame.—41.17

1094 There is one sin which I believe I have never committed. I think that I have never been afraid of any of you, and I hope, by the grace of God, that I never shall be. If I dare not speak the truth on all points, and dare not rebuke sin, what is the good of me to you?—54.91

1095 A celebrated preacher was once told that he had pleased all his hearers. "Ah!" said he, "there is another sermon lost." The most effective sermons are those which make opposers of the gospel bite their lips and gnash their teeth.—44.524

1096 Wherever you are weak, be strong in the pulpit. Give the people a good hearty meal whenever you preach. They will put up with a great many defects if you will only feed them.—56.405

1097 Draw a circle around my pulpit, and you have hit the spot where I am nearest heaven. There the Lord has been more consciously near me than anywhere else. He has ravished my heart while I have been trying to cheer and comfort his mourners.—59.82

1098 I was a few days ago upbraided by a good soul for exposing all her faults from the pulpit. I have been, not merely now and then, but very often thought by some people to be so dreadfully personal that they did not know how they could bear it. And yet I never saw those people, except from the pulpit, and did not know anything at all about them.—60.499

1099 Sometimes, after preaching the gospel, I have been so filled with self-reproach that I could hardly sleep through the night, because I had not preached as I desired. I have sat down and cried over some sermons, as though I knew that I had missed the mark and lost the opportunity. Not once nor twice, but many a time has it happened that within a few days someone has come to tell me that he found the Lord through that very sermon, the shortcoming of which I had deplored. Glory be to Jesus; it was his gentleness that did it.—60.622

1100 God is my witness I have eschewed every idea of trying to be eloquent or oratorical in my preaching. I care nothing whatever about the gaudy show of speechmaking. I only want just to tell you these truths in unvarnished speech.—63.31

Preaching, expository   *See Bible*

1101 I do not believe that God ever fills a cup which was not empty, or that he ever fills a man's mouth with his Word while that man has his mouth full of his own words.—29.424

1102 I cannot help feeling that the man who preaches the Word of God is standing, not on a mere platform, but on a throne.—34.114

1103 I am content to live and die as the mere repeater of scriptural teaching, as a person who has thought out nothing and invented nothing, as one who never thought invention to be any part of his

161

calling, but who concluded that he was simply to be a mouth for God to the people, mourning that anything of his own should come between.—51.4

1104 Saturate your sermons with Bibline, the essence of Bible truth, and you will always have something new to say.—51.7

Preaching, preparation for

1105 I scarcely ever prepare for my pulpit with pleasure. Study for the pulpit is to me the most irksome work in the world.—3.255

1106 There is a story told of me and some person who desired to see me on a Saturday night, when I had shut myself up to make ready for the Sabbath. He was very great and important, and so the maid came to say that someone desired to see me. I directed her to say that it was my rule to see no one at that time. Then he was more important still, and said, "Tell Mr. Spurgeon that a servant of the Lord Jesus Christ desires to see him immediately."
The frightened servant brought the message, but the sender gained little by it, for my answer was, "Tell him I am busy with his Master, and cannot see servants now."—33.646

1107 I have heard of a preacher who thought that whatever came into his head was good enough for his people. On one occasion he

informed one of his officers at the end of his sermon that he had never thought of it before he entered the pulpit. The good elder replied, "I thought so while listening to you."—55.258

Preaching, simplicity of

1108 If I was saved by a simple gospel, then I am bound to preach that same simple gospel till I die, so that others may be saved by it. When I cease to preach salvation by faith in Jesus, put me into a lunatic asylum, for you may be sure that my mind is gone.—26.391

1109 There are a great many ministers who cause their hearers to break the fourth commandment, for the labor involved in hearing them preach is indeed terrible. It must rack the soul instead of resting it.—55.189

Predestination   See Calvinism; Election; Providence; Sovereignty; Will, free

1110 I question whether we have preached the whole counsel of God, unless predestination with all its solemnity and sureness be continually declared.—6.26

1111 I do not doubt that the Lord has settled, concerning every one of his elect, the exact time when they shall pass from death unto life, the precise instrumentality by which they shall be converted, the exact word that shall strike with power on their mind, the period of conviction which they shall undergo, and the instant when they shall burst into the joyful liberty of a simple faith in Christ. It is all settled, all arranged and predetermined in the divine purpose. If the very hairs of our head are all numbered, much more the circumstances of the most important of all events which can occur to us.—13.687

1112 We are no believers in fate, seeing that fate is a different doctrine altogether from predestination. Fate says the thing is and must be, so it is decreed. But the true doctrine is—God has appointed this and that, not because it must be, but because it is best that it should be. Fate is blind, but the destiny of Scripture is full of eyes. Fate is stern and adamantine, and has no tears for human sorrow. But the arrangements of providence are kind and good.— 15.460

1113 "If there are so many that will be saved," says one, "then why do you preach?"

That is why we preach! If there are so many fish to be taken in the net, I will go and catch some of them. Because many are ordained to be caught, I spread my nets with eager expectation. I never could see why that should repress our zealous efforts. It seems to me to be the very thing that should awaken us to energy—that God has a people, and that these

people shall be brought in.— 26.622

1114 If any of you do not believe in the predestination of God, you will probably, in some hour of depression, ascribe your sorrows to cruel fate. The human mind is driven at last to this decision, that some things are beyond the control of man and his will, and that these are fixed by necessity. How much better to see that God has fixed them!—33.189

1115 The foreordination of God in no degree interferes with the responsibility of man. I have often been asked by persons to reconcile the two truths. My only reply is, "They need no reconciliation, for they never fell out." Why should I try to reconcile two friends? The two facts are parallel lines. I cannot make them unite, but you cannot make them cross each other.—33.199

1116 I believe that nothing happens apart from divine determination and decree.—38.66

1117 I do not believe that there ever would have been a man delivered from this present evil world if it had not been according to the will, the purpose, the predestination of God. It needs a mighty tug to get a man away from the world. It is a miracle for a man to live in the world, and yet not to be of it. I am sure it would never have been wrought if it had not been according to the will of God our Father.—42.451

1118 We shall never be able to escape from the doctrine of divine predestination—the doctrine that God has foreordained certain people unto eternal life.—51.457

1119 It is true that everything is predestinated, and that everything that happens is ordered according to the unfailing purpose and will of God.—51.458

Prejudice

1120 I have heard of a lady who was visited by a minister on her deathbed, and she said to him, "I want to ask you one question, now that I am about to die."

"Well," said the minister, "what is it?"

"Oh," she said in a very affected way, "I want to know if there are two places in heaven, because I could not bear that Betsy in the kitchen should be in heaven along with me, she is so unrefined."

The minister said, "Don't trouble yourself about that, madam, for until you get rid of your accursed pride, you will never enter heaven at all."—1.302, 303

Presence, God's   See *God, presence of*

Pride   See *Humility; Self-righteousness; Works*

1121 There is nothing into which the heart of man so easily falls as pride. And yet there is no vice which is more frequently, more emphatically, and more eloquently condemned in Scripture.—2.345

1122 Nothing proves men so mad as pride. For this they have given up rest and ease to find rank and power among men. For this they have dared to risk their hope of salvation, to leave the gentle yoke of Jesus, and go toiling wearily along the way of life, seeking to save themselves by their own works, and at last to stagger into the mire of cruel despair.—2.347

1123 Pride is most likely to meet with destruction, because it is too tall to walk upright. It is most likely to tumble down, because it is always looking upward in its ambition, and never looks to its feet. There only needs to be a pitfall in the way, or even a stone, and down it goes.—2.349

1124 Pride is like the flies of Egypt; all Pharaoh's soldiers could not keep them out. And I am sure all the strong resolutions and devout aspirations we may have cannot keep pride out unless the Lord God Almighty sends a strong wind of his Holy Spirit to sweep it away.—2.350

1125 If any man tells me that he is humble, I know him to be profoundly proud. And if any man will not acknowledge this truth, that he is desperately inclined to self-exaltation, let him know that his denial of this truth is the best proof of it.—3.393

1126 It is a wild, strange thing to think that a man should be proud when he has nothing to be proud of. A living, animated lump of clay—defiled and filthy, a living hell—and yet proud.—4.380

1127 Better to lose your pride than to lose your soul! Why be damned for pride's sake? Why carry your head so high that it must be cut off? Why feed your pride on your soul's blood? Surely there is cheaper stuff than that for pride to drink!—7.216

1128 No matter how dear you are to God, if pride be harbored in your spirit, he will whip it out of you. They that go up in their own estimation must come down again by his discipline.—17.51

1129 Pride is always inconsistent with the true doctrine of the gospel. You may use this test concerning any preaching or teaching that you meet with. If it logically leads a man to boast of himself, it is not true.—22.2

1130 Pride is the devil's dragnet in which he takes more fish than in any other, except procrastination.—27.206

1131 If killed, pride revives. If buried, it bursts the tomb. You may hunt down this fox and think you have destroyed it, and lo, your very exultation is pride.—29.421

1132 Men proudly ask to be humble. They desire to be humble in order that they may be admired for it.—30.532, 533

1133 The gate of heaven, though it is so wide that the greatest sinner may enter, is nevertheless so low that pride can never pass through it.—42.271

1134 Somebody once told John Bunyan that he had preached a delightful sermon. "You are too late," said John, "the devil told me that before I left the pulpit." Satan is adept in teaching us how to steal our Master's glory.—48.292

1135 I remember receiving a warning against pride from a Christian woman who told me that she would pray that I might be kept humble. I thanked her and told her that I would do the same for her. She said that she did not require it, for she had nothing to be proud of, and therefore she was quite sure she never should be proud. Then I told her, gently but decidedly, that I thought she was proud already, or else she would not have uttered such a speech as that.—56.295

Procrastination   See Salvation, urgency of; Time

1136 Procrastination is the thief of time. It steals away our life. And if we knew the hour of our death, we should be no more prepared for it than we are now.—1.147

1137 Men do not get better if left alone. It is with them as with a garden. If you let it alone and permit weeds to grow, you will not expect to find it better in six months, but worse.—1.309

1138 If you were sick, would you send for your physician tomorrow? If your house were on fire, would you call "Fire!" tomorrow? If you were robbed in the street on your road home, would you cry "Stop! Thief!" tomorrow? No. But man is foolish in the things that concern his soul. Unless divine and infinite love shall teach him to number his days, he will still go on boasting of tomorrows until his soul has been destroyed by them.—2.326

1139 Archbishop Tillotson well says, "A man might say, 'I resolve to eat,' but the resolve to eat would never feed his body. A man might say, 'I am resolved to drink,' but the resolve to drink would never slake his thirst." And you may say, "I am resolved before long to seek God," but your resolve will not save you. It is not the forgetful hearer, but the doer of the Word that shall be blessed therein (James 1:25).—4.55

1140 The great mischief of most men is that they procrastinate. It is not that they resolve to be damned, but that they resolve to be saved *tomorrow*. It is not that they reject Christ forever, but that they reject Christ *today*. They might as well reject him forever, as continue perpetually to reject him *now*.—10.688

1141 Remember that if you have missed Christ by just the ticking of a clock, you have missed Christ forever.—13.533

1142 You tell me that nothing endangers your life at this moment. How do you know? The arrows of death often fly imperceptibly. I have stood in congregations preaching on two occasions when the unseen darts of death struck one of my hearers, so that one died on each occasion while listening to the Word of the gospel.—16.681

Note: See the quotation under **Death, suddenness of,** *53.139, for the circumstances surrounding one of these deaths while CHS preached.*

1143 If you resolve that you will repent in a year's time, what is that but a daring defiance of God by declaring that you will continue in sin for twelve months at least? Have you ever looked at it in that light? Even if a man knew that he could live a year, and that on this day twelve months from now he could carry out his resolution to become a Christian, yet if he should make such a resolution, what would it mean but this: "I mean for twelve months to refuse the Savior's claims and remain an enemy to God"? Do you think

166

that he who thus resolves is in a hopeful condition? If he be determined for twelve months to rebel against his Lord, do you not predict that at the end of the year he will be a worse man, and less likely to yield himself to God?—23.188, 189

1144 I met with a striking sentence in the works of William Mason: "Every day of delay leaves a day more to repent of, and a day less to repent in."—26.434

1145 When you see my coffin carried to the silent grave, I should like every one of you, whether converted or not, to be constrained to say, "He did earnestly urge us in plain and simple language not to put off the consideration of eternal things. He did entreat us to look to Christ. Now that he is gone, our blood is not at his door if we perish."—49.600

1146 The road to hell is paved with good intentions. Oh, you lingerers, pull up the paving stones and hurl them at the devil's head. He is ruining you; he is decoying you to your destruction.—61.117

1147 Tomorrow, tomorrow, tomorrow! Alas, tomorrow never comes! It is in no calendar except the almanac of fools.—61.126

Profanity

1148 Filthy speech puts those who are guilty of it among the chief of sinners, and to them will certainly be meted out a terrible vengeance in that day when God shall solemnly curse those who have so glibly cursed themselves.—31.233

1149 Whenever I hear a man swear, I always pray for him. And I have sometimes thought, when I have heard an oath, it has been a warning bell ringing to let me know that it was time for me to pray. It is a horrible thing that men should blaspheme and curse and swear. But I believe that there would be less of these evils if all Christians prayed whenever they heard an oath, for the devil would see that it would not pay him. For, fool though he is, he has some sense left.—44.211

Promises, God's

1150 They are as the granaries which Joseph built in Egypt, or as the golden pot wherein the unrotting manna was preserved. Blessed is he who can take the five barley loaves and fishes of promise and break them till his five thousand necessities shall all be supplied. The promises are the Christian's Magna Charta of liberty, they are his title deeds of his heavenly estate. They are the jewel room in which the Christian's crown treasures are preserved.—8.97

1151 A poor old Christian woman was accustomed to make marginal notes in her Bible, and she placed against one text a "T" and a "P." The minister asked her what they meant, and she said,

"Tried and Proved, for I tried that promise on such and such an occasion and found it true."—16.285

1152 The sacred promises, though in themselves most sure and precious, are of no avail for the comfort and sustenance of the soul unless you grasp them by faith, plead them in prayer, expect them by hope, and receive them with gratitude.—34.161

1153 As you read them over, one after the other, you say to yourselves, "This is my checkbook. I can take out the promises as I want them, sign them by faith, present them at the great Bank of Grace, and come away enriched with present help in time of need." That is the way to use God's promises.—44.322

Prophecy   *See Second Coming*

1154 I think some ministers would do far more for the profit of God's people if they would preach more about the first advent and less about the second.—7.345

1155 Nothing shall induce me to attempt to interpret the prophecies. By God's grace I will be content to expound the gospel. I believe it to be one of the most fatal devices of Satan to turn aside useful gospel ministers from their proper work into idle speculations on the number of the beast and the meaning of the little horn. The prophecies will interpret themselves by their fulfillment, but no expositor has yet arisen who has been able to do it.—12.601

1156 Our business is to save souls. You will hear me expounding the Revelation one day, that is, when there is not another of the elect to save. When all the chosen are saved, we will preach on the deep mysteries of Daniel and Ezekiel, but so long as souls are unsaved, we mean to keep to the plain gospel—Matthew, Mark, Luke, and John.—13.504

1157 In many cases sheer fanaticism has been the result of exclusively dwelling on prophecy, and probably more men have gone mad on that subject than on any other religious question.—21.644

1158 I deeply regret when I see persons so taken up with prophecy that they forget evangelism. Trumpets and vials must not displace the gospel and its invitations.—27.391

1159 A man says to me, "Can you explain the seven trumpets of the Revelation?"

No, but I can blow one in your ear, and warn you to escape from the wrath to come.

Another says, "Can you tell me when the end of the world will come?"

No, but I can tell you how to be so prepared for it that you need not be afraid if it were to come tonight. I can urge you to trust the

Lord Jesus Christ as your Savior, so that you can await it with holy joy.—53.186

Prosperity   *See Money; Trials; Wealth*

1160 It is a very serious thing to grow rich! Of all the temptations to which God's children are exposed, it is the worst, because it is one that they do not dread. Therefore, it is the more subtle temptation.—4.421

1161 Where one man has been ruined by adversity, ten thousand men have been destroyed by prosperity.—14.452

1162 Prosperity is much harder to bear than adversity. As the fining pot to silver and the furnace to gold, so is prosperity to a Christian. Many a man will pass through trouble and praise God under it, who, when he is tried with no trouble, will forget his God, decline in grace, and grow almost a worldling. Believe me, there is no trial as great as no trial.—15.488

Providence   *See Predestination*

1163 A poor harlot determined she would go and take her life on Blackfriars Bridge. Passing by these doors one Sunday night, she thought she would step in, and for the last time hear something that might prepare her to stand before her Maker. The text was, "Seest thou this woman?" (Luke 7:44). I dwelt on Mary Magdalene and her sins, her washing the Savior's feet with her tears, and wiping them with the hair of her head. There stood the woman, melted away with the thought that she should thus hear herself described and her own life painted. Oh, to think of saving a poor harlot from death, and then, as God pleased, to save her soul from going down to hell!—1.344

1164 I was engaged to preach last Wednesday at Halifax, where there was a heavy snowstorm. When I arrived, I found from five thousand to six thousand people gathered to hear the Word. We met together in the afternoon and worshiped God, and again in the evening. In front of me there was a huge gallery, capable of holding two thousand persons.

In the evening when the people were about to retire, and when there was scarcely more than a hundred persons there, a huge beam gave way, and down came a portion of the flooring of the gallery with a fearful crash. Only two persons were injured with broken legs. Had this happened any earlier, not only must many more have been injured, but a panic must necessarily have ensued similar to that which we remember in this place. Had such a thing occurred, I feel certain that I should never have been able to occupy the pulpit again.

But mark another thing. All day long it thawed so fast, that the snow seemed to leave a mass of snow and water together. This ran through the roof on us, to our miserable annoyance, and I was almost ready to complain that we had hard dealing from God's providence. But if it had been a frost instead of a thaw, the place must have fallen several hours before. And then your minister and the greater part of his congregation would probably have been in the other world.—4.177, 178

1165 The keys of providence swing at the girdle of Christ. Believe it, Christian, nothing occurs here without the permit or the decree of your Savior.—13.154

1166 He that has gone to prepare a place for us by his presence has prepared the way to that place for us by his providence.—17.235

1167 "Sir," said one to me, "I had been to bargain about a pair of ducks on Sunday morning, and I passed by the door, and I thought I would just look in. There and then the Lord met with me, and those ducks were forgotten, for I found a Savior."—33.408

1168 Our friends need not be troubled by the flying of a dove. It will soon go out of the window, no doubt. Let us believe that it has come as a messenger of good. Oh, that the blessed Dove would his own self come from heaven and bring salvation in his wings!—41.386

Note: These were CHS's extemporaneous words when he noticed *that some in his congregation were nervous about a dove which had flown into the sanctuary.*

1169 The good old Puritan met his son. When the young man came in, he said, "Father, I had a very special providence as I rode here today. My horse stumbled three times very badly, yet I was not thrown down."

"And I have had an equally special providence in riding here," said the father. "My horse never stumbled all the way, so I was not thrown."—47.125

1170 In connection with that terrible calamity at the Surrey Gardens Music Hall, notwithstanding all the sorrow and suffering that it brought on us, as we now look back on it, we see how God, by means of that calamity, called public attention to the preaching of the Word. And I have no doubt that for every life that was then lost, a thousand souls have since been saved from going down to the pit. So let God's name be praised for that gracious overruling of a terrible crime.—52.595

Note: CHS is referring to the evening of Oct. 19, 1856, when 12,000 people were packed inside the Surrey Gardens Music Hall, and another 10,000 were outside unable to get in. During the service some troublemaker shouted FIRE! The people rushed panic-stricken to the doors, piling on top of one another. Seven were killed, twenty-eight were seri-

ously injured, and many others were hurt. CHS fainted and was carried from his pulpit. He thought he'd never be able to preach again. To learn how the Lord restored him, see the quotation under **Acts 5:31,** *from the source 50.524.*

[1171] On how small an incident the greatest results may hinge! The pivots of history are microscopic.—54.25

[1172] I think it was Mrs. Hannah More who says that she went into a place where they were manufacturing a carpet. She said, "There is no beauty there."

The man said, "It is one of the most beautiful carpets you ever saw."

"Why, here is a piece hanging out, and it is all in disorder."

"Do you know why, ma'am? You are looking at the wrong side of the carpet."—54.498

Punishment *See Condemnation; Damnation; Discipline, God's; Hell; Wrath, God's*

[1173] I fear that in too many places the doctrine of future punishment is rejected and laughed at as a fancy, but the day will come when it shall be known to be a reality. Ahab scoffed at Micaiah, when he said he should never come home alive. The men of Noah's generation laughed at the foolish old man, as they thought him, who told them to take heed, for the world should be drowned. But when they were climbing to the treetops and floods were following them, did they then say that the prophecy was untrue? And when the arrow was sticking in the heart of Ahab, did he then think that Micaiah spoke an untruth?—2.417, 418

[1174] God never punishes his children in the sense of avenging justice. He chastens as a father does his child, but he never punishes his redeemed as a judge does a criminal. It were unjust to exact punishment from redeemed souls since Christ has been punished in their place. How shall the Lord punish twice for one offense?—10.195

Punishment, capital

[1175] As a rule I do not believe in the utility of capital punishment.—3.343

Purgatory *See Catholicism; Mass; Pope*

[1176] What can there be about hell fire to change a man's heart? Surely the more the lost will suffer, the more they will hate God. When God sent plagues on the earth, men blasphemed his name (Rev. 16:8, 9). Men do so now. Are they likely to turn at his rebuke then? Satan has been punished for these six thousand years—do you see any signs of repentance about him? Besides, if the gospel of Christ cannot save you, what can? If the wooings of

Christ's wounds cannot make you love Christ, do you think the flames of hell will?—12.177

1177 When the thief died on the cross, he had but just believed, and had never done a single good work. But where did he go? He ought to have gone to purgatory by rights if ever anybody did. But instead of that the Savior said to him, "Today shalt thou be with me in Paradise" (Luke 23:43). Why? Because the ground of the man's admission into Paradise was perfect.—12.562

1178 If I were a Roman Catholic, I should turn a heretic, in sheer desperation, because I would rather go to heaven than go to purgatory.—18.57

1179 How can God's people go to purgatory? For if they go there at all, they go there for sins which God does not remember, and so he cannot give a reason for sending them there. Does God forgive and forget and yet punish? When you die you shall either go to heaven or to hell, and that immediately. Your state in either case will be fixed eternally without the possibility of change. This doctrine is the cornerstone of Protestantism.—28.585

1180 I heard of one, who said to the preacher, after he had been preaching the doctrine of everlasting punishment, "Sir, I believe that I shall go to hell for a season,

and afterward get round to heaven."

"Man," said the preacher, "even if what you say be true, when there is a straightforward road to heaven, what a fool you must be to want to go round by way of hell!"—45.551

Purpose   *See Church, purpose of*

1181 Your main and principal motive as a Christian should always be to live for Christ. To live for glory? Yes, but for his glory. To live for comfort? Yes, but be all your consolation in him. To live for pleasure? Yes, but when you are merry, sing psalms, and make melody in your hearts to the Lord. To live for wealth? Yes, but to be rich in faith. You may lay up treasure, but lay it up in heaven.—9.148

Quarreling   *See Murmuring; Unity*

1182 Men are always quarreling with God because he will not submit his will to their dictation.—6.34

Reconciliation   *See Salvation*

1183 Our love ought to follow the love of God in one point, namely, in always seeking to produce reconciliation. It was to this end that God sent his Son. Has anybody offended you? Seek reconciliation.

"Oh, but I am the offended party."

So was God, and he went straight ahead and sought reconciliation.—29.119

1184 One of the most glorious evidences of a man being reconciled to God is when he rejoices in God. Suppose he becomes obedient to certain outward precepts. That he may be, and yet be very sorry that he has to be obedient to them. Suppose he begins to repent and mourn to think that he has sinned. He may do that, and yet there may be latent in his heart the wish that he could have his fill of sin without fear of punishment. But when a man feels, "There is no one in the world that I love as I love God. For him I would live, for him I would die; he is everything to me," that man is perfectly reconciled to God. You can see that the enmity in his heart is slain.—44.8

Redeemer   *See Jesus*

1185 Rest assured that there is no meeting with God on our part except through Jesus Christ our Redeemer. I am of Luther's mind when he said, "I will have nothing to do with an absolute God." God out of Christ is a terror to us.—27.65

Redemption   *See Salvation*

Regeneration   *See Conversion; Salvation*

1186 Every regeneration is really instantaneous. Its evidences, its outward manifestations may be gradual, but there must be a time when the man begins to live. There must be a period when the first ray of light darts on the opened eye. There must be a time when the man is condemned, and a period when he is not condemned. And there must be an instant when the change takes place.—12.35

1187 Adoption gives us the *rights* of children, but regeneration alone gives us the *nature* of children.—25.54

1188 Do I address one here who imagines that an orthodox creed will save him? I suppose that no one is more orthodox than the devil, yet no one is more surely lost than he is. You may get a clear head, but if you have not a clean heart, it will not avail you at the last. You may know the Westminster Assembly's Catechism by heart, but unless you are born again, it will not benefit you. Did you say that you believed the thirty-nine articles? There is one article that is essential—"Ye must be born again" (John 3:7). And woe to that man who has not passed through that all-important change.—44.187, 188

Repentance   *See Confession; Conviction*

1189 Christ and we will never be one until we and our sin are two.—5.471

1190 Sin and hell are married unless repentance proclaims the divorce.—6.332

1191 A man may hate sin just as a murderer hates the gallows, but this does not prove repentance. If I hate sin because of the punishment, I have not repented of sin. I merely regret that God is just. But if I can see sin as an offense against Jesus Christ, and loathe myself because I have wounded him, then I have a true brokenness of heart.—10.348

1192 Repentance is a part of salvation, and when Christ saves us, he saves us by making us repent. But repentance does not save. It is the work of God alone.—12.198

1193 What if I say that repentance is like the cry of a newborn babe, which indicates that the child is alive? That cry of "God be merciful to me a sinner!" (Luke 18:13) is as sure a sign of life as the song of cherubim before the throne.—13.328

1194 A Christian must never leave off repenting, for I fear he never leaves off sinning.—14.509

1195 To hate sin because it caused the brow of Christ to be girt with the thorn crown, and the face of Christ to be dishonored with the spittle, and the hands of Christ to be pierced with the nail—this is repentance—not because I am afraid of hell, not because sin brings pains and penalties with it, but because it made Jesus Christ to suffer for me such pangs unutterable.—16.656

1196 If you have not a broken heart, only Christ can give it to you. If you cannot come to him *with* it, come to him *for* it. If you cannot come to him wounded, come to him that he may wound you and make you whole. You need bring nothing to Jesus.—22.379

1197 You are not living to God as you ought unless you repent daily. Remember, we are not saved by a single act of faith which terminates the moment we receive forgiveness, but by a faith which continues as long as we live. And as long as we have faith, we must have repentance, too.—26.715

1198 He that never mourned for sin has never rejoiced in the Lord. If I can look back on my past life and say, "I have no grief over it," then I should do the same again if I had the opportunity. And this shows that my heart is as perverse as ever it was, and I am still unregenerate.—28.524

1199 If you can look on sin without sorrow, then you have never looked on Christ. A faith-look at Jesus breaks the heart, both *for* sin and *from* sin. Try yourself by this test.—34.107

1200 Do you say, "I feel that I can repent whenever I please, and believe in Jesus when I choose"?
Then I must assure you that when you are strong in that way, you are weak. I never yet knew anybody repent who gloried in his

power to repent. I never yet knew a man heartbroken for sin who boasted that he could break his own heart when and where he pleased.—34.591

1201 I learn from the Scriptures that repentance is just as necessary to salvation as faith is, and the faith that has not repentance going with it will have to be repented of.—46.246

1202 Repentance and faith are like Siamese twins. If one is sick the other cannot be well, for they live but one life. If ever you are asked which comes first, repentance or faith, you may answer by another question: "Which spoke of a wheel moves first when the wheel begins to move?"—53.352

1203 Rowland Hill used to say that the only thing that he should be sorry to leave when he went to heaven was that sweet, lovely, sorrowful grace of repentance. He supposed he could not repent in heaven, but it was such a sweet experience to keep on repenting that he would wish to repent forever.—54.257, 258

1204 We cannot find a better definition of repentance than the one many of us learned at our mother's knee:

Repentance is to leave
The sin we loved before,
And show that we in earnest
  grieve
By doing so no more.—56.619

1205 I do not know when I am more perfectly happy than when I am weeping for sin at the foot of the cross.—60.234

Repentance, deathbed

1206 Deathbed repentances are hard to estimate; we must leave them with God. But it is a sorrowful fact that those which seemed to be deathbed repentances have seldom turned out to be worth anything when the men have recovered. In fact, I do not remember a case in which the person who recovered has been at all what he said he would be when he thought that he was on the borders of the grave. So you see, suffering is no help to repentance, and it may be a hindrance.—34.647

1207 My own conviction is that they have been very, very, very, very, very few. We read in Scripture of only one who was saved at the last—the dying thief on the cross. And it has been well said that there was one that none might despair, but only one that none might presume.—52.308

1208 Little hope have I for deathbed repentances. Never trust them, I beseech you.—63.188

Responsibility *See Pastor, responsibility of; Preacher, responsibility of*

Rest, spiritual *See Satisfaction*

1209 Do not tell me that there is no rest for us till we get to heaven. We who have believed in Jesus enter into rest even now. Why should we not do so? Our salvation is complete. The robe of righteousness in which we are clad is finished. The atonement for our sins is fully made. We are reconciled to God, beloved of the Father, preserved by his grace, and supplied by his providence with all that we need. We carry all our burdens to him and leave them at his feet. We spend our lives in his service, and we find his ways to be ways of pleasantness, and his paths to be paths of peace. Oh, yes, we have found rest unto our souls! I recollect the first day that I ever rested in Christ, and I did rest that day. And so will all of you who trust in Jesus as I trusted in him.—47.488

Resurrection   *See Miracles, Jesus'*

1210 The divinity of Christ finds its surest proof in his resurrection (Rom. 1:4). Christ's sovereignty also depends on his resurrection (Rom. 14:9). Again, our justification hangs on Christ's resurrection (Rom. 4:25). Our very regeneration depends on his resurrection (1 Peter 1:3). And most certainly our ultimate resurrection rests here (Rom. 8:11). The silver thread of resurrection runs through all the blessings, from regeneration onward to our eternal glory, and binds them together.—8.219

1211 The resurrection is a fact better attested than any event recorded in any history, whether ancient or modern.—15.185

1212 The electric telegraph, though it be but an invention of man, would have been as hard to believe in a thousand years ago as the resurrection of the dead is now. Who in the days of packhorses would have believed in flashing a message from England to America? Everything is full of wonder till we are used to it, and resurrection owes the incredible portion of its marvel to our never having come across it in our observation—that is all. After the resurrection we shall regard it as a divine display of power as familiar to us as creation and providence now are.—18.477, 478

1213 The resurrection of our divine Lord from the dead is the cornerstone of Christian doctrine. Perhaps I might more accurately call it the keystone of the arch of Christianity, for if that fact could be disproved, the whole fabric of the gospel would fall to the ground.—26.193

Revelation, modern   *See Bible; Signs*

1214 We remember what Rowland Hill said to a lady who knew she was a child of God because she dreamed such and such a thing: "Never mind, ma'am, what you did when you were asleep. Let us see what you will do when you are awake." That is my opinion of dreams.—1.87

1215 All the visions in the world since the days of miracles, put together, are but mere dreams after all, and dreams are nothing but vanity. People eat too much supper and then dream. It is indigestion, or a morbid activity of brain, and that is all. If that is all the evidence you have of conversion, you will do well to doubt it. I beg you never to rest satisfied with it; it is wretched rubbish to build your eternal hopes on.—12.59

1216 Visions and such things belong to the infancy of the church. Nobody thinks of putting a post to support an apple tree which has been there for the last fifty years. In fact, it could hold the stake rather than borrow support from it. When a ship leaves the docks and passes down the river, you will see it towed out till it reaches the sea. But that same vessel will soon spread all her sails, and with a heavenly breeze to bear her along, she will need no tug to tow her to the desired haven. The church of God today is a tree that needs no support of miracle or vision, a vessel that has braved two thousand years the battle and the breeze, and will still, till Christ comes, outride every storm. You have the Word of God, which is better than visions.—26.614

1217 I met the other day a person who was impressed that he was to preach for me. He said that it was revealed to him by the Spirit of God that he should preach for me one Sunday. I told him that he should do so when the Spirit of God also revealed it to me, but that I did not believe in lopsided revelations. I thought that it was needful for the revelation to come to me as well as to him. When it does, I will attend to it.—46.394

1218 "Well," says one, "I heard a voice in the air."
Nonsense! Superstition! It is likely to have been the devil that spoke as anybody else, if indeed it was anybody at all. You are as likely to deceive yourself as anything in the world.—55.149

1219 I have little confidence in those persons who speak of having received *direct* revelations from the Lord, as though he appeared otherwise than by and through the gospel. His Word is so full, so perfect, that for God to make any fresh revelation to you or me is quite needless. To do so would be to put dishonor on the perfection of that Word.—59.21

1220 I am ashamed of such ministers as would encourage their hearers in the conviction that their fancies are to be taken as assurances from God. Why, were you to dream tonight that you were in hell, thank God it would not send you there. Or were you to dream that you were in heaven, it would not carry you there.—63.19

Revival   *See Salvation*

1221 We have felt in our souls, not that we *may* have revival, but that we *must* have it. We must draw near to the angel and wrestle afresh with this determination, that we will not let him go unless he should bless us.—10.614

1222 We have had a continual stream of revival. The cries of sinners have sounded in our ears—every day we have seen souls converted—I was about to say almost every hour of the week these twelve years, and of late we have had a double portion.—12.123

1223 If there be but a dozen men in this, my church, who have set their faces for a revival, we shall surely have it. Of this my heart knows no doubt.—13.76

1224 As a church we have lived in revivals for nearly twenty years. There has never been a time that I can remember when there have not been souls converted in our midst. I do not know that there has ever been a Sabbath without a conversion in this place. I do not think there has been a sermon without a conversion.—55.143

Righteousness   *See Holiness; Saint*

1225 Saints are so righteous in Jesus Christ that they are more righteous than Adam was before he fell, for he had but a creature righteousness, and they have the righteousness of the Creator. He had a righteousness which he lost, but believers have a righteousness which they can never lose, an everlasting righteousness.—28.536

Sabbath   *See Lord's Day*

1226 I am no preacher of the old legal Sabbath. I am a preacher of the gospel. The Sabbath of the Jew is to him a task; the Lord's day of the Christian, the first day of the week, is to him a joy, a day of rest, of peace, and of thanksgiving. And if you Christian men can earnestly drive away all distractions, so that you can really rest today, it will be good for your bodies, good for your souls, good mentally, good spiritually, good temporally, and good eternally.—7.580

Sacrament   *See Ordinance*

Saint   *See Catholicism; Christian; Righteousness*

1227 You cannot make a sinner into a saint by killing him. He who does not live as a saint here will never live as a saint hereafter.—30.459

Salvation   *See Children, salvation of; Christian; Conversion; Evangelism; Forgiveness; Justification; Reconciliation; Regeneration; Revival*

1228 Christ is a great Savior to meet the great transgressions of great rebels. The vast machinery of redemption was never undertaken for a mean or little purpose. There must be a great end in so great a plan, carried out at so great an expense, guaranteed with such great promises, and intended to bring such great glory to God.— 7.145

1229 You may have troubles, but you will never have punishment. You may know affliction, but you shall never know wrath. You may go to the grave, but you shall never go to hell. You shall descend into the regions of the dead, but never into the regions of the damned. The evil one may bruise your heel, but he shall never break your head. You may be in prison under doubts, but you shall never be in prison under condemnation.—8.644

1230 The greatest of all miracles is the salvation of a soul.—12.699

1231 The most important question concerning any man living is this: Is he a saved soul or not? Is he a child of God or an heir of wrath?—18.301

1232 "Oh," says one, "I would give my eyes for salvation."
You shall have it without giving your eyes. Give your heart, no, but take the blessing freely, for freely it is given.—22.370

1233 That one word *saved* is enough to make the heart dance as long as life remains. "Saved!" Let us hang out our banners and set the bells ringing. Saved! What a sweet sound it is to the man who is wrecked and sees the vessel going down, but at that moment discovers that the lifeboat is near and will rescue him from the sinking ship. To be snatched from the devouring fire, or saved from fierce disease, just when the turning point has come, and death appears imminent, these are also occasions for crying "Saved!" But to be rescued from sin and hell is a greater salvation still, and demands a louder joy. We will sing it in life and whisper it in death and chant it throughout eternity— *saved by the Lord!*—23.343, 344

1234 I have never despaired of the salvation of any man since the Lord saved me. I know no heart that God cannot win if he could conquer mine.—24.23

1235 I can bear personal witness that there is hardly a seat in this Tabernacle on which, at some time or another, there has not sat a seeking sinner who has found the Savior. If we marked these seats with golden stars where souls were saved, you would see here many footprints of grace, holy places which angels look on with delight.—26.583

1236 What we mean by salvation is this—deliverance from the love of sin, rescue from the habit of sin, setting free from the desire to sin.—29.449

¹²³⁷ Do you want sparing mercy? Mention him whom God did not spare in the great atoning day. Do you want restoring mercy? Plead him whom God brought again from the dead. Do you want to behold the light of Jehovah's countenance? Plead him who said (Matt 27:46), "Why hast thou forsaken me?"—37.214

¹²³⁸ I am glad that you have given your heart to Christ, but have you learned first this lesson—that he gave his heart for you? We do not find salvation by giving Christ anything. That is the fruit of it. But salvation comes by Christ giving us something. Something, did I say? By Christ giving us everything, by his giving us himself.—38.483, 484

¹²³⁹ God throws his whole self into the work of salvation. His little finger can create the stars and light them up or quench them at his will. But even his right arm is not sufficient for the redemption of his people. Both hands must bear the cruel nails, both feet must be fastened to the accursed tree, the heart of the Son of God must be pierced by the soldier's lance. He must come forth from the bosom of the Father and must descend, and still descend, and yet further descend, till he goes down to the lowest parts of the earth, there to work out the salvation of his people.—40.172

¹²⁴⁰ Human nature's way of salvation is, "Do, do, do." But God's way of salvation is, "Done, done; it is all done." You have but to rely by faith on the atonement which Christ accomplished on the cross.—43.191

¹²⁴¹ A man is never so "fit for believing" as when, in himself, he is most unfit. It is unfitness, not fitness, that is really required. What is fitness for being washed? Filth, and filth alone. What is fitness for receiving alms? Poverty, abject need. What is fitness for receiving pardon? Guilt, and only guilt. If you are guilty, if you are black, if you are foul, you have all the fitness that is required. So come and find in Jesus Christ all that meets your greatest and most urgent need.—49.476

¹²⁴² If I saw you at the very gates of hell—so long as you had not actually crossed the threshold—if I saw you trembling there, and you said to me, "Can Jesus Christ save me now?" I would reply, "Yes, my brother, look unto him, and he will take you from the gates of hell to the gates of heaven in a single moment."—52.154

¹²⁴³ I can certainly endorse Mr. Whitefield's remark, "Jesus Christ is willing to receive the devil's castaways."—53.165

¹²⁴⁴ Nine persons out of ten who go to a place of worship do not know the meaning of the Savior shedding his blood for the remis-

sion of sin. If you press them to tell you how it is that Christ saves, they will tell you that he did something or other by which God is able to forgive sin. Though the grand fact that Christ was actually punished in the place of his chosen people is as clear in the Scripture as noonday, they do not see it.—54.152

1245 Christ is the *A*, and he is the *Z* of the salvation alphabet. He is not only the helper of our salvation, but the God of it, the maker of it, the all-in-all of it. Have any of you a salvation which you have manufactured for yourselves? Then drop it overboard and row away from it as fast as you can, lest it should be a torpedo to work your ruin. The only salvation that can redeem from hell is a salvation which comes from heaven. Eternal salvation must come from an eternal God. Salvation that makes you a new creature must be the work of him who sits on the throne and makes all things new.—58.459

1246 Jesus Christ never saves us *in* our sins, he saves us *from* our sins. "Doctor," says the fool, "make me well, but I'd like to keep my fever." How can a man be saved from his sins while he clings to his sins? What is salvation but to be delivered from sin? Sin-lovers may seek to be saved, but they shall not be able.— 63.186

Salvation, excuses against

1247 "Oh," says one, "I would come to Christ, but I have been too great a sinner."

Self, sir. Your being a great sinner has nothing to do with that. Christ is a great Savior.

Another says, "But I do not feel it enough."

Self again. He does not ask you about your feelings. He simply says, "Look unto me and be ye saved" (Isa. 45:22).

"But sir, I cannot pray."

Self again. You are not to be saved by your prayers. You are to be saved by Christ. He will help you to pray afterwards.

"But," says another, "if I felt as So-and-so did."

Self again. Christ is where you are to look, not yourself.

"Yes," you say, "I think he would receive anybody but me."

Please, who gave you any permission to think at all in the matter? Does he not say, "Him that cometh to me, I will in no wise cast out" (John 6:37)? Why, you are thinking your soul into eternal ruin. Give up thinking, and *believe!*—4.278

1248 You need not trim and dress yourselves to come to Christ. Even your feelings are not the wedding garment. Come naked.

"But sir, I am so careless."
Come careless, then.
"But I am so hard-hearted."
Come hard-hearted, then.
"But I am so thoughtless."

Come thoughtless, then, and trust Christ now.—6.220

1249 "I have no good thing of my own" do you say? Here is every good thing in him.

"I have broken the law."

There is his blood for you. Believe in him; he will wash you.

"Oh, but I dare not."

Do him the honor to dare it.

"Oh, but it seems impossible."

Honor him by believing the impossibility, then.

"Oh, but how can he save such a wretch as I am?"

Christ is glorified in saving wretches.—7.382

1250 If you are never saved until you, an unpardoned sinner, have all objections answered, you will never be saved, because there are a thousand objections to the salvation of any man, which can only be met by one argument, and that is the blood of Jesus.—10.245

1251 "Oh," say you, "but my business occupies so much of my time."

Yes, but do you not know that very likely your business would go on better if you were right with God? Many a time a business goes wrong because the man is wrong. If religion does not make you richer, which it may not do, it will make you more contented with what you have.—36.20

1252 One said to me lately, "Oh, sir, I am the biggest sinner that ever lived!"

I replied, "Jesus Christ came into the world to save sinners" (1 Tim. 1:15).

"But I have not any strength."

"While we were yet without strength, in due time Christ died" (Rom. 5:6).

"Oh, but," he said, "I have been utterly ungodly."

"Christ died for the ungodly" (Rom. 5:6).

"But I am lost."

"Yes," I said, "The Son of Man has come to save that which was lost" (Luke 19:10). I said to this man, "You have the brush in your hand, and at every stroke it looks as if you were quoting Scripture."—38.272

1253 "But I have many sins."

He had many drops of blood.

"But I am a great sinner."

He is a great Savior.

"But I am so old."

Yes, but he can make you to be born again.

"But I have rejected him so often."

He will not reject you.

"But I am the last person in the world to be saved."

Then that is where Christ begins. He always begins at the last man.—51.273, 274

Salvation, urgency of   See Procras-
tination

1254 You stand over the mouth of hell on a single plank, and that plank is rotten. You hang over the jaws of perdition by a solitary rope, and the strands of that rope are snapping one by one. Frailer than the spider's web is your life, and yet that is the only thing which divides you from a world of despair. The slightest insect commissioned by God's providence may end your unhappy life.—10.678

1255 I will have no complicity in that atrocious treason against God's Word which leads men to believe that they may perhaps seek and find him in another state. I believe that of all falsehoods that ever were preached, this is the most dangerous, and likely to do the most hurt to men's souls.—43.440

Satan   *See Devil*

Satisfaction   *See Contentment; Peace; Rest, spiritual*

1256 No heart of a child of God will ever be satisfied with any object or person short of the Lord Jesus Christ. There is room for wife and children, there is room for friend and acquaintance, and all the more room in one's heart because Christ is there. But neither wife nor children nor friends nor kinsfolk can ever fill the believer's heart. He must have Christ Jesus. There is no rest for him elsewhere.—11.365

Science   *See Evolution*

1257 See how often science has altered its very basis. Science is notorious for being most scientific in destruction of all the science that has gone before it. I have sometimes indulged myself in reading ancient natural history, and nothing can be more comic. In twenty years' time some of us may probably find great amusement in the serious scientific teaching of the present hour, even as we do now in the systems of the last century. It may happen that in a little time the doctrine of evolution will be the standing jest of schoolboys.—37.46, 47

Scripture   *See Bible*

Second Coming   *See Prophecy*

1258 Tomorrow Christ may be on this earth, "for in such an hour as ye think not, the Son of Man cometh" (Matt. 24:44). Tomorrow all the glories of the millennial splendor may be revealed.—2.327

1259 Some think that this descent of the Lord will be postmillennial—that is, after the thousand years of his reign. I cannot think so. I conceive that the advent will be premillennial—that he will come first, and then will come the millennium as the result of his personal reign upon earth.—11.249

Note: The above two quotations state that the first event after Christ's return is the millennial reign. This strongly implies that CHS believed the church would pass through the tribula-

tion before the second coming. This would make him a premillennial posttribulationist. The last sentence in the final quotation under this same topic (from 55.318) also leads to this conclusion.

¹²⁶⁰ One reason why I think the world's present state will not wind up for the present is, because all the prophets say it will, and they have always been a lying generation. I mean the prophets who make the business profitable, who only use Scripture as the gypsy uses the cards, who shuffle texts to foretell fortunes for nations and men. We shall go on many a day yet. We may have to wait for another century, yes, another twenty centuries, perhaps. We cannot tell.—11.273

¹²⁶¹ To my great sorrow, I had sent to me this last week two or three copies of a tract purporting to have been written by myself, prophesying the coming of the Lord in the year 1866. Now, you may expect to hear of me being in Bedlam whenever, by my tongue or my pen, I give countenance to such rubbish. The Lord may come in 1866, and I shall be glad to see him, but I do not believe he will. And one reason why I don't believe he will is because all these false prophets say that he will. If they said he would not, I should begin to think he would. But inasmuch as they are all crying as one man that he will come in 1866 or

184

1867, I am inclined to think he will not come at any such time. It seems to me that there are a very great many prophecies which must be fulfilled before the coming of Christ, which will not be fulfilled in the next twelve months.—55.318

Security   *See Assurance; Perseverance*

¹²⁶² As for that sandy gospel which lets you fall away and then come back again, it is the wickedest falsehood on earth.—1.145

¹²⁶³ Take the Bible as it stands, and if you do not see everlasting love there, there is some fault in your eyes, and it is a case rather for the ophthalmic hospital than for me. If you cannot see everlasting, eternal security, blood-bought righteousness there, I am hopeless altogether of your conversion to the truth, while you read it with your present prejudices.—1.148

¹²⁶⁴ As for me, I so deeply believe in the immutable love of Jesus that I suppose that if one believer were to be in hell, Christ himself would not long stay in heaven, but would soon cry, "To the rescue! To the rescue!"—1.201

¹²⁶⁵ What! Did Christ at one tremendous draft of love drink my damnation dry, and shall I be damned after that? God forbid! What! Shall God be unrighteous to forget the Redeemer's work for

us and let the Savior's blood be shed in vain? Not hell itself has ever indulged the thought which has only been worthy of the men who are traitors to God's truth.— 3.272

1266 How can a believer perish if that Scripture be true which says that every believer is a member of Christ's body? If you will only grant me my head afloat above the water, I will give you permission to drown my fingers. Try it, you cannot do it. Christ, the head of the body, is in heaven, and until you can drown the head of the body, you cannot drown the body. And if the head be in heaven and beyond the reach of harm, then every member of the body is alive and secure, and shall at last be in heaven, too.—3.435

1267 I know a man who went so far as to say that although a man might have persevered through grace for sixty years, yet should he fall away the last year of his life, he would perish everlastingly, and all his faith and all the love which God had manifested to him would go for nothing. I am very happy to say that such a notion of God is just the very notion I have of the devil. I could not believe in such a God, and could not bow down before him.—5.422

1268 To suppose that the new nature could die out were to imagine that a member of Christ would die, that a finger, a hand, an arm could rot from the person of Jesus, that he could be maimed and divided. Does not the apostle say (1 Cor. 1:13), "Is Christ divided?" And was it not written, "A bone of him shall not be broken" (John 19:36)?—7.406

1269 Satan took David into the sin of lust, and he found that God would not curse him there, but bless him with a sorrowful chastisement and with a deep repentance. He took Peter into the sin of denying his Master, and he denied him with oaths and curses. But the Lord would not curse him even there, but turned and looked on Peter with a look of love that made him weep bitterly.—7.470

1270 If my good works had put me into Christ, then my bad works might turn me out of him. But since he put me in when I was a sinner, vile and worthless, he will never take me out, though I am a sinner vile and worthless still.— 8.538

1271 We detest the doctrine that a man who has once believed in Jesus will be saved even if he altogether forsook the path of obedience. We deny that such a turning aside is possible to the true believer. No, beloved, a man, if he be indeed a believer in Christ, will not live after the will of the flesh. When he does fall into sin, it will be his grief and misery, and he will never rest till he is cleansed from guilt. But I

185

will say this of the believer, that if he could live as he would like to live, he would live a perfect life.—23.362, 363

1272 Someone said to me "That man has fallen from grace and has been regenerated three times."

"Oh," I said to him, "you need a new word then—re-re-regenerated." I have heard of the new birth, but never of the newer birth. I have heard of being born again, but never of being born again and again and again. I discover no trace of it in the Word of God.—27.483

1273 Nothing binds me to my Lord like a strong belief in his changeless love.

"Oh, but it would be far safer to tell your hearers that they may be overcome by sin and perish!"

I will not tell them what I do not believe. I will not dishonor my Lord by a falsehood. Shall I come to your house and tell your children that if they disobey you, they will cease to be your children? If I were to propound that doctrine, your children would grow angry at such a slander on their father.—35.695

1274 I wonder whether there is any man here who once declared and probably believed that he was a Christian, but who has now given up even the name of Christian. If so, my friend, one of two things is true concerning you—either you never were converted at all, and so have been a mere professor, or else, if you ever were truly converted, you will have to come back again.—52.92

1275 It is a sweet thought to me that even Satan himself can never rob me of my pardon. I may lose my copy of it, and lose my comfort from it, but the original pardon is filed in heaven.—57.283

1276 Did he ordain them to eternal life, and shall they perish? Did he engrave their names on his heart, and shall those names be blotted out? Did he give them to his Son to be his heritage, and shall his Son lose his portion? Did he say, "They shall be mine in the day when I make up my jewels" (Mal. 3:17), and shall he part with them?—57.608

Self-righteousness   See Hypocrite; Pride; Works

1277 I have heard of an army, who, being defeated in battle, endeavored to make good a retreat. The soldiers fled to a certain river, where they expected to find a bridge across which they could retreat and be in safety. But when they came to the stream, there was heard a shriek of terror—"The bridge is broken, the bridge is broken!" All in vain was that cry, for the multitude hurrying on behind pressed upon those that were before and forced them into the river, until the stream was glutted with the bodies of drowned men.

Such must be the fate of the self-righteous. You thought there was a bridge of ceremonies, that baptism, confirmation, and the Lord's Supper made up the solid arches of a bridge of good works and duties. But when you come to die, there shall be heard the cry, "The bridge is broken, the bridge is broken!" It will be in vain for you to turn round then.—5.5

1278 Ever since man became a sinner he has been self-righteous. When he had a righteousness of his own he never gloried in it, but ever since he lost it, he has pretended to be the possessor of it. Martin Luther said he scarcely ever preached a sermon without inveighing against the righteousness of man, and yet, he said, "I find that still I cannot preach it down."—7.17

1279 Nothing can damn a man but his own righteousness; nothing can save him but the righteousness of Christ.—7.216

1280 I do not know of anything against which God's fury burns more than against this, because this touches him in a very tender point—it insults the glory and honor of his Son, Jesus Christ.—9.187

1281 Beware of self-righteousness. The black devil of licentiousness destroys his hundreds, but the white devil of self-righteousness destroys his thousands.—18.444

1282 Self-righteousness is as much an insult to God as blasphemy.—18.506

1283 You may as easily be lost religiously as irreligiously, unless your religion is God's religion and is based on faith in his dear Son.—24.414

1284 There is no venom in the heart of dissolute, debauched men against Christianity that is at all comparable to the poison of asps which lies in the heart of the self-righteous man.—25.561

1285 It is easier to save us from our sins than from our righteousness. Our self-righteousness is that hideous boa constrictor which seems to coil itself round and round our spirit, and to crush out of us all the life that would receive the gospel of the grace of God.—30.489

1286 Conceit of our own righteousness sticks to us as the skin to the flesh. Sooner may the leopard lose his spots than the proud man his self-righteousness.—32.256

1287 The man who clings to his own righteousness is like a man who grasps a millstone to prevent himself from sinking in the flood. Your righteousness will damn you if you trust in it as surely as will your sins, for it is a false, proud lie.—42.78

1288 You know the old story of dear Mr. Hervey, who said to the godly plowman, "Ah, John, it is wonderful when God overcomes sinful self!"

"Yes, Mr. Hervey," answered the plowman, "but it is a greater wonder when he overcomes righteous self."

And so it is. It is easy for the Lord to save a sinner, but it is impossible for a self-righteous man to be saved.—42.90, 91

1289 "As many lives as a cat," and I am sure that self-righteousness has many more lives than that. It is the hardest thing in the world to kill.—44.519

1290 Some of us had, once, a comfortable competence laid by in the Bank of Self-righteousness, and we meant to draw it out when we came to die, and thought we should even have a little spending money for our old age out of the interest which was paid us in the coin of self-conceit. But the bank broke long ago, and now we have not so much as a farthing of our own merits left us, nor a chance of ever having any. And what is worse, we are deeply in debt, and we have nothing to pay. We are insolvent debtors to the justice of God, and unless we are freely forgiven, we must be cast into prison and lie there forever.—53.243

1291 The greatest enemy to human souls is the self-righteous spirit which makes men look to themselves for salvation.—55.146

Separation   *See Worldliness*

Service   *See Ministry*

1292 He is no Christian who does not seek to serve his God. The very motto of the Christian should be "I serve."—5.146

1293 I want every member of this church to be a worker. We do not want any drones. If there are any of you who want to eat and drink and do nothing, there are plenty of places elsewhere where you can do it. There are empty pews about in abundance; go and fill them, for we do not want you.—13.599

1294 I think no servant of God is tired of serving his Master. We may be tired *in* the service, though not tired *of* it.—15.464

1295 I think I know of no delight on earth that is higher than that of knowing that you really are with all your heart adoringly serving God.—15.473

1296 I do believe it is before every Christian either to serve his God with all his heart, or to fall into sin. I believe we must either go forward, or we must fall. The rule is in Christian life, if we do not bring forth fruit unto the Lord our God, we shall lose even our leaves, and stand like a winter's tree, bare and withered.—15.576

1297 As an arrow which falls short of the mark, as a fig tree which yields no figs, as a candle which smokes but yields no light, as a cloud without rain and a well without water, is a man who has not served the Lord. He has led a wasted life—a life to which the flower and glory of existence are lacking. Call it not life at all, but write it down as animated death.—22.302, 303

1298 As long as there is breath in our bodies, let us serve Christ. As long as we can think, as long as we can speak, as long as we can work, let us serve him. Let us even serve him with our last gasp. And, if it be possible, let us try to set some work going that will glorify him when we are dead and gone. Let us scatter some seed that may spring up when we are sleeping beneath the hillock in the cemetery.—40.34

Note: These words were uttered on November 3, 1889. It is gratifying to look back and see how the Lord has been pleased to fulfill the desire CHS expressed in those last two sentences. Still today the seed he scattered is bearing abundant fruit!

1299 He can scarcely be thought to be a Christian, except in name, who lives from week to week with no more spirituality than that which enables him to go sometimes to the house of prayer, but who, neither by his powers nor his gifts nor his time nor by any other means, ever does service to the Lord his God.—57.535

1300 When the physician told John Calvin that he must cease from working so much or he would die because he had a complication of painful diseases, he replied, "Would you have my Master come and find me loitering?"

Oh, it was well said, Master Calvin! It were well said, too, if we could all say it. What have you done for Christ?—58.478

Session, Jesus'   *See Heaven*

1301 Christ is always described in heaven as sitting down. This seems to me to be one material argument for the salvation of the believer—Christ sits in heaven. Now, he never would sit if the work were not fully done.—5.252

Sex, abuse of   *See Fornication; Homosexuality*

1302 I have heard it sometimes said by wicked men that it is unjust that God should condemn men for the use of the powers which he himself has given them. This most subtle evil has often grieved the hearts of those who are weak and ignorant, and have not seen its untruthfulness, for to speak plainly of it, it is a gross lie.

God does not condemn men for the use of the powers he has given them. He condemns them for the misuse of those powers. Not for employing them, but for employing them as they ought not to employ them. Not for thinking, not for speaking, not for doing, but for thinking, speaking, and doing contrary to his law.—3.325

1303 Woe unto the men who lead women astray! I have heard of sailors who, in every port they enter, try to ruin others. I charge you to remember that you will have to face these ruined ones at the day of judgment. You sailed away, and they never knew where you went. But the Lord knew. It may be when you lie in hell, eyes will find you out, and a voice will cry aloud, "Are you here? You are the man that led me to perdition!" You will have to keep everlasting company with those whom you dragged down to hell, and these will forever curse you to your face.

May God grant that you may be stopped altogether, and instead of lusting to pollute others, may you have a desire to save them! May God grant that the channel of evil may be blocked for you, and may you be piloted into the waters of repentance and faith!—37.295

Sickness *See Healing; Pain; Suffering; Trials*

1304 I doubt not that many sickbeds in England are doing more for Christ than our pulpits. Oh, what showers of blessings come down in answer to the prayers and tears of poor godly invalids, whose weakness is their strength, and whose sickness is their opportunity!—15.450

1305 I have often looked gratefully back to my sick chamber. I am certain that I never did grow in grace one-half so much anywhere as I have upon the bed of pain.—17.318

1306 I should not like to have lived forty years in this world without ever having suffered sickness. When I met with a man that never had an ache or a pain or a day's sickness in his life, I used to envy him. But I do not now, because I feel very confident that he is a loser by his unvarying experience. How can a man sympathize with trouble that he never knew? How can he be tender in heart if he has never been touched with infirmity himself? If one is to be a comforter to others, he must know the sorrows and the sicknesses of others in his measure. It was essential to our Lord, and certainly what was essential to him is necessary to those who are to be shepherds of others, as he was.—21.622

1307 I think that health is the greatest blessing that God ever sends us, except sickness, which is far better. I would give anything to be perfectly healthy, but if I had to go over my time again, I could not get on without those sickbeds and those bitter pains and those weary, sleepless nights. Oh, the blessedness that comes to us through suffering!—38.179

1308 It is an atrocious lie that some have uttered when they have said that the sickness is a consequence of the sufferer's sin. I could not select, out of heaven, choicer spirits than some whom I know who have not for twenty years left their bed, and they have lived nearer to God than any of us, and have brought to him more glory than any of us. Although we deeply sympathize with them, we might almost covet their suffering, because God is so greatly glorified in them. All over the world there is a brave band of these burden-bearers.—49.208

Signs *See Revelation, modern*

1309 God has given us more than his word, he has given us his oath. And yet strange is it that we who profess to be his children are vile enough to distrust our own Father. And sometimes if he does not give us signs and evidences, we begin to distrust him, so that after all I am afraid we rather trust the signs than trust God, and put more confidence in evidences than we do in the naked promise, which is an atrocious sin indeed. Many believers cannot be comfortable without signs and evidences.—10.263

Sin *See Carnality; Confession; Conviction; Depravity; Guilt; Heart; Nature, human*

1310 Is sin so luscious that you will burn in hell forever for it?—5.448

1311 You may best measure the sin by the punishment. Depend on it, God will not put his creatures to a single pang more of pain than justice absolutely demands. God does not stretch his creature on the rack like a tyrant; he will give him but what he deserves. And perhaps even when God's wrath is fiercest against sin, he does not punish the sinner so much as his sin might warrant. There will not be a grain more of wormwood in the cup of the lost than naked justice absolutely requires. Then, O my God, if thy creatures are to be cast into a lake that burns with fire and brimstone, if into a pit that is bottomless lost souls must be driven, then what a hideous thing sin must be! I cannot understand that torture, therefore, I cannot understand the guilt that deserves it.—6.106

1312 Doubtless every sin is a God-provoking thing. It stirs him to jealousy. As the blood of Abel cried "Vengeance," so does sin. It is a thorn in the side of justice, a stab at the heart of truth. God's great patience is expended at a tremendous rate by the sins of men.—9.675

1313 Sin is the mother and nurse of all evil, the egg of all mischief, the fountain of bitterness, the root of misery. Here you have the distilled essence of hell, the quintessence, as the old theologians would say, of everything that is unlovely, disreputable, dishonest, impure, abominable—in a word—damnable.—11.134

1314 Out with your knife, man, and cut the throat of every iniquity. Why, there is no sin for which it is worth your while to be damned.—11.307

1315 A genuine Christian dreads sin. He will not say, "Is it not a little one?" for he knows that a little sin is like a small dose of a very potent poison. It is sufficient to destroy our peace and comfort.—12.354

1316 The very least offense against God is so intolerable, that if hell fire were put out, one sin could kindle it again.—12.569

1317 There is no water so deep but fish will swim in it, no pond so foul but frogs will live in it, no mire so filthy but swine will wallow in it, and no sin so damnable but man will commit it.—14.113

1318 Sin, indeed, is hell, hell in embryo, hell in essence, hell kindling, hell emerging from the shell. Hell is but sin when it has manifested and developed itself to the full.—14.556, 557

1319 Sin is like the bale of goods which came from the east to this city in the olden time, which brought the pest in it. Probably it was but a small bale, but yet it contained in it the deaths of hundreds of the inhabitants of London.—16.691

1320 Atlas with the world on his back had a light load compared with a sinner on whom the mountains of sin and wrath are piled.—17.15

1321 It were to be worse than damned to be happy in sin.—17.699

1322 Hell itself is not more horrible than sin. No vision ghastly and grim can ever be so terrible to the spiritual eye as the hideous, loathsome thing called sin.—18.484

1323 "Sin," says Thomas Brooks, "is the only thing that God abhors. It brought Christ to the cross, it damns souls, it shuts heaven, it laid the foundations of hell."—19.77

1324 This day, my God, I hate sin not because it damns me, but because it has done thee wrong. To have grieved my God is the worst grief to me.—19.79

1325 Did you ever find a spider's nest just when the young spiders have all come to life? It is a city of spiders. Now, such is any one sin. It is a colony of iniquities, a living mass of offense. You have but to stir it, and you will see countless sins running out of it. It is an aggregation of evils.—20.545

1326 It were better to die a thousand times than to sin.—22.706

1327 The same sins which put our Lord to death will put us to death if they can. O child of God, you never sin without injuring yourself. The smallest sin that ever creeps into your heart is a robber seeking to kill and to destroy. You never profited by sin, and never can. No, it is poison, deadly poison to your spirit. You know that it injures your faith, destroys your enjoyment, withers up your peace, weakens you in prayer, and prevents your example being beneficial to others.—23.106

1328 Sin is worse than the devil, for sin made the devil a devil. He would have been an angel if it had not been for sin.—25.380

1329 Sin! This casts darkness on the sun, eclipsing its meridian light. Sin is the blast which withers all the flowers of life. Sin is the gall of bitterness. A drop of it would turn an ocean of pleasure into wormwood. Sin would again blight paradise, could it be restored. It would turn heaven into hell, could it enter there. Sin is a burden which an awakened conscience cannot bear; it crushes the spirit into the dust and threatens to bear it down, even to the lowest hell.—32.327

1330 A mouse was caught by its tail in a trap the other day, and the poor creature went on eating the cheese. Many men are doing the same. They know that they are guilty, and they dread their punishment, but they go on nibbling at their beloved sins.—32.480

1331 We could bear disease if we were cured of sin. We could bear the world's troubles if there were not these spiritual sorrows. We could be content to pine in prison on bread and water all the rest of our natural lives if we could be clear from sin. I warrant you that the darkest dungeon would be a bright paradise to a believer, if there he could be exempt from the temptation, from the remembrance, and from the presence of sin.—32.518

1332 A sin may be compared to a honeycomb. There are as many sins within one sin as there are cells within a piece of comb. Sin is a swarming, hiving, teeming thing. You can never estimate its full vileness, nor perceive all its evil bearings. All sorts of sin may hide away in one sin. It would puzzle all the theologians in the world to tell which sin was absent from Adam's first offense. I could take any point you choose, and show that Adam sinned in that direction. Sin is a multitudinous evil, an aggregate of all manner of filthiness, a chain with a thousand deadly links. A sinner is like a man possessed with the devil who cries, "My name is Legion, for we are many" (Mark 5:9). It is one in evil, and yet countless in forms.—32.545

¹³³³ Sin seems all the greater because it was committed against a sin-forgiving God.—32.550

¹³³⁴ You do not know all the pollution of sin unless you have been made to feel yourself to be a polluted thing. If you had fifty leprosies, they would not pollute you like sin, for a poor leper is not really polluted. He may bear a grand and noble soul within that rotting body. Sin alone is real pollution, hellish pollution, abominable pollution. There is nothing in hell that is worse than sin.—32.705

¹³³⁵ I recollect a minister speaking very unguardedly. He said that the child of God lost nothing by sin except his comfort. I thought, "Oh, dear me! Is that nothing?" It is such a loss of comfort that if that were all, it would be the most awful thing in the world. The more God loves you, and the more you love God, the more expensive will you find it to sin. An ordinary sinner sins cheaply; the child of God sins very dearly.—34.416

¹³³⁶ Sin is Christicide.—36.213

¹³³⁷ I come not here to be a fiddler at your feast of sin. I would not set the tune for you to dance by. My music is of another sort. It is a certain sound, which calls you to do battle for your lives against your sins.—36.466

¹³³⁸ Sin! We cannot get away from it. We know more of it than of our most familiar friend. It meets us everywhere, and in everything. Sin! It is the history of humanity. It is the history of the Bible, for why else was it written? It is the history of this building; why else was it built? It is the history of the ordinances of worship; why else were they instituted? Best of all, it is the history of the Christ of God.—37.557, 558

¹³³⁹ Alas, alas! If we had to deal with sane men, our preaching would be easy. But sin is a madness, such a madness that, when men are bitten by it, they would not be persuaded even though one should rise from the dead.—50.467

¹³⁴⁰ I am not so much afraid of dying as I am of sinning; that is ten times worse than death.—42.558

¹³⁴¹ Often that sin of which men think the least, God thinks the most. That spiritual sin of which some say, "Oh, that is a mere trifle!"—that forgetting of the Creator, that ignoring of the only Redeemer—this is the sin of sins, the damning sin which kindles the flames of hell.—43.451

¹³⁴² Even to speak against some sins is to help to spread them. It is dangerous work to handle gunpowder. And even when we need to move it from the magazine, we feel that we must do it with great fear and trembling.—46.341

1343 We can honestly say we would sooner suffer every pain of which the body is capable than we would willfully commit sin. It grates on our ear, it galls our mind, it frets our heart, it aggravates all our spiritual senses. Sin is to us more horrible than death, more diabolical than the devil, more hellish than hell itself, for the pains of hell would lose their sharpness if it were not that sin is the undying worm that causes them.—46.343

1344 It is not the nature of sin to remain in a fixed state. Like decaying fruit, it grows more rotten. The man who is bad today will be worse tomorrow. Every week that he lives, he adds some new evil habit to all that he had before, until the chain, which at first seemed but a silken cord, becomes at last an adamantine fetter, in which he is held fast so that he cannot escape. It is impossible to say how far men will wander away from God!—49.111

1345 A criminal is a person who offends against the laws of men. A "sinner" is a theological term, signifying one who offends against the laws of God. People say, "To be criminals—oh, that is horrible! But to be sinners—well, we are all sinners." They do not appear to think anything of that terrible truth. But unless the grace of God shall change you, the day will come when you will think it would have been better to have been a frog, a toad, a viper, or any other creature, rather than to have been a sinner, for, next to the word *devil,* there is no word which has so much that is dreadful in it as that word *sinner.*—50.311

1346 In the least sin there is more evil than there is even in hell, for hell is at least the vindication of divine justice. But sin defies that justice. Sin is an unlimited and unmitigated evil.—55.354

1347 We can measure the Alps, the Andes have been scaled, but the mountains of sin no man has ever measured yet. They pierce the clouds. Can you think of the mountains of your sin, beloved? Reckon them all up since your birth—sins of childhood, youth, manhood, and riper years; your sins against the gospel and against the law; sins with the body and sins with the mind; sins of every shape and form. What a mountain range they make! And you were on one side of that mountain, and God was on the other. What a distance! An impassable mountain sundered you from your God. It has all gone now. The mountains have sunk into the sea, our transgressions have all gone, but oh, what mountains they were but a little while ago!—62.38

Sin, besetting

1348 There was a man who used to get drunk, and he said that it was his besetting sin. But his

195

brother said, "No, it is your upsetting sin." And so it was. If I were to know that there were thieves at night, yet I walked out on purpose to meet them, you could not say that they had beset me. You would say that I was a fool to walk into their hands. The besetting sin is that which a man fights against and wars against with all his soul, yet he is overcome by it.—42.269

Sin, confession of   *See Confession*

Sin, conviction of   *See Conviction*

Sin, hardening effects of   *See Heart; Heart, hardness of*

1349 The first sin which came into the world hardened man's heart in a most terrific manner, so that he dared to excuse himself and even to charge God as being indirectly the author of his sin, by giving him the woman (Gen. 3:12). He would never have been content with an apron of fig leaves if he had known the full measure of his degradation.—11.158

Sin, original

1350 Some say that children learn sin by imitation. But no, take a child away, place it under the most pious influences, let the very air it breathes be purified by piety, let it constantly drink in drafts of holiness, let it hear

nothing but the voice of prayer and praise, let its ear be always kept in tune by notes of sacred song, and that child may still become one of the grossest of transgressors. Though placed apparently on the very road to heaven, it shall, if not directed by divine grace, march downward to the pit.—1.152

1351 Any man who declares children to be born perfect never was a father. Your child without evil? You without eyes, you mean!—11.104

1352 You never need educate any man into sin. As soon as the young crocodile has left its shell, it begins to act just like its parents, and to bite at the stick which broke the shell. The serpent is scarcely born before it rears itself and begins to hiss. The young tiger may be nurtured in your parlor, but it will develop before long the same thirst for blood as if it were in the forest. So is it with man. He sins as naturally as the young lion seeks for blood or the young serpent stores up venom. Sin is in his very nature that taints his inmost soul.—13.53

1353 An officer in India had tamed a leopard. From the time when it was a kitten he had brought it up, till it went about the house like a cat, and everybody played with it. But he was sitting in his chair one day asleep, and the leopard licked his hand. But as he licked, the skin was broken, and the taste of blood came to the leopard. It rushed forth to kill, and was no more at ease till it reached the jungle. That leopard, though tamed, was a leopard still. So a man, sobered by moral motives but unchanged in heart, is a fallen man still, and the taste of blood, I mean the taste of sin, will soon reveal the tiger in him.—31.54

1354 It may be said that original sin is not our burden, but Adam's. But the burden of the father, if he brings the whole household into poverty, becomes the burden of the family. If the head should ache, it is no use for the hand to say, "It is no business of mine."—59.242

Sin, power of

1355 It would be an awful experiment to set a house on fire, intending to let it burn just so much and no more. Can you say to the fire, "This far you shall come, and no farther"? If you could say it to fire among standing corn, blown by the wind, yet you would say it in vain to sin. Sin swiftly grows from a pygmy to a giant, and, ever increasing in its awful power, it crushes down the man who is in its grip and holds him under its dreadful sway.—43.462

Sin, unpardonable

1356 "I believe I have committed the unpardonable sin," someone says.

My dear brother, I believe you have not. I want you to call one thing to remembrance, and that is that the unpardonable sin is a sin which is unto death. Now a sin which is unto death means a sin which brings death on the conscience. The man who commits it never has any conscience afterwards; he is dead there. Now, you have some feeling. You have enough life to wish to be saved from sin. You have enough life to long to be washed in the precious blood of Jesus. You have not committed the unpardonable sin. Therefore, have hope.— 11.575

Sincerity   *See Honesty; Hypocrite*

1357 Do not tell me that if you are sincere it will little matter which way you take. You know better. If you sincerely believe that you are going to St. Paul's or to London Bridge when you leave this Tabernacle and turn to the right, you will probably find yourselves at Clapham or at Tooting, but not at St. Paul's or London Bridge, with all your sincerity of misbelief. The sincere belief that you will be saved by your good works will by no means avert your damnation if you persist in refusing to trust in Jesus Christ.—15.664

Singing   See Music

Sinner   See Sin

Slander   See Gossip; Honesty; Lying

1358 I am quite certain that the safest way to defend your character is never to say a word about it. If every person in this place chooses to slander me and utter the most furious libels that he pleases, he may rest quite assured he will never have a lawsuit from me. I am not quite fool enough for that.—4.228

1359 The more prominent you are in Christ's service, the more certain are you to be the butt of calumny. I have long ago said farewell to my character. I lost it in the earlier days of my ministry by being a little more zealous than suited a slumbering age. And I have never been able to regain it except in the sight of him who judges all the earth, and in the hearts of those who love me for my work's sake.—11.484

1360 God had a Son that had no fault, but he never had a son that was not found fault with. God himself was slandered in paradise by Satan. Let us not expect, therefore, to escape from the venomous tongue.—18.115

Slavery

1361 From this evil, good Lord, deliver us. If Manchester merchants and Liverpool traders have a share in this guilt, at least let the church be free of this hell-filling crime. Men have tried hard to make the Bible support this sum of all villainies, but slavery, the thing which defiles the Great Republic, such slavery is quite unknown to the Word of God, and by the laws of the Jews it was impossible that it ever could exist. I have known men quote texts as excuses for being damned, and I do not wonder that men can find Scripture to justify them in buying and selling the souls of men.—6.155

Sorrow   See Grief

Soul Winning   See Evangelism

Sovereignty   See Calvinism; Election; Predestination; Will, free

1362 Is there a man here who kicks against divine sovereignty? It is a testing doctrine, and if he does not receive it, it shows that his pride is not out of him.—1.228

1363 There is no attribute of God more comforting to his children than the doctrine of divine sovereignty. On the other hand, there is no doctrine more hated by worldlings, no truth of which they have made such a football, as the great, stupendous, but yet most certain doctrine of the sovereignty of the infinite Jehovah.—2.185

1364 Most men quarrel with this. But mark, the thing that you complain of in God is the very thing that you love in yourselves.

Every man likes to feel that he has a right to do with his own as he pleases. We all like to be little sovereigns. Oh, for a spirit that bows always before the sovereignty of God.—4.82

1365 If I was asked, "Why is a man damned?" I should answer as an Arminian answers, "He destroys himself." I should not dare to lay man's ruin at the door of divine sovereignty. On the other hand, if I were asked, "Why is a man saved?" I could only give the Calvinistic answer, "He is saved through the sovereign grace of God, and not at all of himself." I should not dream of ascribing the man's salvation in any measure to himself.—22.6

1366 Opposition to divine sovereignty is essentially atheism. Men have no objection to a god who is really no God, a god who shall be the subject of caprice, who shall be a servile follower of their will, who shall be under their control. But a God who speaks and it is done, who commands and it stands fast, a God who does as he will among the armies of heaven and among the inhabitants of this lower world, such a God as this they cannot endure. And yet, is it not essential to the very being of God that he should be absolute and supreme? Certainly to the scriptural conception of God, sovereignty is an absolute necessity.—56.292, 293

1367 No doctrine in the whole Word of God has more excited the hatred of mankind than the truth of the absolute sovereignty of God. The fact that "the Lord reigneth" is indisputable, and it is this fact that arouses the utmost opposition in the unrenewed human heart.—58.13

Spirit, Holy   *See Holy Spirit*

Spiritual Gifts   *See Knowledge, spiritual gift of*

Stewardship   *See Giving; Money; Tithing; Wealth*

1368 No man has anything of his own, except his sins.—4.81

1369 There have been many who would do well if they would learn that they have nothing beyond what God has given them. And the more God has given them, the more they are in debt!—5.298

1370 A certain lady, being accosted by a beggar who asked charity of her, gave him a shilling, saying, "Take that shilling; it is more than God ever gave me."
The beggar said, "O madam, but God has given you all your abundance."
"No," said she, "I am right. God has only loaned me what I have. All I have is a loan."—8.631

Substitution   *See Atonement; Blood, Christ's; Cross; Death, Christ's*

1371 Christ, when the sinner is brought to the bar, appears there himself. There stands the man

199

whose hands are pierced; he stands numbered with transgressors. Let the trial proceed. What is the accusation? He stands to answer it. He points to his side, his hands, his feet, and challenges justice to bring anything against the sinners whom he represents.—8.377

1372 In one word, the great fact on which the Christian's hope rests is *substitution*. The vicarious sacrifice of Christ for the sinner, Christ's suffering for the sinner, Christ's being made sin for us that we might be made the righteousness of God in him, Christ offering up a true and proper substitutionary sacrifice in the place of as many as the Father gave him, who are recognized by their trusting in him—this is the cardinal fact of the gospel.—12.280

1373 There is no doctrine that fires my soul with such delight as that of substitution.—12.320

✷ 1374 In the French Revolution there was a young man condemned to the guillotine and shut up in one of the prisons. He was greatly loved by many, but there was one who loved him more than all put together. It was his own father. When the lists were called, the father, whose name was exactly as his son's, answered. And the father rode in the gloomy tumbril out to the place of execution. His head rolled beneath the ax instead of his son's, a victim to mighty love. See here an image of the love of Christ to sinners.—13.211

1375 Substitution is the very marrow of the whole Bible, the soul of salvation, the essence of the gospel. We ought to saturate all our sermons with it, for it is the lifeblood of a gospel ministry.—17.544

1376 I am incapable of moving one inch away from the old faith. One thing I know—the gospel of substitution. And one thing I do—preach it.—23.503

1377 If you put away the doctrine of the substitutionary sacrifice of Christ, you have disembowelled the gospel, and torn from it its very heart.—23.571

1378 Others may preach as they will, but as for this pulpit, it shall always resound with the substitution of Christ.—33.374

1379 Let us cling to the great truth of the vicarious sacrifice, which is the chief teaching of this sacred book. Take this away, and I do not see anything left in the Bible at all which can be called good news.—35.147, 148

1380 You notice that I am always preaching that doctrine of substitution. I cannot help it, because it is the only truth that brought me comfort. I should never have come out of the dungeon of despair if it had not been for that grand truth of substitution.—39.245

1381 An ancient king enacted a law against a certain crime, and the punishment of anyone who committed the crime was that he should have both eyes put out. His own son committed the crime. The king, as a strict judge, said, "I cannot alter the law; I have said that the loss of two eyes shall be the penalty. Take out one of mine and one of his." So he strictly carried out the law. But at the same time, he was able to have mercy in part upon his son.

But the case of Christ goes further than that. He did not say, "Exact half the penalty from me, and half from the sinner." He said, "Put both my eyes out. Nail me to the tree. Let me die. Let me take all the guilt away, and then the sinner may go free."—45.152

1382 I have done with Christianity, I have done with the Bible, I have done with all preaching, if you can once convince me that the substitution of Christ is not a fact. This truth is, to me, the kernel, the core, the marrow, the vital essence of the gospel. With this remedy in my hands I can turn despair into confidence. But take this away, and there remains nothing for me to preach to the despondent and the despairing.—50.283

1383 If you have any question about that great truth, you will have your brain more or less muddled concerning every other doctrine in the Word of God. And I would take this doctrine, just as I would the doctrine of justification by faith, as being the test of a standing or falling church, and of a God-sent ministry.—52.218

1384 I pray God that every stone of this Tabernacle may tumble to its ruin and every timber be shivered to atoms, before there should stand on this platform a man to preach who denies the substitutionary sacrifice of Jesus Christ, or who even keeps it in the background, for this is our watchword.—56.129

1385 If Christ, who was God's Son, suffered so bitterly for sins that were not his own, how bitterly must you, who are not God's sons but God's enemies, suffer for sins that are your own? And you must so suffer unless Christ, the substitute, stands for you.—59.608

Suffering   *See Affliction; Grief; Pain; Persecution; Sickness; Sympathy; Trials*

1386 Men will never become great in theology until they become great in suffering. Said Luther, "Affliction is the best book in my library."—4.461

1387 I met in one of Samuel Rutherford's letters an extraordinary expression, where he speaks of the coals of divine wrath all falling on the head of Christ, so

201

that not one might fall on his people. "And yet," says he, "if one of those coals should drop from his head on mine and did utterly consume me, yet if I felt it was a part of the coals that fell on him, and I was bearing it for his sake and in communion with him, I would choose it for my heaven."—10.137

1388 Better to be taught by suffering than to be taught by sin! Better to lie in God's dungeon than to revel in the devil's palace.—12.438

1389 Suffering is infinitely preferable to sinning. The Lord may therefore send us sorrow to keep us from iniquity.—28.459

1390 There is no learning sympathy except by suffering. It cannot be studied from a book, it must be written on the heart. You must go through the fire if you would have sympathy with others who tread the glowing coals. You must yourself bear the cross if you would feel for those whose life is a burden to them.—32.590

1391 When the pangs shoot through our body, and ghastly death appears in view, people see the patience of the dying Christian. Our infirmities become the black velvet on which the diamond of God's love glitters all the more brightly. Thank God I can suffer! Thank God I can be made the object of shame and contempt, for in this way God shall be glorified.—52.80

Suffering, Jesus' *See Atonement; Substitution*

1392 Christ died, not for one sinner, but tens of thousands, for multitudes whom no man can number. Think, then, what must have been the crushing blows which Jehovah laid on him when those strokes were inflicted to satisfy divine justice for the sins, the crimes, the transgressions of ten thousand times ten thousand of those for whom he died.—59.307

Suicide *See Murder*

1393 He that commits suicide to get out of trouble leaps into the gulf to escape from the water, drowns himself to prevent himself from getting wet, leaps into the fire because he is scorched.—7.528

1394 That crime of all crimes most sure of damnation if a man commit it willfully and in his sound mind, I mean the crime of self-murder.—22.701

Sunday *See Lord's Day; Sabbath*

Sympathy *See Compassion; Sickness; Suffering; Trials; Trouble*

1395 There are none so tender as those who have been skinned themselves.—4.461

Teaching *See Catechism; Children, teaching of; Music*

1396 How hard it is sometimes to state a fact which you perfectly understand yourself in such a way that another man may see it. It is like a telescope. There are many persons who are disappointed with a telescope, because whenever they walk into an observatory and put their eyes to the glass, expecting to see the rings of Saturn and the belts of Jupiter, they have said, "A piece of glass and a grain or two of dust is all I can see!"

"But," says the astronomer, "I can see Saturn in all its glory." Why cannot you? Because the focus does not suit the stranger's eye. By a little skill, the focus can be altered so that the observer may be able to see what he could not see before. So is it with language; it is a sort of telescope by which I enable another to see my thoughts, but I cannot always give him the right focus. The Holy Spirit always gives the right focus to every truth.—6.233

1397 If in doubt, this should be the test of the doctrine: Does it glorify Christ? This should be the test of all our opinions: Do they glorify Christ?—60.594

Temper   *See Anger*

Temptation   *See Trials*

1398 To sin without temptation is to sin like the devil, for the devil was not tempted when he sinned.—5.189

1399 Holy Scripture is full of narratives of temptations. Expect, therefore, Christian, that your life will be as abundantly garnished with them as is a rose with thorns.—12.253

1400 Earnest Christian men are not so much afraid of trials as of temptations. The great horror of a Christian is sin.—15.653

1401 Keep clear of Lucifer's matches. You have got enough mischief in your heart without going where you will get more. If anybody feels that he is so very gracious and good that he can safely enter into temptation, I am sure that he is laboring under a very great mistake. I would say to him, "Brother, there is devil enough in you without your sending out invitation cards to seven more. Go to him who casts out devils."—23.143

1402 I have known what it is to escape from a strong temptation without falling into it. And I think that I have felt as grateful to God as a man would be who had seen a shark after him, had been almost between its jaws, and had just slipped away as he heard the monster close his mouth with a snap. I remember standing under a building which was in course of erection and seeing a mass of stone fall from a great height just in front of me. What a thud it made! How narrow was my escape! How I started! But what joy filled my heart! So it is when one is delivered from temptation which began to overpower the heart.—31.666, 667

1403 You cannot help birds flying over your heads in the air, but do not let them alight and build their nests in your hair. Temptations will come, but do not entertain them. Drive them away.—33.645

Testimony   *See Witnessing*

1404 Many of you feel that you cannot write or preach, and you think you can do nothing. There is one thing you can do for your Master—you can live Christianity. I think there are more people who look at the new life in Christ written out in you than they will in the old life that is written in the Scriptures. An infidel will use arguments to disprove the Bible if you set it before him, but if you live honestly and uprightly in the world, he will say, "Well, I thought the Bible was all hypocrisy, but I cannot think so now, because there is Mr. So-and-so. See how he lives. I could believe my infidelity if it were not for him. The Bible certainly has an effect on his life, and therefore I must believe it."—1.343

1405 Holy Mr. Whitefield, when someone observed, "I should like to hear your dying testimony," said, "No, I shall in all probability bear no dying testimony."

"Why not?" said the other.

"Because I am bearing testimony every day while I live, and there will be the less need of it when I die."

That seraphic apostle preached up to the last afternoon, and then went upstairs to bed and died. There was no need for anyone to ask, "What did he say when he was dying?" No, they knew what he said when he was living, and that was a great deal better.—20.311

1406 Said one to me, "I could almost wish sometimes that I had been an open offender, that I might see the change in my character. But having been always moral from my youth up, I am not always able to see any distinct mark of a change."

This form of evidence is of small use in times of darkness, for if the devil cannot say to a man, "You have not changed your life," he says, "You changed your actions, but your heart is still the same. You turned from a bold, honest sinner to a hypocritical professor."—26.551

Thanksgiving   *See Praise*

1407 A friend said to me on Wednesday, when the sun was shining, "We ought to be grateful for this fine weather."

I replied, "I go farther than that—I *am* grateful for it!"—36.394

Thoughts

1408 Our thoughts, if left to themselves, are as a cage of unclean birds or a den of wild beasts. As Hercules needed to turn a stream of water to cleanse the Augean stable, our Lord Jesus Christ needed to pour rivers of water out of his own heart to cleanse the foul stable of our corrupt thoughts.—57.256

Time   *See Death; Eternity; Procrastination; Waiting*

1409 Listen for one moment to the ticking of that clock! (Here the preacher paused, and amid solemn silence everyone heard the clock with its tick, tick, tick.) It is the beating on the pulse of eternity. It is the footstep of death pursuing you! Each time the clock ticks, death's footsteps are falling on the ground close behind you!—2.47

1410 We confess that we are mortal, but we profess by our actions that we are immortal. Said a man of eighty-two concerning another of seventy, when he wanted to buy his land and could not get it at the price he wished, "Never mind. So-and-so is an old man, and he will soon be dead, and then I'll buy it." Though he was twelve years older than the other, yet the other must of course soon die, while he, in his own thoughts, must live for many a year.—8.656

1411 At what a rate we whirl along! Childhood seems to travel in a wagon, but manhood at express speed. The grey-headed old man looks back upon all his life as being but a day. And I suppose if we could live to be 130 we should feel the same, till like Jacob, we should say, "Few and evil have the days of the years of my life been" (Gen. 47:9). If we could live as long as Methuselah, I doubt not our life would appear shorter still.—8.657

1412 Listen to the ticking of the clock! As the pendulum swings back and forth, it says to some of you, "Now or never! Now or never! Now or never! Now or never!" Will you trust your soul with Jesus?—50.286

1413 Do not believe that you are standing still; you are not. Your pulses each moment beat the funeral marches to the tomb. You are chained to the chariot of rolling time. There is no bridling the steeds or leaping from the chariot.—55.16

Tithing   *See Giving; Money, Stewardship*

1414 It is a blessed thing for a young man to begin business with the rule that he will give the Lord at least his tenth.—14.288

1415 Much has been said about giving the tenth of one's income to the Lord. I think that is a Christian duty which none should for a moment question. If it were a duty under the Jewish law, much more is it so now under the Christian dispensation. But it is a great mistake to suppose that the Jew gave only a tenth. He gave very, very, very much more than that.

The tenth was the payment which he must make. But after that came freewill offerings and all the various gifts at different seasons of the year, so that perhaps he gave a third. Much more nearly that, certainly, than a tenth.—14.567, 568

1416 In the religion of Christ there is no taxation. Everything is of love.—32.213

Total Depravity *See Depravity*

Tragedy *See Affliction; Providence; Suffering; Trials; Trouble*

Trials *See Affliction; Pain; Persecution; Prosperity; Sickness; Suffering; Sympathy; Temptation; Trouble*

1417 Trials make room for consolation. There is nothing that makes a man have a big heart like a great trial. I have found that those people who have no sympathy for their fellows—who never weep for the sorrows of others—very seldom have had any woes of their own. Great hearts can be made only by great troubles.—1.98

1418 If God saves us, it will be a trying matter. All the way to heaven we shall get there only by the skin of our teeth. There will be enough to get you up the hill of difficulty, but only enough then by climbing on your hands and knees. Your trials will be so many that if you had only one trial more, it would be like the last ounce that breaks the camel's back. But nevertheless, though God's love should thus try you all the journey through, your faith will bear the trying. For while God dashes you down to the earth with one hand in providence, he will lift you up with the other in grace.—6.37

1419 The believer takes his daily trials and reads them the opposite way. Trial comes to him and says, "Your hope is dry."

"My hope is not dry," says he. "While I have a trial I have a ground of hope."

"Your God has forsaken you," says tribulation.

"My God has not forsaken me" says he, "for he says, 'In the world ye shall have tribulation' (John 16:33), and I have it!"—9.503

1420 The Christian gains by his losses. He acquires health by his sickness. He wins friends through his bereavements, and he becomes a conqueror through his defeats. Nothing therefore, can be injurious to the Christian, when the very worst things that he has are but rough waves to wash his golden ships home to port and enrich him.—13.20

1421 A man who should live and die without trials would be like a setting sun without clouds. He would have scant opportunity for the display of those virtues with which the grace of God had endowed him.—20.385

1422 Trials from the enemies of Jesus confirm our faith. Those who are never tried usually possess a poor, tottering faith. But trial, especially persecution, is like the rough March wind which goes howling through the forest. While the young oaks are almost torn up by the roots at first, it loosens the soil for them, and they send out more rootlets, till they get such a firm grip that they defy the hurricane. That which shakes them at first strengthens them afterwards.—20.463

1423 Never desire trial! If I were a boy at home, I do not think I should say to my brother, because he had been whipped, "I am afraid I am not my father's child, and fear that he does not love me, because I am not smarting under the rod. I wish he would whip me just to let me know his love." No; no child would ever be so stupid.—24.143, 144

1424 God had one Son without sin, but he never had a son without trial.—26.170

1425 God does not give faith, love, hope, or any grace without meaning to test it. If a man builds a railway bridge, it is that engines may go over it and prove its carrying power. If he only makes a needle, it must be tested by the work it can do. So when God made you to be strong in the Lord, he meant to try every ounce of your strength. Whatever God makes has a purpose, and he will test it to see if it is equal to its design. I do not think that a single grain of faith will be kept out of the fire— all the golden ore must go into the crucible to be tested.—27.355

1426 We talk about our trials. There is another side to that. Think of Christ's trials: How we have grieved him! We must have provoked his spirit ten thousand times, yet he loves us infinitely and does not give us up.—28.347

1427 None of us can come to the highest maturity without enduring the summer heat of trials. As the sycamore fig never ripens if it be not bruised, as the corn does not leave the husk without threshing, and as wheat makes no fine flour till it be ground, so are we of little use till we are afflicted. Why should we be so eager to escape such benefits? We shall have to wait with patience, saying, "The will of the Lord be done." He waited to give grace to us; let us wait to give glory to him.—30.108

1428 You cannot see the stars while the sun shines. Wait till it is dark, and then you shall behold them. And many a Christian grace is quite imperceptible until the time of trial, and then it shines out with great luster. All this supposes that grace is there. But if it be lacking, trial discovers the lack. You know not what spirit you are of till you have been under tribulation.—31.332

1429 I once knew a minister who had never suffered pain or illness in his life. I was unwell in his house, and he most kindly tried to sympathize with me. He did it almost as wonderfully as an elephant picks up a pin. It was a marvel that he could attempt a thing so altogether out of his line. Many of the trials which are experienced by Christians are sent as an education in the art of sympathy.—35.195

1430 Even the road to destruction, broad as it is, has not a path in it which avoids trial. Some sinners go over hedge and ditch to hell. If a man resolves to be a worldling, he will not find the paths of sin are paths of peace. The wicked may well be ill at ease, for God walks contrary to them because they walk contrary to him. No man, be he on the throne or down in a coalpit, can live without affliction.—35.429

1431 I am persuaded that there is no man in this world but has trial in some form, unless it be those whom God permits to have their portion in this life because they will have no portion of bliss in the life that is to come.—42.577

1432 I have looked back to times of trial with a kind of longing, not to have them return, but to feel the strength of God as I have felt it then, to feel the power of faith as I have felt it then, to hang on God's powerful arm as I hung on it then, and to see God at work as I saw him then.—43.477

1433 It is strange that when God gives his children mercies, they generally set their hearts more on the mercies than on the Giver of them. But when the night comes, and he sweeps all the mercies away, then at once they each say, "Now, my God, I have nothing to sing of but thee; I must come to thee, and to thee only."—44.99

1434 The story of Sir James Thornhill painting the inside of the cupola of St. Paul's is probably well known to you. When he had finished one of the compartments, he was stepping backward that he might get a full view of it, and so went almost to the edge of the scaffolding, and would have fallen over if he had taken another step. But a friend who saw his danger wisely seized one of his brushes and rubbed some paint over his picture. The artist in his rage rushed forward to save his painting, and so saved his own life.

We have all pictured life. And as we admired it, we walked further and further away from God and safety, and got nearer and nearer to perilous temptation, when trial came and ruined the picture we had painted. And then, though scarcely knowing why, we came forward and were saved. God had kept us from falling by the trouble he had sent to us.—52.318

1435 You may readily judge whether you are a child of God or a hypocrite by seeing in what direction your soul turns in seasons of severe trial. The hypocrite flies to the world and finds a sort of comfort there. But the child of God runs to his Father and expects consolation only from the Lord's hand.—59.20

Trinity   *See Holy Spirit; Jesus*

1436 A gospel without a Trinity! It is a pyramid built on its apex. A gospel without the Trinity! It is a rope of sand that cannot hold together. A gospel without the Trinity! Then Satan can overturn it. But give me a gospel with the Trinity, and the might of hell cannot prevail against it. No man can any more overthrow it than a bubble could split a rock or a feather break in halves a mountain. Get the thought of the three persons, and you have the marrow of all theology. Only know the Father, the Son, and the Holy Ghost to be one, and all things will appear clear. This is the golden key to the secrets of nature. This is the silken clue of the labyrinths of mystery. And he who understands this will soon understand as much as mortals ever know.—1.29

1437 My firm conviction is that in proportion as we have more regard for the sacred Godhead, the wondrous Trinity in unity, shall we see a greater display of God's power and a more glorious manifestation of his might in our churches.—1.379

1438 Keep the existence of the Trinity prominent in your ministry. Remember, you cannot pray without the Trinity. If the full work of salvation requires a Trinity, so does that very breath by which we live. You cannot draw near to the Father except through the Son and by the Holy Spirit.—37.374

1439 No study in Scripture is more interesting or profitable to the Christian than the revelation which is given to us concerning the sacred Trinity, and the various parts which the divine persons take in the work of salvation.—55.26

1440 The Father gives the great gospel feast, the Son is the feast, and the Spirit not only brings the invitations, he also gathers the guests around the table. Or to use another metaphor, God the Father is the fountain of grace, God the Son is the channel of grace, and God the Holy Spirit is the cup from which we drink of the flowing stream.—58.184

Trouble   *See Affliction; Pain; Suffering; Sympathy; Trials*

1441 We should never know the music of the harp if the strings were left untouched. We should never enjoy the juice of the grape if it were never trodden in the wine press. We should never discover the sweet perfume of cinnamon if it were not pressed and beaten. And we should never know the warmth of fire if the coals were not utterly consumed. The excellence of the Christian is brought out by the fire of trouble.—11.294

1442 I believe that the hardest-hearted, most cross-grained, and most unlovely Christians in all the world are those who never have had much trouble. And those who are the most sympathizing, loving, and Christlike are generally those that have the most affliction. The worst thing that can happen to any of us is to have our path made too smooth, and one of the greatest blessings that ever the Lord gave us was a cross.—12.70, 71

1443 We should never have such fellowship with Jesus as we do if we had not such troubles as we have. We cannot see the stars in the daytime, but they tell us that if we go down into a well we can. Sometimes God sinks wells of trouble and puts his servants into them, and then they see his starry promises.—12.287

1444 Do not imagine that any amount of prayer will have the effect of staving off all trouble, for surely never did anyone else pray like our Lord Jesus Christ did. His agony in Gethsemane was a time of the mightiest prayer that was ever heard in heaven, yet it was followed very closely by his death on the cross.—47.172

Trust *See Faith*

1445 Let us lean on God with all our weight. Let us throw ourselves on his faithfulness as we do on our beds, bringing all our weariness to his dear rest.—8.612

1446 If I might have any choice between having abundant wealth, or being brought to absolute dependence on daily supplies, if, in the latter case I could have greater power to exhibit and to exert faith in Christ, I must confess that I should prefer the mode of living which would give me most room to enjoy the luxury of depending on my God. I believe it is a happier and more divine life to live from hand to mouth, dependent on the providence of God and having confidence and trust in him, than it is to have all the abundance of this world, but to have nothing about which faith may exercise itself.—10.21

1447 A neighbor's dog was very fond of visiting my garden, and as he never improved my flowers, I never gave him a cordial welcome. Walking along quietly one evening I saw him doing mischief. I threw a stick at him and advised him to go home. But how did the good creature reply to me? He turned round and wagged his tail, and in the merriest manner picked up my stick, brought it to me, and laid it at my feet. Did I strike him? No, I am no monster. I should have been ashamed of myself if I had not patted him on the back and told him to come there whenever he liked. He and I were friends directly, because he trusted me and conquered me.

That is just the philosophy of a sinner's faith in Christ. As the dog mastered the man by confiding in him, so a poor guilty sinner does, in effect, master the Lord himself by trusting him, when he says, "Lord, I am a poor dog of a sinner, and thou mightest drive me away, but I believe thee to be too good for that. I believe thou canst save me, and I trust myself with thee." You will never be lost if you thus trust.—23.297

1448 I would trust my God as unreservedly as Alexander trusted his friend, who was also his physician. The physician had mixed a medicine for Alexander, who was sick, and the potion stood by Alexander's bed for him to drink. Just before he drank, a letter was delivered to him in which he was warned that his physician had been bribed to poison him, and had mingled poison with the medicine. Alexander summoned the physician into his presence. When he came in, Alexander at once drank the cup and then handed his friend the letter. What grand confidence was this! He would not let the accused know of the libel till he had proved beyond all dispute that he did not believe a word of it.—25.654, 655

1449 Trust in Christ brings to God greater glory than anything else we can produce.—33.463

1450 If Christ were standing on this platform, and you saw his pierced hands and the wound in his side, you would be ready to fall down and worship him. You can worship him better still by trusting him in his absence.—33.466

1451 If I were a million times as sinful as I am, and then had a million souls, each one a million times more sinful than my own, I would still trust his atoning blood to cleanse me, and himself to save me.—36.95

1452 I do not think I ever finished a sermon except in one way—by trying to explain what is meant by this simple trust in the Lord Jesus Christ.—51.105

1453 When simply to trust Christ saves the soul, to distrust him is the direst and most damnable of sins. It is suicidal.—63.129

Truth *See Bible, truth of; Gospel; Honesty*

1454 Say some, "Tell us how to discern truth."

You may judge it by three things: by God, by Christ, and by man; that is, the truth which honors God, the truth which glorifies Christ, and the truth which humbles man.—54.247

Unbelief *See Agnostic; Atheist; Doubt; Faith*

1455 Oh, believe me, if you could roll all sins into one mass—if you could take murder and blasphemy and lust, adultery, and fornication, and everything that is vile, and unite them all into one vast globe of black corruption, they would not equal even then the sin of unbelief. This is the monarch sin, the quintessence of guilt, the mixture of the venom of all crimes, the dregs of the wine of Gomorrah. It is the A-1 sin, the masterpiece of Satan, the chief work of the devil.—1.19

1456 Many a man would have been a missionary, would have stood and preached his Master's gospel boldly, but he had unbelief. Once make a giant unbelieving, and he becomes a dwarf. Faith is the Samsonian lock of the Christian. Cut it off, and you may put out his eyes. He can do nothing.—1.21

1457 Everything lies in the bowels of this sin, the rejecting of Christ. There is murder in this, for if the man on the scaffold rejects a pardon, does he not murder himself? There is pride in this, for you reject Christ because your proud hearts have turned you aside. There is rebellion in this, for we rebel against God when we reject Christ. There is high treason in this, for you reject a King. You put far from you him who is crowned King of the earth, and you incur therefore the weightiest of all guilt.—4.236

1458 If there be the virus of diabolical guilt in anything, it must be in the unbelief, not of sinners, but of God's own people. For sinners have never seen what saints have seen, have never felt what we have felt, have never known what we have known. If they should doubt, they do not sin against such light, nor do despite to such invincible arguments for confidence as we do.—13.126

1459 If one leak sent the vessel to the bottom, it was no comfort to the crew that their ship leaked only in one place. One disease may kill a man. He may be sound everywhere else, but it will be a sorry comfort to him to know that he might have lived long, had but that one organ been sound. If you should have no sin whatever except only an evil heart of unbelief, if all your external life should be lovely and amiable, yet if that one fatal sin be in you, you can draw small consolation from all else that is good about you.—17.27

1460 This I know, that some men are greater sinners than the devil. "No," say you, "how is that?" I answer that the devil never yet rejected free grace and dying love. The devil never yet struggled against the Holy Spirit in his own conscience. The devil never yet refused the mercy of God.—31.57

1461 A certain skeptical writer, when in prison, was visited by a Christian man who wished him well, but he refused to hear a word about religion. Seeing a Bible in the hand of his visitor, he made this remark, "You do not expect me to believe in that book, do you? Why, if that book is true, I am lost forever."

Just so. Therein lies the reason for half the infidelity in the world, and all the infidelity in our congregations.—34.155

1462 If you do not believe in the Lord Jesus Christ, you set aside the witness of apostles, saints, and martyrs. You also impute foolishness or deceit to your dearest friends, some of whom died in faith, exhorting you to believe in Jesus Christ. Indeed, you make all of us who preach the gospel to be liars, and we are not so. Neither do you think so badly of us when we speak in everyday life.—34.530, 531

1463 I am bowed down with dismay that my Lord's great love, which led him to die for man, should hardly be thought worthy of your hearing, much less of your believing. Here is a heavenly marriage, and right royal nuptials placed within your reach. But with a sneer you turn aside and prefer the witcheries of sin.—34.557

1464 Avoid anxiously the double sin of unbelief. If you do not believe Jesus, you do not believe God. If you reject his Son, you reject himself. If you give the lie to the teaching of Christ, you give the lie to God. Flee from this deadly sin!—36.444

1465 Unbelief calls itself "honest doubt," and not without cause, for we should not have known it to be honest if it had not labeled itself so.—37.117

1466 I have noticed that whenever a person gives up his belief in the Word of God because it requires that he should believe a good deal, his unbelief requires him to believe a great deal more. If there be any difficulties in the faith of Christ, they are not one-tenth as great as the absurdities in any system of unbelief which seeks to take its place.—39.208

1467 O unbelievers, I would not be in your place five minutes for all the world! As the Lord lives, there is but a step between you and hell! Only a breath, and you may be gone. If I were in your place, I should be afraid to eat a morsel of bread tonight, lest a crumb should go the wrong way, and by causing my death should land me in everlasting misery. One might be afraid to shut his eyes tonight as an unbeliever, lest, as he closed them on earth, he shut them forever to all light and hope.—41.563

1468 I think I see you now, O ungodly man! You are standing above the pit of everlasting wrath on a single plank, and that plank is snapping beneath your feet. You are hanging over the awful precipice by a single rope, and each moment the strands of that rope are breaking, and the last one of them will snap before long. And if you are then unsaved, you will learn what eternal destruction from the presence of the Lord and the glory of his power will mean.—48.158

1469 Unbelief will destroy the best of us. Faith will save the worst of us.—62.33

Unconditional Election *See Election, unconditional*

Unction *See Holy Spirit*

1470 There is an old Romish tale of a monk who was detained on his journey and could not reach the congregation in time to conduct the service. The devil thought it was a fine opportunity for him to speak to the people, so, putting on the cowl of the monk, he went into the pulpit and preached about hell—a subject with which he was well-acquainted—and the hearers listened very attentively. Before he finished his discourse, the holy man appeared and made the devil disclose himself in his proper form. "How did you dare preach the truth as you were doing when I came in?" he said.

"Oh," replied Satan, "I did not mind preaching the truth, for there was no unction in it. So I knew that it could not do any hurt to my cause."

It was a curious legend, but there was a great truth at the bottom of it: Where there is no unction, it does not matter what we preach or how we preach it.—46.222, 223

Unity *See Division; Church, denominations of; Quarreling*

1471 It is quite certain we shall never keep the unity of the Spirit if this church shall declare that it is superior to every other. If there be a church which says, "We are *the* church, and all others are mere sects," then it is a troubler in Israel, and must hide its head when the unity of the Spirit is so much as hinted at.—11.8

1472 The church of Christ is always quarreling, but did you ever hear that the devil and his confederates quarrel? They are so united that if at any special moment the great prince of hell wishes to concentrate all the masses of his army at one particular point, it is done to the tick of the clock, and the temptation comes with its fullest force just when he sees it to be the most likely that he will prevail. If we had such unanimity as that in the church of God, if we all moved at the guidance of the finger of Christ, if all the church could move in one great mass to the attack of a certain evil, how much more easily might we prevail! But alas, the powers of hell far exceed us in unanimity.—46.619

Usefulness

1473 God can use inferior persons for grand purposes. He has often done so. Go into his armory and see how he has worked by flies and lice, by worms and caterpillars, by frogs and serpents. His greatest victories were won by a hammer and a tent pin, by an ox goad, by the jawbone of an ass, by a sling and a stone, and such like. His greatest prophets at the first tried to excuse themselves on the ground of unfitness.—36.224

Visions   *See Revelation, modern; Signs*

Waiting   *See Time*

1474 Wait *in prayer.* Call on God and spread the case before him. Express your unstaggering confidence in him. Wait *in faith,* for unfaithful, untrusting waiting is but an insult to the Lord. Believe that if he shall keep you waiting even till midnight, yet he will come at the right time. Wait *in quiet patience,* not murmuring because you are under the affliction, but blessing God for it.—9.653

1475 God kept his Son waiting, and he may very well keep you in like posture, for how long did you delay and cause the Lord of grace to wait on you?

"But I cannot see how I am to be delivered."

Wait.

"Ah, this is such a heavy burden."

Wait.

"But I am ready to die under this terrible load."

Wait! Wait on! He is worth waiting for! *Wait* is a short word, but it takes a deal of grace to spell out its full meaning, and still more grace to put it in practice. Wait, wait.

"Oh, but I have been unfortunate."

Wait.

"But I have believed a promise, and it has not been fulfilled."

Wait, for you wait in blessed company. You may hear Jesus saying, "I waited patiently" (Ps. 40:1). He is teaching us to do the same by his gracious Spirit.—28.455

War

1476 Long have I held that war is an enormous crime. Long have I regarded all battles as but murder on a large scale.—3.343

1477 What a threefold accursed thing is war! I believe with Benjamin Franklin that there never was a good war, and there never was a bad peace. War is unmitigated mischief from end to end, and peace is a thing to rejoice in. Killing and slaying, devastating and burning, are sport for fiends, and for fiends alone. True men, if once called to battle, are the last persons who would lightly enter it again. It is an awful and terrible thing.—26.524

1478 Men have made themselves worse than devils to men. No calamities have ever befallen nations that are so much to be deplored as the atrocities of war.—28.59

1479 As I understand the Word of God, I always rejoice to find a soldier a Christian, but I always mourn to find a Christian a soldier.—59.615

Warfare, spiritual

1480 It strikes me that conflict is the principal feature of the Christian life this side of heaven.—14.43

Wealth   *See Money; Prosperity; Stewardship*

1481 You cannot buy heaven with gold. Why, they pave the streets up there with it.—4.277

1482 I know a brother who, when he had a little money, gave it to the cause of God abundantly! I believe that he is worth a hundred times as much as he was then, and he gives a hundredth part of what he used to when he was poorer. In proportion as his pocket has grown golden, his heart has grown bronzy.—33.21

1483 Saving is good, but the first thing that a man has to do is to see to the saving of his soul. And there are some who always look so much to the saving of their wealth that their soul stands very little chance of being saved.—52.67

1484 I believe it is anti-Christian and unholy for any Christian to live with the object of accumulating wealth. You will say, "Are we not to strive all we can to get all the money we can?"

You may do so. You should do so. I cannot doubt but what, in so doing, you may do good service to the cause of God. But what I said was that to live *with the object* of accumulating wealth is anti-Christian.—59.550

1485 You remember how the old Puritan put it. He had been rich and then was brought to poverty. And he said he didn't find much difference, for when he was rich he found God in all, and now that he was poor he found all in God. Perhaps the latter is the higher state of the two.—62.568

Will, free   *See Election; Grace, irresistible; Nature, human; Predestination; Sovereignty; Will, God's*

1486 Once there was free will in paradise, and a terrible mess free will made there, for it spoiled all paradise and turned Adam out of the garden. Free will was once in heaven, but it turned the glorious archangel out, and a third part of the stars of heaven fell into the abyss. I want nothing to do with free will, but I will try to see whether I have got a free will within. And I find I have. Very free will to do evil, but very poor will to do that which is good.— 1.234

1487 If Jesus Christ were to stand on this platform, what would many people do with him? "Oh," say some, "we would make him a King!"

I do not believe it. They would crucify him again if they had the opportunity. If he were to come and say, "I love you; will you be saved by me?" not one of you would consent if you were left to your will. Not a single person would come to be his disciple. No, it needs the power of the Spirit to make men come to Jesus Christ.—1.305

1488 I will go as far as Martin Luther, where he says, "If any man ascribes anything of salvation, even the very least thing, to the free will of man, he knows nothing of grace, and he has not learned Jesus Christ rightly."— 1.395

1489 We declare on scriptural authority that the human will is so desperately set on mischief, so depraved, so inclined to everything that is evil, and so disin-

clined to everything that is good, that without the powerful, supernatural, irresistible influence of the Holy Spirit, no human will will ever be constrained toward Christ.—4.139

1490 Free will has carried many souls to hell, but yet never a soul to heaven.—4.477

1491 I cannot think why some people are so fond of free will. I believe free will is the delight of sinners, but that God's will is the glory of saints. There is nothing I desire more to get rid of than my own will, and to be absorbed into the will and purpose of my Lord. To do according to the will of him who is most good, most true, most wise, most mighty, seems to me to be heaven. Let others choose the dignity of independence; I crave the glory of being wholly dead in Christ, and only alive in him.—8.605

1492 Free-will doctrine—what does it? It magnifies man into God. It declares God's purposes a nullity, since they cannot be carried out unless men are willing. It makes God's will a waiting servant to the will of man, and the whole covenant of grace dependent on human action. Denying election on the ground of injustice, it holds God to be a debtor to sinners.—9.187

1493 Some set up the will as a kind of deity. It does as it wills with earth and heaven. But in truth the will is not a master but a servant. Men do not will a thing because they will it, but because their affection, their passions, or their judgments influence their wills in that direction. No man can truly say, "I, unbiased and unaided, will to love God and not to love Satan." Such a proud self-assuming language would prove him a liar. The man would be clearly a worshiper of himself.—17.485

1494 Free will I have often heard of, but I have never seen it. I have met with will, and plenty of it, but it has either been led captive by sin or held in blessed bonds of grace.—25.374

1495 It would take a great deal to grind me down into a belief in free will, because it is contrary to my whole experience. I know this, if the Lord had not first loved me, I never should have loved him. And if there is any good thing in me whatsoever, it must have been implanted there by the Holy Spirit.—51.394

Will, God's *See Will, free*

1496 When your will is God's will, you will have your will.—32.281

1497 Absolute submission is not enough. We must go on to joyful acquiescence in the will of God. If the cup be bitter, our acquiescence must take it as cheerfully as if it were sweet.

"Hard lines," say you.

"To hard hearts," say I. But when our hearts are right with God, so well do we love him, that if it ever came to a conflict anywhere, whether it should be our will or his will that should prevail, we should at once end the conflict by saying, "Nevertheless, not as I will, but as thou wilt."—42.365

1498 I certainly do not approve of the practice by which some people say they can tell the Lord's will by just opening the Bible and noticing the first text which catches their eye. I know that Mr. Wesley frequently practiced this plan. But like some other good men, he had his foibles. And I know that others have imitated him, but I should think myself no more justified in seeking guidance in that way than I should in shuffling a pack of cards. I could no more expect to be guided by a text of Scripture, picked out in that haphazard style, than by a gypsy. No, no; we are above all that kind of thing.—52.343

1499 I hardly like to repeat the story of the good woman whose son was ill—a little child near death's door—and she begged the minister to pray for his life. He did pray very earnestly, but he put in, "If it be thy will, save this child."

The woman said, "I cannot bear that. I must have you pray

that the child shall live. Do not put in any ifs or buts."

"Woman," said the minister, "it may be you will live to rue the day that ever you wished to set your will up against God's will."

Twenty years afterward, she was carried away in a fainting fit from under Tyburn gallows, where that son was put to death as a felon. Although she had lived to see her child grow up to be a man, it would have been infinitely better for her had the child died, and infinitely wiser had she left it to God's will.—17.321

Wisdom *See Knowledge*

1500 Some people make use of Christ's gospel to illuminate their heads, instead of making use of it to illuminate their hearts. They are like the farmer Rowland Hill once described. The plowman rushes in and cries, "Thieves! Thieves!" The farmer rises up in a moment, grasps the candle, holds it up to his head, rushes after the thieves, and stumbles over a wheelbarrow, because he holds the light to his head instead of holding it to his feet.

So there are many who just hold religion up to illuminate their intellect, instead of holding it down to illuminate their practice. And so they make a sad tumble of it and cast themselves into the mire. Take care that you make the wisdom of God a thing of true wisdom, directing your feet into his statutes, and keeping you in his ways.—3.208

1501 If we were called on to select a man who, as to his life as a whole, perpetrated the greatest folly, we should mention Solomon. Yet he was the wisest of men. Yes, the cream of wisdom, when curdled, makes the worst of folly.—34.594

Witnessing *See Testimony*

1502 I am sure of this: It is impossible to know the value of salvation without desiring to see others brought in. Said that renowned preacher, Whitefield, "As soon as I was converted, I wanted to be the means of the conversion of all that I had ever known. There were a number of young men that I had played cards with, sinned with, and transgressed with. The first thing I did was, I went to their houses to see what I could do for their salvation. Nor could I rest until I had the pleasure of seeing many of them brought to the Savior."—3.102

1503 Not one of you ever knew a secret Christian, for if it had been a secret, how came you to know it? Then, as you never knew a secret Christian, you are not justified in believing there ever is such a one. You must come out and make a profession.—3.268

1504 I may talk here Sunday after Sunday, and every day in the week, but I cannot preach in so forcible a way as you can, who by your actions are preaching to the world.—4.262

1505 You *must* witness if you be a Christian. You may try to shirk it if you will, but you must witness, for you are *sub poena.* That is to say, you will suffer for it if you do not. Some Christians think they will sneak comfortably into heaven without bearing witness for Christ. I fear they will be mistaken; but this I know, that every Christian who does not come out distinctly and boldly for his Master will lose all choice enjoyments.—11.452

1506 Etiquette nowadays often demands of a Christian that he should not intrude his religion on company. Out on such etiquette! It is the etiquette of hell. True courtesy to my fellow's soul makes me speak to him, if I believe that soul to be in danger.—12.440

1507 How many, my dear friend, were you ever the means of bringing to Jesus? You believe that they must perish everlastingly, unless they have faith in Christ. How many have you personally prayed for? How many did you ever break your heart about? You believe that they must love Christ or be damned. How many have you ever talked to concerning him who is the only Savior?—15.452

1508 Having joined the church of God, are any of you satisfied to be silent? Are you content to let those around you sink to hell? What! Never tell of Christ's love? What! Never speak of salvation to your own children? Can this be right? In God's name, wake up! What are you left on this earth for? If there is nothing for you to do, why are you in this sinful world?—34.384

1509 If you are a husband, you will never be content till you have told your wife and family. And if you are a mother, I am sure you will be eager to make the gospel known to your children. It is a great and holy fire that will burn and not smolder.—50.369

1510 Some of you that come to hear me on Sunday nights ought not to come. If you have got the grace of God in your heart, come and get enough spiritual meat to feed you, but remember that London is perishing for the lack of the gospel. How dare you, then, sit still to enjoy the gospel while men are perishing?—63.82

Works *See Covenant; Faith; Gospel; Grace; Law; Legalism; Pride; Self-righteousness*

1511 Some of the Indian tribes use little strips of cloth instead of money, and I would not find fault with them if I lived there. But when I come to England, strips of cloth will not suffice. So honesty, sobriety, and such things may be very good among men. But all these things put together, without faith, do not please God. Virtues without faith are whitewashed sins.—1.20, 21

1512 Ralph Erskine did not say amiss when he remarked, "I have got more hurt by my good works than my bad ones. My bad works always drove me to the Savior for mercy. My good works often kept me from him, and I began to trust in myself."—1.297

1513 Go home and make yourself a mixture of fire and water; endeavor to keep in your house a lion and a lamb. And when you have succeeded in doing these, tell me that you have made works and grace agree, and I will tell you that you have told me a lie even then. The two things are so essentially opposite that it cannot be done.—2.128

1514 Augustine well said, "Good works, as they are called, in sinners are nothing but splendid sins."—2.131

1515 Says one, "Do you find fault with good works?"
Not at all. Suppose I see a man building a house, and he were fool enough to lay the foundation with chimney pots. If I should say, "I do not like these chimney pots to be put into the foundation," you would not say I found fault with the chimney pots, but with the man for putting them in the wrong place. So with good works

and ceremonies. They will not do for a foundation.—4.276

1516 I like the saying of a man who declared to his minister that God had done his part in his salvation, and he had done the rest. "Well," said the minister, "what part did you do?"
"Why," said the poor man, "God did it all, and I stood in the way." That is about all that you and I shall ever do in our own strength.—15.345

1517 I was like a man in a bog. The more he struggles, the more he sinks. Or like a prisoner upon the treadmill, who rises no higher, but only wearies himself by his climbing. No good can result from efforts made apart from faith in Jesus.—20.281

1518 The attempt to perform good works apart from God is like the effort of a thief to set his stolen goods in order. His sole duty is to return them at once. The very same pride which leads men away from God may be seen in their self-conceited notion that they can improve themselves while still they refuse to return to him.—20.477

1519 I said the other evening to an esteemed member of this church who lies dying, "Dear brother, you have been a good soldier of Jesus Christ."
He replied, "You say so, but I think nothing of what I have

done. I am looking to Christ alone."

Just so. That is the ground of salvation.—24.584, 585

1520 Perhaps your chosen hope is that you will be saved by doing your best. Alas, no man does his best! And the best acts of a rebel must be unacceptable to his king.—32.142

1521 The cardinal error against which the gospel of Christ has to contend is the effect of the tendency of the human heart to rely on salvation by works. The great antagonist to the truth as it is in Jesus is that pride of man which leads him to believe that he can be, at least in part, his own savior. This error is the prolific mother of multitudes of heresies.—47.397

Worldliness

1522 Put your finger on any prosperous page in the church's history, and I will find a little marginal note reading thus: "In this age men could readily see where the church began and where the world ended." Never were there good times when the church and the world were joined in marriage. The more the church is different from the world in her acts and in her maxims, the more true is her testimony for Christ, and the more potent is her witness against sin.—6.154

1523 Our being so much like the world—our trading as the world trades, our talking as the world talks, our always insisting on it that we must do as other people do—this is doing more mischief to the world than all our preachers can hope to effect good. I cannot imagine a man professing to be a Christian, and then acting as the world acts, and yet honoring Christ.—6.156

1524 It were better that you had never been born than that you should go back to the world.—12.346

1525 The Christian is the most contented man *in* the world, but he is the least contented *with* the world. He is like a traveler in an inn, perfectly satisfied with the inn and its accommodation, considering it as an inn, but putting quite out of all consideration the idea of making it his home.—16.50

1526 I believe that one reason why the church of God at this present moment has so little influence over the world is because the world has so much influence over the church.—32.339

1527 Worldliness has gone a long way to destroy the church of God. I judge it to be the worst cankerworm that assails us.—37.57

1528 Surely the fish, were it asked if it did not wish to fly, would reply, "I am not unhappy because I am not allowed to fly. It is not my element." So the Christian can say, "I am not unhappy because I do not spend my nights in worldly society, because I do not join in their revelry and wantonness. It is not my element, and I could not enjoy it."—50.463, 464

1529 I sometimes hear people say as an excuse for professors going to doubtful places of amusement, "You know they must have some recreation."

Yes, I know. But the re-creation which the Christian experienced when he was born again has so completely made all things new to him, that the vile rubbish called recreation by the world is so vapid to him, that he might as well try to fill himself with fog as to satisfy his soul with such utter vanity.—53.321

1530 He that follows the world with all his heart and thinks that the best, is a reasonable man in following it. But he who thinks the world to come the best, and yet follows this present evil world—why, what a fool is he, and who shall plead for him? When he stands before God, his prayers will damn him, if nothing else will, for his prayers will be swift witnesses against him that he did know, did feel, and yet he would not act on his knowledge.—62.416

Worry

1531 It does not matter how heavy troubles are if you can cast them on the Lord. The heavier they are, so much the better, for the more you have gotten rid of, and the more there is laid on the rock.—1.280, 281

Worship   See Music; Praise; Prayer

1532 All places are places of worship to a Christian. Wherever he is, he ought to be in a worshiping frame of mind.—13.500

1533 Soul worship is the soul of worship, and if you take away the soul from the worship, you have killed the worship. It becomes dead and barren after that.—20.63

1534 There should be some preparation of the heart in coming to the worship of God. Consider who he is in whose name we gather, and surely we cannot rush together without thought. Consider whom we profess to worship, and we shall not hurry into his presence as men run to a fire. Moses, the man of God, was warned to put off his shoes from his feet when God only revealed himself in a bush. How should we prepare ourselves when we come to him who reveals himself in Christ Jesus, his dear Son? There should be no stumbling into the place of worship half asleep, no roaming here as if it were no more than going to a playhouse. We cannot expect to profit much if we bring with us a swarm of idle thoughts and a heart crammed with vanity. If we are full of folly, we may shut out the truth of God from our minds.—31.350

1535 The best worship that we ever render to God is far from perfect. Our praises, how faint and feeble they are! Our prayers, how wandering, how wavering they are! When we get nearest to God, how far off we are! When we are most like him, how greatly unlike him we are!—40.330

1536 My happiest moments are when I am worshiping God, really adoring the Lord Jesus Christ, and having fellowship with the ever-blessed Spirit. In that worship I forget the cares of the church and everything else. To me it is the nearest approach to what it will be in heaven.—46.142

Worship, false   *See Worship*

1537 By semi-dramatic performances they make houses of prayer to approximate to the theater. They turn their services into musical displays, and their sermons into political harangues or philosophical essays. In fact, they exchange the temple for the theater, and turn ministers of God into actors, whose business it is to amuse men.—34.560

Wrath, God's   *See Anger; Condemnation; Damnation; Discipline, God's; Hell; Judgment, God's; Punishment*

1538 I remember well the time when I thought there was no reason why the flames of hell should not consume me, and why the crushing weight of God's wrath should not roll over me forever and forever. I think every sinner who has really come to Christ has been made to feel that however angry God may be with sin, he is not one whit too angry.—11.416, 417

1539 If there be a man before me who says that the wrath of God is too heavy a punishment for his little sin, I ask him, if the sin be little, why does he not give it up?—12.670

1540 The wrath of God does not end with death. This is a truth which the preacher cannot mention without trembling, nor without wondering that he does not tremble more. The eternity of punishment is a thought which crushes the heart. You have buried the man, but you have not buried his sins. His sins live and are immortal. They have gone before him to judgment, or they will follow after him to bear their witness as to the evil of his heart and the rebellion of his life. The Lord God is slow to anger, but when he is once aroused to it, as he will be against those who finally reject his Son, he will put forth all his omnipotence to crush his enemies.—36.652

Zeal   *See Evangelism; Prayer, fervent; Prayer, importunate*

1541 If you never have sleepless hours, if you never have weeping eyes, if your hearts never swell as if they would burst, you need not anticipate that you will be called zealous. You do not know the beginning of true zeal, for the foundation of Christian zeal lies in the heart. The heart must be heavy with grief and yet must beat high with holy ardor. The heart must be vehement in desire, panting continually for God's glory, or else we shall never attain to anything like the zeal which God would have us know.—11.393

1542 One of the first requisites of an earnest, successful, soul-winning man, must be zeal. As well a chariot without its steeds, a sun without its beams, a heaven without its joy, as a man of God without zeal.—14.529

Quotations Applicable to Specific Scripture Texts
(Genesis to Revelation)

Genesis 1:2 *"And the earth was without form, and void."*

1543 Such is the state of every human heart till God the Holy Spirit visits it. So far as spiritual things are concerned, the human heart is in a state of chaos and disorder. There is no thought of faith, of love, of hope, of obedience. It is spiritually a confused mass of dead sinfulness, in which everything is misplaced. It is void or utterly empty.—11.637

Genesis 2:17 *"In the day that thou eatest thereof thou shalt surely die."*

1544 Man is a suicide. Our sin slays the race. We die because we have sinned. How this should make us hate sin!—6.142

Genesis 2:21 *"And he took one of his ribs."*

1545 Adam was laid asleep, and God took a rib and made it into a helper suitable for him. If God shall take anything from you, though it lies near your heart, do not mourn as one that has no hope. In patience rest in the Lord, for he will bring it to pass that out of all this shall come a spiritual life power, which in after days shall gladden your heart and make you the joyful parent of much good to others in this world of sin and woe.—12.285

Genesis 3:6 *"She took of the fruit . . . and gave also unto her husband . . . and he did eat."*

1546 Some have said, "Surely the sin of Adam was but a little one;

he did but take an apple and eat it." Yes, but in its littleness was its greatness. If it was but a little thing to take the forbidden fruit, with how little trouble might the sin have been avoided! And because it was so small an act, there was couched within it the greater malignity of guilt.—57.279

Genesis 4:9   *"Am I my brother's keeper?"*

1547 I put it to the consciences of many silent Christians, who have never yet made known to others what God has made known to them—How can you be clear from guilt in this matter? Do not say, "Am I my brother's keeper?" for I shall have to give you a horrible answer if you do. I shall have to say, "No, Cain, you are not your brother's keeper, but you are your brother's killer." If, by your effort you have not sought his good, by your neglect you have destroyed him.—33.672

Genesis 5:24   *"Enoch walked with God."*

1548 He walked with God 400 years. This implies perseverance. You have received Christ; persevere in receiving him. You have come to trust him; keep on trusting him. You hang about his neck as a poor, helpless sinner; remain hanging there. Abide in him.—8.679

Genesis 7:23   *"They were destroyed from the earth: and Noah only remained alive."*

1549 Very likely some of them, when the rains descended and the floods came, as they were sinking in the waters, could say, "I helped to caulk her and to tar her. I helped, when the beasts were coming in, to take fodder into the ark, and now I am lost myself." You subscribed to the building of a house of prayer and never pray. You help to support the ministry, yet have no share in the good truth.—55.452

Genesis 8:8   *"He sent forth a dove."*

1550 The Christian's heart is like Noah's dove. It flies over the wide waste, and cannot rest the sole of its foot until it comes back to Christ. He is the true Noah, who puts out his hand and takes in the weary, fluttering dove, and gives it rest. There is no peace the whole world over but with Christ.—13.418

Genesis 9:13   *"I do set my bow in the cloud."*

1551 I should not wonder but what the first shower of rain that fell after he came out of the ark frightened Noah. And if it had not been that he saw the bow of God in the cloud, he would have trembled lest once again the fair world would be buried in the deeps. But his fears were all in

228

vain. I do not suppose that there is now a man existing who is afraid of a general flood. Child of God, you must get rid, once for all, of all fear that God's wrath can ever be let loose on you, for it can never come on the justified. As the waters of Noah shall no more go over the earth, so if you believe in the Lord Jesus Christ, the Lord will never be angry with you so as to destroy you or count you his enemy. His great wrath is over.—22.428

Genesis 19:17 *"Escape for thy life."*

1552 Lot must not stop to argue, nor must you. You have objections, to which my one solitary answer is, "Escape, escape, escape for your life!" That drowning man will not clutch the rope until I have explained to him the doctrine of specific gravity. O fool, what do you have to do with specific gravity when you are drowning? Lay hold of that rope and live!

So there are some who must have election or predestination explained to them. They must have this or that opened up to them and made clear as daylight. I beseech you, do not be such madmen. Do not trifle with your souls, but escape for your life. That is the one business of the present hour. See to that first, and let other matters wait awhile till you are in a fit condition to consider them.—41.76

Genesis 22:12 *"Thou hast not withheld thy son, thine only son, from me."*

1553 What faith and obedience made man do, love constrained God himself to do.—4.67, 68

1554 You admire Abraham's giving up his son to God. Much more admire Jehovah's giving up his Son for sinners.—29.437

Genesis 27:15 *"And Rebekah took . . . raiment of her . . . son Esau . . . and put them upon Jacob."*

1555 Jacob put on his brother Esau's clothes, and he obtained the blessing of his father. We, too, have put on the garments of Christ, and have won the blessing.—16.379

Genesis 27:19 *"Jacob said unto his father . . . eat of my venison, that thy soul may bless me."*

1556 He sold his birthright for a mess of pottage, and he thought he would buy it back by giving his father a mess of pottage. "There," he says, "I will hunt venison for my father, and he will readily give me my birthright again."

That is what sinners say: "I have lost heaven by my evil works; I will easily get it again by reforming."—5.119

Genesis 29:20 *"Jacob served seven years for Rachel; and they seemed . . . but a few days."*

1557 As Jacob forgot all his toils when at last he could call the beloved Rachel his own, so should we count nothing hard, laborious, or trying, so long as souls are saved. Oh, to bring souls to God!—33.472

Genesis 32:11 *"Deliver me, I pray thee, from the hand of . . . Esau: for I fear him."*

1558 Note concerning Jacob's fear, that it probably arose out of the recollection of his old sins. Old sins, like old sores, are very apt to break out again. The very mention of the name of Esau brought up before his mind the day when his mother took his brother's raiment and put it on Jacob, that he might deceive his father into the belief that he was his very son, Esau. Jacob remembered all that, and felt that Esau had good reason to be angry, for he had supplanted him twice and done him grievous wrong. He was afraid of Esau on the principle that "conscience doth make cowards of us all."—49.64

Genesis 37:4 *"When his brethren saw that their father loved him more . . . they hated him."*

1559 Do you hope, if you are the Lord's Josephs, that you shall escape envy? I tell you, no. That green-eyed monster, envy, creeps into God's church. It is hardest of all to be envied by one's brethren. If the devil hates us, we can bear it. If the foes of God's truth speak ill of us, we buckle up our harness and say, "Away, away to the conflict." But when the friends within the house slander us, when brethren who should uphold us turn our foes, and when they try to tread down their younger brethren, then there is some meaning in the passage, "The archers have sorely grieved him, and shot at him, and hated him" (Gen. 49:23). —1.127

Genesis 39:9 *"How then can I do this great wickedness, and sin against God?"*

1560 Do you tremble before God? There is something in that. I do not ask you whether you tremble at hell. That would be no sign of grace, for what thief will not tremble at the gallows? I do not ask if you are afraid of death. What mortal man is not, unless he has a good hope through grace? But do you tremble in the presence of God because you have offended him, and do you tremble in the presence of sin lest you should again offend him? Does it ever come over you thus—"How can I do this great wickedness and sin against God?"—25.151

Genesis 39:20 *"And Joseph's master took him, and put him into the prison."*

1561 Joseph never said a word about Potiphar's wife. It seemed necessary to his own defense, but he would not accuse the woman. He let judgment go by default, and left her to her own conscience and her husband's cooler consideration. This showed great power. It is hard for a man to say nothing when his character is at stake. So eloquent was Joseph in his silence that there is not a word of complaint throughout the whole record of his life. We may often repent of speech, but I think very seldom of silence.—27.421

Genesis 42:8 *"Joseph knew his brethren, but they knew not him."*

1562 Perhaps you will think that Joseph seemed for a while to afflict and tantalize his brothers. By no means! He was seeking their good. The love he bore them was wise and prudent. God, who is far more loving than Joseph, frequently afflicts us to bring us to repentance and to heal us of many evils. Joseph wished to bring his brothers into a right state of heart. And he succeeded in it, though the process was more painful to him than to them.—27.420, 421

Exodus 8:8 *"Entreat the LORD, that he may take away the frogs from me."*

1563 The Lord began with the proud monarch by turning the waters into blood. But it may be that Pharaoh said in his heart, "What a great man I am! If Jehovah comes forth against me, he must work a terrible miracle in order to conquer." He goes his way to his house unhumbled.

This time the Lord will deal with him in another style. In Pharaoh's estimation the croaking frogs were a mean sort of adversary. The Lord seemed by this to say, "Who are you that I should do great things to conquer you? I will even vanquish you by frogs."—59.61, 62

Exodus 17:12 *"But Moses' hands were heavy."*

1564 We never read that Joshua's hand was weary with wielding the sword, but Moses' hand was weary with holding the rod. The more spiritual the duty, the more apt we are to tire of it. We could stand and preach all day, but we could not pray all day. We could go forth to seek the sick all day, but we could not be in our closets all day one half so easily.—3.47

1565 Moses grew weary, and then his friends assisted him. When at any time your prayer flags, let faith support one hand, and let holy hope uplift the other. And with prayer seating itself on the stone of Israel, the rock of our salvation will continue and prevail. Beware of faintness in devotion. If Moses felt it, who can escape it? It is far easier to fight with sin in public than to pray against it in private.—12.535, 536

1566 I wish that some of our pastors were sustained as they should be by their Aarons and their Hurs. Alas, I know many a fainting brother whose hands are hanging down, who finds an Aaron to pull them lower still, and a

231

Hur to depress his spirits yet more.—12.538

Exodus 20:3–17 *(The Ten Commandments)*

1567 The law with its ten black horses drags the plowshare of conviction up and down the soul from end to end of the field, till there is no one part of it left unfurrowed. And, deeper than any plow can go, conviction goes to the very core and center of the spirit, till the whole heart is wounded. The plowers make deep furrows indeed when God puts his hand to the plow. The soil of the heart is broken in pieces in the presence of the Most High.—12.86

1568 Neither the Jewish law of ten commands nor its law of ceremonies was ever intended to save anybody. By a set of pictures it set forth the way of salvation, but it was not itself the way. It was a map, not a country; a model of the road, not the road itself.—20.553

Exodus 20:4 *"Thou shalt not make . . . any likeness of any thing that is in heaven."*

1569 I have seen, to my horror, a picture of God the Father represented as an old man, whereas the Lord has declared that we should make no image of him or represent him in any way. The attempt is blasphemous.—55.526

Exodus 20:8 *"Remember the sabbath day, to keep it holy."*

1570 There are some persons who have been in the habit of carrying on their trade on the Sabbath. But when they have become Christ's disciples, they have shut up their shop on that day, and people have said to them, "You will be ruined. You will never get a living. You know, we must live."

I have often heard that last little sentence, but I do not believe it. I do not see any necessity for us to live. There is a necessity for us to be true to Christ, but not for us to continue to live. It is a great deal better that we should die than that we should do a wrong thing. And we should be prepared at any time to say, "If need be, we will let our trade go, and we will be poor, but we will keep a clear conscience."—45.569

Exodus 20:17 *"Thou shalt not covet."*

1571 I think that it was St. Francis de Sales who said that, among all those who came to him confessing their sins, not one ever confessed to being covetous.—45.414

Exodus 33:18 *"I beseech thee, show me thy glory."*

1572 The glory of God is only to be seen in the face of Christ Jesus. On the top of Tabor, Moses saw the Son of God transfigured, and his prayer was there and then answered to its utmost bounds. In the transfiguration God showed to Moses his full glory, for he was then made able to behold it.—36.255

1573 This seems to me the greatest stretch of faith that I have either heard or read of. Had Moses requested a fiery chariot to whirl him up to heaven, had he asked to cleave the waterfloods and drown the chivalry of a nation, had he prayed to the Almighty to send fire from heaven to consume whole armies, a parallel to his prayer might possibly have been found. But when he offers this petition, "I beseech thee, show me thy glory," he stands alone, a giant among giants, a colossus even in those days of mighty men. This is the highest elevation that faith ever gained.—54.565

Exodus 33:20 *"Thou canst not see my face . . . and live."*

1574 When Augustine read those words, "Thou canst not see my face and live," he was bold enough to answer, "Let me die to see thy face."—34.280

Exodus 34:30 *"Behold, the skin of his face shone."*

1575 I am afraid, brethren, that God could not afford to make our faces shine. We should grow too proud. It needs a very meek and lowly spirit to bear the shinings of God. We only read of two men whose faces shone, and both were very meek. The one is Moses, in the Old Testament; the other is

Stephen in the New Testament, whose last words proved his meekness. When the Jews were stoning him, he prayed, "Lord, lay not this sin to their charge" (Acts 7:60). Gentleness of nature and lowliness of mind are a fine background on which God may lay the brightness of his glory.—36.254

1576 Learn the exceeding glory of our Lord Jesus Christ. This was, so to speak, the transfiguration of Moses, and all it came to was that his *face* shone. But when Christ came, he was transfigured as to his whole person. Not only his face shone, but his whole person and garments also. Moses could veil his face, but the shining of our Lord could not be thus veiled, for it streamed through his raiment, which became "white and glistering" (Luke 9:29).—36.263

Leviticus 5:17 *"If a soul sin . . . though he wist it not, yet is he guilty."*

1577 I know that I cannot keep the law of God, and my text makes it impossible beyond all other impossibility, because the law accuses me of doing wrong even when I do not intend it and am not conscious of it. You who hope to be saved by works, how can you ever enjoy a moment's peace? If you think your righteousness will save you if it is perfect, how can you ever be sure that it is perfect? You may have sinned ignorantly, and that will spoil it all.—23.671

Leviticus 10:3   *"And Aaron held his peace."*

¹⁵⁷⁸ Aaron held his peace when his two sons died. He got as far as that in submission to the will of the Lord. But it will be better still if, instead of simply holding your peace, you can bless and praise and magnify the Lord even in your sharpest trouble.—46.132

Numbers 22:28   *"And the* LORD *opened the mouth of the ass."*

¹⁵⁷⁹ An old author named Stuckley said, "There were some professed Christians who were not so good as Balaam's ass, for Balaam's ass once rebuked the mad prophet for his sin. But there were some Christians who never rebuked anyone all their lives long."—6.483

Joshua 2:13   *"Save alive my father, and my mother, and my brethren, and my sisters."*

¹⁵⁸⁰ I like this in Rahab, that she did not bargain for her own safety alone. Her sin had not hardened her heart as sin does in many cases. She thought of her father, her mother, her brothers, and her sisters. Wherever there is a real child of God there will be anxiety for his family. If you do not want to have your children saved, you are not saved yourself.—18.407

Joshua 6:4   *"The seventh day ye shall compass the city seven times."*

¹⁵⁸¹ Unconverted men and women, you are our Jericho; we wish to conquer you for Christ. Our desire is to win you to Jesus for your own good and for his glory. Joshua was bidden to go round the city seven times. We would preach to you the gospel of Christ, not seven times, but seventy times seven. They were to blow the rams' horns. The ram's horn was most common as to matter, most dull as to sound, and the least showy as to appearance. So, not with enticing words of man's wisdom, but in simplicity do we warn you with the rough sound of our ram's horn, that unless you repent, you must perish.—14.94

Joshua 6:5   *"All the people shall shout."*

¹⁵⁸² We are not only to sound the ram's horn of warning and to bear round and round the sinner's conscience the ark of Christ's grace, but *all the host must engage in this work.* Did you notice that the whole of the people were to compass the city? It would not fall else. And they were to shout, too, at the last. I want you, my fellow members, to unite in our earnest efforts to win souls for Christ.—14.96

Judges 7:20   *"The sword of the* LORD, *and of Gideon."*

¹⁵⁸³ The true war cry of the church is Gideon's war cry, "The sword of the Lord!" God must do it, it is his work. But we are not to be idle; instrumentality is to be

used—"The sword of the Lord *and* of Gideon!" If we only cry, "The sword of the Lord!" we shall be guilty of an idle presumption, and shall be tempting God to depart from his fixed rule of procedure. This is the cry of every lazy lie-abed. What good ever comes from saying, "The Lord will do his own work; let us sit still"? Nor must it be "The sword of Gideon" alone, for that were idolatrous reliance on an arm of flesh. We can do nothing of ourselves.—10.167

Ruth 2:3 *"And she went, and came, and gleaned in the field."*

[1584] I have now to invite you to other fields than these. I would bring you to the field of gospel truth. My Master is the Boaz. See here, in this precious Book is a field of truthful promises, of blessings rich and ripe. The Master stands at the gate and affords us welcome. Strong men full of faith, like reapers, reap their sheaves and gather in their armfuls. O that you were all reapers, for the harvest truly is plenteous! But if not reapers, may you be as the maidens of Boaz. I see some servants who do not so much reap themselves as partake of that which others have reaped.—8.447

1 Samuel 1:15 *"I am a woman of a sorrowful spirit."*

[1585] Hannah's sorrow prepared her to receive further blessings, for after the birth of Samuel she had three more sons and two daughters (1 Sam. 2:21), God giving her five for the one that she had dedicated to him. This was grand interest for her loan: five hundred percent! Parting with Samuel was the necessary preface to the reception of other little ones. God cannot bless some of us till first of all he has tried us.—26.47

1 Samuel 3:10 *"Speak; for thy servant heareth."*

[1586] Do you ever get alone and sit still and say, as Samuel did, in the dead of night, "Speak, Lord, for thy servant heareth"? If you never do that, the little child Samuel may well rebuke you. He was willing that God should speak to him. But, oh, we are so busy! So busy! So sadly busy!—26.394

[1587] Samuel was asleep, yet he heard God's voice. But I know some people who are awake, yet have not heard it.—54.110

1 Samuel 3:15 *"Samuel feared to show Eli the vision."*

[1588] Samuel loved his foster father, and for him to mention the tremendous doom pronounced on Eli's house must have caused him great grief of spirit. But he bravely repeated the dread words of the Most High.

There are certain truths in God's Word which we tremble to think on. Do you dream that we have any pleasure in the doctrine of eternal punishment? We speak

235

of the wrath to come with fear and trembling, but we speak of it because we cannot escape from the conviction that it is taught in the Word of God. As Samuel was compelled to tell Eli of the unalterable curse that God had pronounced on his household, so must God's faithful servants speak of the doom of the wicked and never flinch from warning them. We must speak all the gospel, or else the blood of souls will stain our skirts at the last great day. However painful a duty it may be, it is nonetheless binding on us.—37.31

1 Samuel 5:4 *"Behold, Dagon was fallen upon his face."*

1589 Where the Holy Spirit enters, he is able to subdue all things unto himself. When the ark came unto the Philistine temple, down went Dagon. And when the Holy Ghost enters the soul, sin falls and is broken. If the Holy Spirit be within, we may rest assured he will tolerate no reigning sin.—18.225

1 Samuel 7:12 *"Samuel . . . called the name of it Ebenezer."*

1590 A good old woman used to hear people speak about their Ebenezers, or stones of help, in remembrance of God's mercy. But she said that when she looked back on hers, she thought she was looking back on a wall. They were set so closely together that they seemed to make a wall on the right hand and on the left of all her pathway. Well, that is just like mine. I am such a debtor to divine mercy that if I could but pay half a farthing to the pound, I should need to give 50 million times more than I am, or ever hope to be worth. Oh, what I owe him!—39.7

1 Samuel 10:6 *"Thou shalt . . . be turned into another man."*

1591 I do not think that Saul ever did really in his inmost soul know the Lord. After Samuel anointed him, he was "turned into another man," but he never became a new man, and the sense of God's presence that he had was not comparable to that presence of God which a true saint enjoys.—48.521

1 Samuel 20:39 *"But the lad knew not any thing."*

1592 I believe a very large majority of churchgoers know no more of what the preaching is about than did Jonathan's lad when he ran after the arrows. Their flight David well understood, but the lad knew nothing of the matter. Too many are merely the stolid, unthinking, slumbering worshipers of an unknown God.—11.496

2 Samuel 6:22 *"And I will yet be more vile than thus."*

1593 David would more and more abase himself before the Lord. He felt that whatever Michal's opinion of him might be, it could not be more humbling than his own view of himself. If any man thinks ill of you, do not be angry with him, for you are worse than he thinks you to be. If he charges you falsely on some point, yet be satisfied, for if he knew you better he might change the accusation, and you would be no gainer by the correction. If you have your moral portrait painted and it is ugly, be satisfied, for it only needs a few blacker touches, and it would be still nearer the truth.—34.367

2 Samuel 12:23 *"I shall go to him, but he shall not return to me."*

1594 Where did David expect to go? Why, to heaven, surely. Then his child must have been there, for he said, "I shall go to him." I do not hear him say the same of Absalom. He did not stand over his corpse and say, "I shall go to him." He had no hope for that rebellious son. Over this child it was not, "O my son! Would to God I had died for you!" No, he could let this babe go with perfect confidence, for he said, "I shall go to him."—7.509

2 Samuel 23:16 *"He would not drink thereof, but poured it out unto the* LORD.*"*

1595 David felt he could not drink the water that the brave warriors who broke through the host of the Philistines brought to him from the well at Bethlehem, because it seemed to him as though it were the blood of the men that went in

jeopardy of their lives. He poured it out before the Lord. It was too precious a draft for him, when men's lives had been hazarded for it. But the good Shepherd not only hazarded his life, but even laid it down for his sheep.—17.327

1 Kings 3:5 *"God said, Ask what I shall give thee."*

1596 If in a vision of the night the Lord should say to us as he did to Solomon, "Ask what I shall give you," I do not think any of us would hesitate. I cannot imagine myself asking for riches or honor or even for wisdom, unless it were wisdom of a far higher order than is commonly esteemed among men. The gift which I feel I should crave beyond every other boon is holiness, pure and immaculate holiness. The one thing I desire beyond everything else is to be perfectly free from sin, and to lead an unblemished life without sin of omission or sin of commission.—18.411, 412

1 Kings 17:4 *"I have commanded the ravens to feed thee."*

1597 There was a poor man who had no bread for his family, and they were almost starving. One of his children said to him, "Father, God sent bread to Elijah by ravens."

"Ah yes," he replied, "but God does not use birds in that way now." He was a cobbler, and a short time after he spoke these words there flew into his workshop a bird, which he saw was a rare one, so he caught it and put it in a cage. A little later, a servant came in and said to him, "Have you seen such-and-such a bird?"

"Yes," he answered, "it flew into my shop, so I caught it and put it into a cage."

"It belongs to my mistress," said the maid.

"Well then, take it," he replied, and away she went. When the girl took the bird to her mistress, the lady sent her back to thank the cobbler for his care of her pet, and to give him half a sovereign. So, if the bird did not actually bring the bread and meat in its mouth, it was made the medium of feeding the hungry family although the father had doubted whether such a thing could be.—46.234

1598 The ravens owe their own meat day by day to God's providing, and yet he employs them for the supply of his servant. So poor saints, deeply dependent on God for their humblest needs, he enables to help saints yet poorer still. His prophet shall be sustained by ravens, who, perhaps, have little ones that cry for their food. The Lord will provide. We know not how, but he has his own ways and methods.—57.401

1 Kings 18:21 *"How long halt ye between two opinions?"*

1599 How many more sermons do you want? How many more Sundays must roll away wasted? How many warnings, how many sicknesses, how many tollings of the bell to warn you that you must die? How many graves must be dug for your family before you will be impressed? How many plagues and pestilences must ravage this city before you will turn to God in truth? "How long halt ye between two opinions?"—3.219

1 Kings 19:4 *"O Lord, take away my life."*

1600 The man who did pray that he might die never died at all. How foolish he was to pray that he might die, when God had intended that he should go to heaven by a whirlwind with a chariot and horses of fire!—40.164

1601 Elijah failed in the very point at which he was strongest, and that is where most men fail. In Scripture it is the wisest man who proves himself to be the greatest fool, just as the meekest man, Moses, spoke hasty and bitter words. Abraham failed in his faith, and Job in his patience. So he who was the most courageous of all men fled from an angry woman. Elijah could stand face to face with that woman's husband. Yet he was afraid of Jezebel, and he fled from her and even requested that he might die. This was to show us that Elijah was not strong by nature, but only in the strength imparted to him by God, so that when the divine strength was gone, he was of no more account that anybody else.—47.206, 207

1602 Elijah prayed that he might die. Why? Because he was afraid that he should die! This was very inconsistent on his part, but we always are inconsistent when we are unbelieving. There is nothing in the world more ridiculous than unbelieving fears!—47.210

2 Kings 5:13 *"If the prophet had bid thee do some great thing . . . ?"*

1603 Believe in Jesus Christ. "It is so simple," says one.

Yes, and that is the reason why it is so hard. If it were hard, people would do it, but because it is so simple, they won't have it. It was a very hard thing for Naaman to go and wash in the Jordan; and why hard? Because it was so easy! If it had been a difficult thing it would not have been hard; he would have done it.—19.418

2 Kings 6:5 *"Alas, master! for it was borrowed."*

1604 It would be bad enough to lose your own ax, but it was not his own. Therefore he doubly deplored the incident. I know this would not operate on thievish minds. There are some who, if it was another man's, and they had borrowed it, would have no further care about it. "Let the lender get it back if he can." But we speak to honest men, and with them it is always a strong argument: Your body is another's; do

it no injury. As for our spirit, that too is God's, and how careful we should be of it.—17.439, 440

2 Kings 20:17 *"All that is in thine house . . . shall be carried unto Babylon."*

1605 Isaiah threatened to make the same persons the means of his punishment who had been the means of his sin. "You were so pleased while you showed these Babylonians your treasures, that these very men shall take them away." And so the things in which we confide shall be our disappointment. If we take our hearts away from God and give them to any earthly thing, it will be a curse to us. Our sins are the mothers of our sorrows.—12.442

2 Chronicles 28:23 *"They were the ruin of him, and of all Israel."*

1606 Ahaz ruined all Israel as well as himself. This man perished not alone in his iniquity. If you perish in your sin, you will not perish alone. That is one of the most terrible things about evil. Are there not many men who will be the ruin of their children's souls? And are there not mothers who train their daughters for gaiety and frivolity, who will have to answer for the ruin of their souls? O, we all have vastly more influence than we reckon on! The workingman in the shop thinks that he is the victim of his companions' bad example. But if he had more backbone, he might be the master and leader of them.—44.175, 176

239

2 Chronicles 33:1 *"Manasseh was twelve years old when he began to reign."*

1607 Manasseh was born three years after his father's memorable sickness. His days were prolonged by fifteen years. In the third year of those fifteen his son Manasseh was born to him. Had he known, I think, what sort of a son would have risen up in his stead, he might have been content to die rather than to be the father of such a persecutor of God's people and such a setter up of idolatry in the land. Alas, often we know not what we pray for!—62.145, 146

Esther 4:14 *"If thou altogether holdest thy peace at this time. . . ."*

1608 We are very much in our position as a church as Esther was to the Jews. If she did not do her part, Mordecai told her God would do it by somebody else, and put her away. And so it is with us. If we lag and loiter in work for Christ, he will put us away as a Christian church—not from his eternal love, for that he will never do—but from our position of honor and usefulness. May it please him to remove me, his unworthy servant, and give me rest from my labors, before such a catastrophe as that should overwhelm us.—13.408

Job 1:20 *"Then Job . . . fell down upon the ground, and worshipped."*

1609 After the patriarch had fallen down upon the ground, he "worshipped." Not, "he grumbled," not "he lamented," much less that he began to imprecate and use language unjustifiable and improper. But he "fell down upon the ground, and worshipped." O dear friend, when your grief presses you to the very dust, worship there!—42.134

Job 1:21 *"The LORD gave, and the LORD hath taken away."*

1610 I believe that Satan intended to make Job feel that it was God who was at work when his messenger said, "The fire of God is fallen from heaven, and hath burned up the sheep."

"Ah," said Satan, "he will see that God is against him!" The devil did not succeed as he thought, for Job could see that it was God's hand, and that took away the sting of the stroke. "The LORD hath taken away."—42.140

Job 1:21 *"Blessed be the name of the LORD."*

1611 Suppose your best beloved should sicken and die. You can bless a giving God; could you bless a taking God? Suppose that your riches took to themselves wings, and every one of them should fly away. Could you still praise the God who is as good when he takes as when he gives?—12.67

1612 When Job blessed God on the dunghill, even the devil himself could not insinuate that Job was a hypocrite. When Job prospered, the devil said, "Doth Job serve God for naught?" But when he lost his all and yet said, "Blessed be the name of the LORD," then the good man shone like a star when the clouds are gone. Oh, let us be sure to praise God when things go ill with us!—61.438

Job 1:22 *"In all this Job sinned not, nor charged God foolishly."*

1613 As I read the verse through, it looked too dry for me, and so I wetted it with a tear. I, who have suffered so little, have often sinned, and in times of anguish have charged God foolishly. Is not this true of some of you? If so, let your tear follow mine. But yet the tear will not wash out the sin. Fly to the fountain filled with blood, and wash therein from sins of impatience, sins of petulance, sins of rebellion, sins of unbelief.—36.611

Job 7:15 *"My soul chooseth strangling, and death rather than my life."*

1614 I think I know, as well as most men, what physical pain means. But I would sooner lie bedridden, suffering all the pains that could be crowded into a human body, and lie like that for seventy years, than endure the tortures of a guilty conscience or the pangs of a soul under the sentence of condemnation. I know that when I was under conviction of sin, I could sympathize with Job when he said, "My soul chooseth strangling, and death rather than my life."—50.279

Job 13:15 *"Though he slay me, yet will I trust in him."*

1615 The text holds the plain supposition that Job shall be tried extremely. He does not say, "Though I die. . . ." That would be a great trial. Death is not a pleasant thing. It is no child's play even to the strongest believer. Job does not say, "Though I die," but "Though he slay me." That is more. He does not say, "Though he permit me to be slain," but "Though he *slay* me; though he should seem to be so much my enemy as to turn round and kill me, though I may not believe his action, I will believe himself. I will believe his infallible word, even though he slay me." It is not, "Though he make me hunger," or "Though he put me in prison, though he allow me to be mocked, though he allow me to be banished from all my friends and to live a solitary and wretched life." No, it is more than that: "Though he slay me."—57.413

Job 14:4 *"Who can bring a clean thing out of an unclean? not one."*

1616 How then, can he be pure who is born of a woman who is herself sinful? How can we, who are impure, be the parents of pure children? Such a thing is not possible.—53.362

241

Job 23:10 *"When he hath tried me, I shall come forth as gold."*

1617 Trials are no evidence of being without God, since *trials come from God!* Job says, "When *he* hath tried me." He sees God in his afflictions. It was God who tried Job, and it is God who tries us. No trouble comes to us without divine permission. All the dogs of affliction are muzzled until God sets them free.—35.429

Job 42:10 *"The LORD gave Job twice as much as he had before."*

1618 Did you ever notice that when God gave Job twice as much substance as he had before, he gave him only the same number of children as he formerly had? The Lord gave him twice as much gold, and twice as much property, but he gave him only the exact number of children that he had before. Why did he not give the patriarch double the number of children? Because God reckoned the first ones as being his still. They were dead to Job's eye, but they were visible to Job's faith. God numbered them still as part of Job's family. And if you count up how many children Job had, you will find that he had twice as many in the end as he had in the beginning.—46.44

Psalm 7:11 *"God is angry with the wicked every day."*

1619 He is angry with you this moment—and always. You go to sleep with an angry God gazing into your face. You wake in the morning, and if your eye were not dim, you would perceive his frowning countenance. He is angry with you even when you are singing his praises, for you mock him with solemn sounds upon a thoughtless tongue. He is angry with you on your knees, for you only pretend to pray; you utter words without heart. As long as you are not a believer, he must be angry with you every moment.—17.538

Psalm 9:17 *"The wicked shall be turned into hell."*

1620 "Oh," you say, "that is not me."

No, I did not mean that for you; I have not finished the verse yet. This is the part for you: "and all the nations that forget God." What did they do? They did not do anything. They merely fell into a little matter of neglect. That is all. They forgot something—God. Neglect destroys men. Only sit still and allow matters to take their course, and your damnation is sure.—26.578, 579

Psalm 14:1 *"The fool hath said in his heart, There is no God."*

1621 That passage is wrongly translated. It should be, "The fool has said in his heart, no God—I don't want any, I wish there were none." And who amongst us has not been so foolish as to desire that there were no God?—1:151

Psalm 23:1 *"The* Lord *is my shepherd."*

1622 This sweetest of the Psalms sings of many mercies which the happy soul of the believer receives, and it traces all those benefits to one source—the good Shepherd himself. "I shall not want." Why? Because *the Lord* is my Shepherd. I lie down in delicious repose in green pastures. Why? Because *he* maketh me. I march onward making holy progress beside the still waters. Why? Because *he* leadeth me. In the prospect of death I am calm and free from fear. Why? Because *he* is with me, *his* rod and staff comfort me.—19.721

1623 One would think from the look on your doubtful face that it said, "The Lord has forgotten to be my Shepherd. He has given me over to the wolf. He has driven me into a wilderness and left me among the dark mountains. I perish in a dry and thirsty land, where there is no water."—30.515

Psalm 23:4 *"Though I walk through the valley of the shadow of death. . . . "*

1624 A shadow was cast across my road, but I passed through it, and scarcely perceived that it was there. Why was that? Because I had my eye fixed on a strong light beyond, and I did not notice the shadow which otherwise would have distressed me. Believers are so rejoiced by the presence of the Lord and Master that they do not observe that they are dying. They rest so sweetly in the embrace of Jesus that they hear not the voice of wailing. When they pass from one world into another, it is something like going from England to Scotland. It is all one kingdom, and one sun shines in both lands.—36.572

Psalm 31:15 *"My times are in thy hand."*

1625 If our times are in God's hand, here is a grand argument for future blessedness. He that takes care of our times will take care of our eternity.—37.287

Psalm 34:8 *"O taste and see that the* Lord *is good."*

1626 Those who rejoice that they have tasted that the Lord is gracious yet confess it with a deep blush, because *they have only tasted.* I would to God that all of us would go to Jesus and feed on him to the full. Oh, for a divine hunger which would make us eat abundantly! I would be ravenous for Christ!—36.561

Psalm 42:1 *"As the hart panteth after the water brooks. . . . "*

1627 A camel does not pant after water brooks, because it carries its own water within. But the hart does, because it has no inward resources. After being hunted on a hot day, it has no inward supplies; it is drained of its moisture. So are we. We do not carry a store of grace within of our own on which

243

we can rely. We need to come again and again and again to the divine fountain and drink of the eternal spring. Hence it is because we have a new life, and that life is dependent on God, and has all its fresh springs in him, that therefore we pant and thirst after him.—14.417

Psalm 46:1 *"God is our refuge and strength."*

1628 It is all very well for me to stand here and talk about this, but the sweetness lies in getting under the refuge. It is of no use to know, when you are climbing the storm-beaten Alp, that there is a refuge on the hillside against the storm, unless you get into it. Beloved believer, get into your God!—14.187

Psalm 51:5 *"In sin did my mother conceive me."*

1629 It is a most villainous thing that some persons try to slander David's mother, and to suppose that there was something irregular about his birth which made him speak as he has done, whereas there cannot be the slightest imputation on that admirable woman. David himself speaks of her with intense respect and says, "Save the son of thine handmaid," as though he felt it no discredit to be the son of such a woman. She was, doubtless, one of the excellent of the earth, and yet, excellent as she was, it could not but be

otherwise that in sin her son was conceived.—11.103

Psalm 51:14 *"Deliver me from bloodguiltiness, O God."*

1630 It is pleasing to observe in David's penitence that he plainly names his sin. He does not call it manslaughter; he does not speak of it as an imprudence by which an unfortunate accident occurred to a worthy man. He calls it by its true name, bloodguiltiness. He did not actually slay the husband of Bathsheba; it was by another hand that Uriah died. But still it was planned in David's heart that Uriah should be slain, and he was before the Lord the murderer of Uriah. He calls a spade a spade.

Let us learn in our confessions to be honest with God. Do not give fair names to foul sins. Call them what you will, they will smell no sweeter. What God sees them to be, labor to feel them to be, and with openness of heart acknowledge their true character.—12.541

Psalm 51:17 *"A broken and a contrite heart, O God, thou wilt not despise."*

1631 When St. Augustine lay dying, he had this verse always fixed on the curtains, so that as often as he awoke, he might read it: "A broken and a contrite heart, O God, thou wilt not despise." When you despise yourselves, God honors you. But as long as you honor yourselves, God despises you. A whole heart is a scentless thing.

But when it is broken and bruised, it is like that precious spice which was burned as holy incense in the ancient tabernacle.—6.347

Psalm 84:11   *"No good thing will he withhold from them that walk uprightly."*

1632 It does not say, "I will force all my children to enjoy every good thing." No, but, "No good thing will he withhold." There are thousands of mercies that we do not enjoy, not because they are withheld, but because we do not take them. We are not confined in God, but in ourselves. We are empty because we do not accept the fulness of Christ.—28.276

1633 I have often thought of the large promise written in the Bible—I do not know where there is a larger one—"No good thing will he withhold from them that walk uprightly."—53.489

Psalm 91:16   *"With long life will I satisfy him."*

1634 No believer dies an untimely death. Long life is not to be reckoned by years as men count them. He lives longest who lives best. Many a man has crowded half a century into a single year. God gives his people life, not as the clock ticks, but as he helps them to serve him, and he can make them to live much in a short space of time. There are no untimely figs gathered into God's basket. The great Master of the vineyard plucks the grapes when they are ripe and ready to be taken, and not before.—18.102, 103

Psalm 103:1   *"Bless the LORD, O my soul: and all that is within me, bless his holy name."*

1635 I believe that David uttered a great truth when he said, "Bless the Lord, O my soul: and all that is within me, bless his holy name." There is nothing in man that God has put there which may not be employed in God's service. Some may ask me whether anger can be brought in. I answer, yes. A good man may serve God by being angry against sin, and to be angry against sin is a high and holy thing. You may ask me whether ridicule can be employed. I answer, yes. I believe we may even rightly employ it in the preaching of God's Word. I always intend to use it, and if by a laugh I can make men see the folly of an error better than in any other way, they shall laugh. Every power that God has implanted in man—I will make no exception—may be used for God's service and honor.—3.325

1636 The whole life of the Christian should be a psalm, of which the contents should be summed up in this sentence, "Bless the Lord, O my soul: and all that is within me, bless his holy name."—21.536

1637 Notice that the psalm begins, "Bless the Lord, O my soul,"

245

and it ends in the same way, "Bless the Lord, O my soul," as if to show us that praise is the Alpha and Omega of a Christian life. Praise is the life of life. Oh, that our infancy would bless the Lord, and our childhood and our youth bless the Lord, and our manhood and our old age bless the Lord!—36.1

Psalm 103:13   *"The* LORD *pitieth them that fear him."*

¹⁶³⁸ Some of you he does not pity at all. You that do not fear him, but trifle with him, you that hate him, you that despise him, you that are careless about him, you that never think of him—you have none of his pity. When you are sick, he looks on your sickness as something you deserve. When you go astray, he looks upon your wandering as a mere matter of course of your guilty nature, and he is angry with you. Your afflictions are not strokes of his rod, they are cuts of his sword. Your sins are not things that he overlooks, but if you die as you now are—guilty and unsaved—justice shall look on you with a tearless eye and say to you, "You knew your duty, but did it not." Think not that this text shall afford you any consolation in this life or in that which is to come. You shall not have even a drop of water to cool your tongues in hell. No pity shall be shed upon you there.—45.440, 441

Psalm 119:11   *"Thy word have I hid in mine heart."*

¹⁶³⁹ The place for God's Word is not an outside place, but an inside place. It is infinitely better to have it hidden in your heart than it is to have many copies of it laid among the furniture of your house. It may be that your having the Word of God so plentifully at home may increase your damnation, rather than lead to your salvation.—44.398

Psalm 136:1   *"His mercy endureth for ever."*

¹⁶⁴⁰ It ought to be a great encouragement to you who are not God's people. You have gone to the utmost extreme of sin, but "his mercy endureth for ever." You have resisted his Spirit, you have stifled your conscience, you have been disobedient to Christ, but "his mercy endureth for ever." You have indulged every evil passion, you have broken loose from every bond that ought to have held you to the way of right, but "his mercy endureth for ever." The last day of your life is almost come, but his mercy still endures, and will endure till you die.—22.180

Psalm 139:17   *"How precious also are thy thoughts unto me, O God!"*

¹⁶⁴¹ If God's thoughts are so precious to us, how very precious his words ought to be!—57.187

246

Proverbs 16:33 *"The lot is cast . . . but the whole disposing thereof is of the* LORD.*"*

1642 If the disposal of the lot is the Lord's, whose is the arrangement of the whole life? When Achan had committed a great sin, the tribes were assembled and the lot fell on Achan (Josh. 7). When Jonah was in the ship, they cast lots and the lot fell on Jonah (Jonah 1). And when Jonathan had tasted the honey, they cast lots and Jonathan was taken (1 Sam. 14). When they cast lots for an apostle who should succeed the fallen Judas, the lot fell on Matthias, and he was separated to the work (Acts 1). If the simple casting of a lot is guided by God, how much more the events of the entire life!—1.257

Ecclesiastes 8:2 *"I counsel thee to keep the king's commandment."*

1643 This is admirable counsel for every Christian. If the commandment were of men, we might break it. But if it be the King who gives the command, even the Lord Jesus Christ, then the advice is wise and weighty. Perhaps some of you would ask me, "What is the best course for me to pursue in certain difficult cases?"

"I counsel thee to keep the King's commandment."

"But I am a young man just beginning life, and may get into trouble if I am rigidly scrupulous in doing that which is right."

"I counsel thee to keep the King's commandment."

"But at this present time I may lose my situation if I keep all his statutes. Could I not forget one of the commandments for a little while?"

"I counsel thee to keep the King's commandment." If he be a King, then it is a solemn hazard to your soul if you come short of the least of his commandments. One treason makes a traitor.—28.712, 713

Song of Solomon 1:1 *"The Song of songs, which is Solomon's."*

1644 The historical books I may compare to the outer courts of the temple; the gospels, the epistles, and the psalms bring us into the holy place, or the court of the priests; but the Song of Solomon is the most holy place—the holy of holies, before which the veil still hangs to many an untaught believer.—10:133

1645 This book of the Canticles seems to us to belong to the secret place of the tabernacle of the Most High. We see our Savior's face in almost every page of the Bible, but here we see his heart and feel his love to us.—11.349

1646 We take it for granted that the Song of Solomon is a sacred marriage song between Christ and his church.—26.133

247

Song of Solomon 5:16 *"He is altogether lovely."*

1647 Think of his name. It is Jesus, the Savior. Is not that lovely? Think of his work. He is come to seek and to save that which was lost. Is not that lovely? Think of what he has done. He has redeemed our souls with blood. Is not that lovely? Think of what he is doing. He is pleading before the throne of God for sinners. Think of what he is giving at this moment. He is exalted on high to give repentance and remission of sins. Is not this lovely? Under every aspect Christ Jesus is attractive to sinners who need him. Come, then, come and welcome! There is nothing to keep you away; there is everything to bid you to come.—17.408

Song of Solomon 7:10 *"I am my beloved's, and his desire is toward me."*

1648 A Christian is never strong for service when he does not know whether Christ loves him or not. If that be a question, you have put out the fire by which alone the force can be generated which must work the machinery of your spirit. You must know beyond question that Jesus loved you and gave himself for you.—18.459

Isaiah 3:10 *"Say ye to the righteous, that it shall be well with him."*

1649 I was about to say of the Christian that it is so well with him that I could not imagine it to be better, for he is well-fed; he feeds on the flesh and blood of Jesus. He is well-clothed—"Bring forth the best robe, and put it on him" (Luke 15:22). He is well-housed; he dwells in God who has been the dwelling place of his people in all generations. He is well-married, for his soul is knit in bonds of marriage union to Christ. He is well-provided for in the present; the Lord is his Shepherd, and he shall not want.—13.20

Isaiah 6:5 *"I dwell in the midst of a people of unclean lips."*

1650 I do not think a man can be a good missionary if he winks at the sin that surrounds him. Unless it stinks in his nostrils, unless it makes his soul boil with holy indignation, unless like Paul his heart is stirred in him, how can he speak as he should speak the message of his God?—23.247

Isaiah 9:6 *"The everlasting Father."*

1651 Jesus is not the child of eternity, but the Father of it. Eternity did not bring him forth from its mighty bowels, but he brought forth eternity.—12.677

Isaiah 38:3 *"Remember ... O Lord ... how I have walked before thee ... with a perfect heart."*

1652 Some degree of self-righteousness is, we think, manifest in Hezekiah's prayer when he turned his face to the wall. He was diseased we fear at that time with two diseases. Not merely a swelling boil, but a swelling self-conceit, and God let him see that he was a poor silly sinner after all.—12.438

Isaiah 38:17 *"Thou hast cast all my sins behind thy back."*

1653 Where is God's back? Is there any place behind his back? He is everywhere present, and everywhere seen. It must be nowhere at all. Our sins are thrown into the nowhere.—38.561

Isaiah 41:10 *"Fear thou not; for I am with thee. . . . "*

1654 Five times in this verse you get some form of the pronoun *thou*, and five times you get the pronoun *I*. Whatever there may be of you, there shall be as much of God. Whatever there may be of your weakness, there shall be as much of God's strength. Whatever there may be of your sin, there shall be as much of God's mercy to meet it all.—16.273

Isaiah 45:22 *"Look unto me, and be ye saved, all the ends of the earth."*

1655 The text was "Look unto me, and be ye saved, all the ends of the earth." He was an ignorant man. He could not say much; he was obliged to keep to his text. Thank God for that. He began, " 'Look,' that is not a hard word. A fool can do that. It does not need a wise man to look. A child can do that. How simple." Then he went on, " 'Look unto *me.'* Do not look to yourselves, but to

Christ." And then he went on in his own simple way to put it thus: "Look unto me; I am sweating great drops of blood for you. Look unto me; I am scourged and spit upon. I am nailed to the cross. I die, I am buried, I rise and ascend, I am pleading before the Father's throne, and all this for you."

Stooping down, he looked under the gallery and said, "Young man, you are very miserable."

So I was, but I had not been accustomed to be addressed in that way.

"Ah," said he, "and you will always be miserable if you don't do as my text tells you, that is, look unto Christ." And then he called out, with all his might, "Young man, look! In God's name look, and look now!"

I did look, blessed be God! I know I looked then and there, and he who but that minute before had been near despair had the fulness of joy and hope. And that instant he who was ready to destroy himself could have stood up there and then to sing!—7.224

Note: In the above quotation CHS describes his conversion experience on Sunday morning, January 6, 1850, when he was 15 years old. A heavy snowfall prevented him from reaching the church which his mother recommended, and he turned into a Primitive Methodist Chapel in Colchester. The preacher himself was snowbound, and a layman who made no claims to educa-

tion preached extemporaneously on Isaiah 45:22 to fifteen people, one of whom was CHS. Who could have guessed that God would use this seemingly insignificant occasion to make history? Preachers and Sunday school teachers, take heart!

1656 Standing in one of the halls of the orphanage is the very pulpit from which I savingly heard the gospel of our Lord Jesus Christ. Though I have no reverence for relics of any sort, yet a flood of grateful memories flows before me as I look on the platform whereon stood the unknown brother who pointed me to Jesus. Who he was I shall never know till the Day of Judgment. But the text, "Look unto me, and be ye saved, all the ends of the earth," was the voice of God to my soul.—32.555

Isaiah 49:16 *"I have graven thee upon the palms of my hands."*

1657 I may illustrate this by our Savior's hands. What are these wounds in thy hands, these sacred *stigmata*, these ensigns of suffering? The graver's tool was the nail, backed by the hammer. He must be fastened to the cross, that his people might be truly graven on the palms of his hands. There is much consolation here. We know that what a man has won with great pain he will keep with great tenacity. Child of God, you cost

Christ too much for him to forget you.—61.16, 17

Isaiah 53:5 *"With his stripes we are healed."*

1658 No sprinkling can wash out sin. No confirmation can confer grace. No masses can propitiate God. Your hope must be in Jesus, Jesus smitten, Jesus bruised, Jesus slain, Jesus the substitute for sinners. Whoever believes in him is healed, but all other hopes are a lie from top to bottom.—18.491

1659 Do not scourge yourself. "With *his* stripes we are healed." I beg you, do not think that by some kind of spiritual mortification or terror or horror into which you force yourself you shall be healed. Your healing is in *his* stripes, not in your own, in *his* griefs, not in your griefs. I implore you, do not make your repentance into a rival of the stripes of Jesus, for so it would become an antichrist. When your eye is full of tears, look through them to Christ whom you may see, whether your eye be wet or dry. In the Christ on the cross there are five wounds, but you have not to add even another one of your own to them. In him, and in him alone, is all your healing; in him who, from head to foot, becomes a mass of suffering, that you, diseased from head to foot, might from the crown of your head to the sole of your foot be made perfectly whole.—43.19, 20

Isaiah 53:6   *"All we like sheep have gone astray."*

¹⁶⁶⁰ Man is here compared to a beast, for sin brings out the animal part of us, and while holiness allies us to angels, sin degrades us to brutes. We are not likened to one of the more noble and intelligent animals, but to a silly sheep. All sin is folly; all sinners are fools.—16.205, 206

Isaiah 53:6   *"The LORD hath laid on him the iniquity of us all."*

¹⁶⁶¹ Sin I may compare to the rays of some evil sun. Sin was scattered throughout this world as abundantly as light, and Christ is made to suffer the full effect of the baleful rays which stream from the sun of sin. God as it were holds up a burning glass and concentrates all the scattered rays in a focus upon Christ. That seems to be the thought of the text, "The Lord hath focused upon him the iniquity of us all." That which was scattered abroad everywhere is here brought into terrible concentration.—12.314

Isaiah 53:7   *"He openeth not his mouth."*

¹⁶⁶² In his questioning our Lord Jesus said not a word in self-defense. He knew that it availed not for a lamb to plead with wolves. He was well-aware that whatever he said would be mis-construed and made a fresh source of accusation. What power he thus exerted in remaining silent! Perhaps nothing displays more fully the omnipotence of Christ than this power of self-control.—9.99

Isaiah 53:10   *"It pleased the LORD to bruise him."*

¹⁶⁶³ If God were to lay his finger on any one of us, only his finger, we should be struck with sick-ness, paralysis, and death. Then think of God smiting! God must smite sin wherever he sees it. So when he saw our sin laid on his Son, he smote him with the blows of a cruel One, till beneath that smiting his Son cried out, "My God, my God, why hast thou forsaken me?" (Matt. 27:46).—18.487

Isaiah 55:7   *"Let the wicked forsake his way, and the unrighteous man his thoughts."*

¹⁶⁶⁴ "But thoughts are free," says some unthinking person. "I shall never be hanged for my thoughts."

No, perhaps not, but have you never heard that old saying, "A man may not be hanged for his thoughts, but he may be damned for his thoughts"? In thought is often the very essence of sin. A deed might in itself be colorless, but the motive for doing it—the thought at the back of it—puts the venom and virus and guilt into the deed.—48.450

251

Isaiah 55:7 *"He will abundantly pardon."*

1665 You have abundant sin, fatally abundant! But here is abundant pardon. You mourn your abundant hardness of heart. Yes, but abundant pardon will dissolve the stone. How abundant that pardon is the Lord does not tell, but certainly it is superabundant.—35.357

Isaiah 55:8 *"For my thoughts are not your thoughts."*

1666 God's thoughts are love, pity, tenderness; ours are forgetfulness, ingratitude, and hardheartedness. He is tender of our comfort, but we are not tender of his honor. He considers our interests, but we think not of his glory. He watches over our safety, but we are not watchful to keep his statutes. He loads us with benefits, but we only load him with our sins. He has given us all that we have, but we bring him cold thanks in return.—23.675, 676

Isaiah 55:11 *"My word . . . shall not return unto me void."*

1667 My first student, Mr. Medhurst, went out to preach on Tower Hill, Sunday after Sunday. He was not then my student, but one of the young men in the church. He came to me and said, "I have been out preaching now for several months on Tower Hill, and I have not seen one conversion."

I said to him, rather sharply, "Do you expect God is going to bless you every time you choose to open your mouth?"

He answered, "Oh, no, sir! I do not expect him to do that."

"Then," I replied, "that is why you do not get a blessing." We ought to expect a blessing." God has said, "My word shall not return unto me void," and it will not. We ought to look for a harvest.—38.341

Isaiah 59:1 *"The Lord's hand is not shortened . . . neither his ear heavy."*

1668 Your accusation against God may be turned against you. You thought that God's hand was shortened, that it could not save. But it is your hand that is shortened, for you have not laid hold on Christ. You said that God's ear was heavy. No, no, no; it is your ear that is heavy. You have not heard what God the Lord has been saying to you; you have not been obedient to the heavenly message. All the mischief lies with yourself, not with God. And at the last, if you are not saved, the blame will not rest on the Savior, but on yourself.—41.209

Isaiah 65:1 *"I am found of them that sought me not."*

1669 If the Lord is thus found by those that seek him not, how much more surely will he be found by those who seek him! If he saved Saul who hated him, much more will he listen to him

252

who cries, "God be merciful to me, a sinner." If he called careless, curious Zacchaeus, much more will he speak to you, my anxious, earnest hearers, who are saying, "Oh, that he would speak to me!"—54.30

Jeremiah 8:20   *"The harvest is past, the summer is ended, and we are not saved."*

1670 You Sunday school teachers and other beloved laborers for Christ, I trust you will not have to cry at the last, "Our harvest is past, and our summer is ended, and none of our children are saved. Oh, that we had talked to our boys and girls more solemnly! Oh, that we had entreated them with tears to flee from the wrath to come!" I pray God that such may not be your dying lamentations, but that each of us may live for God at the rate which eternity will justify.—13.669

Jeremiah 13:23   *"Can the Ethiopian change his skin?"*

1671 Even if an Ethiopian could change his skin, that would be a far smaller difficulty than the one with which a sinner has to deal, for it is not his skin, but his heart which has to be changed.—43.458

Jeremiah 15:16   *"Thy words were found, and I did eat them."*

1672 It is not "I did hear them," for that he might have done and yet have perished. Herod heard John gladly, and yet became his murderer. He does not say, "I did learn them by heart." Hundreds have committed chapters to memory and were rather wearied than benefited thereby. The scribes fought over the jots and tittles of the law, but were blind leaders of the blind notwithstanding. It is not, "Thy words were found, and I did repeat them," for that he might have done as a parrot repeats language it is taught. Nor is it even, "Thy words were found, and I remembered them," for though it is an excellent thing to store truth in the memory, yet the blessed effect of the divine words comes rather to those who ponder them in their hearts. What is meant by *eating* God's words? The phrase signifies more than any other word could express. It implies *an eager study*— "I did eat them." I could not have too much of them, could not enter too thoroughly into their consideration.—17.148, 149

Jeremiah 17:9   *"The heart is deceitful above all things."*

1673 The devil is one of the "things." Therefore, the heart is worse than the devil.—1.290

Jeremiah 17:9   *"The heart is . . . desperately wicked."*

1674 There is within our nature that which would send the best saint to hell if sovereign grace did not prevent. There is a little hell within the heart of every child of God, and only the great God of heaven can master that mischievous indwelling sin.—18.414

Jeremiah 29:13 *"... seek me ... search for me with all your heart."*

[1675] If you are not seeking the Lord, the devil is seeking *you*. If you are not seeking the Lord, judgment is at your heels.—2.92

[1676] Men seek after gold as if they had a thousand hearts. But they seek after grace as if their heart were cut into a thousand pieces, and only one solitary thousandth part of it went after the blessing.—38.484

Jeremiah 31:3 *"I have loved thee with an everlasting love."*

[1677] Columbus, when he discovered America, could not have been so overjoyed as my heart was when I learned the lesson of those words, "Yea, I have loved thee with an everlasting love: therefore with lovingkindness have I drawn thee."—13.295

Jeremiah 31:33 *"I will ... write ... in their hearts."*

[1678] Perhaps you have never had anything written on your heart. Then lay your heart before the Lord with this simple prayer, "Lord, write on it!" And if he writes on it that one word *Jesus*, it will be all that you can want.—38.525

Jeremiah 31:34 *"I will remember their sin no more."*

[1679] It is a wonderful thing when omnipotence overcomes omniscience, when omnipotent love will not allow omniscience to recollect.—39.329

Lamentations 1:12 *"Is it nothing to you!"*

[1680] One thing I would say to all of you to whom it seems to be nothing that Jesus should die— that personally to me it is something that he should die. It is more than something, it is everything, and I will tell you why. It is much to me that Jesus died, for I know I slew him. But then I know another thing, that by that death I am delivered from the very guilt that put him to death.—59.304

Ezekiel 3:17 *"Son of man, I have made thee a watchman unto the house of Israel."*

[1681] The burden of the Lord hangs heavily on me. I must deliver myself from the blood of some of you who are living in impenitence, and who will probably die in it, and when, if you die unwarned, having often listened to my voice, may be able to reproach me in another world if I do not faithfully and earnestly bear my solemn testimony concerning the wrath to come.—12.169

Ezekiel 16:63   *"When I am pacified toward thee."*

1682 When I am *peace*-ified; when I am made peace toward thee. God thinks of nothing but peace toward his children. "Peace, peace," says he. He is the God of peace (Phil. 4:9), the fruit of his Spirit is peace (Gal. 5:22), the very name of his Son is peace (Isa. 9:6). The heaven to which he is bringing us is everlasting peace. And even now the peace of God which passeth all understanding keeps our hearts and minds through Jesus Christ (Phil. 4:7).—22.220

Ezekiel 36:26   *"A new heart also will I give you."*

1683 True religion begins, then, with the heart, and the heart is the ruling power of manhood. You may enlighten a man's understanding and you have done much, but as long as his heart is wrong, the enlightenment of the understanding only enables him to sin with a greater weight of responsibility resting on him. He knows good to be good, but he prefers the evil. He sees the light, but he loves the darkness, and turns from the truth because his heart is alienated from God.—19.481

Daniel 3:25   *"Lo, I see four men loose, walking in the midst of the fire."*

1684 Shadrach, Meshach, and Abednego lost something in the fire—not their coats, not one hair

of their heads. The fire did not hurt them, but it snapped their bonds. Blessed loss! A true Christian's losses are gains in another shape. Many of God's servants never know the fulness of spiritual liberty till they are cast into the midst of the furnace.—11.666

Daniel 3:25   *"Lo, I see four men . . . and . . . the fourth is like the Son of God."*

1685 You must go into the furnace if you would have the nearest and dearest dealings with Christ Jesus. Whenever the Lord appears, it is to his people when they are in a militant posture. Moses saw God at Horeb, but it was in a burning bush (Exod. 3). Joshua saw him, but it was with a drawn sword in his hand, to show that his people are still a militant people (Josh. 5). And here where the saints saw their Savior, it was as himself being in the furnace. The richest thought that a Christian perhaps can live on is this, that Christ is in the furnace with him. When you suffer, Christ suffers.—11.670

Daniel 3:27   *"Neither were their coats changed, nor the smell of fire had passed on them."*

1686 A man who has been in the furance and has come out of it is a marked man. I think I should know Shadrach, Meshach, and Abednego even now if I were to meet them. Though the smell of fire had not passed on them, I feel sure that it left a glow on their countenances and a glory on their persons which we find nowhere else. They are henceforth called "the three holy children."—38.57

Daniel 5:6 *"His knees smote one against another."*

1687 Belshazzar's knees knocked together, and the joints of his loins were loosened when he saw the handwriting on the wall which declared his condemnation. What joy would have filled his despairing spirit, if suddenly that writing had been blotted out and another hand had written, "I have loved thee with an everlasting love!" Can you conceive the joy of that astonished monarch? Yet this morning I have as good news to tell the penitent as though such were their position, and such the act of pardoning mercy. Jesus has blotted out the handwriting which was against us, and written words of love concerning us.—13.374

Daniel 6:10 *"When Daniel knew that the writing was signed, he went into his house. . . . "*

1688 If a man were to lose his soul in order to save his life, he would make a wretched bargain. So Daniel felt that the risk of being put into a den with lions was nothing to the risk of being put into hell. He chose the smaller risk, and in the name of God he went straight on.—20.56

Daniel 6:22 *"My God . . . hath shut the lions' mouths."*

1689 When Daniel came out the next morning, so far from being a loser, he was a gainer. The king approved him, admired him, loved him. Everybody in the city had heard that Daniel had been put into the lions' den. He was a great man, and it was like putting the prime minister into the lions' den. And when he came out, with what awe they looked on him! The king was not regarded as half as much a god as Daniel. Daniel has a smooth time of it afterward. The counselors never troubled him again. The lions had taken care of them.—20.58, 59

Hosea 4:17 *"Ephraim is joined to idols: let him alone."*

1690 God has said to all the agents that might do that man good, "Let him alone!" But he will not say that to the agents which can to him harm. He has not said to the devil, "Let him alone!" He will not say to death, "Let him alone!" He will not say to judgment, "Let him alone!" nor will he say to the flames of hell, "Let him alone!"—19.620

Hosea 6:1 *"Come, and let us return unto the LORD: for he hath torn, and he will heal."*

1691 This believing heart in my text actually finds an argument in the blows of God why we should trust him. When a physician finds a man's bone badly set and breaks it again, what am I sure that he is going to do? Why, to set it, and set it right next time. Now, God is the great Surgeon of men's souls, and sometimes he has to put man on the table and cut to the very bone, but he never means to kill. He never takes the knife of discipline except with the intent to bind up every wound he makes, and set the man on his feet again.—24.68

Hosea 14:4   *"I will love them freely."*

1692 When God says, "I will love them freely," he means that no prayers, no tears, no good works, no alms are an inducement to him to love men. Not only nothing in themselves, but nothing anywhere else was the cause of his love to them, not even the blood of Christ. Not even the groans and tears of his beloved Son. These are the fruits of his love, not the cause of it. He does not love because Christ died, but Christ died because the Father loved. Remember that this fountain of love has its spring in itself, not in you, nor in me, but only in the Father's own gracious, infinite heart of goodness.—9.171, 172

Hosea 14:8   *"Ephraim shall say, What have I to do any more with idols?"*

1693 If I had a favorite knife and with it a murderer had killed my wife, do you think I would use it at my table or carry it about with me? Away with the accursed thing! How I should loathe the very sight of it. And sin has murdered Christ! Our idols have put our Lord to death! Stand at the foot of the cross and see his murdered, mangled body, bleeding with its five great wounds, and you will say, "What have I to do any more with idols?"—23.106

Amos 3:3   *"Can two walk together, except they be agreed?"*

1694 If two men walk together, there must be a place where they meet each other. Do you know where that is? It is at the cross. Sinner, if you trust in Jesus, God will meet you there. That is the place where true at-one-ment is made between God and sinners.—12.454

1695 "Walking together" is not only activity, but continuance. So, true communion with Christ is not a mere spasm, not just an excitement of ecstasy. It also implies progress, for in walking together we do not lift up our feet and put them down in the same place. We proceed nearer to our journey's end. He that has true communion with Christ is making progress.—46.145

Amos 4:12   *"Prepare to meet thy God."*

1696 There are no more joyous words under heaven than these in some aspects, none more solemn

257

out of hell in others: "Prepare to meet thy God."—16.182

Amos 7:14 *"I was . . . a gatherer of sycomore fruit."*

1697 It was the trade of Amos to be a bruiser of sycamore figs. They were struck with a long staff, and then after being wounded, they sweetened. How like many of us! How many, many of us seem as if we never would be sweet till first we have been dipped in bitterness, never would be perfected till we have been smitten! We may trace many of our sharp trials, our bereavements, and our bodily pains to the fact that we are such sour fruit, nothing will ripen us but heavy blows. Blessed be the Lord that he does not spare us!—16.451

Jonah 1:3 *"Jonah . . . found a ship going to Tarshish."*

1698 When Jonah went down to flee unto Tarshish, he found a ship going there. Was not that a remarkable providence? Perhaps he said to himself, "I felt some doubt about whether I was right in going there, but when I got down to the seashore, there was a ship, and there was just room for me to go as a passenger, and the fare was just the amount that I possessed, and so I felt that it must be of the Lord." Nonsense, Jonah! It is of the Lord for you to do what is right.—46.395

Jonah 1:17 *"Now the* Lord *had prepared a great fish to swallow up Jonah."*

1699 Just let me know that God says something is true, and that is enough for me. I do not quite join with the poor old woman in her words, but I agree with her spirit, who put her implicit faith in Scripture. When someone ridiculed her for believing that the whale swallowed Jonah, "Dear," said she, "if the Word of God had said that Jonah swallowed the whale, I would have believed it."—26.644

Jonah 2:4 *"I am cast out of thy sight."*

1700 That was not true. Poor Jonah! The mariners cast him out, but God did not. He was cast out of the ship, but not out of the sight of God. "Him that cometh to me I will in no wise cast out" (John 6:37).—30.666

Jonah 2:9 *"Salvation is of the* Lord.*"*

1701 There is an obverse to this truth. If salvation is of the Lord, then damnation is of man. If you are damned, you will have no one to blame but yourself. If you perish, the blame will not lie at God's door. If you are lost and cast away, you will forever lie in hell and reflect, "I made a suicide of my soul. I can lay no blame on God."—3.200

Jonah 4:9   *"And he said, I do well to be angry, even unto death."*

1702 I was greatly struck with a story a dear sister told me yesterday. She was very nearly being removed from the church. She had quarreled with the Lord for taking away her husband, and she would not go to any place of worship, she felt so angry about her loss. But her little child came to her one morning and said, "Mother, do you think Jonah was right when he said, 'I do well to be angry, even unto death'?"

She replied, "O child, do not talk to me," and put the little one away. But she felt the rebuke, and it brought her back to her God and her church again, humbly rejoicing in him who had used this instrumentality to set her right with her Lord.—31.93, 94

Habakkuk 2:4   *"The just shall live by his faith."*

1703 This one sentence, "The just shall live by his faith," produced the Reformation.—29.614

Habakkuk 3:16   *"When I heard, my belly trembled; my lips quivered at the voice. . . . "*

1704 The period of my conviction of sin is burned into my memory as with a red-hot iron. Its wounds are cured, but the scars remain. As Habakkuk has well put it, "When I heard, my belly trembled; my lips quivered at the voice, rottenness entered into my bones, and I trembled in myself."

Oh, it's a burden, this load of sin, a burden which might crush an angel down to hell. There I stood, and seemed like another staggering Atlas, bearing up a world of sin on these shoulders, and fearing every moment lest I should be crushed into the abyss and justly lost forever. Only let a man once feel sin for half an hour, really feel its tortures, and I warrant you he would prefer to dwell in a pit of snakes than to live with his sins.—18.485

Zephaniah 2:5   *"The word of the* LORD *is against you."*

1705 You will soon be dead, and you pass into another world. You will come to the seat of judgment. You will want witnesses in your favor, and this book will be called to give its testimony. If the book could speak, it would say, "Great God, he never read me. I bear witness to his neglect of thee, for he never read me." And many a text of Scripture would rise up in that last day and say, "I was preached to him. His mother quoted me to him. His sister wrote this in a letter. A friend sent him this verse and pleaded with him to take it to heart, but he heeded none of it." If "the Word of the Lord is against you," the law will say, "He knew me, and he broke me." The gospel will say, "He knew me, and he refused me." The Bible itself will say, "He understood something of me, but he ridiculed me."—37.644

Zephaniah 3:17 *"The* LORD *thy God . . . will joy over thee with singing."*

¹⁷⁰⁶ I think this is the most wonderful text in the Bible in some respects—God himself singing! I can imagine, when the world was made, the morning stars shouting for joy, but God did not sing. He said it was "very good," and that was all. There was no song. But, oh, to think of it, that when all the chosen race shall meet around the throne, the joy of the eternal Father shall swell so high, that God, who fills all in all, shall burst out into an infinite godlike song!—11.335, 336

Zechariah 12:10 *"They shall look upon me whom they have pierced, and they shall mourn."*

¹⁷⁰⁷ Repentance is not a preparation for looking to Christ. Do you not see that? The looking is put first, and the mourning afterwards. Yet you have said, "We must mourn for sin, and then look to Christ to pardon it." That is not God's order. There will never be a tear of acceptable repentance in your eye till you have first looked to Jesus Christ. If you weep for sin without fixing your gaze on Christ, you will have to weep again over your repentance, for it is itself another sin.—50.450

Malachi 1:3 *"I hated Esau."*

¹⁷⁰⁸ Why does God hate any man? I defy anyone to give an answer but this: because that man

deserves it. No reply but that can ever be true.—5.118

Malachi 1:13 *"Ye said also, Behold, what a weariness is it!"*

¹⁷⁰⁹ When we listen to the reading of the Word of God or the preaching of his truth, shall that be a weariness? Yes, when we have no part or lot in it, when it is like reading a will in which we have no legacy. But if the gospel be preached as our gospel, the gospel of *our* salvation, and we have a share in it, what can so inspire our soul with joy?—13.500

¹⁷¹⁰ If God had been weary of us we need not have wondered. But we ought to blush and be silent for shame, because we have wearied of him. Are we tired of God? If not, how is it that we do not walk with him from day to day? Really spiritual worship is not much cared for in these days, even by professing Christians. Many will go to a place of worship if they can be entertained with fine music or grand oratory, but if communion with God is the only attraction, they are not drawn thereby.—32.212

Matthew 1:23 *"They shall call his name Emmanuel, which being interpreted is, God with us."*

¹⁷¹¹ John Wesley died with this on his tongue, and let us live with it on our hearts—"The best of all is God with us."—21.720

1712 Do you know what "God with us" means? Has it been God with you in your tribulations by the Holy Ghost's comforting influence? Has it been God with you in searching the Scriptures? Has the Holy Spirit shone on the Word? Has it been God with you in conviction, bringing you to Sinai? Has it been God with you in comforting you, by bringing you again to Calvary? Do you know the full meaning of that name, Emmanuel, "God with us"? No, he who knows it best knows little of it. He who knows it not at all is so ignorant that his ignorance is not bliss, but will be his damnation. "God with us"— it is eternity's sonnet, heaven's hallelujah, the shout of the glorified, the song of the redeemed, the chorus of angels, the everlasting oratorio of the great orchestra of the sky.—40.610

Matthew 4:19   *"Follow me, and I will make you fishers of men."*

1713 There are three words which have been running in my mind for the last few days and have seemed to work themselves into me. I hope I may long keep them. One word is Work, another is Wait, and the other is Pray. Work, work, work! Wait, wait, wait! Pray, pray, pray! I think that these three words will enable a man to be, under God, a true and successful fisher of men.—12.417

1714 When Christ calls us by his grace we ought to think of what he can make us. It is "Follow me, and I will *make* you." It is not "Follow me, because of what you are already." It is not "Follow me, because you may make something of yourselves," but "Follow me, because of what I will make you."

It did not seem a likely thing that lowly fishermen would develop into apostles, that men so handy with the net would be quite as much at home in preaching sermons and in instructing converts. One would have said, "How can these things be? You cannot make founders of churches out of peasants of Galilee." But that is exactly what Christ did!—32.337

1715 We cannot be fishers of men if we remain in the same element with them. Fish will not be fishers. The sinner will not convert the sinner. The ungodly man will not convert the ungodly man. And what is more to the point, the worldly Christian will not convert the world.—32.339

Matthew 5:3   *"Blessed are the poor in spirit: for theirs is the kingdom of heaven."*

1716 Learn this lesson—not to trust Christ because you repent, but trust Christ to make you repent; not to come to Christ because you have a broken heart, but to come to him that he may give you a broken heart; not to come to him because you are fit to come, but to come to him because you are unfit to come. Your fitness is your unfitness. Your qualification is your lack of qualification.—47.427

Matthew 5:6 *"Blessed are they which do hunger and thirst after righteousness."*

1717 Never does the Lord work in any man a firm resolution to find the Savior and yet allow him to perish.—26.188

1718 He is blessed because in the presence of this hunger many meaner hungers die out. One master passion, like Aaron's rod, swallows up all the rest. He hungers and thirsts after righteousness, and therefore he is done with the craving of lust, the greed of avarice, the passion of hate, and pining of ambition.—35.487

Matthew 5:13 *"If the salt have lost his savor . . . it is . . . good for nothing."*

1719 The teacher said, "Boys, here's a watch. What is it for?"

The children answered, "To tell the time."

"Well," said he, "suppose my watch does not tell the time. What is it good for?"

"Good for nothing, sir."

Then he took a pencil. "What is this pencil for?"

"It is to write with, sir."

Suppose the pencil won't make a mark. What is it good for?"

"Good for nothing, sir."

Then the teacher asked, "What is the chief end of man?" and they replied, "To glorify God."

"But suppose a man does not glorify God. What is he good for?"

"Good for nothing, sir."—29.71

Matthew 5:28 *"Whosoever looketh on a woman to lust after her hath committed adultery."*

1720 The commandment, "Thou shalt not commit adultery," means more than the mere act. It refers to fornication and uncleanness of any shape, in act, word, and thought. So with every commandment. The bare letter is nothing compared with the whole stupendous meaning and severe strictness of the rule. The commands are like stars. When seen with the naked eye, they appear to be brilliant points. If we could draw near to them, we would see them to be infinite worlds.—6.105

Matthew 6:6 *"When thou prayest, enter into thy closet."*

1721 Public prayer is no evidence of piety. It is practiced by an abundance of hypocrites. But private prayer is a thing for which the hypocrite has no heart.—17.207

Matthew 6:13 *"Lead us not into temptation."*

1722 Very stupid people have tried to alter the petition into *"Leave* us not into temptation."

The Savior never said that.—11.363

Matthew 6:19 *"Lay not up for yourselves treasures upon earth."*

1723 Hold not earth's treasures with too firm a grasp. Our bereavements would not be half so sharp if we always viewed our friends as being lent to us. A man does not cry when he has to return a tool which he has borrowed.—14.488

Matthew 6:24 *"No man can serve two masters."*

1724 This is often misunderstood. Some read it, "No man can serve *two* masters." Yes he can; he can serve three or four. The way to read it is this: "No man can serve two *masters."* He can serve two, but they cannot both be his master.—3.51

1725 When the Romans erected the statue of Christ and put it up in their pantheon, saying that he should be one among their gods, their homage was worthless. And when they turned their heads, first to Jupiter, then to Venus, and then to Jesus Christ, they did no honor to our Lord; they did but dishonor him. Their service was not acceptable. And so if you imagine in your heart that you can sometimes serve God and sometimes serve self and be your own master, you have made a mistake.—6.183

Matthew 6:26 *"Behold the fowls of the air."*

1726 You know what Luther said the little bird said to him. He sat on the spray of the tree and sang,

Mortal, cease from toil and sorrow;

God provideth for tomorrow.

And it chirped and picked up its little grain, and sang again. Yet it had no granary. It had not a handful of wheat stored up anywhere, but it kept on with its chirping—

Mortal, cease from toil and sorrow;

God provideth for tomorrow.—3.300

1727 A little London girl who had gone into the country once said, "Look, mamma, at that poor little bird. It has no cage!"

That would not have struck me as being any loss to the bird. And if you and I were without our cage, the box of seed, and the glass of water, it would not be much of a loss if we were cast adrift into the glorious liberty of a life of humble dependence on God. It is that cage of carnal trust and that box of seed we are always laboring to fill that make the worry of this mortal life. But he who has grace to spread his wings and soar away and get into the open field of divine trustfulness may sing all the day, and ever have this for his tune:

Mortal, cease from toil and sorrow;

263

God provideth for tomorrow.—40.109

Matthew 6:33 *"Seek ye first the kingdom of God."*

1728 When I had resolved to enter college, walking across Midsummer Common, just outside of Cambridge, revolving in my mind the joys of scholarship and the hope of being something in the world, that text came to my heart, "Seekest thou great things for thyself? Seek them not" (Jer. 45:5); "Seek first the kingdom of God and his righteousness, and all these things shall be added unto you." All was given up, everything was renounced, the finest prospects seemed to melt into thin air, merely on the strength of that text, believing that God would most certainly fulfill to me his promise if I could keep his precept.—8.101

Note: If CHS had not been sensitive to the voice of God in Scripture, his preaching career would have been postponed for several years. We can only guess how history itself would have been altered as a result.

Matthew 7:7 *"Ask . . . seek . . . knock."*

1729 Faith asks, hope seeks, and love knocks.—19.31

1730 There was a nailhead for the knocker to drop on, and people used to smite it so heavily that some remarked that such blows on the head were killing. Hence arose the mirthful proverb, "as dead as a doornail." It betokens a hearty kind of knocking, which I would have you imitate in prayer. Knock at heaven's gate as earnestly as people knocked at doors in the olden time.—29.308

Matthew 7:13 *"Broad is the way, that leadeth to destruction."*

1731 The road is so wide that there may be many independent tracks in it, and the drunkard may find his way along it without ever ruffling the complacency of the hypocrite. The mere moralist may pick a clean path all the way, while the immoral wretch may wade up to his knees in mire throughout the whole road. Behold how sinners disagree and yet agree in this, that they are opposed to God! It is a broad road.—15.138

Matthew 7:23 *"I never knew you."*

1732 Not passionately or angrily, but in stern, sad, solemn tones he said, "I never knew you."

"But we used thy name, good Lord."

"I know you did, but I never knew you, and you never truly knew me."

I can almost imagine someone turning around in that day and saying to some Christians who used to sit in that same pew, "You knew me."

"Yes," they will reply, "we knew you, but that is of no avail, for the Master did not know you."

I can picture some of you crying out to your minister, "Pastor, did not you know us? Surely you recollect what we used to do."

What can he reply? "Ah, yes, sorrowfully do I own that I know you, but I cannot help you. It is only Christ's knowing you that can be of any avail to you."—48.584, 585

Matthew 7:26 *"Every one that heareth these sayings of mine, and doeth them not. . . . "*

1733 If any soul will be lost emphatically, it is he who has been for years a hearer only, a hearer where thousands have believed unto eternal life. Over the cell of such a man write, "He knew his duty, but he did it not," and that cell will be built in the very center of Gehenna. It is the innermost prison of hell. Willful rejection of Christ ensures woeful rejection from Christ.—31.359

Matthew 8:11 *"Many shall come."*

1734 The devil says, "They shall not come," but they shall come. Their sins say, "You can't come"; God says, "You shall come." You yourselves say, "We won't come"; God says, "You shall come." Yes, there are some here who are laughing at salvation, who can scoff at Christ and mock the gospel; but I tell you that some of you shall come yet.

"What," you say, "can God make me become a Christian?"

I tell you yes, for herein rests the power of the gospel. It does not ask for your consent, but it gets it. It does not say, "Will you have it?" but it makes you willing in the day of God's power. Not against your will, but it makes you willing. It shows you its value, and then you fall in love with it, and immediately you run after it and have it.—1.304

Matthew 9:9 *"Jesus . . . saw a man, named Matthew."*

1735 Matthew has put this story immediately after a miracle. "There," said he, "I will tell them one miracle about the Savior having made the paralyzed man take up his bed and walk, and then I will tell them of another miracle—a greater miracle still— how there was another man who was more than paralyzed, chained to his gains and to an injurious traffic, yet who, nevertheless, at the command of Christ left that occupation and all his gains, that he might follow his divine Master."

Whenever you think about your own conversion, regard it as a miracle, and always say within yourself, "It is a wonder of grace."—42.566

Matthew 10:3 *"Philip, and Bartholomew. . . . "*

1736 Bartholomew's name is never mentioned alone. He is always spoken of as doing some good thing with somebody else.

He is never the principal actor, but always second. Well, let this be your feeling, that if you cannot do all yourself, you will help to do what you can.—13.600

Matthew 10:29 *"Are not two sparrows sold for a farthing?"*

[1737] In another passage Jesus says, "Are not five sparrows sold for two farthings? And not one of them is forgotten by God" (Luke 12:6). Do you notice that? Two for a farthing, and five for two farthings. So there is an odd one thrown in for taking a double quantity. Only a sparrow! Nobody cares about the sparrow, but not one of them is forgotten by your heavenly Father—not even the odd sparrow. And so no stray thought of yours, no imagination, no trifle which you have quite forgotten, which indeed you never took any heed of, has escaped your heavenly Father's notice.—22.98

Matthew 10:30 *"The very hairs of your head are all numbered."*

[1738] If God so values me that he counts the very hairs of my head, ought I not to give to God my whole self even to the minutest detail? Should I not give him, not merely my head, but my hair, as that penitent woman did who unbound her tresses that she might make a towel of them with which to wipe the feet that she had washed with her tears? Ought we not to consecrate to God the very least things as well as the greater things?—34.56

Matthew 11:24 *"It shall be more tolerable for . . . Sodom in the . . . judgment, than for thee."*

[1739] God is more angry with some of you than he is with some in hell. Are you startled by the assertion? "It shall be more tolerable for Sodom in the day of judgment than for thee." The sins you have already committed are greater than those of Sodom, and the anger is in proportion to the guilt.—16.681

Matthew 11:28 *"Come unto me."*

[1740] The cry of the Christian religion is the simple word, *come.* The Jewish law said, "Go, and break the commandments, and thou shalt perish. Go, and keep them, and thou shalt live." The law was a dispensation of the whip, which drove men before it. The gospel is just the opposite. It is the Shepherd's dispensation. He goes before his sheep, and he bids them follow him, saying, "Come." The law repels; the gospel attracts.—5.433

[1741] An old Puritan says, "Come to Jesus, sinner, and if you are lame, come lame. If you say you have no feet, come on your stumps. Come as you can, for he cannot reject you till he denies himself.—15.204

[1742] If you cannot come *with* a broken heart, come *for* a broken

266

heart. If you cannot come *with* faith, come *for* faith. If you cannot come repenting, come and ask the Lord to give you repentance. Come empty-handed, bankrupt, ruined, condemned, and you will find rest.—28.654

1743 Perhaps no verse in the whole of Scripture has been handled in the pulpit more frequently than this, and yet it has not been exhausted, and never can it be. It is a great soul-saving text.—59.205

Note: CHS preached nine sermons on Matthew 11:28 in his 63-volume set of published messages.

Matthew 11:30 *"For my yoke is easy."*

1744 I might call to witness all those who have ever proved this. Never did a man wear the yoke of Christ but he always loved to wear it.—18.53

Matthew 12:30 *"He that is not with me is against me."*

1745 Unless you are converted you are enemies to Jesus. You deny it! I ask you why then do you not believe in him?—13.311

1746 What must it be to be against the Lord? Banished from his love and light and life and peace and rest and joy! What a loss will this be! Think of it— forever hating Jesus, forever plotting against him, forever gnashing your teeth against him—this

is hell, this is the infinite of misery, to be against the Lord of love and life and light. Turn from this fatal course! Believe on him!—23.528

Matthew 12:32 *"Whosoever speaketh against the Holy Ghost, it shall not be forgiven him."*

1747 He that sins against the Holy Ghost may find himself waterlogged by sin, so as to be no longer able to move his vessel toward the shores of salvation. Nothing hardens like the gospel when it is long trifled with.— 31.234

Matthew 13:58 *"He did not many mighty works there because of their unbelief."*

1748 There are two things that God always hears. Mark this! The first is the voice of faith, and the second is the voice of unbelief. As much as God loves faith, so much he loathes unbelief. When we are strong in faith, the Lord can do anything with us and for us, and he can make us equal to all difficulties. But when we give way to unbelief, Christ himself can do nothing with us.—29.297

Matthew 15:19 *"Out of the heart proceed evil thoughts, murders, adulteries. . . ."*

1749 Sin is not a splash of mud on a man's exterior; it is filth generated within himself.—32.402, 403

Matthew 15:22 *"My daughter is grievously vexed with a devil."*

1750 A gracious God used the devil himself to drive this woman to Jesus, for her daughter was "grievously vexed with a devil," and she could not bear to stay at home and see her child in such misery. Oh, how often does a great sorrow drive men and women to Christ, even as a fierce wind compels the mariner to hasten to the harbor! May your boy's sickness work your health! Yes, may your girl's death be the means of the father's spiritual life!—36.85, 86

Matthew 15:23 *"He answered her not a word."*

1751 He was himself the word (John 1:1), and yet he did not give her the word she wanted.—44.554

Matthew 15:27 *"And she said, Truth, Lord."*

1752 If the Lord reminds you of your unworthiness and your unfitness, he only tells you what is true, and it will be your wisdom to say, "Truth, Lord." Scripture describes you as having a depraved nature. Say, "Truth, Lord." It describes you as going astray like a lost sheep, and the charge is true. It describes you as having a deceitful heart, and just such a heart you have. Therefore, say, "Truth, Lord." It represents you as "without strength" (Rom. 5:6) and "without hope" (Eph. 2:12).

Let your answer be, "Truth, Lord."—36.88

Matthew 15:27 *"Yet the dogs eat of the crumbs which fall from their masters' table."*

1753 When the door is shut in her face, she knocks at it, and when Christ calls her "Dog," she only picks up what Christ has said, as a good dog will pick up his master's stick, and bring it right to his feet. She had such faith—shall I not say such dogged faith—in the Lord Jesus Christ, that she could even get comfort out of being called a dog.—42.2

Matthew 16:24 *"Let him . . . take up his cross."*

1754 You have to bear the cross, but not the curse. Your Lord endured both cross and curse, but to you there is not so much as a drop of divine anger in all that you are suffering. Your Lord sends you a cross, but not a crush. It is meant to bear you down, but not to break you and grind you in the dust. Your cross is proportioned to your strength. Your cross is not a loss.—15:271, 272

Matthew 16:28 *"Some standing here . . . shall not taste of death, till they see the Son of man."*

1755 This tasting of death here may be explained by a reference to the second death, which men will not taste of till the Lord comes. And what a dreadful sentence that was, when the Savior said—

perhaps singling out Judas as he spoke—"Verily I say unto you, there be some standing here, who shall never know what that dreadful word 'death' means, till the Lord shall come."—10.576

Matthew 17:15 *"Lord, have mercy on my son; for he is lunatic."*

1756 Learn the lesson that you cannot have gone too far from Christ. Believe that your extremities are only extremities to you and not to him. The highest sin and the deepest despair together cannot baffle the power of Jesus. If you were between the very jaws of hell, Christ could snatch you forth. If your sins had brought you even to the gates of hell, so that the flames flashed into your face, if then you looked to Jesus, he could save you. If you are brought to him when you are at death's door, yet still eternal mercy will receive you.—14.407

Matthew 18:20 *"Where two or three are gathered . . . in my name, there am I in the midst."*

1757 What the moon is to the night or the sun to the day or the Nile to Egypt or the dew to the tender herb or the soul to the human frame, that is the presence of Jesus to his church.—18.86, 87

Matthew 21:9 *"The multitudes . . . cried, saying, Hosanna to the Son of David."*

1758 Those same tongues which were that day crying, "Hosanna!" those same tongues which cried, "Blessed is he that cometh in the name of the Lord," within that same week said, "Crucify him! Crucify him!" I say not all, but some. It was the mob of Jerusalem that brought him in as their king. Expect not, therefore, when many hearts are impressed with the gospel, that all will be steadfast toward Christ. Do not reckon that every pious feeling will end in genuine conversion.—18:132

Matthew 21:19 *"When he saw a fig tree . . . he came to it, and found nothing . . . but leaves."*

1759 The first Adam came to the fig tree for leaves, but the second Adam looks for figs. He searches our character through and through to see whether there is any real faith, any true love, and living hope, and joy which is the fruit of the Spirit, any patience, any self-denial, any fervor in prayer, any walking with God, any indwelling of the Holy Spirit. And if he does not see these things, he is not satisfied with churchgoing, prayer meetings, communions, sermons, and Bible readings, for all these may be no more than leafage. If our Lord does not see the fruit of the Spirit on us, he is not satisfied with us, and his inspection will lead to severe measures. What Jesus looks for is not your words, your resolves, your avowals, but your sincerity, your inward faith, your being indeed wrought on by the Spirit of God to bring forth fruits suitable for his kingdom.—35.535

Matthew 21:22 *"All things, whatsoever ye shall ask in prayer, believing, ye shall receive."*

[1760] Prayer without faith! What sort of prayer is it? It is the prayer of a man who does not believe in God.—25.415

Matthew 23:37 *"How often would I have gathered thy children together . . . and ye would not!"*

[1761] Believe me, if you have but a spark of desire after Christ, he has a whole furnace of desire after you. Oh, that you would have him as your Savior!—44.611

Matthew 25:18 *"He that had received one . . . digged in the earth, and hid his lord's money."*

[1762] He knew that it was but one talent, and for that reason he was the less afraid to bury it. Perhaps he argued that the interest on one talent could never come to much and would never be noticed side by side with the result of five or ten talents, and he might as well bring nothing at all to his Lord as bring so little. Perhaps he might not have wrapped it up if it had not been so small that a napkin could cover it. The smallness of our gifts may be a temptation to us. We are consciously so weak and so insignificant compared with the great God and his great cause, that we are discouraged and think it vain to attempt anything.—32.484

Matthew 25:25 *"I . . . hid thy talent in the earth: lo, there thou hast that is thine."*

[1763] We ought to observe that the unprofitable servant did not spend that talent on himself or use it in business for his own benefit. He was not a thief, nor in any way a misappropriator of money placed under his charge. In this he excels many who profess to be the servants of God and yet live to themselves only. And yet he was cast into outer darkness. What then will become of some of you?—26.328, 329

Matthew 25:35, 36 *"Ye gave me meat . . . ye took me in . . . ye clothed me . . . ye visited me."*

[1764] They fed the hungry, but sovereign grace had first fed them. They clothed the naked, but infinite love first clothed them. They went to prison, but free grace had first set them free from a worse prison. They visited the sick, but the good Physician in his infinite mercy first came and visited them.—21.287

Matthew 26:16 *"And from that time he sought opportunity to betray him."*

[1765] As long as the church exists, I suppose she will have traitors among her number, for if Judas intruded under the watchful eye of the Chief Shepherd, we may be pretty sure that many a Judas will elude the far less watchful eyes of the minor shepherds.—22.75

Matthew 26:74   *"Then began he to curse and swear."*

[1766] Peter not only denied his Master, but as if he knew that a true Christian would not swear, he did it. He cursed and swore to convince them that he was not a disciple of Jesus Christ.—48.136, 137

Matthew 27:19   *"I have suffered many things . . . in a dream because of him."*

[1767] In her dream Pilate's wife may have seen her husband brought forth to judgment, himself a prisoner to be tried by the just One, who had earlier been accused before him. She may have awoke, startled at the shriek of her husband as he fell back into the pit that knows no bottom.— 28.124

Matthew 27:30   *"And they spit upon him."*

[1768] Of all the things that ever existed, sin is the most shameful. It deserves to be spit on. It deserves to be crucified. And because our Lord had taken on himself our sin, he must be put to shame. If you want to see what God thinks of sin, see his only Son spat on by the soldiers when he was made sin for us. In God's sight sin is a shameful, horrible, loathsome, abominable thing, and when Jesus takes it he must be forsaken and given up to scorn.—25.426, 427

Matthew 27:45   *"From the sixth hour there was darkness over all the land."*

[1769] Sin is there, and all its innumerable offspring, spitting forth the venom of asps and fixing their poison fangs in the Savior's flesh. Death is there, and his cruel dart rends its way through the body of Jesus even to his inmost heart. Hell comes with all its coals of juniper and fiery darts. But chief and head among them is Satan. Remembering well the ancient day when Christ hurled him from the battlements of heaven, he rushes with all his malice, yelling to the attack. The darts shot into the air are so countless that they blind the sun.—5.387

[1770] When Jesus was born midnight turned to midday, and when he died midday turned to midnight. When he was born heaven was lit up with splendor, and from angelic choirs the Bethlehem song was heard. But when he died heaven put out her brightest light.—61.374

Matthew 27:46   *"My God, my God, why hast thou forsaken me!"*

[1771] Jesus was deserted by God. And if he, who was only imputedly a sinner, was deserted, how much more shall you be? Oh, sinner, if God hides his face from Christ, how much less will he spare you?—9.132

[1772] Our Lord's lament is an address to God. The godly, in their anguish, turn to the hand which smites them. The Savior's outcry is not *against* God, but *to* him. "My God, my God." He makes a double effort to draw near. True sonship is here.—36.138

1773 Some years ago I preached a sermon to you from the text, "My God, my God, why hast thou forsaken me?" In a mournful degree I felt what I preached as my own cry. I felt an agony of spirit, for I was under an awful sense of being forsaken by God, and yet I could not understand why I was surrounded by such thick darkness. I wished to clear myself if any sin remained on me, but I could not discover any evil which I was tolerating.

When I went back into the vestry, I learned the secret of my personal distress, for there was an elderly man in a horror of great darkness, who said to me, "I have never before met with any person who has been where I am. I trust there is hope for me." I bade him sit down, and I talked with him. I saw him afterward, and I hope I conducted him from the verge of insanity into the open, healthy place of peace through believing. I fear I would never have touched his case if I had not been in the miry clay myself. Then I understood why I must feel like one forsaken.—37.335, 336

1774 I have read that Martin Luther sat down in his study to consider this text. Hour after hour that mighty man of God sat still, and he was so absorbed in his meditation that those who waited on him almost thought he was a corpse. He moved neither hand nor foot and neither ate nor drank, but sat with his eyes wide open, like one in a trance, thinking over these wondrous words: "My God, my God, why hast thou forsaken me?" And after many long hours in which he seemed to be utterly lost to everything that went on around him, he rose from his chair, and someone heard him say, "God forsaking God! No man can understand that."—48.517, 518

1775 I will tell you what is a much more awful thing even than crying out, "My God, my God, why hast thou forsaken me?" To be without God and not to care about it, to be living like some whom I am now addressing—without God and without hope—yet that never concerns them at all. I can pity the agony of the man who cannot bear to be without his God. But at the same time I can bless the Lord that he feels such agony as that, for that proves to me that his soul will never perish.—48.525

Matthew 27:51, 52 *"The earth did quake . . . the rocks rent . . . graves were opened . . . bodies . . . arose."*

1776 Sin abounded so much that it put out the light of the sun. So heavy was it that it cracked the solid earth and rent the rocks asunder and caused the graves to open, while the great veil of the temple was rent in two from the top to the bottom. Yet "where sin abounded, grace did much more abound" (Rom. 5:20).—58.256

Matthew 27:53 *"And came out of the graves."*

1777 Those persons who received life in due time left their graves. What living men would wish to stay in their graves? And you, if the Lord quickens you, will not stay in your graves. If you have been accustomed to strong drink or to any other besetting sin, you will leave it. You will not feel any attachment to your sepulcher. If you have lived in ungodly company and found amusement in questionable places, you will not stop in your graves.—34.703

Matthew 28:2 *"The angel . . . rolled back the stone . . . and sat upon it."*

1778 That stone was a boundary appointed. On that side what see you? The guards stiffened with fear like dead men. On this side what see you? The timid trembling women, to whom the angel softly speaks, "Fear not ye: for I know that ye seek Jesus" (Matt. 28:5). That stone became the boundary between the living and the dead, between the seekers and the haters, between the friends and the foes of Christ.

To his enemies his resurrection is "a stone of stumbling, and a rock of offense" (1 Peter 2:8), as of old on Mars Hill, when the sages heard of the resurrection and mocked. But to his own people the resurrection is the headstone of the corner. Our Lord's resurrection is our triumph and delight. The resurrection acts much in the same manner as the pillar which Jehovah placed between Israel and Egypt. It was darkness to Egypt, but it gave light to Israel.—15.186, 187

Mark 1:23 *"And there was in their synagogue a man with an unclean spirit."*

1779 The miracle seems to me to teach that the power of Christ to save from sin does not lie in the person saved. It lies wholly in Jesus himself. Further, I learn that though the person to be saved be so far gone that you could scarcely expect faith from him, yet the gospel coming to him can bring faith with itself and do its own work. The gospel is a seed that makes its own soil! It is a spark that carries its own fuel with it, a life which can implant itself within the ribs of death, yes, between the jaws of destruction.—30.95

Mark 2:17 *"I came not to call the righteous, but sinners to repentance."*

1780 Some of you may say, "You seem to think us a bad lot," and so I do.

Others exclaim, "How can you talk to us in this way? We are

273

honest, moral, and upright people."

If so, then I have no gospel to preach to you. You may go elsewhere if you will, for you may get moral sermons in scores of chapels if you want them. But I have come in my Master's name to preach to sinners, and so I will not say a word to you Pharisees except this: By so much as you think yourself righteous and holy, by so much shall you be cast out of God's presence at last.—1.184, 185

1781 The Pharisees said, "They are sinners, we are not."

"Very well," said Christ, "I endorse the distinction you have made. In your own opinion you are not sinners. Well, you shall stand exempt for now from being called sinners. But I beg to inform you that I came to save those very persons who, in their own estimation and in yours, are reckoned to be sinners."

It is my belief that the doctrine of the text is this—Christ receives not the self-righteous, not the good, not those who dream that they do not need a Savior, but the broken in spirit, the contrite in heart, those who are ready to confess that they have broken God's laws and have merited his displeasure.—4.434

1782 Why send a physician to a man who is not sick? Why offer alms to a man who is not poor? If you can save yourselves by your works, go and do so, fools that you are, for you might as well hope to drink dry the Atlantic. If you believe in self-salvation, I am hopeless of doing you any good till you are exhausted of your strength. When you are weak and sick and ready to die, then you will be willing to accept the free salvation of Christ. But remember, Christ came to save the ungodly. The guilty alone are objects of mercy.—19.678, 679

1783 I know that to many this is a very unpalatable doctrine. Well, friend, you had better have your palate altered, for you will never be able to alter the doctrine. It is the truth of the everlasting God and cannot be changed. The very best thing you can do, since the gospel looks toward sinners, is to get where the gospel looks. You will only be in your right place when you get there.—23.176

Mark 5:19 *"Go home ... and tell them how great things the Lord hath done for thee."*

1784 Cannot you imagine the scene, when the poor demoniac went home? He had been a raving madman, and when he came and knocked at the door, don't you see his friends calling to one another in fear, "Oh, there he is again," and the mother running upstairs and locking all the doors, because her son who was raving mad, had come back, and the little ones crying because they knew how he cut himself with stones, because he was possessed by devils?

And can you picture their joy when the man said, "Mother! Jesus Christ has healed me. Let me in, I am no longer a lunatic!" And when the father opened the door he said, "Father! I am not what I was. All the evil spirits are gone. I shall live in the tombs no longer. I want to tell you how the glorious man who wrought my deliverance accomplished the miracle. I have come home healed and saved."

Oh, if such a one, possessed with sin, were here and would go home to his friends to tell them of his release, I think the scene would be somewhat similar.—3.22

Mark 5:28   *"For she said, If I may touch but his clothes, I shall be whole."*

1785 The poor woman who touched the hem of his garment made a mistake, I suppose, in imagining that power must necessarily dwell in his raiment. But nevertheless the Lord went with her mistake and let the virtue go even out of his robe as well as out of himself. He will meet you, dear friend, where you are, and grasp the hand of even your blind and lame faith, and save you.—24.201

Mark 5:30   *"Jesus, immediately knowing in himself that virtue had gone out of him. . . . "*

1786 He perceived that virtue had gone out of him, but he did not perceive it by any pain he felt. I believe that he perceived it by the pleasure which it caused him. Something gave him unusual joy. A faith-touch had reached him through his clothes, and he rejoiced to respond by imparting healing virtue from himself. You will not defile my Lord if you bring him all your sin.—30.617

Mark 6:3   *"Is not this the carpenter?"*

1787 He toiled in his father's workshop. "Fit place," a quaint author says, "for Jesus, for he had to make a ladder that should reach from earth to heaven."—1.78

Mark 6:6   *"He marvelled because of their unbelief."*

1788 There were but two occasions when our Lord Jesus is recorded to have marveled at all, and both of these were concerning faith. First, he marveled at the centurion: "I have not found so great faith, no, not in Israel" (Luke 7:9). And on the second occasion, he marveled at the absence of faith where it might have been expected to be found, namely, in his own fellow townsmen: "He marvelled because of their unbelief" (Mark 6:6). So you see that in both instances it was faith or the absence of it that caused Christ to wonder. See the importance of faith! Never place that precious grace in a secondary position.—16.325, 326

Mark 6:20 *"Herod feared John ... and heard him gladly."*

1789 Though Herod loved John, he never looked to John's Master. John never wanted anybody to be his disciple, but he cried, "Behold the Lamb of God" (John 1:29). Herod was, after a sort, a follower of John, but never a follower of Jesus. It is easy for you to hear the preacher and love and admire him, and yet the preacher's Master may be all unknown to you. The goal of all our ministry is Christ Jesus. You will be Herods, and nothing more, unless grace leads you to Jesus Christ.—26.404

Mark 7:21, 22 *"Out of the heart ... proceed evil thoughts, adulteries, fornications. ..."*

1790 It reads like a grim sarcasm, that sinners should be proud. What have such creatures to be proud of? What! Adulteries, murders, thefts, and yet pride? One would have said that such sins would have forbidden pride. What a misalliance! A person infamous, and yet puffed up! Alas, the worse a man becomes, the more is he filled with a sort of vainglory, by the force of which he justifies his own iniquities and refuses to see his own vileness.—32.401

Mark 7:23 *"All these evil things come from within, and defile the man."*

1791 If sin had not been in you, it could not have come out. All the trouble in the world does not put sin in the Christian. It brings it out.—12.70

Mark 7:28 *"Yet the dogs under the table eat of the children's crumbs."*

1792 Think of this faith. To have the devil cast out of her daughter was the greatest thing she could imagine. And yet she had such a belief in the greatness of the Lord Christ, that she thought it would be no more to him to make her daughter well than for a great housekeeper to let a poor little dog eat a tiny crumb that had been dropped by a child. Is not that splendid faith? And now, can you exercise such faith?—36.95

Mark 9:18 *"He teareth him; and he foameth, and gnasheth with his teeth."*

1793 This child possessed with an evil spirit is a most fitting emblem of every ungodly and unconverted man. Though we be not possessed with devils, yet by nature we are possessed with devilish vices and lusts, which will most certainly destroy our souls. Never a creature possessed with an evil spirit was in a worse plight than the man who is without God, without Christ, and without hope in the world.

The casting out of the unclean spirit was, moreover, a thing impossible to man and only possible to God. And so is the conversion of an ungodly sinner a thing beyond the reach of human ability, and only to be accomplished by the might of the Most High.

The dreadful bellowings, foamings, and tearings caused in this unhappy child by the unclean spirit are a picture of the sins, iniquities, and vices into which ungodly men are continually and impetuously hurried.—2.369

Mark 9:24 *"Lord, I believe; help thou mine unbelief."*

1794 It is very noticeable that he does not say, "Lord, I believe; help thou my child." Nor does he say, "Lord, I believe; now cast the devil out of my boy." Not at all. He perceives that his own unbelief was harder to overcome than the devil, and that to heal him of his spiritual disease was a more needful work than even to heal his child of the sad malady under which he labored!—18.71

Mark 10:14 *"Suffer the little children to come unto me, and forbid them not."*

1795 Too young to be saved! Is anyone too young to be happy? Too young to be a Christian! Is anyone too young to get the richest treasure that can make human hearts glad?—13.531

Mark 10:45 *"The Son of man came not to be ministered unto, but to minister."*

1796 Does not this suit you who never did serve him, you who could not as you are minister to him? Well, he did not come to get your service, he came to give you his services. Not that you might first do him honor, but that he might show you mercy. Oh, you need him so very much! And since he has come not to look for treasures, but to bestow unsearchable riches, not to find specimens of health, but instances of sickness on which the healing art of his grace may operate, surely there is hope for you.—62.472

Mark 10:49 *"Jesus stood still."*

1797 I have heard of Joshua, who made the sun and the moon stand still, but I rank the blind beggar above Joshua, for he causes the Sun of Righteousness to stand still! Yes, he who created both sun and moon stood still, and the Lord listened to the voice of a man.—27.135

Mark 10:50 *"He, casting away his garment, rose, and came to Jesus."*

1798 The poor blind beggar cast away his garment. Now, if you would be saved you must resolve in your soul, by the blessing of the Holy Spirit, that every sin and every habit of yours which hinders your finding Christ at once shall be cast away. There is no pleasure worth keeping at the price of your soul.—23.707

Mark 12:30 *"Thou shalt love the Lord thy God."*

1799 We must give the Lord our love, or that love will go somewhere else. We are so created that we must love something or other. If the ever-blessed One does not win our love, the world, the flesh, or the devil will gain it.—22.188

Mark 12:34 *"Thou art not far from the kingdom of God."*

1800 The great danger is that though you are not far from the kingdom, *you are not in it!* A man was in a sinking ship. He almost leaped into the lifeboat, but just missed it and was drowned. The manslayer was flying for his life, and the avenger of blood was close behind him. He had almost reached the city of refuge, but he was overtaken by his adversary just outside the gate, and so was slain.

Almost saved is altogether lost. There are many in hell who once were almost saved, but who are now altogether damned. Think of that, you who are not far from the kingdom. It is being *in* the kingdom that saves the soul, not being *near* the kingdom.—52.258

Mark 15:1 *"The chief priests . . . bound Jesus."*

1801 He could have snapped those bonds as easily as Samson did the Philistines' bonds. There were other cords that bound him, invisible to carnal sense—the bonds of covenant engagements, the bonds of his own oath and promise, the bonds of his love to you and to me, and the mighty bonds of his marriage union to our souls, which constrained him without a word to yield himself as a lamb to the slaughter.—12.651

Mark 15:21 *"And they compel one Simon . . . to bear his cross."*

1802 And where was that other Simon? What a silent but strong rebuke this would be to him. Simon Peter, where were you? Another Simon has taken your place. Sometimes the Lord's servants are backward where they are expected to be forward, and he finds other servants for a time. If this has ever happened to us, it ought gently to rebuke us as long as we live.—28.561, 562

Mark 16:16 *"He that believeth not shall be damned."*

1803 When a thousand years of hell's torments shall have passed away, you shall see written in burning letters of fire, "He that believeth not shall be damned."

"But, Lord, I am damned."

Nevertheless it says, "shall be" still. And when a million ages have rolled away, and you are exhausted by your pains and agonies, you shall turn up your eye and still read, "SHALL BE DAMNED," unchanged, unaltered. And when you shall have thought that eternity must have spun out its last thread, you shall still see it written up there, "SHALL BE DAMNED."—1.4

1804 We can have no hope for those who receive not Christ. We pity them, we love them, we pray for them, we plead for them, that they may be brought to this, but we dare not deceive them. We dare not tell them that God will hear their prayers, if they will not come to him through Jesus Christ. No, we will be as tolerant as Jesus was, but Jesus himself said, "He that believeth not must be damned."—5.164

1805 The other day an inquirer said to me, "I cannot believe," and I gave him no answer but this—"Then you must be damned." Had I nothing else to say? No, nothing else. I had no comforts to offer, no hopes to present to an unbeliever. "He that believeth not shall be damned."—20.695

Luke 1:18   *"Whereby shall I know this?"*

1806 Zacharias had asked for a sign, and by a sign he was chastened. God often makes us gather the twigs from which he makes the rod with which he scourges us. Our own sins are the thorns which cause us to smart. Zacharias asked for a sign, and he has this sign: "Thou shalt be dumb, and not able to speak, until the day that these things shall be performed, because thou believest not my words" (Luke 1:20). "You did not believe what was spoken to you by the Lord, and now you are unable to repeat it to others, for the Lord will not employ an unbelieving messenger. If you will not believe when an angel speaks, you shall not speak yourself."

Many a dumb Christian, I am afraid, has had his mouth sealed through unbelief.—24.176

Luke 1:46   *"My soul doth magnify the Lord."*

1807 I should like to be able to say as long as I live, "My soul doth magnify the Lord." I should like to have this as the one motto of my life from this moment until I close my eyes in death: "My soul doth magnify the Lord." I would gladly preach that way. I would gladly eat and drink that way. I would even sleep that way, so that I could truthfully say, "I have no wish but that God should be great, and that I should help to make him great in the eyes of others." Will not you also make this the motto of your life?—51.309

Luke 2:7   *"There was no room . . . in the inn."*

1808 Have *you* room for Christ?

"Well," says one, "I have room for him, but I am not worthy that he should come to me."

I did not ask about worthiness. Have you room for him?

"Oh, but the room I have in my heart is so base!"

So was the manger.

"But it is so despicable!"

So was the manger.

"But my heart is so foul!"

So, perhaps, the manger may have been.

"Oh, but I feel it is a place not at all fit for Christ!"

Nor was the manger, and yet there he was laid.

"Oh, but I have been such a sinner. I feel as if my heart had been a den of beasts and devils!"

Well, the manger had been a place where beasts had fed. Have you room for him? Never mind what the past has been. He can forget and forgive. It matters not what even the present state may be if you mourn it. If you have room for Christ, he will come and be your guest. Do not say, "I hope I shall have room for him." The time has come that he shall be born. Mary cannot wait months and years. Oh, if you have room for him, let him be born in your soul today!—8.707

1809 If Jesus Christ was born in a manger in a rock, why should he not come and live in our rocky hearts? If he was born in a stable, why should not the stable of our souls be made into a habitation for him? If he was born in poverty, may not the poor in spirit expect that he will be their Friend?—40.605

Luke 2:16   *"And they . . . found . . . the babe lying in a manger."*

1810 We never find that the shepherds lost their way. No, God guides the shepherds, and he did direct the wise men, too. But they lost their way. It often happens that while shepherds find Christ, wise men miss him.—1.78

Luke 2:19   *"Mary kept all these things, and pondered them in her heart."*

1811 There was an exercise on the part of this blessed woman of the three great parts of her being: her memory—she kept all these things; her affections—she kept them in her heart; and her intellect—she pondered them, considered them, weighed them, turned them over. Memory, affection, and understanding were all exercised about these things.—11.715, 716

Luke 2:20   *"Glorifying . . . God for all the things that they had heard and seen. . . ."*

1812 They praised God for the agreement between what they had heard and what they had seen. Observe the last sentence: " . . . as it was told unto them." Have you not found the gospel to be in yourselves just what the Bible said it would be? Jesus said he would give you grace. Have you not had it? He promised you rest. Have you not received it? He said that you should have joy and comfort and life through believing in him. Have you not had all these?—11.719

Luke 2:34   *"This child is set for the fall and rising . . . of many."*

1813 Never does a man hear the gospel but he either rises or falls under that hearing.—15.710

Luke 4:1, 2 *"Jesus, being full of the Holy Ghost . . . tempted of the devil."*

[1814] He was full of the Holy Ghost, yet he was tempted. Why? Because the Holy Spirit is never given in vain, and if given to us, it is as a preparation for conflict, in order that we may have strength proportioned to our need.—52.353

Luke 5:8 *"Depart from me; for I am a sinful man, O Lord."*

[1815] Would it not be better to say, "Come nearer to me, for I am a sinful man, O Lord"? "I am a sinful man," here is humility. "Come nearer to me," here is faith, which prevents humility from degenerating into unbelief and despair.—60.247

Luke 5:19 *"They went upon the housetop, and let him down through the tiling."*

[1816] Some of you say, "We cannot be of any use. We wish we could preach."

These men could not preach! They did not need to preach. They lowered the paralytic, and their work was done. They could not preach, but they could hold a rope. We want in the Christian church not only preachers, but soul winners who can bear souls on their hearts and feel the solemn burden; men who, it may be, cannot talk, but who can weep; men who cannot break other men's hearts with their language, but who break their own hearts with their compassion.—17.163

Luke 6:38 *"Give, and it shall be given unto you."*

[1817] We may so give for God as to get in the giving, so spend as to increase in the spending, so die for God as to live more than ever.—31.82

Luke 7:37, 38 *"Behold, a woman . . . began to wash his feet with tears . . . and kissed his feet."*

[1818] Eyes which were full of adultery were now founts of repentance. Lips which were doors of lascivious speech now yield holy kisses. The profligate was a penitent, the castaway a new creature. All the actions which are attributed to this woman illustrate the transforming power of divine grace.—14.162

Luke 7:45 *"Thou gavest me no kiss."*

[1819] Simon shows how self-righteous men love the Savior. They do not even wash his feet or kiss his cheeks. But those who are saved by grace love Jesus, and therefore kiss his feet and bathe them with their tears, and would willingly lay down their lives for him. Law! There is no power for holiness in it! Law drives our spirits to rebellion, but love has magic in it.—19.682

Luke 7:47 *"Her sins, which are many, are forgiven; for she loved much."*

[1820] I do not say that love is always in proportion to the amount of sin forgiven. But I do say that it is in proportion to the consciousness of sin forgiven. A man may be less of a sinner than another, but he may be more conscious of his sin. He will be the man who loves Christ most.—26.716

Luke 7:50 *"Thy faith hath saved thee."*

1821 Faith saves us just as the mouth saves from hunger. If we be hungry, bread is the real cure. But still it would be right to say that eating removes hunger, seeing that the bread itself could not benefit us unless the mouth should eat it. Faith is the soul's mouth, whereby the hunger of the heart is removed.—20.148, 149

1822 "But," says someone, "was it not the Lord Jesus Christ who saved her?"

Yes, certainly it was. But do you see what Christ does? He is so fond of faith that he takes the crown from his own head and puts it on the head of faith, as he says to the woman, "Thy faith hath saved thee." Is that a safe thing for Christ to do? Oh, yes! Because faith at once removes the crown from her own head and puts it back on Christ's, saying, "Not unto me, but unto thy name be all the glory." Christ loves to crown faith because faith loves to crown Christ. As for boasting, faith cannot tolerate that for a moment. She hurls it out of the window and will have nothing to do with it.—48.124, 125

Luke 8:5 *"Some fell by the way-side . . . and the fowls of the air devoured it."*

1823 It is easy for birds to pick up seed which lies exposed on a trodden path. If the soil had been good and the seed had entered it, he would have had far greater difficulty. He might even have been foiled. But a hard heart does the devil's work for him in great measure. He need not use violence or craft. There lies the unreceived word on the surface of the soul, and he takes it away. The power of the evil one largely springs from our own evil.—25.99

1824 Notice how zealous the devil is. We may be careless about souls, but he never is. Although the seed lay there on the surface and had never penetrated the soil, and although that grain had been trodden on, Satan was not satisfied. He said, "There may be life in it, and if there is, it is dangerous to have it lying there, for it may grow." So he comes and takes it away altogether.—49.380, 381

Luke 8:43, 44 *"A woman having an issue of blood twelve years . . . Came behind him."*

1825 The poor sick soul had a faith which assured her that Christ could bless her when his back was turned. Can you also reach this point? Some of God's own children can hardly trust him when they see the light of his countenance. I would to God that we had such confidence in Jesus that we would not doubt under any circumstances his power and willingness to save all who trust him.—53.12

Luke 10:21 *"Jesus rejoiced in spirit."*

1826 God never did a sovereign act yet that the loving Christ himself could not rejoice in. Be content, therefore, to leave everything that you do not understand in the hand of God.—26.684

Luke 10:33 *"But a certain Samaritan . . . had compassion on him."*

1827 Our Lord Jesus Christ has done better than the Good Samaritan, because our case was worse. The wounded man could not blame himself for his sad estate. It was his misfortune, not his fault. But you and I are not only half-dead, but altogether dead in trespasses and sins, and we have brought many of our ills on ourselves. The thieves that have stripped us are our own iniquities; the wounds which we bear have been inflicted by our own suicidal hand. 23.358, 359

Luke 10:40 *"Martha was cumbered about much serving."*

1828 It was not her fault that she had much serving. We cannot do too much. Let us do all that we possibly can. Head and heart and hands, let every single power and passion of our nature be engaged in the Master's service. But her fault was that she grew *cumbered* with much serving, so that she forgot *him* and remembered only the service. She overrode her union with Christ by her service to Christ, and herein was the mischief.—55.457, 458

Luke 11:1 *"Lord, teach us to pray."*

1829 Though the disciples often heard Christ preach, they never said, "Lord, teach us to preach." But when they heard him pray, they said to him, "Lord, teach us to pray." They were so astonished with such praying as the Savior's that though they thought they might emulate his preaching, his praying seemed too masterly, too infinitely above them, and they could not help exclaiming, "Oh, God, show us how to pray like that!"—61.605

Luke 12:14 *"Who made me a judge or a divider over you?"*

1830 For each one of us there is a special vocation in which we can follow Christ. I do not believe that all of you would be following him if you were to attempt to preach. Even Christ never attempted to do what his Father did not intend him to do. A man once asked him to officiate as a lawyer or judge, but he replied, "Who made me a judge or a divider over you?" One beauty of Christ's life was that he kept to his calling and did not go beyond his commission. And you will be wise if you do the same.—53.448

Luke 12:24   *"Consider the ravens."*

1831 Consider the ravens as they cry. With harsh, inarticulate, croaking notes they make known their wants, and your heavenly Father answers their prayer and sends them food. You, too, have begun to pray and to seek his favor; are you not much better than they? Does God care for ravens, and will he not care for you?—12.50

Luke 13:3   *"Except ye repent, ye shall all likewise perish."*

1832 How did those Galileans perish? I am solemnly afraid that some of you will perish just as they did. Think of it—your blood on your hymn singing and on your prayers, because you have not yielded yourselves up to God or obeyed the word of his gospel! If my blood must be spilled through an act of divine vengeance, let it fall anywhere but on my religion, for that would seem a doubly dreadful thing. Yet I fear that this must and will be the lot of some here who never forsake the gatherings of God's people, and yet have never yielded their hearts to God.—43.589

Luke 13:8   *"Let it alone this year."*

1833 There was no reason in that tree why he should plead for it, and there is no reason in you why Christ should plead for you, yet he does it. This very morning, perhaps, he is crying, "Spare him yet a little while. Let him hear the gospel again. Let him be entreated once more. Oh, let him have another sickness, that it may make his conscience feel! Let me have another endeavor with his hard heart. It may be that he will yield."

O sinner, bless God that Jesus Christ pleads for you in that way.—8.381

1834 Our text represents the gardener as only *asking* to have the tree spared, but Jesus Christ did something more than ask. He pleaded, not with his mouth only, but with pierced hands and pierced feet and pierced side. And those prevailing pleas have moved the heart of God, and you are still spared.—11.527

Luke 13:16   *". . . whom Satan hath bound, lo, these eighteen years."*

1835 As in Job's case there was a limit, so was there here. Satan had bound this woman, but he had not killed her. He might bend her toward the grave, but he could not bend her into it. He might make her droop over till she was bent double, but he could not take away her poor feeble life. With all his infernal craft he could not make her die before her time. Moreover, she was still a woman, and he could not make a beast of her, notwithstanding that she was thus bowed down in the form of a brute. Even so the devil cannot destroy you, O child of God. He can smite you, but he cannot slay you.—24.427

Luke 14:22 *"Yet there is room."*

1836 We have a word of warning to say to you. There is room in the precious blood of Christ. There is room at the gospel feast. There is room in the church on earth. There is room in heaven. But if you will not occupy this room, I must solemnly tell you that *there is room in hell!* There may hardly be prisons enough for all the criminals on earth, but there is room for them in hell. There are nations that forget God, there are myriads that hate him, there are millions that neglect his great salvation. But there is room for them all in hell if they will not repent and believe the gospel.— 56.524, 525

Luke 14:26 *"If any man come to me, and hate not his father, and mother. . . . "*

1837 Sometimes we think we could say with St. Jerome, "If Christ should bid me go this way, and my mother did hang about my neck to draw me another, and my father were in my way, bowing at my knees with tears entreating me not to go, and my children plucking at my skirts should seek to pull me the other way, I must unclasp my mother, I must push to the very ground my father, and put aside my children, for I must follow Christ."—6.415, 416

Luke 15:3 *"And he spake this parable unto them, saying. . . . "*

1838 The doctrine of free will has not a single specimen to show to prove itself. There is not a sheep in all the flock that came back to the shepherd unsought. There is not a single piece of money which leaped again into the woman's purse; she swept the house to find it. There is not even a single prodigal son in the entire family who did ever say, "I will arise, and go unto my Father" till first the Father's grace, veiling itself in the afflicting providence of a mighty famine, had taught the prodigal the miserable results of sin.—11.686

Luke 15:4 *"What man of you, having a hundred sheep, if he lose one of them. . . . "*

1839 To be lost to Christ may seem to you who are careless and thoughtless a trifling matter. If the wandering sheep could have spoken, it might have said, "I do not want to belong to the shepherd. I know that he values me, and that he is seeking me because I am his, but I do not care about that." No, poor sheep, but if you had been the shepherd, you would have cared. And, poor sinner, if you did but know even a little of what Christ feels, you also would begin to care about your own soul.—49.112

Luke 15:10 *"There is joy in the presence of the angels of God. . . . "*

1840 We often say of the angels that they rejoice over one sinner that repents. I doubt not that they do, but the Bible does not say so. The Bible says, "There is joy in the presence of the angels of God over one sinner that repenteth." What means the presence of the angels? Why, that the angels see the joy of Christ when sinners repent. Hear them say to one another, "Behold, the Father's face! How he rejoices! Gaze on the countenance of the Son! What a heaven of delight shines in those eyes of his! Jesus wept for these sinners, but now he rejoices over them."—37.251

Luke 15:20 *"His father saw him, and had compassion, and ran."*

1841 The prodigal son was resolved to come, yet he was half-afraid. But we read that his father ran. Slow are the steps of repentance, but swift are the feet of forgiveness. God can run where we can scarcely limp, and if we are limping toward him, he will run toward us. Though the father was out of breath, he was not out of love.—37.650

Luke 15:20 *"His father . . . ran, and fell on his neck, and kissed him."*

1842 If ever there was a soul that knew itself to be far off from God, I was that soul. And yet in a moment, no sooner had I turned my eyes to Jesus crucified, than I felt my perfect reconciliation with God. I knew my sins to be forgiven. There was no time for getting out of my heavenly Father's way. It was done, and done in an instant. And in my case at least, he ran and fell on my neck to kiss me.—10.505

Luke 15:24 *"This my son was dead, and is alive again; he was lost, and is found."*

1843 We are happy when God blesses us, but not so happy as God is. We are glad when we are pardoned, but he that pardons us is gladder still. The prodigal going back to his home was very happy, but not so delighted as his father, who could say, "This my son was dead, and is alive again; he was lost, and is found." The father's heart was by far the larger heart, so that it could hold more joy.—34.428

Luke 15:32 *"It was meet that we should make merry, and be glad."*

1844 The father in the parable was glad when his prodigal son was found. But he would have been gladder still had a brother found him.—34.376

Luke 16:24 *"That he may . . . cool my tongue; for I am tormented in this flame."*

1845 It was not a metaphorical tongue, and it was not a metaphorical flame. It was not metaphorical water that he wanted. Real, positive, actual flames tormented the body of that rich man in hell. Wicked man, those very hands of yours that now grasp the wine cup shall grasp the cup of your damnation. The eyes that look on the spectacles of lust—it is no figure, sir—those same eyes shall see murderous spectacles of misery. The same head which has often here throbbed with headache shall there beat with pains you have not yet felt. Your heart for which you care so little shall become an emporium of miseries, where demons shall empty the scalding boilers of woe. It is not a fiction!—11.636

Luke 16:27, 28 *"Send him . . . for I have five brethren . . . lest they also come into this place."*

1846 Was not the rich man afraid to see them there, because their recriminations would increase his misery? It will be a horrible thing for a man who has been a debauched villain to confront his victims whom his lusts dragged down to hell! How will he quail as he hears them lay their damnation at his door!—15.587

Luke 16:31 *"Neither will they be persuaded, though one rose from the dead."*

1847 Though one should rise from the grave with all the scars of his torments upon him, with his hair crisp by the hot fire of vengeance, his body scorched in the flames, though he should tell you with a tear at every word and a groan as a

stop at every sentence and a deep sigh on every syllable how horribly he feels, how damnably he is tormented, still you would not repent.—2.92

1848 Do not say in your heart, "I never will believe there is a hell unless one should come from it." If one should come from it then you would not believe at all. You would say, "If one person came from hell, then another may, and I may myself."—7.501

Luke 17:6 *"Say unto this sycamine tree, Be thou plucked up . . . and it should obey you."*

1849 You say, "My bad temper is rooted in me. As a sycamore tree takes hold of the earth by its roots, so an ill temper has gone into the very depth of my nature. Constitutionally quick-tempered am I." If you have faith, you can say to that sycamore tree within you, "Be thou plucked up by the roots."—22.574

Luke 17:18 *"There are not found that returned to give glory to God, save this stranger."*

1850 One would have thought that all who prayed would praise, but it is not so. Cases have been where a whole ship's crew in time of storm prayed, and yet none of that crew have sung the praise of God when the storm has become a calm. Multitudes of our fellow citizens pray when they are sick and near dying, but when they grow better, their praises grow sick unto death.—32.686, 687

Luke 18:1 *"Men ought always to pray, and not to faint."*

1851 We must continue incessantly and constantly, and know no pause to our prayer till we win the mercy to the fullest possible extent. Week by week, month by month, year by year, the conversion of that dear child is to be the father's main plea. The bringing in of that unconverted husband is to lie on the wife's heart night and day till she gets it. She is not to take even ten or twenty years of unsuccessful prayer as a reason why she should cease.—15.100

1852 "We ought always to pray, and not to faint" because we are always sinning.—17.211

1853 I feel so grateful to the Holy Spirit that this text does not say, "Saints ought always to pray," because then I might ask myself, "Am I a saint?" Perhaps I might have to answer, "No, I am far from it." But the text does not say "saints," and it does not even say, "Tender-hearted, penitent persons ought always to pray." No, there is no description of character given in the text, for which I am deeply grateful.—43.254

1854 "Men ought always to pray." It is always the wisest thing they can do. "Men ought always to pray." It is sometimes the only thing they can do. "Men ought always to pray," or else they take the matter out of God's hand. "Men ought always to pray," for they always need God's help, whether they think they do or not.—43.259

Luke 18:13 *"Standing afar ... [he] would not lift ... his eyes ... but smote upon his breast."*

1855 His heart had sinned, and he smote it. His eyes had led him astray, and he made them look down to the earth. And as he himself had sinned by living far off from God, he banished himself far from the manifest presence. Every gesture and posture is significant, and yet all came spontaneously. He had no book of directions how to behave himself in the house of God. His sincerity guided him. If you want to know how to behave yourselves as penitents, be penitents. The best rubrics of worship are those which are written on broken hearts.—33.116

Luke 18:13 *"God be merciful to me a sinner."*

1856 The prayer of the publican is my everyday prayer. I have what I may call a Sunday prayer, a prayer for high days and holidays. But my everyday prayer, the one that I can use all through the week, the one that I can pick up when I cannot pick up anything else, is the publican's prayer: "God be merciful to me, a sinner."—43.447, 448

1857 I never feel so well in spiritual health as when I cry out, "God be merciful to me, a sinner."—59.147, 148

Luke 19:5 *"Zacchaeus . . . come down; for to-day I must abide at thy house."*

1858 Why call Zacchaeus? There were many better men in the city than he. Why call him? Simply because the call of God comes to unworthy sinners. There is nothing in man that can deserve this call, nothing in the best of men that can invite it. But God quickens whom he will, and when he sends that call, though it should come to the vilest of the vile, down they come speedily and swiftly. They come down from the tree of their sin and fall prostrate in penitence at the feet of Jesus Christ.—5.132

Luke 19:9 *"This day is salvation come to this house."*

1859 Often the most unlikely persons are the first to receive the Savior. The least likely person in the city of Jericho to receive Christ was this rich little tax-gatherer, Zacchaeus. When Christ went to his house they all murmured, saying that he was to be the guest of a man that was a sinner. Yet he was the one person in that place who did entertain the Lord Jesus Christ. And many a time since has Christ been shut out of good men's doors, or the doors of those who have reckoned themselves as good men. But he has found shelter within the gates of sinners, and such sinners as have been reputed among men to be utterly given over and hopeless.—46.542

Luke 19:10 *"The Son of man is come to seek and to save that which was lost."*

1860 If you would win souls, you must seek them. The sportsman knows that his game will not come to the window of his house to be shot. The fisherman knows that the fish will not come swimming up to his house. Do they not go abroad and seek their prey? And so must you and I.—6.374

1861 Martin Luther speaks in his book on Galatians of cutting the devil's head off with his own sword: "There," says Martin to the devil, "you say I am a great sinner. I thank you for that, for Jesus Christ came into the world to save sinners, and so I feel he came to save me." And if the devil says to you, "You are lost altogether," off with his head, my brother, with his own sword. Rejoice that "the Son of Man is come to seek and to save that which was lost."—19.144

1862 They are so lost that they need saving, but they are also so lost that they need *seeking.* Persons may be so lost on land or on sea as to need saving and not seeking, but we were spiritually lost, so as to need both saving and seeking.—58.319

1863 Mr. Whitefield's brother had once been a very sad backslider. He had gone far from the way of Christ. At last, his conscience was pricked, and he fell into despair. Sitting at tea one day with the Countess of Huntingdon, he said, "I know what you have said is very proper, and I believe in the infinite mercy and goodness of God. But I do not believe in its application to me, for I am a lost man."

The countess put down the tea and said, "I am glad to hear it, Mr. Whitefield!"

"Madam," he said, "I did not think you would rejoice and glory in a thing so terrible as that."

"I am glad to hear you say you are lost, Mr. Whitefield," she said, "for it is written that 'Jesus Christ came to seek and to save that which was lost.' "

His eyes sparkled, and he said, "I thank God for that text, and for the extraordinary power with which it has now come into my heart." He died that night, and God had just sent him the word of peace in time to gather him into the fold.—59.573

Luke 19:37 *"The whole multitude of the disciples began to rejoice and praise God."*

1864 While the praise was multitudinous, it was quite select. It was the whole multitude *of the disciples.* The Pharisees did not praise him; they were murmuring. All true praise must come from true hearts.—12.124

Luke 19:41 *"He beheld the city, and wept over it."*

1865 Even if I knew that my hearers must be lost, I would pray to God to help me weep over them, because our Savior's tears over Jerusalem were accompanied with a distinct indication that it would be destroyed (Luke 19:44). Still he wept.—23.240

Luke 22:19 *"This do in remembrance of me."*

1866 Remember the Lord Jesus that you may follow him. In sickness recollect him in his patience. When you are persecuted, recollect him in his gentleness. In holy service remember him with his burning zeal. In your times of solitude remember him and his midnight prayers. And when you are in public and have to bear witness, remember him and his lionlike declarations of the gospel. Remember him so that he becomes your pattern, and you are the reproduction of himself, and so the best memorial of him.—34.449

Luke 22:44 *"His sweat was as it were great drops of blood falling down to the ground."*

1867 Jesus is so utterly oblivious of self that instead of his agony driving his blood to the heart to nourish himself, it drives it outward to bedew the earth. The agony of Christ, inasmuch as it pours him out on the ground, pictures the fulness of the offering which he made for men.—9.81

Luke 22:61, 62 *"And the Lord . . . looked upon Peter . . . And Peter went out, and wept bitterly."*

¹⁸⁶⁸ Observe the power there is in people's eyes. What a power there was in that maid's eye when she gazed earnestly on Peter! It was that earnest gaze of the girl that made Peter deny his Master. But then see the power for good that there was in Christ's eyes. Eyes can say far more than lips can. Often there is more heart-affecting eloquence in the eye than there is in the tongue. If the Lord will manage your eyes for you, you will find that they will be potent messengers of love for him. God give you to have those sanctified eyes which can work wonders for him!—48.141

Luke 22:63–65 *"Men that held Jesus mocked . . . blindfolded him . . . and . . . blasphemously spake."*

¹⁸⁶⁹ Was Jesus held captive? Then he shall hold me fast and never let me go. My Lord, I surrender myself, my life, my all to thee, to be thy willing captive forever! Then next, as they did despise him, I will despise the world that did despise my Lord and Savior. And as they blindfolded Jesus, what then? Why, I will be blindfolded too. I will henceforth see no charm, no attraction anywhere but in my Lord. And inasmuch as these men said many other things blasphemously against him, let us say many things in his praise.—49.167

Luke 23:9 *"He answered him nothing."*

¹⁸⁷⁰ Herod had already silenced the voice, and no wonder that he could not hear the word. For what was John? He said, "I am the voice of one crying in the wilderness" (John 1:23). What was Jesus but the word (John 1:1)? He that silences the voice may well be denied the word.—28.103

Luke 23:18 *"Away with this man, and release unto us Barabbas."*

¹⁸⁷¹ The perfect, loving, tender, sympathizing Savior was met with the words, "Crucify him!" and Barabbas, the thief, was preferred.

"Well," says one, "that was atrocious."

The same thing is put before you, and every unregenerate man will make the same choice that the Jews did. Only men renewed by grace will act on the contrary principle. This day I put before you Christ Jesus or your sins. The reason why many come not to Christ is because they cannot give up their lusts, their pleasures, their profits. Sin is Barabbas. Sin is a thief. It will rob your soul of its life. It will rob God of his glory. Sin is a murderer. It stabbed our father, Adam. It slew our purity.

Sin is a traitor. It rebels against the king of heaven and earth.—9.107

Luke 23:28 *"Weep not for me, but weep for yourselves."*

[1872] You need not weep because Christ died one tenth as much as because your sins rendered it necessary that he should die. You need not weep over the crucifixion, but weep over your transgression, for your sins nailed the Redeemer to the accursed tree. To weep over a dying Savior is to lament the remedy. It were wiser to bewail the disease. To weep over the dying Savior is to wet the surgeon's knife with tears. It were better to bewail that spreading tumor which that knife must cut away.—22.595

Luke 23:34 *"Father, forgive them; for they know not what they do."*

[1873] What an example our Lord herein presents to us! Let us continue in prayer as long as our heart beats. Let no excess of suffering drive us away from the throne of grace, but rather let it drive us closer to it.—15.589

[1874] On that day when Peter stood up with the eleven and charged the people that with wicked hands they had slain the Savior, three thousand of these persons who were thus justly accused of his crucifixion became believers in him (Acts 2). That was

292

an answer to Jesus' prayer.—15.595

[1875] Christ prays for you when you do not pray for yourselves. "Father, forgive them" was a prayer for those who had never sought forgiveness for themselves. And when under a sense of sin you dare not lift so much as your eyes toward heaven, he is pleading for you. And when you *cannot plead*, when the language of supplication seems to blister your lips because you feel yourself to be so unworthy, he still pleads for you. Oh, what encouragement this ought to give you!—23.654, 655

[1876] Say, "Father, forgive me." Shall my Master say, "Father, forgive him," and will not you pray for yourself? Do not use Christ's plea; that is his, not yours. He could say, "Father, forgive them; for they know not what they do." You must use another plea: "Father, forgive me through thy Son's precious blood."—53.585

Luke 23:35 *"He saved others; let him save himself."*

[1877] Perhaps this dying thief read the gospel out of the lips of Christ's enemies. They said, "He saved others."

"Ah!" thought he, "Did he save others? Why should he not save me?"

What a grand bit of gospel that was for the dying thief!—32.53

Luke 23:42 *"Lord, remember me when thou comest into thy kingdom."*

1878 The thief does not even seem to have had an instruction, an invitation, or an expostulation addressed to him, and yet this man became a sincere and accepted believer in the Lord Jesus Christ. There are many who have been instructed from their childhood, who have been admonished and warned and entreated and invited, and yet they have not come to Christ, while this man, without any of these advantages, nevertheless believed in the Lord Jesus Christ and found eternal life. You who have lived under the sound of the gospel from your childhood, the thief does not comfort you, he accuses you!—32.51

John 1:17 *"The law was given by Moses, but grace and truth came by Jesus Christ."*

1879 When it was demanded of Moses to prove whether or not he was sent by God, he took the wonder-working rod in his hand and achieved marvels. But they were all miracles of judgment, not of mercy. Moses, the type of the law, has his credentials in judgment. How different from Jesus. He is full of grace and truth, and the seals of his ministry must be acts of mercy and kindness.

He turns not the water into blood, but water into wine. He slays not their fish, but multiplies a few small fish and feeds thousands with them. He does not smite their wheat with hail, but he multiplies their bread and gives them many blessings. He sends no boils, but he heals their sicknesses. Instead of striking the first-born dead, he heals the dying and rescues from the grasp of death some who had even gone down to the grave!—6.373

1880 Moses came to show how the holy should behave, but Jesus comes to reveal how the unholy may be cleansed.—23.171

John 1:29 *"Behold the Lamb of God."*

1881 It is the preacher's principal business, his only business, to cry, "Behold the Lamb of God!" I think the minister who has failed to cry, "Behold the Lamb of God," may expect at the last to be cut in pieces and to have his portion with the tormentors.—18.385

1882 God-sent servants do not say, "Look to the priest, look to the altar, look to the sacraments, look to yourself; come and confess your sins, and I will give you absolution." No, no, no, no. Forever and ever no! The priests of antichrist do that, but the servants of Christ cry, "Behold the Lamb of God." Our great difficulty is to get men's eyes off themselves, off their works, off their forms and ceremonies, off mere creed religion, and to get them to look at the living Christ.—45.520

John 1:36 *"Looking upon Jesus as he walked, he saith, Behold the Lamb of God!"*

1883 Notice in the text the attitude of the preacher, for it is very instructive. The preacher's eye should be *on* his Master while he points *to* his Master. They preach Christ best who see him best.—18.386

John 1:43, 45 *"Jesus . . . findeth Philip . . . Philip found him."*

1884 Once when I was a little child I thought I saw a needle moving across the table. I should have been wondering who made the needle march as it did, but I was old enough to understand that somebody was moving a magnet underneath the table. Thus the Lord, with his mighty magnet of grace, is often at work on the hearts of men, and we think that their desire after God and their faith in Christ are of themselves. In a sense these are their own. But there is a divine force that is at work on them, producing these results. Philip thinks he is finding Jesus, but behind the veil it is Jesus finding Philip.—40.403

John 2:9 *"Water . . . was made wine."*

1885 Jesus Christ commenced the gospel dispensation, not with a miracle of vengeance, like that of Moses, who turned water into blood, but with a miracle of generosity, turning water into wine. He does not only supply necessities, but also gives luxuries. Here he not only gives sinners enough to save them, but also he gives abundantly, grace upon grace.—26.494

John 3:7 *"Ye must be born again."*

1886 There are the flames of hell. Would you escape them? You must be born again. There are heaven's glories sparkling in their own light. Would you enjoy them? You must be born again. This is the one condition that never moves. God never alters it. You must, *must*, MUST. Which shall it be? Bow yourselves down and say, "Lord, I must, then I will. And it has come to this—I must tonight."—11.288

1887 I was staying one day at an inn in one of the valleys of Northern Italy, where the floor was dreadfully dirty. I had it in my mind to advise the landlady to scrub it, but when I perceived that it was made of mud, I reflected that the more she scrubbed, the worse it would be. The man who knows his own heart soon perceives that his corrupt nature allows no opportunity of improvement. There must be a new nature implanted, or the man will be washed only to deeper stains. You must be born again.—13.184, 185

1888 Is a man a Christian because he lives in England? Is a rat a horse because it lives in a stable? That is just as good reasoning. A man must be born again, or he is no child of God.—13.640

1889 The most unpopular truth in the world is this sentence which fell from the lips of Christ: "Ye must be born again."—42.247

John 3:16 *"For God so loved the world, that he gave his only begotten Son. . . ."*

1890 Who in this congregation would object to giving anything to the Queen? Not a soul of us. And yet, perhaps, there is no person in the world who so little needs our gifts. We can always give to those who do not require anything, for we feel that there is some honor conferred on us, an honor bestowed by the reception. Now look to Jesus. When he gives to his friends, he gets no honor from them. The honor is in his own free heart that should lead him to give to such poor worms.—5.181

1891 Perhaps there is no greater soul-saving text in the Bible than this. I must have conversed with more than a hundred persons who have found the Lord through this blessed verse. I am speaking very moderately, for I think I might say that I have known several hundred who have been guided into liberty by this polestar text.—32.440

1892 I sometimes think that if I never had a gleam of love from God's face again, I would live on this one text.—35.418

John 3:18 *"He that believeth on him is not condemned."*

1893 What would I have given ten or eleven years ago if I could have known this text was sure to me, that I was not condemned. I thought if I could feel I was once forgiven and had to live on bread and water and be locked up in a dungeon and every day be flogged with a cat-o'-nine-tails, I would gladly have accepted it, if I could have once felt my sins forgiven.—7.119

1894 If I were to meet an angel, and he should say, "Charles Spurgeon, I have come from heaven to tell you that you are pardoned," I would say to him, "I know that without your telling me anything of the kind. I know it on a great deal better authority than yours." And if he asked me how I knew it, I would reply, "The Word of God is better to me than the word of an angel, and he has said, 'He that believeth on him is not condemned.' I do believe on him, and therefore I am not condemned, and I know it without an angel to tell me so."—12.60

1895 This is the whole Bible in miniature. It is the essence of the gospel, the good news in brief.—16.673

John 3:18 *"He that believeth not is condemned already."*

1896 I have heard some ministers talk of men being in a state of probation. No such thing. You are condemned already. You are not today, my unregenerate hearers, prisoners at the bar about to be tried for your lives. No, your trial is over, your sentence is passed already, and you are now this day condemned.—5.483

1897 You are in the position of the courtier at the feast of Dionysus, with the sword over your head suspended by a single hair. Condemned already!—7.515

John 3:36 *"The wrath of God abideth on him."*

1898 Till you have believed, your danger is of the most imminent kind. You are not in danger of something future only; you are in peril even now, for the wrath of God *abideth* on you. You are not like a city which is to be attacked by troops yet at a distance. The Judge is even at the door. You are actually besieged.—16.480

John 4:27 *"His disciples . . . marvelled that he talked with the woman."*

1899 How could these disciples marvel that he spoke with anybody after having chosen *them* and called *them?* Surely when they frowned on others, they forgot the dunghills where they grew. If they had only remembered where they were when he found them, and how often they had grieved him by their perverseness, they would have reserved their surprise for their own cases. Ever since the Lord spoke with

me, I have never marveled that he spoke with anybody.—28.495

John 6:11 *"Jesus took the loaves; and . . . distributed to the disciples."*

1900 When Jesus took the loaves, it was not only to multiply, but also to dispose of them. They were distributed by Christ. He did not believe in multiplication unless it was attended by division. Christ's additions mean subtraction, and Christ's subtractions mean additions. He gives that we may give away. If you have received the truth from Christ, tell it out!—37.416

John 6:37 *"Him that cometh to me I will in no wise cast out."*

1901 Let it ring down the corridors of hell, and let every devil dance for joy as he hears that Christ has broken his promise and is untrue to his character, whenever you hear of one who comes to him whom he casts out. I challenge all time, I challenge heaven and earth and hell to bring a case in which my Lord and Master ever cast out a soul that put its trust in him. It cannot be.—26.189

1902 If Jesus Christ casts any one of you out when you come to him, please let me know, for I do not want to go up and down the country telling lies. If my Lord does cast out one poor soul that comes to him, let me know it, and I will give up preaching.—33.419

John 6:44 *"No man can come to me, except the Father . . . draw him."*

1903 You see a mother with her babe in her arms. You put a knife in her hand and tell her to stab that babe to the heart. She replies truthfully, "I cannot." Now, so far as her bodily power is concerned, she can if she pleases. There is the knife, and there is the child. But she is quite correct when she says she cannot do it.

It is even so with a sinner. Coming to Christ is so obnoxious to human nature that although, so far as physical and mental forces are concerned, men could come if they would, it is strictly correct that they cannot and will not unless the Father who sent Christ draws them.—4.138

John 6:47 *"He that believeth on me hath everlasting life."*

1904 According to a certain theology a man may have life in Christ one day and lose it the next. How, then, is it everlasting life? That which comes to an end could not have been everlasting. But we teach with the authority of Christ that the man who believes in Christ has at this moment within him a life that can never expire. The man may die after the flesh, but he can never die after the spirit.—28.66

John 7:37 *"If any man thirst, let him come unto me, and drink."*

1905 Come if you do thirst, and come if you think you do not thirst but wish you did, for that wish to thirst is the very thirst you wish for. Your lack of a power to feel your lack is your greatest lack. Consciousness of your own unconsciousness is the truest consciousness. Your groaning because you cannot groan is the deepest groaning that ever is groaned. The more unfit you feel yourself to be, the more are you invited to come. Your very unfitness is your fitness for coming to Jesus.—31.682

John 8:34 *"Whosoever committeth sin is the servant of sin."*

1906 Sin drives men mad. Against their reason, against their best interests, they follow after that which they know will destroy them. They are slaves, though they wear no fetters of iron; captives, though no walls enclose them. The magic arts of evil have taken them in a net and wrapped them about with invisible bonds, from which they cannot escape.—27.27

John 8:56 *"Your father Abraham. . . ."*

1907 However good a man may be personally, he cannot possibly ensure that his descendants will be like him. It was to the carping, unbelieving Jews that our Lord said, "Your father Abraham." Abraham was a clear-eyed saint, whose gaze pierced through those twenty centuries and beheld his Lord. Yet after the flesh he was the father of a bleary-eyed generation that could not see the light eternal, even when it flashed directly on their eyeballs. I think there is nothing that is more full of warning than this to you who are descended from godly parents.—45.590, 591

John 9:4 *"I must work the works of him that sent me."*

[1908] There are plenty of people who say, "I must work," but there are very few who say,"I must work the works of him that sent me."—13.341

John 9:7 *"He went his way . . . and washed, and came seeing."*

[1909] If the blind man had remained blind, he might have continued a tolerably happy beggar. He seems to have had very considerable mental resources, and he might have made his way in the world as well as others of the begging confraternity. But *you* cannot be happy or safe unless the Lord Jesus opens your eyes. There remains for you nothing but the blackness of darkness forever, unless light from heaven visits you. You must have Christ or die.—33.449

John 9:35 *"Dost thou believe on the Son of God?"*

[1910] I am convinced that this question is the most important question that a man can ever have to answer.—55.89

John 10:9 *"I am the door."*

[1911] You may knock at a thousand doors; you may cry and pray and groan and agonize and sweat, even to drops of blood, but there is only one door to heaven, and that door is faith in Jesus Christ. If you will not enter by that door, God himself will not open another.—20.695, 696

John 10:10 *"I am come that they might have life . . . more abundantly."*

[1912] Christians should have such abundant life that their circumstances should not be able to overcome them, such abundant life that in poverty they are rich, in sickness they are in spiritual health, in contempt they are full of triumph, and in death full of glory.—20.11

John 10:28 *"They shall never perish."*

[1913] What if they should live to be very aged and then fall into sin?

"They shall never perish."

But perhaps they may be assaulted in quarters where they least expect it, or they may be surrounded by temptation.

"They shall never perish."

But a man may be a child of God and yet go to hell.

How so, if he can *never* perish?—12.704

John 11:24 *"I know that he shall rise again in the resurrection at the last day."*

[1914] Is it hard to believe that Lazarus can rise four days after his death? It is a great deal harder to believe that bodies can be quickened which have been dead several thousand years. Yet Martha did believe that the dead would rise on the resurrection day—not only those who were stinking, but those whose bodies had been dissolved by corruption! She believed the miracle on the grand scale. But when it came home to the one person who had been dead only four days, she could not believe it.—26.646

John 11:35 *"Jesus wept."*

¹⁹¹⁵ Love made him weep. Nothing else ever compelled him to tears. I do not find that all the pains he endured, even when scourged or fastened to the cruel tree, fetched a single tear from him. But for love's sake, "Jesus wept." The Jews recognized, even with their unfriendly eyes, that his tears were drawn from him by love alone (John 11:36). From this rock of our salvation no rod but that of love could bring forth water floods.—33.53

John 11:36 *"Behold how he loved him!"*

¹⁹¹⁶ Truly you might say the like with deeper emphasis. There was nothing in you to make him love you, but he left heaven's throne for you. As he came down the celestial hill, I think the angels said, "Oh, how he loved them!" When he lay in the manger an infant, they gathered round and said, "Oh, how he loves!" But when they saw him sweating in the garden, when he was put into the crucible and began to be melted in the furnace, then indeed the spirits above began to know how much he loved us.—6.313

John 11:43 *"Lazarus, come forth."*

¹⁹¹⁷ There is a man who says, "I have been living fifty years in sin, and tonight I am worse than ever. My old habits bind me hand and foot, and I have no hope of being delivered."

Now, if tonight Jesus says, "Lazarus, come forth," you will come forth in an instant.

"But" say you, "I am corrupt."

Yes, but Christ is mightier than your corruption.

Do you say, "I am dead"? Christ is life. Do you say, "I am bound hand and foot and in a dungeon of darkness"? Christ is a light in darkness, and he will disperse the gloom. You say, perhaps, "I do not deserve it," but Jesus cares nothing for deserving. The dead body of Lazarus was putrid and deserved only to have the stone cover it forever.

"Roll away the stone," says Christ. And there may be some from whom Jesus Christ may have rolled away the stone tonight. They may be standing at their own graves and feeling themselves loathsome and offensive. But still, offensive as you are, Jesus asks no merit of you. He will give you his merits. It is only for him to say, "Come forth," and you will come forth from your grave and be made alive in Christ.—44.55

John 11:44 *"He that was dead came forth, bound hand and foot with graveclothes."*

[1918] When we first obtain spiritual life, how many graveclothes there are hanging about us! A man who has been a drunkard, even though he becomes a living child of God, will sometimes find his old habits clinging to him.—44.56

John 12:31 *"Now is the judgment of this world."*

[1919] We find in the Greek, "Now is the *crisis* of this world." The world had come to a solemn crisis. This was the great turning point of all the world's history. Should Christ die, or should he not? If he should refuse the bitter cup of agony, the world is doomed. If he should pass onward, do battle with the powers of death and hell, and come off a victor, then the world is blessed, and her future shall be glorious. Then this world shall yet see times when there shall be "a new heaven and a new earth, wherein dwelleth righteousness" (2 Peter 3:13). Now is the crisis of the world!—3.257

John 12:32 *"And I, if I be lifted up from the earth, will draw all men unto me."*

[1920] I would stake what reputation I may have in spiritual things on this—that a man cannot, under God's Holy Spirit, contemplate the cross of Christ without a broken heart.—1.338

[1921] Drawing is very different from driving. The way by which Jesus leads his followers is by soft, gentle influences.—13.573

[1922] I have often asked when I have looked on you congregated here by thousands year after year, and know that my speech has nothing in it remarkable, why it is that you gather so continually. Many others have asked the secret why this house is always thronged. The true answer is that I preach Jesus Christ to you, and it is written, "I, if I be lifted up, will draw all men unto me." I have no other theme, and I want no other. It is not worn out and never will be. Though I should stand here the next six thousand years, I believe the house would still be filled if the testimony were the same. Despite London's sin, nothing strikes London's heart like the name of Jesus Christ.—16.282, 283

[1923] This it is—the unique, unrivaled love—which draws men to Jesus. The pierced heart of Christ is a lodestone to draw all other hearts.—29.234

1924 If a thousand persons were to believe in Jesus this morning, I should not be in the least surprised. For this I surely can claim, that I have these many years preached nothing among you but the cross of Christ.—32.556

1925 We slander Christ when we think that we are to draw the people by something else but the preaching of Christ crucified. We know that the largest crowd in London has been held together these thirty years by nothing but the preaching of Christ crucified. Where is our music? Where is our oratory? Where is anything of attractive architecture or beauty of ritual? "A bare service" they call it. Yes, but Christ makes up for all deficiencies. Preach Christ, and men will be drawn to him, for so the text says.—39.596

1926 I believe that Christ will save some out of this congregation, though I know not who they may be. You are like a heap of steel filings and ashes before me. It is no business of mine to separate you. My business is to thrust in the magnet, and that will do it.—54.588

John 13:1 *"He loved them unto the end."*

1927 Jesus will know his people to the utmost end of their unloveliness. Their sinfulness cannot travel so far but what his love will travel beyond it. Their unbelief even shall not be extended to so great a length but what his faithfulness shall still be wider and broader than their unfaithfulness.—14.273

John 13:35 *"By this shall all men know that ye are my disciples, if ye have love."*

1928 I am told that Christians do not love each other. I am very sorry if that be true, but I rather doubt it, for I suspect that those who do not love each other are not Christians.—12.6

John 14:2 *"In my Father's house are many mansions."*

1929 Some have doubted whether there will be recognition in heaven. There is no room for doubt, for it is called "my Father's house," and shall not the family be known to each other?—15.476

John 14:2 *"I go to prepare a place for you."*

1930 Our Lord Jesus Christ prepares heaven for his people by going there. Suppose you were to be lifted up to a state which was looked on as heavenly, but Jesus was not there. It would be no heaven to you. But wherever I may go, when I do go, if Jesus is already there, I do not care where it is. To be with Christ is far better than to be anywhere else. Well, then, the first thing that Christ had to do in order to prepare heaven for his people was to go to heaven. That made it heaven.—47.522

1931 The place is prepared; are *you* prepared for it? Do you believe on the Lord Jesus Christ? If so, your preparation has begun. Do you love the Lord and love his people? If so, your preparation is going on. Do you hate sin, and do you pant after holiness? If so, your preparation is progressing. Is Jesus your all in all? Then you are almost ready. May the Lord keep you in that condition and before long swing up the gates of pearl and let you into the prepared place!—47.526

John 14:6 *"I am the way, the truth, and the life."*

1932 Christ is "the way," but if you will not tread it, you shall not reach the end. Christ is "the truth," but if you will not believe him, you shall not rejoice. Christ is "the life," but if you will not receive him, you shall abide among the dead.—11.444

1933 A minister in America was going up the aisle of his church during a revival, when a young man earnestly cried to him, "Sir, can you tell me the way to Christ?"

"No," was the answer, very deliberately given, "I cannot."

The young man answered, "I beg your pardon; I thought you were a minister of the gospel."

"So I am," was the reply.

"Then how is it that you cannot tell me the way to Christ?"

"My friend," said the minister, "there is no way to Christ. He himself is the way. Christ is here."—31.309

John 14:19 *"Because I live, ye shall live also."*

1934 God gave Noah a token that he would not destroy the earth—it was the rainbow. But the rainbow is not often seen. There are peculiar circumstances before the bow is placed in the cloud. You, brother, have a token of God's covenant given you in the text which can always be seen. Neither sun nor shower are needful to its appearance. The living Christ is the token that you live too.—17.11

1935 When Christ can die, then can the believer perish. When it shall be possible for Christ to be cast out of heaven, for his power and glory to be taken from him, and for his very deity to wax old and grow effete with age, then may the believer's life be quenched. But not till then.—51.454

John 14:26 *"He shall teach you all things, and bring all things to your remembrance."*

1936 It is part of the Spirit's work to make us understand what Jesus taught. If he were merely to bring to remembrance the words of Jesus, it would do us little good, even as a child learns his catechism and does not understand it. But if you first teach him their meaning and then bring the words to remembrance, you have conferred on him a double boon. Now, we can, as far as the letter goes, learn from the Scriptures the words of Jesus for ourselves. But to understand these teachings is the gift of the Spirit of God, and of no one else.—18.556, 557

1937 The Comforter is the Instructor, and Jesus is the Lesson.—23.690

John 15:2 *"Every branch that beareth fruit, he purgeth."*

1938 Do you know that the promise of the old covenant was prosperity, but the promise of the new covenant is adversity? If you bring forth fruit, you will have to endure affliction.—11.537

1939 You have no right to say, when a man is afflicted, that it is because he has done wrong. On the contrary, "every branch that beareth fruit he purgeth." Just the branch that is good for something gets the pruning knife.—13.562

1940 Many trials are not sent for chastisements at all, but as preparations for higher usefulness. "Every branch that beareth fruit, he purgeth," evidently not because of any offense in the branch, but because the branch is good and does bear fruit! Therefore, it is allowed the special privilege of the pruning knife that it may bring forth more fruit.—23.424

John 15:5 *"Without me ye can do nothing."*

1941 "Do nothing," and the world dying around us! Africa in darkness! China perishing! India sunk in superstition, and a church which can do nothing! Ministers, evangelists, churches, salvation armies—the world dies for need of you, and yet "ye can do nothing" if your Lord is away.—27.601

1942 My heart said, "Lord, what is there that I want to do without thee? There is no pain in this thought to me. If I can do without thee, I am sorry to possess so dangerous a power. I am happy to be deprived of all strength except that which comes from thee. It charms, it exhilarates and delights my soul to think that thou art my all."—27.602, 603

1943 If this be true of apostles, much more of opposers! If Jesus' friends can do nothing without him, I am sure his foes can do nothing against him.—27.604

John 15:13 *"Greater love hath no man than this. . . ."*

1944 But greater love a man may have than to lay down his life for his friends, namely, if he dies for his enemies. And herein is the greatness of Jesus' love, that though he called us "friends," the friendship was all on his side at the first. He called us friends, but our hearts called him enemy.—19.476

John 15:26 *"The Comforter . . . even the Spirit of truth."*

1945 As the Holy Spirit is the Comforter, Christ is the comfort. The Holy Spirit consoles, but Christ is the consolation. The Holy Spirit is the Physician, but Christ is the medicine. He heals the wound, but it is by applying the holy ointment of Christ's name and grace. He takes not of his own things, but of the things of Christ.—7.1

John 16:8 *"He will reprove the world of sin."*

1946 I know the preacher has thought within himself, "I have only to put the truth in a reasonable way, and the man will see it." But sinners are not reasonable; they are the most unreasonable of all creatures. None act so madly as they do.

"But," says he, "if I were to tell them of the love of Christ in an affectionate way, that would reach them."

Yes, but you will find that all your affection and your tears and earnest description of the love of Jesus will be powerless against human hearts, unless the eternal Spirit shall drive home your appeals.—17.472

1947 It is absolutely necessary that men should be convinced of sin. The fashionable theology is, "Convince men of the goodness of God. Show them the universal fatherhood, and assure them of unlimited mercy. Win them by God's love, but never mention his wrath against sin or the need of an atonement or the place of punishment. Comfort and encourage, but never accuse and threaten."

That is the way of man, but the way of the Spirit of God is very different. He comes on purpose to convince men of sin, to make them feel that they are so guilty that they are lost and ruined and undone. He comes to remind them not only of God's loveliness, but of their own unloveliness. The Holy Ghost does not come to make sinners comfortable in their sins, but to cause them to grieve over their sins. He does not help them to forget their sin or think little of it, but he comes to convince them of the horrible enormity of their iniquity. It is no work of the Spirit to pipe to men's dancing.—29.125

1948 One comforting thought is that he who alone can pierce sinners' hearts is named "The Comforter." The Spirit who convicts us is also the Spirit who consoles. The same divine Spirit is both Wounder and Healer.—54.261

John 16:14 *"He shall glorify me."*

1949 You say that you want to glorify Christ. That is also what the Holy Spirit wants to do. That is what he has long been doing, and still is doing. Therefore, cast

304

in your lot with him. My sister, do not go to that Sunday school class of yours again until you have asked the Holy Spirit to go with you. My brother, do not go up those pulpit stairs again, nor even up the stairs of that infirmary where you visit the sick, without first saying, "Spirit of God, it is thy business to glorify Christ, and that is also my business. So wilt thou graciously go with me, and go in me?"—55.33

John 16:14 *"He shall receive of mine, and shall show it unto you."*

1950 Preachers, do not try to be original. Be content to take the things of Christ and show them to the people, for that is what the Holy Ghost himself does.—37.239

John 16:20 *"Your sorrow shall be turned into joy."*

1951 Your sorrow itself shall be turned into joy. Not the sorrow to be taken away, and joy to be put in its place, but the very sorrow which now grieves you shall be turned into joy. God not only takes away the bitterness and gives sweetness in its place, but turns the bitterness itself into sweetness!—52.184

John 16:33 *"In the world ye shall have tribulation."*

1952 This is as sure a promise as that other, "In me ye shall have peace" (also John 16:33). The trials of God's servants are sometimes extremely severe.—18.112

John 17:24 *"Father, I will that they . . . be with me where I am."*

1953 Do you know why the righteous die? Shall I tell you what kills them? It is Christ's prayer in this verse. It is that which fetches them up to heaven. They would stop here, if Christ did not pray them to death.—41.596

John 18:18 *"Peter stood with them, and warmed himself."*

1954 It is a great deal easier to warm your hands than your hearts. A few coals in a brazier sufficed to warm Peter's hands, but even the infinite love of Jesus did not just then warm his heart. There was a furnace at the other end of the hall, a furnace of love divine! If Peter had but looked at his Master's face, marred with agony, and seen on it the mark of his terrible night sweat, surely had his heart been right, it must have burned within him.—56.44

John 18:37 *"To this end was I born . . . that I should bear witness unto the truth."*

1955 Do we feel this? I do not believe that you came into the world to be a merchant or an auctioneer, and nothing else. I do not believe that God created you to be merely and only a seamstress, a nurse, or a housekeeper. Immortal souls were not created for merely mortal ends.—18.707

John 19:28 *"I thirst."*

1956 Who was this that said, "I thirst"? It was he who balanced the clouds and filled the channels of the mighty deep. *He* said, "I thirst," and yet in him was a well of water springing up to eternal life! Yes, he who guided every river in its course and watered all the fields with grateful showers— he it was, the King of kings and Lord of lords, before whom hell trembles and the earth is filled with dismay, he whom heaven adores and all eternity worships— he it was who said, "I thirst"! Matchless condescension—from the infinity of God to the weakness of a thirsting, dying man! And this was for you.—59.604

1957 Once when he sat on the well of Samaria, he said to the poor harlot who met him there, "Give me to drink" (John 4:7). And he got drink from her—drink that the world knew nothing about, when she gave her heart to him. Christ is always thirsting after the salvation of precious souls. On the cross he saw the multitude and cried to his God, "I thirst." He thirsted to redeem mankind, he thirsted to accomplish the work of our salvation. This very day he thirsts still.—59.605

1958 If the Lord Jesus Christ thirsted when he only carried the sins of others, what thirst will be on you when God shall punish you for your own sins? Either Christ must thirst for you, or you must thirst forever and ever and ever.—59.607

John 19:30 *"It is finished."*

1959 There is nothing for God to do. "It is finished." There is nothing for you to do. "It is finished." Christ need not bleed. "It is finished." You need not weep. "It is finished." God the Holy Spirit need not delay because of your unworthiness, nor need you delay because of your helplessness. "It is finished." Every stumbling block is rolled out of the road; every gate is opened. The bars of brass are broken, the gates of iron are burst asunder. "It is finished." Come and welcome; come and welcome!—7.592

1960 There is no mortgage on the saints.—20.162

1961 The general religion of mankind is "Do," but the religion of a true Christian is "Done." "It is finished," is the believer's conquering word.—30.164

John 20:13 *"Woman, why weepest thou?"*

1962 When a soul is seeking Christ, nothing but Christ's own word will satisfy it. This holy woman was not content with what the angels said. Though they said to her, "Woman, why weepest thou?" those shining ones do not appear to have comforted her at all. She went on weeping. She told them why she wept, but she did not, therefore, cease her tears. And believe me, if the angels of heaven cannot content a heart which is seeking after Jesus, the angels of the churches cannot do so. We may preach as best we can, but the words of man will never satisfy the cravings of the heart. The seeker needs Jesus: Jesus only, but Jesus certainly.—35.676

John 20:27, 28 *"Reach hither thy finger. . . . Thomas answered . . . My Lord and my God."*

1963 Here faith went beyond what the finger revealed. The eye and hand showed a wounded man, but faith could see Godhead and authority, and therefore bowed and accepted the risen Man as being henceforth her Lord and her God.—12.363

1964 On a day which I had given up to prayer, I sat before the Lord in holy peacefulness, wrapped in solemn contemplation. And though I did not see a vision or wish to see one, yet I so realized my Master's presence that I was borne away from all earthly things, and knew of no man save Jesus only. Then a sense of his Godhead filled me till I would gladly have stood up where I was and have proclaimed aloud, as with the voice of a trumpet, that he was my Lord and my God. Such times you also have known.—30.214

John 21:15 *"Yea, Lord; thou knowest that I love thee" . . . "Feed my lambs."*

1965 When Peter said, "Yea, Lord; thou knowest that I love thee," you half thought that the Lord would answer, "Ah, Peter, and I love you," but he did not say so. And yet he did say so. Perhaps Peter did not see his meaning, but we can see it. Jesus did in effect say, "I love you so that I trust you with that which I purchased with my heart's blood. The dearest thing I have in all the world is my flock. I make you a shepherd to my sheep. I gave everything for them, even my life. Now, Simon, take care of them for me."—28.574, 575

John 21:16 *"Lovest thou me?"*

1966 Our Lord deals with the most vital point. The question is not, "Simon, son of Jonas, knowest thou me?" though that would not have been an unreasonable question, since Peter had said, "I know not the man" (Matt. 26:74). He might have asked, "Simon, knowest thou the deep mysteries of God?" Our great Bishop of souls did not examine him with regard to his mental endowments, nor on his other spiritual qualifications, but only on this one: "Simon, lovest thou me? If so, then feed my sheep." Does not this plainly show us that the chief endowment of the pastor is to love Christ supremely? Only such a man as that is fit to look after Christ's sheep.—56.398

Acts 1:1 *". . . of all that Jesus began both to do and teach."*

1967 When our biographies shall be written at last, God grant that they may not be all sayings, but a history of our sayings *and* doings! And may the good Spirit so dwell in us that it may be seen that our doings did not clash with our sayings! It is one thing to preach, but another thing to practice. And unless preaching and practice go together, the preacher is himself condemned, and his practice may be the means of condemning multitudes through his leading them astray.—6.245

Acts 1:8 *"Ye shall be witnesses unto me . . . in Jerusalem."*

1968 The invitations of the gospel seem to select the worst sinners first. What did the Savior say? "Begin at Jerusalem."

But, Lord, the men live there who crucified thee.

"Begin at Jerusalem."

But, Lord, it was in Jerusalem that they shed thy blood and thrust out the tongue and laughed at thee and made a mockery of thy prayers.

"Begin at Jerusalem"—the worst first, just as the surgeon in a battle is accustomed to look to the worst cases first.—10.382

1969 Remember, if you are not witnesses for God, you will be prisoners at his bar. You must either occupy the witness stand for God, or else take the prisoner's place, to be tried and found guilty. Oh, I wish you would try our God, whose witnesses we are. If we had found him untrue, we would tell you. If we had found that Christ could not save, we would tell you. If we had found that God could not pardon, we would tell you. But we have no such disclosures to make. We bear our willing testimony for God.—55.491

Acts 1:8 *"Ye shall be witnesses . . . unto the uttermost part of the earth."*

1970 I think the "ends of the earth" imply those who have gone the farthest away from Christ.—2.55

Acts 2:2 *"Suddenly there came a sound from heaven as of a rushing mighty wind."*

1971 No doubt this wind was intended to show the irresistible power of the Holy Ghost, for simple as the air is, and apparently feeble, yet set it in motion, and you feel that a thing of life is among you. Make that motion more rapid, and who knows the power of the restless giant who has been awakened? See, it becomes a storm, a tempest, a hurricane, a tornado, a cyclone.—27.523, 524

Acts 2:36 *"God hath made that same Jesus, whom ye have crucified, both Lord and Christ."*

1972 If there was ever an occasion when a preacher of the gospel might have forgotten to speak of Christ, it was surely when Peter spoke so boldly of him. Might it not have been said, "Talk not of Jesus. They have recently brought him to death. Preach the truth, but do not mention his name. Deliver his doctrine, but withhold the mention of his person, for you will excite them to madness. You will put your own life in jeopardy. You will scarcely do good while they are so prejudiced, and you may do much mischief"?

But instead of this, let them rage as they would, Peter would tell them about Jesus Christ, and about nothing else. He knew this to be the power of God unto salvation, and he would not flinch from it.—14.194

Acts 2:37 *"When they heard this, they were pricked in their heart."*

1973 A bleeding Savior makes men's hearts bleed. When he is pierced, they also are pierced. Of one thing I am sure, that nothing ever pierced my heart like the discovery of God's boundless love in giving his beloved Son to die for me.—54.260

Acts 2:41 *"The same day there were added unto them about three thousand souls."*

1974 Three thousand in one day under Peter's sermon! Why not three thousand again? Why not thirty thousand? Why not three hundred thousand in a day? There is nothing too great for us to ask for or for God to grant.— 12.82

Acts 4:12 *"Neither is there salvation in any other."*

1975 Some are foolish enough to put their confidence in ministers. I cannot even save myself; what can I do for others? There died in London not long ago a tradesman of much wealth. When he came near to death, though I had never seen the man in my life, he importunately asked for me. I could not go. My brother went to see him, and after setting before him the way to salvation, he inquired, "What made you wish to see my brother?"

"Well," he said, "whenever I have a doctor, I always like to get the best. And when I employ a lawyer, I like the man who is high in the profession. Money is no object. I want the best possible help."

I shuddered at being so regarded. The best help he could get! That best is nothing—less than nothing, and vanity. What can we do for you if you will not have a Savior? We can stand and weep over you, and break our hearts to think that you reject him, but what can we do?— 31.116, 117

Acts 4:20 *"We cannot but speak the things which we have seen and heard."*

1976 What said John Bunyan after he had lain in prison many years simply for preaching the gospel? The magistrates said, "John, we will let you out, but you must promise not to preach again. There are the regular clergymen of the country; what have you, as a tinker, to do with preaching?"

John Bunyan did not say, "Well now, I can see that this preaching is a bad thing. It has got me into prison, and I have had hard work to sell enough laces to keep my wife and that poor blind child of mine. I had better get out of this place and stick to tinkering."

No, he did not talk like that, but he said to the magistrates, "If you let me out of prison today, I will preach again tomorrow, by the grace of God." And when they told him that they would not let him out unless he promised not to preach, he bravely answered, "If I lie in jail till the moss grows on my eyelids, I will never conceal the truth which God has taught me."—48.604

Acts 5:31 *"Him hath God exalted with his right hand to be a Prince and a Saviour."*

1977 Many years ago, when this great congregation first met in the Surrey Music Hall and the terrible accident occurred, when many were either killed or wounded in the panic, I did my best to hold the people together—till I heard that some were dead. Then I broke down like a man stunned, and for a fortnight or so I had little reason left. I felt so broken in heart that I thought I should never be able to face a congregation again.

I went down to a friend's house to be very quiet and still. I was walking round his garden, and I well remember the spot, and even the time when this passage came to me: "Him hath God exalted with his right hand to be a Prince and a Saviour."

This thought came into my mind at once: "You are only a soldier in the great king's army, and you may die in a ditch. But it does not matter what becomes of you as long as your King is exalted." And so I thought, "He is exalted. What matters it about me?" In a moment my reason was perfectly restored. I came back to preach to my congregation on the following Sabbath, restored only by having looked to Jesus and having seen that he was glorious.—50.524

Note: See the quotation and note under **Providence,** *from the source 52.595 for another way in which God worked through this tragic experience.*

Acts 5:31 *"Him hath God exalted . . . to give repentance."*

1978 We are to tell of the source of repentance, namely, that the

Lord Jesus Christ is exalted on high to *give* repentance. Repentance is a plant that never grows on nature's dunghill. The nature must be changed, and repentance must be implanted by the Holy Spirit, or it will never flourish in our hearts. We preach repentance as a fruit of the Spirit, or else we greatly err.—29.374

Acts 7:55 *"He . . . saw . . . Jesus standing on the right hand of God."*

1979 Stephen saw his Lord *standing*. Our Lord is generally described as sitting, but it was as if the sympathizing Lord had risen up to draw near to his suffering servant, eager both to sustain and to receive him when the conflict was over. Jesus rose from his throne to gaze upon himself suffering again in the person of one of his beloved members.—20.307

1980 A man is generally much grieved with anyone who injures his children. I have known a man behave patiently to his neighbors and put up with a great deal from them, but when one of them has struck his child, I have seen him incensed to the last degree. He has said, "I cannot stand that. I will not look on and see my child abused."

The Lord says, "He that touches you touches the apple of my eye" (Zech. 2:8). Jesus rises from his throne in glory and stands up indignantly while his servant Stephen is being stoned.—30.120

Acts 7:58 *"The witnesses laid . . . their clothes at a . . . man's feet, whose name was Saul."*

1981 No doubt Stephen's mantle was among them. So, as surely as Elijah left his mantle to Elisha, the mantle of Stephen was lying at the feet of Saul. He did not put it on at once, but he did put it on afterward. I have often been asked, "What is to be done with the Tabernacle, the College, and the Orphanage when you are gone?" Dear me, the Lord got on very well before I was born, and I am sure he will when I am dead. That question never troubles me.—51.392

Acts 7:59 *"They stoned Stephen, calling upon God, and saying, Lord Jesus. . . ."*

1982 It is an infallible proof of our Lord's divinity that he may be addressed in prayer.—22.193

Acts 7:60 *"Lord, lay not this sin to their charge."*

1983 In speaking of his conversion, surely Paul must have thought within himself that it was the prayer of Stephen that was the means of changing Saul the persecutor into Paul the apostle of the crucified Son of God.—13.150

1984 When one of the martyrs was being tortured and tormented in a horrible way, the tyrant who had caused his suffering said to him, "And what has your Christ ever done for you that you should bear this?"

He replied, "He has done this for me, that in the midst of all my pain, I do nothing else but pray for you."—22.563

Acts 9:4 *"Saul, Saul, why persecutest thou me?"*

[1985] As all the rivers run into the sea, so all the streams of the church's suffering run into Christ. If the clouds be full of rain, they empty themselves on the earth. And if the Christian's heart be full of woes, it empties itself into the breast of Jesus.—4.300

[1986] When Saul was most at enmity against Christ, then was his turning point. As though some strong hand had suddenly seized by the bridle a horse that had broken loose and was about to leap down a precipice, and had thrown it back on its haunches and delivered it at the last moment from the destruction on which it was impetuously rushing, so Christ interposed and saved the rebel of Tarsus from being his own destroyer.—54.28

Acts 9:5 *"And he said, Who art thou, Lord?"*

[1987] Saul of Tarsus was not on his knees in prayer, but hastening to shed innocent blood. Yet the Lord brought him down and made him seek salvation. Beloved, our Lord knows how to reach inaccessible persons. They may shut *us* out, but they cannot shut *him* out! This should much encourage us in pleading for souls.—24.381

Acts 9:11 *"Behold, he prayeth."*

[1988] These words are the hallmark of genuine conversion. "Behold, he prayeth" is a surer witness of a man's conversion than "Behold, he singeth" or "Behold, he readeth the Scripture" or "Behold, he preacheth." These things may be admirably done by men who are not regenerate. But if, in God's sense of the term, a man really *prays*, we may know of a surety that he has passed from death into life.—31.505

[1989] If we could have stood outside the door and listened, we should have understood why the Lord said, "Behold, he prayeth." Before, you might have heard him repeating words, but now he utters groans, cries, sobs, and tears. Before, you might have said to yourself, "He is saying his prayers," but this time it was as when a man wrestles for his life. All previous prayer was sham, but this was real. All the rest was but a performance, but now he did real business with the Most High. "Behold, he prayeth."—31.514, 515

Acts 10:14 *"Not so, Lord."*

1990 "Not so, Lord" is an odd jumble of self-will and reverence, of pride and humility, of contradiction and devotion. Surely when you say, "Not so," it ought not to be said to the Lord. And if you say, "Lord," you ought not to put side by side with such an ascription the expression, "Not so."—31.85

Acts 12:5 *"Peter . . . was . . . in prison: but prayer was made without ceasing of the church."*

1991 I do not find that they met to petition Herod. It would have been of no avail to ask that monster to relent. They might as well request a wolf to release a lamb which he has seized. No, the petitions were to the great invisible God. It looked as if they could do nothing, but they felt they could do everything by prayer. They thought little of the fact that sixteen soldiers had him in charge. What are sixteen guards? If there had been sixteen thousand soldiers, these believing men and women would still have prayed Peter out.—21.436

Acts 13:48 *"As many as were ordained to eternal life believed."*

1992 Trouble not yourself about election, but rather encourage yourself with it. This is sure evidence of your election, that you believe in Jesus, for "as many as were ordained to eternal life believed."—34.539

Acts 15:11 *"Through the grace of the Lord Jesus Christ we shall be saved, even as they."*

1993 You expect to hear Peter say to these gentlemen, "These Gentile dogs, as you call them, can be saved, even as you." No, he turns the tables and says to them, "We believe that you may be saved, even as they." Suppose some of our members should say, "Yes, we believe that a drunkard may be saved, and a person who has been a harlot, may, perhaps, be saved, too." But imagine now that I were to stand up and reply, "My dear brethren, I believe that you may be saved even as these." What a rebuke it would be! This is precisely what Peter meant.—13.450

Acts 16:30 *"What must I do to be saved?"*

1994 Ah, you trifle with subtleties while you neglect certainties! More questions have been asked concerning the origin of evil than anything else. Men have puzzled their heads and twisted their brains to understand what men can never know—how evil came into this world, and how its entrance is consistent with divine goodness. The broad fact is this: There is evil, and your question should be, "How can I escape from the wrath to come, which was produced by this evil?"—3.90

313

Acts 16:31 *"Believe on the Lord Jesus Christ, and thou shalt be saved, and thy house."*

1995 Does the father's faith save the family? Yes! No! *Yes*, it does in some way, namely, that the father's faith makes him pray for his family, and God hears his prayer, and the family is saved. *No*, the father's faith cannot be a substitute for the faith of the children. They must believe too.—6.249

1996 "Ah," says one, "but you do not know what children mine are."

No, but I know that if you are a Christian, they are children that God has promised to bless.

"O, but they are such unruly ones, they break my heart."

Then pray God to break their hearts, and they will not break your heart any more.

"But they will bring my grey hairs with sorrow to the grave."

Pray God then that he may bring their eyes with sorrow to prayer and to the cross, and then they will not bring you to the grave.

"But," you say, "my children have such hard hearts."

You think they cannot be saved? Look at yourself. He that saved you can save them.—6.252

Acts 17:30 *"God . . . now commandeth all men every where to repent."*

1997 So it is not left optional to you whether or not you will accept the gospel. It is not said to you, "You may, if you will, accept it, or you may, if you please, reject it." You cannot reject it without incurring the guilt of disobedience to a divine command.—48.530

Acts 20:21 *"Testifying . . . repentance toward God, and faith toward our Lord Jesus Christ."*

1998 Repentance and faith must go together to complete each other. I compare them to a door and its post. Repentance is the door which shuts out sin, but faith is the post on which its hinges are fixed. A door without a doorpost to hang on is not a door at all, while a doorpost without the door hanging on it is of no value whatever. What God hath joined together let no man put asunder, and these two he has made inseparable—repentance and faith.—35.122

Acts 24:25 *"When I have a convenient season, I will call for thee."*

1999 A man that waits for a more convenient season for thinking about the affairs of his soul is like the countryman in Aesop's fable, who sat down by a flowing river, saying, "If this stream continues to flow as it does now for a little while, it will empty itself, and then I shall walk over dry-shod." But the stream was just as deep when he had waited day after day as it was before. And so shall it be with you.—6.121

Acts 26:14 *"It is hard for thee to kick against the pricks."*

2000 All your kickings against the pricks will be among your sharpest stings when you feel the judgment of God in another world. "Remember," says conscience, "you were warned. You did not sin without knowing it was sin. You did not choose the downward path without understanding it to be the path that led to ruin. You felt the pricks of warning, but you kicked against them, and now you receive your portion in the lake that burns with fire and brimstone, with this aggravation above all others: You knew your duty, but you did it not."—12.503

Acts 26:24 *"Much learning doth make thee mad."*

2001 "Oh," they say, "the man is mad!"

But why is he mad? Because you do not understand him. Are you so conceited as to suppose that all wisdom and all learning must rest with you? I would hint to you that the madness is on the other side. And though you may say of him, "Much learning doth make thee mad," we would reply, "It is quite as easy to be made mad with none at all!"—2.357

Acts 26:28 *"Almost thou persuadest me to be a Christian."*

2002 Almost persuaded to be a Christian is like the man who was almost pardoned, but he was hanged; like the man who was almost rescued, but he was burned in the house. A man that is almost saved is damned.—14.427

Acts 27:25 *"I believe God, that it shall be even as it was told me."*

2003 Since the apostle Paul truly believed God, he was not ashamed to say so. He said openly to all those around him, "There shall not a hair of your heads perish, for I believe God." It is not so easy to thrust out your faith and expose it to rough men. Many a man has believed the promise but has not quite liked to say so, for there has been a whisper in his soul, "Suppose it should not come true. Then how the enemy will rejoice!"

Thus does the devil cause faith to be dumb, and God is robbed of his honor. Under the name of prudence there lurks an unbelieving selfishness. Brother, lend me your ear that I may whisper in it, "You do not believe at all."—23.52

Romans 2:4 *"The riches of his goodness and forbearance and longsuffering."*

2004 God's "goodness" may refer to the way in which he has overlooked all our past sins, so that he has not yet dealt with us in justice concerning them. His "forbearance" may refer to our present sins. And his "longsuffering" may refer to our future sins, for he knows that we shall continue to sin, yet he does not destroy us, but bears with us still.—55.350

315

Romans 2:5 *"[Thou] treasurest up unto thyself wrath against the day of wrath."*

2005 God's wrath, though it come not on you yet, is like a stream that is dammed up. Every moment it gathers force. It bursts not the dike, yet every hour it is swelling it. Each moment of each day in which you remain an unbeliever you are treasuring up wrath against the day of wrath when the measure of your iniquity is full.—16.682

Romans 3:20 *"By the law is the knowledge of sin."*

2006 Some fancy that they have done a great many good works. In cherishing that delusion, they are like a Hindu of whom I once heard. He believed that he must not eat any animal substance, and that if he did he would perish. A missionary said to him, "That idea is ridiculous. Why, you cannot drink a glass of water without swallowing thousands of living creatures." He did not believe it, so the missionary took a drop of water and put it under a microscope. When the man saw the innumerable living creatures in the drop of water, he broke the microscope. That was his way of settling the question.

So when we meet with persons who say, "Our works are pure and clean and excellent," we bring the great microscope of the law of the Lord, and we bid them look through that. When they do look through it and discover that even one sinful thought destroys their hope of salvation by self-righteousness, and when they see a whole host of sins in one of their prayers or acts or thoughts, then they are angry with the preacher. They try to break the microscope!

But for all that, the truth remains, "By the deeds of the law there shall no flesh be justified in his sight; for by the law is the knowledge of sin."—54.139

Romans 3:23 *"For all have sinned, and come short of the glory of God."*

2007 I have heard of Robert Burns, that on one occasion when at church, he sat in a pew with a young lady whom he observed to be much affected by certain terrible passages of Scripture which the minister quoted in his sermon. The wicked wag scribbled on a piece of paper a verse which he passed to her. I fear that the substance of that verse has been whispered into many of your ears often:

Fair maid, you need not take the hint,
Nor idle texts pursue;
'Twas only sinners that he meant,
Not angels such as you.

This sermon is meant for those who think themselves angels as well as for those who know themselves to be sinners. Cease from all dreamy confidences. Arouse yourselves from proud self-content, and come to Jesus the Savior, who alone can save from sin and death.—28.263

Romans 5:1 *"We have peace with God."*

2008 If you are to have peace with God, there must be war with Satan.—24.214

2009 I hear poor souls crying, "I do believe, but I do not enjoy peace." I think I can tell you how it is. You make a mistake as to what this peace is. You say, "I am so dreadfully tempted. Sometimes I am drawn this way and sometimes the other, and the devil never lets me alone." Did you ever read in the Bible that you were to have peace with the devil? Look at the text: "Being justified by faith, we have peace *with* God."—25.68

Romans 5:5 *"The love of God is shed abroad in our hearts by the Holy Ghost."*

2010 Only by the Holy Ghost could this have been done. Would you ever have been charmed with the love of God through the influence of the devil?—32.322

Romans 5:6 *"Christ died for the ungodly."*

2011 Your sense of unworthiness, if it be properly used, should drive you to Christ. You are unworthy, but Jesus died for the unworthy.—14.148

2012 Never did the human ear listen to a more astounding and yet cheering truth.—20.494

2013 I would not mind if I were condemned to live fifty years more and never allowed to speak but these five words, if I might be allowed to utter them in the ear of every man, woman, and child who lives. "Christ Died for the Ungodly" is the best message that even angels could bring to men.—20.503

2014 I love to think that the gospel does not address itself to those who might be supposed to have helped themselves a little out of the mire, to those who show signs of lingering goodness. It comes to men ruined in Adam and doubly lost by their own sin. It comes to them in the abyss where sin has hurled them and lifts them up from the gates of hell.—22.21

2015 The devil often tells me, "You are not this, and you are not that," and I feel bound to own that the accuser of the brethren makes terrible work of my spiritual finery, so that I have to abandon one ground of glorying after another. But I never knew the devil himself dare to say, "You are not a sinner." He knows I am, and I know it too. And as "in due time Christ died for the ungodly," I just rest in him, and I am saved.—24.311, 312

317

Romans 5:10 *"When we were ene-mies, we were reconciled to God by the death of his Son."*

²⁰¹⁶ No more love to God is there in an unrenewed heart than there is life within a piece of granite. No more love to God is there within the soul that is unsaved than there is fire within the depths of the ocean's waves. And here is the wonder, that when we had no love for God, he should have loved us!—42.27

Romans 5:11 *"We also joy in God through our Lord Jesus Christ."*

²⁰¹⁷ Joy in God is the happiest of all joys. There are other sweets, but this is the virgin honey drip-ping fresh from the comb. Joy in God is also a most elevating joy. Those who joy in wealth grow avaricious. Those who joy in their friends too often lose nobility of spirit. But he who boasts in God grows like God. It is a solid joy, and he who joys in God has good reasons for rejoicing. He has argu-ments which will justify his joy at any time. It is an abiding joy. In a word, it is celestial joy.—18.215

Romans 5:12 *"Sin entered into the world, and death by sin."*

²⁰¹⁸ Ask Noah as he looks out of his ark, "Does sin bring bitter-ness?" and he points to the float-ing carcases of innumerable thou-sands that died because of sin (Gen. 7:21). Turn to Abraham. Does sin bring bitterness? He points to the smoke of Sodom and Gomorrah that God destroyed because of their wickedness (Gen. 19). Ask Moses, and he reminds you of Korah, Dathan, and Abi-ram, who were swallowed up alive (Num. 16).—12.669

Romans 5:19 *"As by one man's dis-obedience many were made sinners. . . ."*

²⁰¹⁹ It is a happy circumstance for us that we did fall and were condemned in the bulk in our representative, because had we been individually put on the like probation, we would to a cer-tainty all have fallen. But then it must have ended finally and fatally, for when the angels fell by sinning individually, there was no hope of restoration for them. But we, happily, had fallen through a representative, and therefore we could be restored by another representative.—47.434

Romans 5:20 *"The law entered, that the offense might abound."*

²⁰²⁰ A stick is crooked, but you do not notice how crooked it is until you place a straight rule by the side of it. You have a handker-chief, and it seems to be quite white. You could hardly wish it to be whiter. But you lay it down on the newly fallen snow, and you wonder how you could ever have thought it to be white at all. So the pure and holy law of God, when our eyes are opened to see its purity, shows up our sin in its true blackness, and in that way it makes sin to abound. But this is

for our good, for that sight of our sin awakens us to a sense of our true condition, leads us to repentance, drives us by faith to the precious blood of Jesus, and no longer permits us to rest in our self-righteousness.—54.507

Romans 6:1, 2 *"Shall we continue in sin, that grace may abound? God forbid."*

²⁰²¹ It is a precious doctrine that the saints are safe, but it is a damnable inference from it that therefore they may live as they like. It is a glorious truth that God will keep his people, but it is an abominable falsehood that sin will do them no harm. Remember that God gives us liberty, not license, and while he gives us protection, he will not allow us presumption.—12.259

²⁰²² The faith which saves is not an unproductive faith, but is always a faith which produces good works and abounds in holiness. Salvation *in* sin is not possible; it always must be salvation *from* sin. As well speak of liberty while the irons are still on a man's wrists, or boast of healing while the disease waxes worse and worse, or glory in victory when the army is on the point of surrendering, as to dream of salvation in Christ while the sinner continues to give full swing to his evil passions.—16.685

²⁰²³ It would be nothing less than devilish for a man to say, "I have been forgiven, therefore I will sin again." There is no remission where there is no repentance. The guilt of sin remains on that man in whom the love of sin still remains.—25.345

²⁰²⁴ Says one, "I may live as I like."

Listen! If you are God's child, I will tell you how you will like to live. You will desire to live in perfect obedience to your Father, and it will be your passionate longing from day to day to be perfect, even as your Father in heaven is perfect. The nature of sons which grace implants is a law unto itself. The Lord puts his fear into the hearts of the regenerate so that they do not depart from him.—30.694

Romans 6:6 *"Our old man is crucified with him."*

²⁰²⁵ One of the best men I ever knew said, at eighty years of age, "I find the old man is not dead yet." Our old man is crucified, but he is long at dying. He is not dead when we think he is. You may live to be very old, but you will have need still to watch against the carnal nature, which remains even in the regenerate.—36.350, 351

Romans 6:6 *". . . that the body of sin might be destroyed."*

²⁰²⁶ I may say of our sins what a Scottish officer said to his soldiers: "My lads, there are the enemy! Kill them, or they will kill you." And so must I say of all

sins. There they are! Destroy them, or they will destroy you.—12.63

[2027] Christian, here is your practical lesson: Fight with your sins! Hack them in pieces, as Samuel did Agag. Let not one of them escape. Take them as Elijah took the prophets of Baal—hew them in pieces before the Lord. Revenge the death of Christ on your sins, but keep to Christ's cross for power to do it.—15.418

Romans 6:14 *"Sin shall not have dominion over you."*

[2028] Has sin dominion over you? If so, then you are not a believer. I did not say, "Do you sin?" for "if we say we have no sin, we deceive ourselves and the truth is not in us" (1 John 1:8). But I did say, "Has sin *dominion* over you?"—15.638

Romans 6:17, 18 *"Ye were the servants of sin, but . . . ye became the servants of righteousness."*

[2029] As long as the blood-red flag of Christ's cross floats over the castle of your heart, Satan may get possession of eye-gate and ear-gate and mouth-gate for a while, but Christ is still king. Your will is still good toward righteousness. Sin has not dominion over you.—15.644

Romans 6:23 *"The wages of sin is death."*

[2030] This whole world has been for ages a vast burying place. Men whine out their abhorrence of God's justice and hold in contempt the idea of future punishment with the question, "Would a father do thus and thus with his children?" The question needs no other reply than fact. All men die. Would a father allow his children to die when it was in his power to prevent it? Certainly not. Since, then, the great God evidently permits much pain and even death to happen to his creatures, he is evidently not Father merely, but something more. To ungodly men Jehovah reveals himself in the light of a Judge whose stern severity has brought to pass the terrible doom of death on every man of woman born.—12.170

[2031] That sin must die, or you will perish by it. Depend on it, that sin which you would save from slaughter will slaughter you.—28.646

Romans 6:23 *"The gift of God is eternal life through Jesus Christ our Lord."*

[2032] You may offer whatever terms you please, but God will never sell Christ. Judas did that, but the Father never will.—46.353

Romans 7:7 *"Is the law sin? God forbid."*

[2033] Augustine placed the truth in a clear light when he wrote, "The law is not at fault, but our evil and wicked nature; even as a heap of lime is still and quiet until water is poured on it, but then it begins to smoke and burn, not from the fault of the water, but from the nature of the lime which will not endure it."—1.286

Romans 7:13 *"... that sin ... might become exceeding sinful."*

²⁰³⁴ Paul here calls sin "exceeding sinful." Why didn't he say, "exceeding black" or "exceeding horrible" or "exceeding deadly"? Because there is nothing in the world so bad as sin. When he wanted to use the very worst word he could find to call sin by, he called it by its own name, and reiterated it: "Sin ... exceeding sinful."—59.469

Romans 7:23 *"I see another law in my members, warring against the law of my mind."*

²⁰³⁵ It is some comfort when we feel a war within the soul to remember that it is an interesting phase of Christian experience. Such as are dead in sin have never made proof of any of these things. These inward conflicts show that we are alive. There is some life in the soul that hates sin, even though it cannot do as it would. Do not be depressed about it. Where there is pain there is life.—18.419

Romans 7:24 *"O wretched man that I am! who shall deliver me from the body of this death?"*

²⁰³⁶ This proves that he was not attacking his sin, but that this sin was attacking him. I do not seek to be delivered from a man against whom I lead the attack. It is the man who is opposing me from whom I seek to be delivered. And so sometimes the sin that dwells in believers flies at us, like some foul tiger of the woods, or some demon, jealous of the celestial spirit within us.—2.235

²⁰³⁷ I went to that same Primitive Methodist Chapel where I first received peace with God through the simple preaching of the Word. The text happened to be, "O wretched man that I am! who shall deliver me from the body of this death?"

"There," I thought, "that's a text for me." I had got as far as that, when the minister began by saying, "Paul was not a believer when he said this." I knew I was a believer, and it seemed to me from the context that Paul must have been a believer, too. Now I am sure he was. The man went on to say that no child of God ever did feel any conflict within. So I took up my hat and left the place, and I do not think I have frequented such places since.—8.167

Romans 8:1 *"There is therefore now no condemnation to them which are in Christ Jesus."*

²⁰³⁸ I like the old translation. There was a martyr once summoned before Bonner. After he had expressed his faith in Christ, Bonner said, "You are a heretic and will be damned."

"No," said he, quoting the old

321

version, "There is therefore now no damnation to them that believe in Christ Jesus."—5.31

[2039] Oh, for faith to lay hold on this! Oh, for an overpowering faith that shall get the victory over doubts and fears, and make us enjoy the liberty with which Christ makes men free! You that believe in Christ, go to your beds this night and say,"If I die in my bed, I cannot be condemned!" Should you wake the next morning, go into the world and say, "I am not condemned!" When the devil howls at you, tell him, "You may accuse, but I am not condemned!" And if sometimes your sins rise, say, "I know you, but you are all gone forever. I am not condemned!"—7.112

[2040] As "there is therefore now no condemnation to them that are in Christ Jesus," so we may solemnly say, "There is therefore now a most weighty condemnation on you who are not in Christ Jesus, who are walking, not after the Spirit, but after the flesh."—53.233, 234

Romans 8:3 *"God sending his own Son ... condemned sin in the flesh."*

[2041] God had condemned sin before, but never so efficiently as in the person of his Son.—12.374

Romans 8:7 *"The carnal mind is enmity against God."*

[2042] Paul uses a noun, not an adjective. He does not say that the carnal mind is opposed to God merely, but it is the positive enmity. It is not black, but blackness. It is not at enmity, but *enmity* itself. It is not corrupt, but corruption. It is not rebellious; it is rebellion. It is not wicked; it is wickedness itself. The heart, though it be deceitful, is positively deceit. It is evil in the concrete, sin in the essence. It is the distillation, the quintessence of all things that are vile.—1.150

Romans 8:9 *"... the Spirit of God ... the Spirit of Christ."*

[2043] He is called in the first part of the verse, "the Spirit of God," and then he is styled, "the Spirit of Christ." Christ and God are essentially one. The Holy Ghost stands in intimate relationship both to the Father and to the Son, and is rightly called by either name.—19.530

Romans 8:9 *"If any man have not the Spirit of Christ, he is none of his."*

[2044] If it were possible (which it is not) for you to produce the same virtues in yourself which are produced by the Holy Spirit, yet even those would not suffice, for the text is absolute. It does not say, "If any man have not the works of the Spirit" or "the influences of the Spirit" or "the general character which comes from the indwelling of the Spirit." It goes deeper and declares, "If any man have not *the Spirit* of Christ, he is none of his." The difference between the regenerate and the unregenerate is not one of degree, but of kind.—19.534

Romans 8:13 *"If ye live after the flesh, ye shall die."*

2045 If you will not have death unto sin, you shall have sin unto death. There is no alternative. If you do not die to sin, you shall die for sin. If you do not slay sin, sin will slay you.—15.419

Romans 8:26 *"The Spirit itself maketh intercession for us."*

2046 It is a mark of wondrous condescension that God should not only answer our prayers when they are made, but should make our prayers for us. That the king should say to the petitioner, "Bring your case before me, and I will grant your desire," is kindness. But for him to say, "I will be your secretary. I will write out your petition for you. I will put it into proper words so that your petition shall be framed acceptably," this is goodness at its utmost stretch. But this is precisely what the Holy Ghost does for us poor, ignorant, wavering, weak men. Jesus in his agony was strengthened by an angel; you are to be helped by God himself. Aaron and Hur held up the hands of Moses, but the Holy Ghost himself helps your infirmities.—12.617, 618

Romans 8:28 *"All things work together for good to them that love God."*

2047 To the sinner, however, all things work together for evil. Is he prosperous? He is as the beast that is fattened for the slaughter. Is he healthy? He is as the blooming flower that is ripening for the mower's scythe. Does he suffer? His sufferings are the first drops of the eternal hailstorm of divine vengeance. Everything to the sinner, if he could but open his eye, has a black aspect.—6.151

2048 Did you ever hear of a man who got his health by being sick? That is a Christian. He gets rich by his losses, he rises by his falls, he goes on by being pushed back, he lives by dying, he grows by being diminished, and becomes full by being emptied. Well, if the bad things work him so much good, what must his best things do? If he can sing in a dungeon, how sweetly will he sing in heaven!—9.502

2049 When that eminent servant of God, Mr. Gilpin, was arrested to be brought up to London to be tried for preaching the gospel, his captors made mirth of his frequent remark, "Everything is for the best." When he fell from his horse and broke his leg, they were especially merry about it. But the good man quietly remarked, "I have no doubt but that even this painful accident will prove to be a blessing."

323

And so it was, for, as he could not travel quickly, the journey was prolonged, and he arrived at London some days later than had been expected. When they reached Highgate, they heard the bells ringing merrily in the city down below. They asked the meaning and were told, "Queen Mary is dead, and there will be no more burning of Protestants!"

"Ah," said Gilpin, "you see, it is all for the best." It is a blessing to break a leg if thereby a life is saved. How often our calamities are our preservatives!—31.562, 563

Romans 8:31 *"If God be for us, who can be against us?"*

²⁰⁵⁰ There is an opposite to this, and it belongs to some who are here: If God be *against* you, who can be *for* you? If you are an enemy to God, your very blessings are curses to you. Your pleasures are only the prelude to your pains. Whether you have adversity or prosperity, so long as God is against you, you can never truly prosper. Take half an hour this afternoon to think this over: If God be *against* me, what then? What will become of me in time and eternity? How shall I die? How shall I face him in the day of judgment? It is not an impossible "if" but an "if" which amounts to a certainty, I fear, in the case of many who are sitting in this house today.—10.411, 412

Romans 8:34 *"Who is he that condemneth?"*

²⁰⁵¹ Why, Paul, Satan will bring thundering accusations against you. Are you not afraid?

"No," says he, "I can stop his mouth with this cry: 'It is Christ that died!' That will make him tremble, for he crushed the serpent's head in that victorious hour. And I can shut his mouth again: 'yea, rather, that is risen again,' for he took him captive on that day. And I will add, 'who sitteth at the right hand of God.' I can foil him with that, for he sits there to judge him and to condemn him forever. Once more I will appeal to his advocacy: 'Who maketh intercession for us.' I can stop his accusation with the perpetual care of Jesus for his people."—5.255

Romans 8:34 *"It is Christ that died."*

²⁰⁵² If any confront you with other confidences, still keep to this almighty plea: "Christ has died." If one says, "I was christened and confirmed," answer him by saying, "Christ has died." Should another say, "I was baptized as an adult," let your confidence remain the same: "Christ has died." When another says, "I am a sound, orthodox Presbyterian," stick to this solid ground: "Christ has died." And if still another says, "I am a red-hot Methodist," answer him in the same way: "Christ has died."

Whatever may be the confidences of others, and whatever may be your own, put them all away, and keep to this one declaration: "It is Christ that died."—38.38

Romans 8:37 *"We are more than conquerors through him that loved us."*

2053 Jesus is the representative man for his people. The head has triumphed, and the members share in the victory. While a man's head is above the water you cannot drown his body.—12.263

Romans 8:38, 39 *"I am persuaded, that neither death, nor life. . . ."*

2054 Someone asked me the other day, "What persuasion are you of?" and the answer was, "I am persuaded that neither death, nor life, nor angels, nor principalities, nor powers, nor things present, nor things to come, nor height, nor depth, nor any other creature, shall be able to separate us from the love of God, which is in Christ Jesus our Lord."—29.276

Romans 9:3 *"I could wish that myself were accursed from Christ for my brethren."*

2055 I have sometimes felt willing to go to the gates of hell to save a soul, but the Redeemer went further, for he suffered the wrath of God for souls.—18.201

2056 What would be the result, if we felt as Paul did? Likeness to Christ. After that manner he loved. He did become a curse for us (Gal. 3:13). He did enter under the awful shadow of Jehovah's wrath for us. He *did* what Paul could *wish.*—24.418

Romans 9:15 *"I will have mercy on whom I will have mercy."*

2057 It is equally true that he *wills* to have mercy, and has already had mercy on every soul that repents of sin and puts its trust in Jesus.—13.309

2058 If there is one doctrine in the world which reveals the enmity of the human heart more than another, it is the doctrine of God's sovereignty. When men hear the Lord's voice saying, "I will have mercy on whom I will have mercy," they gnash their teeth and call the preacher an Antinomian, a High Calvinist, or some other hard name. They do not love God except they can make him a little God. They cannot bear for him to be supreme. They would gladly take his will away from him and set up their own will as the first cause.—18.214

Romans 10:13 *"Whosoever shall call upon the name of the Lord shall be saved."*

2059 I have often thought that if I had read in Scripture that "if Charles Haddon Spurgeon shall call upon the name of the Lord, he shall be saved," I would not have felt as sure of salvation as I do now, because I would have concluded that there might have been somebody else of that name, and I would have said, "Surely it did not mean me." But when the Lord says, "Whosoever," I cannot get out of that circle!—39.458

Romans 12:1 *"Present your bodies a living sacrifice . . . which is your reasonable service."*

²⁰⁶⁰ I scarcely like this word *sacrifice*, because it involves nothing more than a reasonable service. If we gave up all we had and became beggars for Christ, it would display no such chivalrous spirit or magnanimous conduct after all. We would be gainers by the surrender.—16.659

Romans 12:2 *"Be not conformed to this world."*

²⁰⁶¹ Nothing worse can happen to a church than to be conformed to this world.—57.606, 607

Romans 12:21 *"Be not overcome of evil, but overcome evil with good."*

²⁰⁶² The text appears to give us a choice between two things, and bids us choose the better one. You must either be overcome by evil, or you must yourself overcome evil. One of the two. You cannot let evil alone, and evil will not let you alone. You *must* fight, and in the battle you must either conquer or be conquered.—22.553

²⁰⁶³ This text inculcates not merely passive non-resistance, but it teaches us active benevolence to enemies. "Overcome evil with good," with direct and overt acts of kindness. If any man has done you a wrong, do not only forgive it, but also avenge it by doing him a favor.—22.560

²⁰⁶⁴ You know the old saying: Returning evil for good is devil-like, evil for evil is beastlike, good for good is manlike, and good for evil is God-like. Rise to that God-like point.—27.101

Romans 13:11 *". . . for now is our salvation nearer than when we believed."*

²⁰⁶⁵ Oh, you unconverted men, must I read the text as it would have to run if it were written to you? "It is high time that you should awake out of sleep, for now is your damnation nearer than when you first heard the gospel and rejected it." God grant you grace to take heed and believe in Christ.—24.660

Romans 14:7 *"None of us liveth to himself, and no man dieth to himself."*

²⁰⁶⁶ I think the first instinct of one who has been himself called by grace is to go and call others. When Christ appears to Mary, Mary runs to the disciples to tell them that the Lord has spoken to her. Samuel is chosen that he may carry the message to Eli. And let each believer feel that he is favored by God that he may take a blessing to others, "for none of us liveth to himself, and no man dieth to himself."—43.338

Romans 14:23 *"Whatsoever is not of faith is sin."*

2067 Do nothing about which you have need to ask a question. Be quite sure about it, or leave it alone. Whatsoever you cannot do with the confidence that you are doing right is sin to you. Though the deed may be right to other people, if you have any doubt about it yourself, it is evil to you.—13.634

1 Corinthians 1:23 *"We preach Christ crucified."*

2068 Those who would preach Christ, but not Christ crucified, miss the very soul and essence of our holy faith.—13.137

2069 If a man can preach one sermon without mentioning Christ's name in it, it ought to be his last, certainly the last that any Christian ought to go to hear him preach.—13.489

2070 The one topic of every Sabbath day in this place is Jesus Christ crucified.—18.333

2071 I am bound to preach Jesus Christ and him crucified, for I do not know anything else to preach. My simplicity is my safeguard.—20.94

2072 I do not believe it would be possible to retain year after year a mass of attentive hearers, and send them away longing for more, with any theme except Jesus Christ and him crucified.—22.325

2073 We preach Christ crucified, and every sermon shakes the gates of hell. We bring sinners to Jesus by the Spirit's power, and every convert is a stone torn down from the wall of Satan's mighty castle.—22.665

2074 Oh, that my memorial might be, "He preached Christ crucified!"—34.525

1 Corinthians 1:23 *"We preach Christ crucified, unto the Jews a stumblingblock."*

2075 How doubly foolish you are to be offended with Christ, who is the only one who can save you! As well might the drowning man be offended with the rope which is cast to him and which is the only means of his escape. As well might the dying patient be offended with the cup of medicine which is put to his lips, and which alone can save his body from death. As well might the man whose house is burning be offended with the fireman who roughly puts the ladder against his window, as that you should be offended with Christ.—44.523

1 Corinthians 2:2 *"I determined not to know any thing among you, save Jesus Christ . . . crucified."*

2076 I have often felt to be of Paul's mind here. Some are wise to interpret prophecies. I am not. Enough for me to know about the cross.—20.94

327

2077 Paul does not merely determine to keep his preaching to that point, but he resolves not even to *know* any other subject. He would keep his mind closed to any thought but Jesus Christ and him crucified.—21.639

1 Corinthians 2:9 *"Eye hath not seen . . . the things . . . God hath prepared for them that love him."*

2078 Hell is horrible, for we may say of it, "Eye hath not seen, nor ear heard, neither hath it entered into the heart of man to conceive the horrors which God hath prepared for them that hate him."—4.310

1 Corinthians 2:14 *"The natural man receiveth not the things of the Spirit of God."*

2079 Before my conversion I was accustomed to read the Scriptures to admire their grandeur, to feel the charm of their history, and wonder at the majesty of their language. But I altogether missed the Lord's intent therein. But when the Spirit came with his divine life and quickened all the page to my newly enlightened soul, the inner meaning shone forth with quickening glory.—17.147

2080 My brother, you think you will put the gospel so clearly that they *must* see it, but their blind eyes overcome you. You think you will put it so zealously that they *must* feel it, but their clay-cold hearts defeat you. You may

think you are going to win souls by your pleadings, but you might as well stand on the top of a mountain and whistle to the wind, unless the Holy Spirit be with you. After all your talking, your hearers will, perhaps, have caught *your* idea, but the mind of the Spirit, the real soul of the gospel, you cannot impart to them. This remains, like creation itself, a work which only God can accomplish.—23.18

1 Corinthians 3:11 *"Other foundation can no man lay than that is laid, which is Jesus Christ."*

2081 You must imagine two redemptions before you can conceive of two groundworks for our confidence. Who will dream of two atonements, two Saviors, two Christs? Yet must such a thing be before there can be two foundations. None but Jesus, the divine Savior, could sustain the weight of a single soul with all its sins, much less of all the souls which are built up into the temple of God.—25.518

1 Corinthians 3:23 *"Ye are Christ's."*

2082 I like to think, in church matters especially, that we are all Christ's. If we have any ability, it is Christ's ability—to be laid at his feet. If we have any substance, it is Christ's money—to be used in spreading his church. Our Sunday school is Christ's nursery, and the little ones are

Christ's lambs. Our work out of doors in preaching at the corners of the streets is Christ's mission. It is his trumpet that is blown when the gospel is preached, and every form of agency is not ours; it is Christ's.—18.460, 461

1 Corinthians 4:2 *"It is required in stewards, that a man be found faithful."*

2083 When anyone dies, I ask myself, "Was I faithful? Did I speak all the truth? And did I speak it from my very soul every time I preached?"—17.79

2084 Oh, unhappy men, if we be found unfaithful! Of criminals the chief, murderers of immortal souls, if we have not preached the pure gospel. We shall be wholesale poisoners of the bread of men, the bread which their souls require. We, if we be not true to God, are the choice servants of Satan. Judas himself was not more the son of perdition than the man who calls himself an ambassador for Christ, and yet dares to be unfaithful to the souls of men.—19.604

1 Corinthians 4:7 *"What hast thou that thou didst not receive?"*

2085 Will a man who is very deeply in debt say, "I have reason to be proud more than you because I owe ten times as much as you do"? Yet that is just the condition of every man who has any grace—he owes it all to God. And he who has the most grace is the most in debt to his Lord.—44.484

1 Corinthians 6:19 *"Ye are not your own."*

2086 It is a great privilege not to be one's own. Does any man think it would be a pleasure to be his own? Let me assure him that there is no ruler so tyrannical as self. He that is his own master has a fool and a tyrant to be his lord.—17.438, 439

2087 God has a right to do whatever he wills with you. If we must suffer week after week bedridden with pain, he has a right to lay us there and chasten us in every limb. If the Lord says, "Go into your room and cough all the winter through, and then melt away," we must bow before his decree, remembering these words, "Ye are not your own." Or if he says, "Come down from your position of comfort into hard work and poverty," again you must remember, "Ye are not your own." Or if he says, "Migrate across the seas. Go to a new country. Cut every tie and break the fondest connections," you must cheerfully obey, for "ye are not your own."—26.478

1 Corinthians 7:39 *"She is at liberty to be married to whom she will; only in the Lord."*

2088 There is no wiser precept in Holy Scripture than that which commands Christians to marry "only in the Lord." It never can

329

lead to the comfort of any Christian man or woman to be unequally yoked together with an unbeliever. You had far better remain in the cold of your bachelor or spinster life than warm your hands at the fire of unhallowed marriage.—56.42

1 Corinthians 9:16 *"Woe is unto me, if I preach not the gospel!"*

2089 It was good advice of a venerable minister to a young man who aspired to be a preacher, when he said to him, "Don't become a minister if you can help it." The man who could very easily be a tradesman or a merchant had better not be a minister. A preacher of the gospel should always be a volunteer, and yet he should always be a pressed man, who serves his King because he is omnipotently constrained to do so. Only he is fit to preach who cannot avoid preaching, who feels that woe is on him unless he preaches the gospel, and that the very stones would cry out against him if he should hold his peace.—18.613, 614

1 Corinthians 9:22 *"I am made all things to all men, that I might by all means save some."*

2090 What good will it be to a man to be educated when he comes to be damned? Of what service will it be to him to have been amused when the trumpet sounds, and heaven and earth are shaking, and the pit opens wide her jaws of fire and swallows up the soul unsaved? What profit even to have moralized a man if still he is on the left hand of the Judge, and if still "Depart, ye cursed" (Matt. 25:41) shall be his portion? Blood-red with the murder of men's souls will be the skirts of professing Christians, unless the drift and end and aim of all their work has been to "save some."—25.676

2091 How indefatigably did Paul labor! With what vehemence did he pray! With what energy did he preach! Slander and contempt he bore with the utmost patience. Scourging or stoning had no terrors for him. Imprisonment, yes, death itself he defied. Nothing could daunt him. Because the Lord had saved him, he felt that he must by all means save some. He could not be quiet.—59.388

1 Corinthians 10:31 *"Whatsoever ye do, do all to the glory of God."*

2092 Says one, "How can I do God's business? I have no talent. I have scarce money enough to pay my rent. I could not teach in a Sunday school."

Brother, have you a child? Well, there is a door of usefulness for you. Sister, you are very poor. No one knows you. You have a husband, and however drunken he may be, there is a door of usefulness for you.—3.127

2093 The Christian's aim in life is to live for God's glory. If he does so, no persecution can ever shake him. If his goods be spoiled, he says, "If it glorifies God for me to lose my property, I am no loser. I gave my goods to God years ago." If he is put in prison, he says, "I have lost my liberty, but I am no loser. I gave up my liberty to God long ago." If they tell him that he will die, he says, "I am no loser, for I gave him my life long ago. I am altogether Christ's."—21.633

1 Corinthians 11:24 *"This do in remembrance of me."*

2094 Remember Jesus till you feel that he is with you, till his joy gets into your soul, and your joy is full. Remember him till you begin to forget yourself, your temptations, and your cares. Remember him till you begin to think of the time when he will remember you and come in his glory for you. Remember him till you begin to be like him.—54.320

1 Corinthians 15:3 *"Christ died for our sins."*

2095 As Martin Luther gloried to put it, "Jesus Christ never died for our good works. They were not worth dying for. But he gave himself for our sins, according to the Scriptures." What did our Savior himself say? "I came not to call the righteous, but sinners to repentance" (Mark 2:17).—52.56

1 Corinthians 15:6 *"He was seen of above five hundred brethren at once."*

2096 Our Lord was careful to show himself after his resurrection to those who, having known him before his decease, would be able to answer for the identity of his person. Had he merely showed himself to strangers who had not known him before, they might have been able to say that they had seen such a one, but they could not have affirmed that he was the same person who had been buried. But showing himself to men like Thomas, and bidding them to put their fingers into the print of the nails and thrust their hand into his side, he gave to men the most absolute proofs of his resurrection, and received from the most competent witnesses the most assured evidence that no deception had been practiced.—8.217

1 Corinthians 15:29 *"What shall they do which are baptized for the dead?"*

2097 The meaning I like best is, "What shall they do who are baptized with the certainty that immediately after baptism they will be dragged away to die— baptized in the very teeth of death?" For as soon as anyone was baptized, the Romans would be looking after him, to drag him away to death. Thus they were baptized as if they were being washed for their burial and dedicating themselves to the grave.— 2.111

331

1 Corinthians 15:44 *"It is sown a natural body, it is raised a spiritual body."*

2098 These very eyes which have wept for sin shall see the King in his beauty. And these hands which here have served the Lord shall embrace him in his glory. Do not think that death will destroy the identity of the resurrection body. It will be as much the same as the full-blown flower is the same as the seed out of which it grew. There will be a mighty development, but it will still be the same. *It* is sown a natural body, and the same *it* is raised a spiritual body.—13.441

2 Corinthians 1:4 *"Who comforteth us . . . that we may be able to comfort them . . . in any trouble."*

2099 Do not believe that any man will become a physician unless he walks the hospitals. And I am sure that no one will become a minister or a comforter unless he lies in the hospital as well as walks through it, and has to suffer himself.—4.461

2 Corinthians 1:9 *". . . that we should not trust in ourselves, but in God."*

2100 I have heard men say several times, "I am sure there is no likelihood that I should ever trust in myself. I know better." Brother, you are trusting in yourself when you say so. The subtle poison is in your veins even now.—26.268

2 Corinthians 1:10 *"Who delivered us from . . . death, and doth deliver . . . he will yet deliver us."*

2101 We shall always be in danger as long as we are here. "The Lord delivered, doth deliver, and he will deliver," so we shall always need divine deliverance while we are in this world. We must not expect here to be ever out of gunshot of the enemy.—47.128, 129

2 Corinthians 2:15 *"We are unto God a sweet savour of Christ."*

2102 Paul compares the preaching of Christ to a sweet-smelling savor. You cannot say to a perfume, "Be quiet. Do not load the air with sweets. Do not affect men's nostrils." It cannot do otherwise. The fragrance must fill the chamber. Even so, Christ must be a savor, either of life unto life, or of death unto death, but a savor he must be wherever he comes. It is no more possible for you to restrain the working of the gospel than to forbid the action of fire.—15.710

2 Corinthians 2:16 *"To the one . . . the savour of death . . . to the other the savour of life."*

2103 The gospel has a hardening power over those who reject it. The sun shines out of the heavens on wax and softens it, but at the same time it shines on clay and hardens it. The sunlight of the gospel shining on hearers either melts them into repentance or else hardens them into greater obstinacy. You cannot be hearers of the gospel without its having some effect on you. Some of you have attended this place ever since it was built, and if you are not the better for it, you certainly are the worse.—19.484

2 Corinthians 3:17 *"Where the Spirit of the Lord is, there is liberty."*

2104 There is no overcoming a man who has climbed into this spirit. "I will banish you," said a persecutor of the saints.

"But you cannot do that," said he, "for I am at home wherever Christ is."

"I shall take away all your property," said he.

"But I have none," said the other, "and if I had, you could not take away Christ from me, and as long as he is left I shall be rich."

"I will take away your good name," cried the persecutor.

"That is gone already," said the Christian, "and I count it joy to be considered the offscouring of all things for Christ's sake."

"But I will put you in prison."

"You may do as you please, but I shall always be free, for where Christ is, there is liberty."

"But I shall take away your life," said he.

"Then I shall be in heaven, which is the truest life, so that you cannot hurt me."—19.71

2 Corinthians 4:4 *"The god of this world hath blinded the minds of them which believe not."*

2105 Beware lest that blindness becomes the herald of your doom. Before Haman was hanged, the first thing that the servants did was to cover his face (Esth. 7:8). And when a man is about to be lost forever, the first thing the devil does is to blind his eyes so that he cannot see. Now the poor blind Samson will make sport for the Philistines. Now they hope that they can kill him whenever they please. Beware of a blinded conscience; it is the prelude to eternal destruction!—39.188

2 Corinthians 4:13 *"I believed, and therefore have I spoken."*

2106 This is a text which should be written over every minister's study door, and over his pulpit, too. What have we to say if we have a doubt about it? How can we move others if we have no fulcrum for our lever, if we are not ourselves sure and certain? If there is no element of dogmatism in our message because of our confidence concerning what we have to deliver, in God's name let us go to bed and hold our tongues until we do believe it.—39.98, 99

2 Corinthians 5:7 *"We walk by faith, not by sight."*

2107 Those who walk by sight walk alone. Walking by sight is just this—"I believe in myself," whereas walking by faith is, "I believe in God."—12.116

2 Corinthians 5:14 *"The love of Christ constraineth us."*

²¹⁰⁸ The gospel to the Christian is a thing of power. What is it that makes the young man devote himself as a missionary to the cause of God, to leave father and mother and go into distant lands? It is a thing of power that does it—the gospel. What is it that constrains the minister in the midst of cholera to climb up that creaking staircase and stand by the bed of some dying creature who has that dire disease? It must be a thing of power which leads him to venture his life. It is love of the cross of Christ which bids him to do it.—1.58

²¹⁰⁹ With some people, when they give Christ anything or do anything for him, it is dreadfully forced work. They say, "The love of Christ *ought* to constrain us." I do not know that there is any such text in the Bible. I do remember one that runs thus: "The love of Christ constraineth us." If it does not constrain us, it is because it is not in us. It is not merely a thing which ought to be; it *must* be.—16.720

2 Corinthians 5:17 *"If any man be in Christ, he is a new creature."*

²¹¹⁰ The new creation is as much and entirely the work of God as the old creation.—18.290

²¹¹¹ One of the early saints, I think it was Augustine, had indulged in great sins in his younger days. After his conversion he met a woman who had been the sharer of his wicked follies. She approached him winningly and said to him, "Augustine," but he ran away from her with all speed. She called after him and said, "Augustine, it is I."

He turned around and said, "But it is not I. The old Augustine is dead, and I am a new creature in Christ Jesus."—19.353

²¹¹² We are saved, not by evolution, but by creation.—34.500

2 Corinthians 5:20 *"We are ambassadors for Christ, as though God did beseech you by us."*

²¹¹³ As I came along this morning I felt as if I could bury my head in my hands and weep as I thought of God beseeching anybody. He speaks, and it is done. Myriads of angels count themselves happy to fly at his command. And yet man has so become God's enemy that he will not be reconciled to him. God would make him his friend, and spends the blood of his dear Son to cement that friendship, but man will not have it. See how the great God turns to beseeching his obstinate creature! In this I feel a reverent compassion for God. Must he beseech a rebel to be forgiven? Angels, do you hear it? He who is the King of kings veils

his sovereignty and stoops to beseeching his creature to be reconciled to him!—32.395

2 Corinthians 6:2 *"Behold, now is the accepted time; behold, now is the day of salvation."*

²¹¹⁴ Dream not that you will ever obtain eternal life hereafter unless you receive it in this life. Unless you are partakers of it now, tremble for the consequences. Where death finds you, eternity will leave you.—33.74

²¹¹⁵ I spoke to one the other day to whom I said, "Your brother is very anxious about your soul."

He said, "I know he is."

And then I said to him, "And so am I. I wish you were a believer in Jesus."

He answered me, "My time is not yet come."

"No," I replied, "but God's time has, for he says, 'Now is the accepted time; behold, now is the day of salvation.' "—48.261

2 Corinthians 6:14 *"Be ye not unequally yoked together with unbelievers."*

²¹¹⁶ Let me admonish you young people not to be unequally yoked together. Marriage without the fear of God is a fearful mistake. Those ill-assorted unions between believers and unbelievers rob our churches of more members than any other popular delinquency I know of. Seldom—I might almost say never—do I meet with a woman professing godliness who becomes joined in wedlock to a man of the world but that she goes away. She ceases to follow Jesus, and we hear no more of her. I counsel every young man or woman that chooses to be unequally yoked, that you communicate your intention to your minister and renounce your membership in the church before you seal your vows. Give up all profession of religion voluntarily. Do not wait to be excommunicated. Do not sneak away without giving an account of yourself. You had better count the cost and pay the price of your own presumption.—50.605, 606

²¹¹⁷ "But," says one, "I do not intend to depart from Christ, though I am about to marry an unconverted person."

Rest assured that you are departing from Jesus by that act. I have never yet met with a single case in which marriages of this kind have been blessed by God. I know that young women say, "Do not be too severe, sir. I shall bring him around." You will certainly fail. You are sinning in marrying under that idea.—53.322

2 Corinthians 7:10 *"The sorrow of the world worketh death."*

²¹¹⁸ You are afraid of damnation, but you are not afraid of sinning. You are afraid of being cast into the pit, but not afraid to harden your hearts against God's commands. It is not the soul's state

that troubles you, but hell. If hell were extinguished, your repentance would be extinguished. Be not deceived. Examine yourselves whether you are in the faith. Ask yourself if you have that which is "repentance unto life," for you may humble yourselves for a time, and yet never repent before God.—1.333

2 Corinthians 8:9 *"Though he was rich, yet for your sakes he became poor."*

2119 A lady was out in the snow one night and was so very cold that she cried out, "Oh, those poor people that have such little money, how little warmth they have, and how pinched they must be! I will send a hundred weight of coals to twenty families or more." When she reached her own living room there was a fine fire burning, and she sat there with her feet up and enjoyed an excellent tea. She said to herself, "Well, it is not very cold, after all. I do not think I shall send those coals; at any rate, not now."

The *sufferer* thinks of the sufferer, even as the poor help the poor. The divine wonder is that this Lord of ours, "though he was rich, yet for our sakes he became poor." And now he takes delight in helping the poor. Having been tempted, he helps the tempted. His own trials make him desire to bless those who are tried.—33.417

2 Corinthians 8:9 *"... that ye through his poverty might be rich."*

2120 If Christ in his poverty made us rich, what will he do now that he is glorified? If the Man of sorrows saved my soul, will the Man now exalted permit it to perish? If the dying Savior availed for our salvation, will not the living, interceding Savior abundantly secure it?—3.355

2 Corinthians 9:7 *"God loveth a cheerful giver."*

2121 One thing I know, that a cheerful giver always wishes that he could give ten times as much.—14.569

2 Corinthians 12:7 *"There was given to me a thorn in the flesh."*

2122 Paul reckoned his great trial to be a gift. It is well-put. He does not say, "There was *inflicted* on me a thorn in the flesh," but "There was *given* to me." This is holy reckoning. Child of God, among all the goods of your house, you have not one single article that is a better token of divine love to you than your daily cross.—18.678

2 Corinthians 12:8 *"For this thing I besought the Lord thrice."*

2123 Anything is a blessing which makes us pray. This thorn compelled Paul to cry unto God, and having commenced to pray, he resorted to prayer again and again.—18.682

2 Corinthians 12:9 *"My grace is sufficient for thee."*

2124 If you were to tell your child that you would grant him anything he asked for, you would not intend by that to give him a poisonous drug, if someone should delude him into the idea that it would be useful to him. You would mean that you would give your child all that was really good for him. God, therefore, knowing that this thorn in the flesh was a sacred medicine to Paul, would not take it away, even though most urgently requested to do so. So, though refused, Paul was answered.—18.682

2125 Whatever would be good for you, Christ's grace is sufficient to bestow. Whatever would harm you, his grace is sufficient to avert. Whatever you desire, his grace is sufficient to give, if it be good for you. Whatever you would avoid, his grace can shield you from it if his wisdom shall dictate.—22.196, 197

2 Corinthians 13:5 *"Examine yourselves, whether ye be in the faith."*

2126 Can you not bear a little self-examination? How will you bear that God-examination? If the scales of earth tell you that you are lacking, what message will the scales of heaven give you?—12.512

Galatians 1:4 *"Who gave himself for our sins."*

2127 Christ died for our sins, not for our virtues. It is not your efficiencies, but your deficiencies which entitle you to the Lord Jesus. It is not your wealth, but your lack. It is not what you have, but what you have not. It is not what you can boast of, but what you mourn over that qualifies you to receive the gospel of the Lord Jesus Christ.—30.484

Galatians 1:6 *"Another gospel."*

2128 We have not only "another gospel," but we have fifty other gospels now preached.—16.558

Galatians 2:20 *"I am crucified with Christ."*

2129 The Roman Catholic hangs the cross on his bosom; the true Christian carries the cross in his heart. And a cross inside the heart is one of the sweetest cures for a cross on the back. If you have a cross in your heart—Christ crucified in you—all the cross of this world's troubles will seem to you light enough, and you will easily be able to sustain it.—4.428, 429

Galatians 2:20 *". . . who loved me, and gave himself for me."*

2130 Jesus loved *me*, and gave himself for *me*. Can you say this? If you can, you can say more than Demosthenes or Cicero were ever

337

able to say with all their eloquence.—10.210

Galatians 2:21 *"I do not frustrate the grace of God."*

²¹³¹ This is a sin so gross that even the heathen cannot commit it. They have never heard of the grace of God, and therefore they cannot put a slight on it. When they perish it will be with a far lighter doom than those who have been told that God is gracious and ready to pardon, and yet they wickedly boast of innocence and pretend to be clean in the sight of God. This is a sin which devils cannot commit. With all the obstinacy of their rebellion, they can never reach to this. They have never had the sweet notes of free grace and dying love ringing in their ears, and therefore they have never refused the heavenly invitation.—26.246

Galatians 3:13 *"Christ hath redeemed us from the curse . . . being made a curse for us."*

²¹³² You must either be cursed by God or else you must accept Christ as bearing the curse instead of you. This is the truth which the apostles preached, and suffered and died to maintain. It is this for which the Reformers struggled. It is this for which the martyrs burned at Smithfield. It is the grand basic doctrine of the Reformation, and the very truth of God.—15.311

Galatians 3:24 *"The law was our schoolmaster to bring us unto Christ."*

²¹³³ The law is meant to lead the sinner to faith in Christ by showing the impossibility of any other way. It is the black dog to fetch the sheep to the shepherd, the burning heat which drives the traveler to the shadow of the great rock in a weary land.—22.651

Galatians 5:6 *"Faith which worketh by love."*

²¹³⁴ There are some who do many works as the result of a kind of faith, who, nevertheless, are not justified, as, for instance, Herod, who believed in John and did many things, and yet murdered him (Mark 6:17–28). His faith did work, but it worked by dread and not by love. He feared the stern language of the second Elijah, and the judgments which would come upon him if he rejected the Baptist's warnings, and his faith worked through fear. The great test of the working of saving faith is this: It "worketh by love." If you are led by your faith in Jesus Christ to love him and so to serve him, then you have the faith of God's elect.—26.458

Galatians 5:17 *"The flesh lusteth against the Spirit, and the Spirit against the flesh."*

²¹³⁵ I know in my own soul that I feel myself to be like two distinct men. There is the old man, as base as ever, and the new man, that cannot sin, because he is born of

God. I cannot myself understand the experience of those Christians who do not find a conflict within, for my experience goes to show this, if it shows anything, that there is an incessant contention between the old nature—O that we could get rid of it—and the new nature—for the strength of which God be thanked! Do you not find it so?—15.174

Galatians 6:1 *"Considering thyself, lest thou also be tempted."*

2136 In these days of epidemics, if we knew that a certain house was tainted with disease, and if we saw a person who had come from it with the marks of the disease in his face, what should we feel? Should we not take it as a warning to keep clear of the house, because we ourselves are as likely to take the disease as he was? So when we see a sinner transgressing, we should say to ourselves, "I also am a man, and a fallen man. Let me abhor every evil way, and guard myself jealously, lest I also fall into sin."—17.184, 185

Galatians 6:7 *"Whatsoever a man soweth, that shall he also reap."*

2137 It is taken for granted in the world that young persons ought to be allowed to sow their "wild oats," and then it is hoped that they will settle down. But these wild oats are more easily sown than reaped, and many men might weep tears of blood to think of

what a harvest has sprung from them.—12.544

Galatians 6:14 *"God forbid that I should glory, save in the cross of our Lord Jesus Christ."*

2138 Paul might have gloried in the *life* of Christ. Was there ever such another, so benevolent and blameless? He might have gloried in the *resurrection* of Christ. It is the world's great hope concerning those who are asleep. He might have gloried in our Lord's *ascension,* for he "led captivity captive" (Eph. 4:8), and all his followers glory in his victory. He might have gloried in his *second advent,* and I doubt not that he did. Yet the apostle selected beyond all these that center of the Christian system, that point which is most assailed by its foes, that focus of the world's derision—the cross. Learn, then, that the highest glory of our holy religion is the cross. The history of grace begins earlier and goes on later, but in the middle point stands the cross.—31.494, 495

Ephesians 2:8 *"By grace are ye saved."*

2139 I could wish that every time the clock struck, it said, "By grace are ye saved." I could wish that there were a trumpet voice ringing out at daybreak both on sea and on land, over the whole round globe the words, "By grace are ye saved." The larger portion of mankind do not believe that salvation is by grace. Another part of them profess to believe it, but do not understand its meaning. And many who do understand it have never surrendered to it and embraced it.—27.182

Ephesians 2:8 *". . . and that not of yourselves: it is the gift of God."*

²¹⁴⁰ If the faith whereby I have laid hold on Christ to be my Savior be altogether wrought in me by the Holy Ghost through grace, then I defy the devil to take away that which he never gave me or to crush that which Jehovah himself created in me. I defy my free will to fling away what it never brought to me. What God has given, created, introduced, and established in the heart, he will maintain there.—36.197

²¹⁴¹ God has not granted his love, his favor, his mercy to me because he foresaw that I would repent of my sin and trust in his dear Son. Nothing in my disposition or character could move his heart to me. His heart must have moved spontaneously. It must have welled up because of its own deep love.—49.254

Ephesians 2:10 *"We are his workmanship."*

²¹⁴² You have seen a painter with his palette on his finger, and he has ugly little daubs of paint on the palette. What can he do with those spots? Go in and see the picture. What splendid painting!

In an even wiser way does Jesus act toward us. He takes us, poor smudges of paint, and he makes the blessed pictures of his grace out of us. It is neither the brush nor the paint he uses, but it is the skill of his own hand which does it all.—26.236, 237

Ephesians 2:12 *"Ye were without Christ . . . aliens . . . strangers . . . having no hope . . . without God."*

²¹⁴³ I saw on a board this morning words announcing that an asylum was to be built on a plot of ground for a class of persons who are described in three terrible words—"HELPLESS, HOMELESS, HOPELESS." These are the kind of people whom God receives; to them he gives his mercy. Are you helpless? He will help you. Are you homeless? He will house you. Are you hopeless? He is the hope of those who have no other confidence. Come then to him at once!—37.130, 131

Ephesians 3:20 *"Unto him that is able to do exceeding abundantly above all that we ask."*

²¹⁴⁴ God will give us much more than we ask. Abraham thought, "I cannot expect that Sarah will bear a child in her old age. God has promised me a seed, and surely it must be this child of Hagar. 'O that Ishmael might live before thee' " (Gen. 17:18). God granted him that, but he gave him Isaac as well, and all the blessings of the covenant.

There is Jacob. He kneels down to pray, and asks the Lord to give him bread to eat and raiment to put on. But what did his God give him? When he came back to Bethel he had two bands, thousands of sheep and camels, and much wealth.

It is said of David, "The king asked life of thee, and thou gavest him length of days for ever and ever" (Ps. 21:4). He gave him not only length of days himself, but a throne for his sons throughout all generations.

"Well," say you, "but is that true of New Testament prayers?"

Yes, it is so with New Testament pleaders, whether saints or sinners. They brought a man to Christ sick of the palsy and asked him to heal him, and he said, "Son . . . thy sins be forgiven thee" (Matt. 9:2). He had not asked that, had he? No, but God gives greater things than we ask for.

Hear that poor dying thief's humble prayer, "Lord, remember me when thou comest into thy kingdom" (Luke 23:42). Jesus replies, "Today shalt thou be with me in paradise" (Luke 23:43). He had not dreamed of such an honor.

Even the story of the prodigal teaches us this. He resolved to say, "I am not worthy to be called thy son; make me as one of thy hired servants" (Luke 15:19). What was the answer? "Bring forth the best robe and put it on him; put a ring on his hands, and shoes on his feet" (Luke 15:22).

Once you get into the position of an asker, you shall have what you never asked for, and never thought to receive.—28.551

Ephesians 4:12 *"For the perfecting of the saints, for the work of the ministry."*

2145 I believe that no Christian church can have prosperity if only a part of the members are active for the conversion of souls.—14.173

Ephesians 4:15 *"Speaking the truth in love."*

2146 Henry the Eighth would listen to Hugh Latimer though he denounced him to his face, and even sent him on his birthday a handkerchief, on which was marked the text, "Whoremongers and adulterers God will judge" (Heb. 13:4). Henry cried, "Let us hear honest Hugh Latimer." Even bad men admire those who tell them the truth.—26.403

Ephesians 4:32 *"Forgiving one another."*

2147 Does he say, "forgiving *another*"? No, that is not the text. It is "forgiving *one another.*" That means that if you have to forgive today, it is very likely that you will yourself need to be forgiven tomorrow, for it is "forgiving *one another.*"—24.692

341

Ephesians 6:11 *"Put on the whole armour of God."*

²¹⁴⁸ What do you want armor for at all? Because you are weak; because you are in danger. Then think to yourself, "It is because this head may be smitten with a deadly blow that I put on this helmet of salvation." When you buckle on your breastplate of righteousness, think to yourself, "This poor heart of mine would soon be wounded with mortal sin if it were not for God's infinite love in providing me this breastplate of impenetrable metal." When you fit on those shoes, when you receive "the preparation of the gospel of peace," think to yourself, "What a feeble creature I am! Even a poor thorn would lame me for my pilgrimage if God had not provided me with these protecting sandals." As you take each piece of armor, look at it and say to yourself, "I cannot be proud, for my need of this proves that I am a poor, weak creature."—20.521, 522

Ephesians 6:12 *"We wrestle not against flesh and blood."*

²¹⁴⁹ Have you never noticed in religious controversies how men will fall foul of each other and make personal remarks and abuse each other? What is that but forgetting what Christ's war is? We are not fighting *against* men; we are fighting *for* men.—3.42

342

Philippians 1:6 *"Confident . . . that he which hath begun a good work in you will perform it."*

²¹⁵⁰ A good old minister was once asked whether he believed in the final perseverance of the saints. "Well," said he, "I do not know much about that, but I firmly believe in the final perseverance of God, that where he has begun a good work he will carry it on until it is complete." To my mind, that truth includes the final perseverance of the saints. They persevere in the way of salvation because God keeps them in it.—44.585

Philippians 1:21 *"To me to live is Christ, and to die is gain."*

²¹⁵¹ Could I now have the greatest favor conferred on me that mortals could desire, I would ask that I might die. I never wish to have the choice given to me, but to die is the happiest thing man can have, because it is to lose anxiety, it is to slay care, it is to have the peculiar sleep of the beloved. To the Christian, death must be acceptable.—1.327

²¹⁵² It seems to me to be the highest stage of man to have no wish, no thought, no desire but Christ—to feel that to die were bliss if it were for Christ, that to live in penury and woe and scorn and contempt and misery were sweet for Christ, to feel that it did not matter what became of one's self, so that one's Master was but

exalted, to feel that though, like a leaf, you are blown in the blast, you are quite free from anxiety, as long as you feel that the Master's hand is guiding you according to his will. Though like the diamond you must be cut, you care not how sharply you may be cut, so that you may be made fit to be brilliant in *his* crown.—2.380

2153 It is not death to die if the death of Christ be but the life of the soul.—27.541

Philippians 2:12 *"Work out your own salvation."*

2154 We must work out our own salvation with fear and trembling, but not till he has worked *in* us can we work it *out.*—53.525

Philippians 3:8 *"Christ Jesus my Lord: for whom I have suffered the loss of all things."*

2155 Since you have not had to suffer the loss of all things, do you hold all things at God's disposal? Are you ready to part with comfort and honor for him? Since God has left your worldly comforts to you, have you used all things for his sake?—23.323, 324

Philippians 3:19 *". . . whose glory is in their shame."*

2156 It is an awful thing when a man is no longer conscious of shame, but a more awful thing still when he comes to glory in his shame, for then his damnation is not far off.—24.632

Philippians 4:4 *"Rejoice in the Lord always."*

2157 Sorrow for sin should be the keenest sorrow; joy in the Lord should be the loftiest joy.—18.533

Philippians 4:11 *"I have learned, in whatsoever state I am, therewith to be content."*

2158 There was another lesson which Paul had learned, but he does not tell us so. I have no doubt he had learned in whatsoever state he was, there*without* to be content, which is a good deal more.—21.8

Philippians 4:13 *"I can do all things through Christ which strengtheneth me."*

2159 We know not how much capacity for usefulness there may be in us. That ass's jawbone lying on the earth, what can it do? Nobody knows. It gets into Samson's hands. No one knows what it *cannot* do now that a Samson wields it. And you have often thought yourself to be as contemptible as that bone. You have said, "What can I do?" But when Christ by his Spirit grips you, what can you not do? Truly you may adopt Paul's language and say, "I can do all things through Christ which strengtheneth me."—11.154

Philippians 4:19 *"My God shall supply all your need."*

2160 He says to them, "You have helped me, but my God shall supply you. You have helped me

343

in one of my needs—clothing and food. I have other needs in which you could not help me. But my God shall supply *all* your need. You have helped me out of your deep poverty, but my God shall supply all your need out of his riches in glory. You have sent Epaphroditus to me with your offering. God shall send a better Messenger to you, for he shall supply all your needs by Christ Jesus."—29.170

²¹⁶¹ This precious text is one which, when we built the Orphanage, I caused to be cut on one of the pillars of the entrance. You will notice it inside the first columns on either side whenever you go there. This I took for the foundation of the Institution, and set my seal to it as true. And it has been so.—29.176

²¹⁶² My friend, Dr. Pierson, sent me an imitation of an American banknote, and on one side of it were these words: "My God shall supply all your need, according to his riches in glory by Christ Jesus." A splendid note that! It had our friend's name on the back, "Arthur T. Pierson," and he said to me, "If the Lord does not pay you, I will, for I have endorsed the note." I shall never have to look my brother Pierson up and tell him that the note he endorsed is of no value. There it stands, and stands forever. God will keep his word.—38.199

²¹⁶³ God knows how to make our enemies minister to our good, both temporally and spiritually. Once in old Popish times a good woman condemned to starve was asked by the judge in derision, "Now that you are condemned to starve, what can your God do for you?"

She boldly answered, "He can feed me from your table if he pleases."

It so happened that the judge's wife, melted to compassion by the boldness of one of her own sex, daily abstracted a portion of her own food to give to the poor woman in prison. And so her life was prolonged.—57.401

Colossians 1:19 *"It pleased the Father that in him should all fulness dwell."*

²¹⁶⁴ "All fulness." It tells us that Christ is substance and not shadow, fulness and not foretaste. This is good news for us, for nothing but realities will meet our case. What joy these words give to us when we remember that our vast necessities demand a fulness—"all fulness"—before they can be supplied!—17.122, 123

1 Thessalonians 1:8 *"From you sounded out the word of the Lord."*

²¹⁶⁵ It is the vocation of faith to be a speaker. When the heart believes, the mouth follows suit and makes confession. Faith made Noah a preacher, and it caused it to be said of Abel, "He being dead

yet speaketh" (Heb. 11:4). A silent faith is a questionable grace. Faith first speaks *to* Christ and then *for* Christ. It hears his voice and then acts as an echo by repeating it.—26.618

1 Thessalonians 2:4 *"So we speak; not as pleasing men, but God."*

2166 A minister said to me, "If I were to preach in your bold style, I would lose some of my richest people and offend the rest." And if he did, would he not have an easy conscience, and is not that worth more than money? The minister who cares for any man's opinion when he is doing his duty is unworthy of his office.—20.359

1 Thessalonians 4:13 *". . . that ye sorrow not, even as others which have no hope."*

2167 Tears are permitted to us, but they must glisten in the light of faith and hope. Jesus wept, but Jesus never repined. We, too, may weep, but not as those who are without hope, nor yet as though forgetful that there is greater cause for joy than for sorrow in the departure of our brethren.—18.98, 99

1 Thessalonians 4:17 *"Then we which are alive and remain shall be caught up . . . to meet the Lord."*

2168 I hear some brethren rejoicing that perhaps the Lord will come, and that therefore they will not die. I would sooner die, had I my choice. I see no comfort in the hope of not dying. If I die not I shall have lost what thousands will have who die, namely, actual fellowship with Christ in the grave.—14.599

1 Thessalonians 5:17 *"Pray without ceasing."*

2169 As you are tempted without ceasing, so pray without ceasing."—18.142

1 Thessalonians 5:18 *"In every thing give thanks."*

2170 I have not always found it easy to practice this duty; this I confess to my shame. When suffering extreme pain some time ago, a brother in Christ said to me, "Have you thanked God for this?" I replied that I desired to be patient, and would be thankful to recover. "But," said he, "in everything give thanks, not after it is over, but while you are still in it, and perhaps when you are enabled to give thanks for the severe pain, it will cease." I believe that there was much force in that good advice.—19.64

1 Thessalonians 5:25 *"Brethren, pray for us."*

2171 If I were allowed to offer only one request to you, it would be this: "Brethren, pray for us." Of what use can our ministry be without the divine blessing, and how can we expect the divine blessing unless it be sought for by the church of God? I would say it even with tears, "Brethren, pray

345

for us." Do not restrain prayer. On the contrary, be abundant in intercession, for only so can our prosperity as a church be increased, or even continued.—19.169

2172 Dismiss me or else intercede for me.—29.155

2 Thessalonians 3:10 *"If any would not work, neither should he eat."*

2173 The rule of the Christian life is, "If any man will not work, neither shall he eat." If you will not serve God as Christians, you shall not feed on the sweet things of the kingdom to your own soul's comfort.—20.70

1 Timothy 1:15 *"Christ Jesus came into the world to save sinners; of whom I am chief."*

2174 Between that word *save* and the next word, *sinners*, there is no adjective. It does not say, "penitent sinners," "sensible sinners," "grieving sinners," or "alarmed sinners." No, it only says, "sinners."—7.108

2175 "But I have been a thief!"
I suppose a thief is a sinner.
"But I have been a drunkard!"
A drunkard is a sinner.
"But I have lived in uncleanness!"
You are a sinner, then.
"But I have such a hard heart!"
Well, to have a hard heart is one of the greatest sins in the world.
"But I am unbelieving!"
Well, that is sin too.—8.380

2176 If I only had about a dozen words to speak and knew I must die, I would say, "This is a faithful saying and worthy of all acceptation, that Christ Jesus came into the world to save sinners"—11.178

2177 There is nothing but sham salvation for sham sinners. But you real sinners, you who have broken God's law and know it, feeling that you could not say a word against divine justice if you were now executed, come and welcome, for Jesus Christ came to save such as you are. Confess your sin, and when you have done so rest on the salvation provided in Christ Jesus.—24.311

2178 This is one of the "little Bibles," as Luther used to call them, the gospel in a verse, the essence of the whole Bible is here.—39.134

2179 I am not going to dispute with the apostle, and yet if he were here, I should be a little dubious as to his right to the title of "chief of sinners." I would ask him whether, if he were chief, I was not the next.—39.140

2180 The only qualification a physician seeks in his patient is that he is sick. The qualification for pardon from Christ is guilt. The qualification for imparting his fulness is your emptiness. That is all. And if you feel yourself to be so empty that you do not even feel your emptiness, if you feel yourself to be so hard that you do not even think you feel your hardness, then you are just the kind of man that Jesus Christ came to save.—47.426

2181 Christ Jesus came into the world to save sinners, but he never came here to spare their sins.—48.446

2182 Many people imagine that they cannot be saved because they are sinners, but that is the very reason why they can be saved. You remember how Martin Luther puts it. He says,"The devil came to me and said, 'Martin Luther, you are a big sinner. You are so great a sinner that you cannot be saved.' "
Luther replied, "I will cut off your head with your own sword, for I am a sinner, and I know that it is so. Christ Jesus came into the world to save sinners, so I believe he came to save me, and I have trusted my soul to him for time and eternity."—50.212

2183 When the devil wanted to make the biggest sinner that ever lived, he took an apostle to be the raw material, namely Judas, and made him the son of perdition. But when Christ wanted the greatest of preachers and the best of all apostles, he went right into the devil's camp and laid hold of "the chief of sinners," and made him become the mighty winner of souls.—60.285

1 Timothy 2:3, 4 *"God our Saviour; who will have all men to be saved."*

2184 You never have to drag mercy out of Christ, as money from a miser. It flows freely from him, like the stream from the fountain or the sunlight from the sun. If he can be happier, he is made happier by giving his mercy to the undeserving.—18.728

1 Timothy 2:5 *"There is ... one mediator between God and men, the man Christ Jesus."*

2185 Are you afraid to come to God through Christ, and do you want someone to speak to Christ for you? Oh, foolish heart! You do need a mediator in coming to God, but you do not need any in coming to Christ. Go to him just as you are, without making yourself any better. Go immediately, rags and sin and leprosy and blotches and sores and all.—5.166

1 Timothy 3:16 *"Without controversy great is the mystery of godliness. . . ."*

2186 Out of these six articles of Paul's creed, they all speak of Christ, from which I gather that if we are to preach the gospel faithfully, we must preach much concerning Jesus Christ. This must be the first, the midst, and end of our ministry. That man of whom it cannot be said that he preaches Christ does not behave himself rightly in the house of God. He evidently is not a messenger sent from heaven.—13.705

347

2187 I think it was Dr. Priestley, who was a Unitarian, and who had a brother who was a sound Calvinist minister. He agreed to let him preach for him on condition that he would promise not to preach on any controversial subject. The good man gave the promise, but repented afterward that he had done so. Yet he managed to redeem his promise and also to clear his conscience, for he preached from this text: "Without controversy great is the mystery of godliness: God was manifest in the flesh," from which he proved that the godhead of Christ is a truth about which no controversy could be allowed!—51.317, 318

1 Timothy 4:12 *"Let no man despise thy youth."*

2188 I recollect a young man going into a pulpit to address a congregation, and he began by saying that he hoped they would pardon his youth and forgive his impertinence in coming to speak to them. Some foolish old gentleman said, "How humble that young man is to talk like that!" But another said, "What a dishonor to his Lord and Master! If God sent him with a message to those people, what does it matter whether he is young or old? Such mock modesty as that is out of place in the pulpit." I think that second man was right. A true minister of the gospel is an ambassador for Christ, and do our ambassadors go to foreign courts with apologies for carrying messages from their sovereign?—56.488

2 Timothy 1:9 *"Who hath saved us, and called us . . . according to his own purpose."*

2189 It is a strange thing that men should be so angry against the purpose of God. We ourselves have a purpose. We permit our fellow creatures to have some will of their own, and especially in giving away their own goods. But my God is to be bound and fettered by men, and not permitted to do as he wills with his own.—12.427

2 Timothy 1:12 *"I know whom I have believed."*

2190 Paul does not say, "I know *what* I have believed," though that would have been true. He does not say, "I know *when* I have believed," though that would have been correct. Nor does he say, "I know *how much* I have believed," although he had well-weighed his faith. He does not even say, "I know *in whom* I have believed." He says expressly, "I know *whom* I have believed," as much as to say, "I know the person into whose hand I have committed my present condition and my eternal destiny. I know who he is, and I therefore, without any hesitation, leave myself in his hands."—32.422

2 Timothy 2:22 *"Flee also youthful lusts."*

²¹⁹¹ Sins of the flesh are never to be reasoned or parleyed with. There is no more reasoning with them than with the winds. Understanding is nonplused, for lust, like a hurricane of sand, blinds the eyes. We must fly. It is true valor in such a case to turn the back.—12.535

²¹⁹² What would you think of a man who went as near as he could to burning his house down, just to test how much fire it would stand? Or of one who cut himself with a knife to see how deep he could go without mortally wounding himself? Or of another who experimented as to how large a quantity of poison he could take? These are extreme follies, but not so great as that of a man who tries to see how much sin he may indulge in and yet be saved. I pray you, do not attempt such perilous experiments.—31.160

2 Timothy 3:16 *"All Scripture is given by inspiration of God."*

²¹⁹³ Whatever is in Scripture we accept as infallible truth.—19.634

2 Timothy 4:2 *"Preach the word . . . reprove, rebuke, exhort."*

²¹⁹⁴ I am sometimes accused of saying sharp things. The charge does not come home to my conscience with very great power. If anybody said I spoke smooth things, I think it would oppress me a great deal more. As long as there are evils in this world, God's ministers are bound to protest against them.—19.103

²¹⁹⁵ Little is that ministry worth which never chides you. If God never used his minister as a rod, depend on it, he will never use him as a pot of manna, for the rod of Aaron and the pot of manna always go together (Heb. 9:4), and he who is God's true servant will be both to your soul.—20.259

Titus 3:5 *"According to his mercy he saved us."*

²¹⁹⁶ If salvation be of mercy only, it is clear that our sin is by no means an impediment to our salvation. If it were of justice, our transgression of the law would render our salvation utterly impossible.—18.435

Hebrews 3:13 *"The deceitfulness of sin."*

²¹⁹⁷ If we preach against hypocrisy, hypocrites say, "Admirable! Admirable!" If we deal out threatenings against secret sin, secret sinners feel a little twinge, but forget it all and say, "An excellent discourse." They have hardened their neck against God's Word, have made their brows like flints and their hearts like adamant stones, and now they might just as well stay away from the house of God as not, for their soul has become hardened through the de-

ceitfulness of sin. And yet would I have them refrain from the means of grace? No, for with God nothing is impossible.—11.163, 164

2198 Man loves his own ruin. The cup is so sweet that though he knows it will poison him, yet he must drink it. And the harlot is so fair, that though he understands that her ways lead down to hell, yet like a bullock he follows to the slaughter till the dart goes through his liver. Man is fascinated and bewitched by sin.—13.268

Hebrews 3:18 *"And to whom sware he that they should not enter into his rest . . . ?"*

2199 God has never taken an oath, that I know of, against any class of persons, except unbelievers.—17.539

Hebrews 4:7 *"Harden not your hearts."*

2200 "Harden not your hearts." There is no need; they are hard enough already. "Harden not your hearts." There is no excuse, for why should you resist love? "Harden not your hearts." There can be no good in it. A man is the less a man in proportion to his loss of tenderness. "Harden not your hearts." You cannot soften them, but you can harden them. "Harden not your hearts," for this will be your ruin. It is suicide of soul.—26.441

Hebrews 4:12 *"The word of God is . . . sharper than any two-edged sword."*

2201 As you have seen hanging up in the butcher's shop the carcasses of animals cut right down in the center, so the Word of God is "piercing to the dividing of soul and spirit, of joints and marrow." It opens a man to himself and makes him see himself.—25.200

2202 The Word of God is like the sword of Goliath, which had been laid up in the sanctuary, of which David said, "There is none like it, give it me" (1 Sam. 21:9). Why did he like it so well? I think he liked it all the better because it had been laid up in the holy place by the priests. But I think he liked it best of all because it had stains of blood on it—the blood of Goliath. I like my own sword because it is covered with blood right up to the hilt—the blood of slaughtered sins and errors and prejudices has made it like the sword of Don Rodrigo, "of a dark and purple tint." The slain of the Lord have been many by the old gospel.—34.119

Hebrews 4:12 *"The word of God . . . is a discerner of the thoughts and intents of the heart."*

2203 Many and many a time have persons written to me or spoken with me and said, "Did you intend in the sermon to make a personal allusion to me?"

I have said, "Yes, I most certainly did. But I never saw you in my life and never knew anything about your case; only he that sent me commanded me to say this and that, and he knew who would be there to hear it, and he took care to guide my thoughts and words, so as to suit your case exactly, so that there could be no mistake about it."—26.399

Hebrews 4:15 *"But was in all points tempted like as we are, yet without sin."*

2204 This does not make Christ less tender, but more so. Anything that is sinful hardens, and inasmuch as he was without sin, he was without the hardening influence that sin would bring to bear on a man.—38.178

Hebrews 5:9 *"He became the author of eternal salvation unto all them that obey him."*

2205 But mark, not to one more. No soul that refuses to obey Christ shall have any part or lot in this matter.—20.275

Hebrews 6:4–6 *"It is impossible . . . to renew them again unto repentance."*

2206 I have met with persons of whom I have been told that they have been born again three or four times. After experiencing regeneration, they had fallen from grace altogether, and yet had been renewed again unto repentance. I must confess I have not believed what I have been told, for it is contrary to those many Scriptures which declare that "if these shall fall away, it is impossible to renew

them again unto repentance."—20.630

Hebrews 7:25 *"He is able to save them to the uttermost."*

2207 An Englishman, who had in a state of drunkenness committed a murder, was confined to prison for life. Here is the story of his conversion:

"A man called to see me and brought with him a parcel of books. I was thankful for anything. After I had read several of the books, I found a sermon preached by C. H. Spurgeon from the words, 'Wherefore he is able to save them to the uttermost.' Mr. Spurgeon referred to Palmer, who was then lying under sentence of death in Stafford Gaol. In order to bring home this text to his hearers, he said that if Palmer had committed many other murders, if he repents and seeks God's pardoning love in Christ, even he will be forgiven. I then felt that if Palmer could be forgiven, so might I. I sought, and blessed be God, I found! I am pardoned; I am free! I am a sinner saved by grace. Though a murderer, I have not yet sinned beyond 'the uttermost.' "

It made me very happy to think that a poor condemned murderer could thus be converted. Surely there is hope for every hearer and reader of this sermon, however guilty he may be.—33.719

Note: It was on June 8, 1856, at the age of 21, when CHS preached the sermon which God used to

351

convert this murderer. It is #84 in the complete sermon series. In this case, CHS was able to see this piece of spiritual fruit that had come from his preaching. But surely only eternity will reveal the full harvest of every faithful preacher's labors.

Hebrews 7:25 *"He ever liveth to make intercession for them."*

²²⁰⁸ If Christ appears in heaven for us, let us be glad to appear on earth for him. He owns us before God and the holy angels. Let us not be ashamed to confess him before men and devils. If Christ pleads with God for men, let us not be backward to plead with men for God. If he by intercession saves us to the uttermost, let us hasten to serve him to the uttermost. If he spends eternity in intercession for us, let us spend our time in intercession for his cause.—23.659

Hebrews 7:27 *"He offered up himself."*

²²⁰⁹ This truth leads us who accept it to be ready for self-sacrifice. It makes the believing man say, "As he offered himself for me, I must give myself for him."—46.454

Hebrews 9:22 *"Without shedding of blood is no remission."*

²²¹⁰ If the doctrine of the atonement be kicked at, the answer of Christ's minister should be to preach the atonement again and again and again in the plainest terms, and declare with even greater vigor and frequency the glorious substitutionary sacrifice of our Lord Jesus Christ in the place of his people. This is the very heart of the gospel, and it should be preached in your hearing every Sabbath day at the least. Leave that out? You have left out the life of the gospel.—24.89

²²¹¹ Now and then we meet with some squeamish person who says, "I cannot bear the mention of the word *blood.*" Such individuals will be horrified this morning, and it is intended that they should be. Sin is such a horrible thing that God has appointed blood to wash it away, that the very horror which the thought of it causes may give you some notion of the terrible nature of sin as God judges it. It is not without a dreadful bloodshedding that your dreadful guilt could by any possibility be cleansed. Sin-bearing and suffering for sin can never be pleasant things; neither should the type which sets it forth be pleasing to the observer. On great days of sacrifice the courts of the tabernacle must have seemed like a shambles, and fitly so, that all might be struck with the deadly nature of sin.—30.173

Hebrews 9:26 *"He appeared to put away sin."*

²²¹² He could not come to put away sin from those who had

352

none or from those who by their own efforts could put that sin away by themselves. It must be, then, for such as you are, who are hopelessly sinful.—16.37

Hebrews 9:27 *"It is appointed unto men once to die."*

²²¹³ As surely as you live you will die.—23.506

Hebrews 10:31 *"It is a fearful thing to fall into the hands of the living God."*

²²¹⁴ We are sometimes accused of using language too harsh, too ghastly, too alarming with regard to the world to come, but we shall not soon change our note. We solemnly believe that if we could speak thunderbolts, and our every look were a lightning flash, and if our eyes dropped blood instead of tears, no tones, words, gestures, or similitudes of dread could exaggerate the awful condition of a soul which has refused the gospel and is delivered over to justice.—16.186

Hebrews 11:6 *"Without faith it is impossible to please him."*

²²¹⁵ Some of the Indian tribes use little strips of cloth instead of money. I would not find fault with them if I lived there, but when I come to England, strips of cloth will not suffice. So honesty, sobriety, and such things may be very good among men, and the more you have of them the better. But all these things put together, without faith, do not please God.

Virtues without faith are white-washed sins.—1.20, 21

Hebrews 12:2 *"Looking unto Jesus."*

²²¹⁶ How frequently you who are coming to Christ look to yourselves. "Oh," say you, "I do not repent enough!" That is looking to yourself. "I do not believe enough!" That is looking to yourself. "I am too unworthy." That is looking to yourself. "I cannot discover," says another, "that I have any righteousness." It is quite right to say that you have not any righteousness, but it is quite wrong to look for any.—2.53

Hebrews 12:2 *"Who for the joy that was set before him endured the cross."*

²²¹⁷ What was "the joy that was set before him"? Oh, it's a thought that melts a rock. It makes a heart of iron move. The joy set before Jesus was principally joy of saving you and me!—5.95

Hebrews 12:6 *"Whom the Lord loveth he chasteneth."*

²²¹⁸ We ought to thank God that he will not let us sin without chastisement. If any of you are sinning and find pleasure without penalty in the self-indulgence, do not congratulate yourself on the apparent immunity with which you violate the laws of virtue, for *that* is the badge of the reprobate. To sin and never smart is the mark of those who will be damned; their smart, like their

doom, being in reserve and stored up for sorer judgment.—13.158

2219 I remember once being very, very ill, and a man who had no godliness but who was full of wicked wit accosted me thus: "You see, 'whom the Lord loveth he chasteneth.' "

"Yes," I said, "I am suffering greatly."

"Well," said he with a sneer, "I can do very well without such love, as long as I get off such chastening."

I burst into tears, and my very soul boiled over as I cried, "If the Lord were to grind me to powder, I would accept it at his hands, so that I might but have his love. It is you who need to be pitied, for sound as your health may be and merry as you look, you are a poor creature, since you have missed the only thing worth living for." I let fly a volley at him; I could not help it. I felt forced to stand up for my Master.—22.82

Hebrews 12:14 *"Follow ... holiness."*

2220 You will not gain holiness by standing still. Nobody ever grew holy without consenting, desiring, and agonizing to be holy. Sin will grow without sowing, but holiness needs cultivation. Follow it; it will not run after you. You must pursue it with determination, with eagerness, with perseverance, as a hunter pursues his prey.—16.390

Hebrews 12:14 *"... holiness, without which no man shall see the Lord."*

2221 If you occasionally get drunk, or if you now and then let fall an oath, or if in your business you would make twice two into five or three, according as your profit happens to run, do not talk about being a Christian. Christ has nothing to do with you, at least no more to do with you than he had to do with Judas Iscariot. You are very much in the same position. If without holiness, then much more without morality can no man expect to see the face of God with acceptance.—24.629, 630

2222 God smote an angel down from heaven for sin, and will he let man in with sin in his right hand? God would sooner extinguish heaven than see sin despoil it. It is enough for him to bear with your hypocrisies on earth. Shall he have them flung in his own face in heaven?—50.465

Hebrews 13:5 *"I will never leave thee, nor forsake thee."*

2223 These words are remarkably forcible in the original. You probably have heard that in the Greek there are no less than five negatives. We cannot well translate them into English except in such language as that of the verse we were singing just now:

The soul that on Jesus hath leaned for repose,

I will *not,* I will *not* desert to his foes;

That soul, though all hell should endeavor to shake,

I'll *never,* no *never,* no *never* forsake.—55.305

Note: Those words are from the hymn, "How Firm a Foundation" (author unknown).

Hebrews 13:8 *"Jesus Christ the same yesterday, and today, and for ever."*

2224 He is immutable; he will not change. He is all-wise; he need not change. He is perfect, he cannot change.—3.405

James 2:19 *"The devils also believe, and tremble."*

2225 If there be a faith (and there is) which leaves a man just what he was, and permits him to indulge in sin, it is the faith of devils. Perhaps not so good as that, for "the devils believe and tremble," whereas these hypocrites profess to believe and yet dare to defy God and seem to have no fear of him whatsoever.—27.682

James 2:26 *"Faith without works is dead."*

2226 We believe that men are saved by faith alone, but not by a faith which is alone. They are saved by faith without works, but not by a faith which is without works.—21.25, 26

2227 If that tree stands in the orchard, and when the springtime comes there is no bud, and when the summer comes there is no leafing or fruit bearing, but the next year and the next it stands there without bud or blossom or leaf or fruit, you would say it is dead, and you would be correct. It is not that the leaves could have made it live, but that the absence of the leaves is a proof that it is dead. So too is it with the professor. If he has life, that life must give fruits. If his faith has a root but no works, then depend on it, the inference that he is spiritually dead is certainly a correct one.—60.570

James 4:2 *"Ye lust, and have not."*

2228 See the boy hunting the butterfly, which flits from flower to flower while he pursues it ardently. At last it is within reach, and with his cap he knocks it down. But when he picks up the poor remains, he finds the painted fly spoiled by the act which won it. Thus may it be said of multitudes of men, "Ye lust, and have not."—28.542, 543

James 4:4 *"Know ye not that the friendship of the world is enmity with God?"*

2229 Let me imagine a man entering heaven without a change of heart. He comes within the gates. He hears a sonnet. He starts! It is to the praise of his *enemy.* He sees a throne, and on it sits one who is glorious, but it is his *enemy.* He walks streets of gold, but those streets belong to his *enemy.* He sees hosts of angels, but those hosts are the servants of his *enemy*. He is in an *enemy's* house, for he is at enmity with God. If the unregenerate man could enter heaven, I mention the oft-repeated saying of Whitefield, "he would be so unhappy in heaven that he would ask God to let him run down into hell for shelter."—1.155, 156

2230 I know a beloved sister in Christ who was baptized. She had moved in high circles, but after her baptism she received the cold shoulder. When I heard it, I said, "Thank God for it," for half her temptations were gone. If the world has turned its back on her, she will be all the more sure to turn her back on the world and live near to her Lord. The friendship of the world is enmity to God. Why should we seek it?—17.191

James 4:7 *"Submit yourselves therefore to God. Resist the devil, and he will flee from you."*

2231 If you do not submit to God, you never will resist the devil. And you will remain constantly under his tyrannical power. Which shall be your master, God or devil? One of these must. No man is without a master.—22.68

2232 If you will not submit, your faith is a lie, your hope is a delusion, your prayer is an insult, your peace is presumption, your end will be despair.—24.213

2233 Satan has no weapons of defense, and so when we resist him he must flee. A Christian man has both defensive and offensive weapons. He has a shield as well as a sword. But Satan has fiery darts and nothing else. I never read of his having any shield whatever. So when we resist him, he is bound to run away. He has no defense for himself, and the fact of our resistance is in itself a victory.—29.213

James 4:17 *"To him that knoweth to do good, and doeth it not, to him it is sin."*

2234 In a certain sense all offenses against the law of God come under the head of sins of omission, for in every sin of commission there is an omission—an omission, at least, of that godly fear which would have prevented disobedience. Our Lord has told us that the whole law is summarized in these two commandments: "Thou shalt love the Lord thy God with all thine heart, and thy neighbor as thyself" (Matt. 22:37–40). Since, then, every sin must be a breach of this comprehensive law, every sin must, from a certain aspect, be a sin of omission. Consider then, how multitudinous have been your omissions and mine! Have we loved the Lord our God with all our hearts? Perhaps you have omitted to love him at all.—14.602

2235 I am afraid that many are content because they can say, "We do not drink. We do not swear. We do not gamble. We do not lie." Who said you did? You ought to be ashamed of yourselves if you did any of those things. But is this enough? What are you actually *doing*? "To him that knoweth to do good, and doeth it not, to him it is sin."—33.671

2236 I do not know any subject that so much depresses me, humbles me, and lays me in the dust as the thought of my omissions. It is not what I have done about which I think so much, as of what I have *not* done. "You have been very useful," says one. Yes, but might I not have been ten times more useful?—44.20

James 5:11 *"Ye have heard of the patience of Job."*

2237 Did Job learn patience among his flocks or with his camels or with his children when they were feasting? No, he learned it when he sat among the ashes, and scraped himself with a potsherd, and his heart was heavy because of the death of his children. Patience is a pearl which is found only in the deep seas of affliction, and only grace can find it there, bring it to the surface, and adorn the neck of faith with it.—32.314

James 5:15 *"The prayer of faith shall save the sick."*

2238 You cannot always pray the prayer of faith in reference to any one thing. That prayer is often the distinct gift of God for an occasion. Others may ask your prayers, and sometimes you may plead very prevalently for them. But at another time that power is absent. You feel no liberty to offer a certain petition, but on the contrary feel held back in the matter. Well, be guided by this inward direction, and follow rather than press forward in such a case.—24.256

2239 I shall never forget the faith of a certain member of this church, who is still living. About eighteen or nineteen years ago I was very ill indeed. Most people thought that I would die. But one morning very early this good brother came down to my house and asked to see my wife. It was just about daybreak, and when she saw him he said to her, "I have spent all this night wrestling with God for your husband's life. We cannot afford to lose our pastor, and I feel sure that he is going to live. So I thought I would just walk here and tell you so."

"Thank you, thank you," said my wife, "I am very grateful for your prayers and for your faith."

It is not everybody who can pray to God like that, and we fail to obtain the blessings that we seek because we do not pray like that.—52.128, 129

1 Peter 1:8 *"Ye rejoice with joy unspeakable and full of glory."*

2240 Why is this joy of the Christian so unspeakable and full of glory? I think it is because it is so altogether divine. It is God's own joy; it is Christ's own joy.—12.369

1 Peter 1:19 *"The precious blood of Christ."*

2241 Two soldiers were on duty in the citadel of Gibraltar. One of them had obtained peace through the precious blood of Christ; the other was in very great distress of mind. It happened to be their turn to stand, both of them, sentinel the same night. There are many long passages in the rock, which are adapted to convey sounds a very great distance.

The soldier in distress of mind was ready to beat his breast for grief. He felt he had rebelled against God, and he could not find how he could be reconciled. Suddenly there came through the air what seemed to him to be a mysterious voice from heaven saying, "The precious blood of Christ." In a moment he saw it all. It was that which reconciled us to God, and he rejoiced with joy unspeakable and full of glory.

Who was it that had spoken these words? The other sentinel at the far end of the passage was meditating, when an officer came by. It was his duty to give a word for the night, and with soldier-like promptitude he did give it. But instead of giving the proper word, he was so taken up with his meditations that he said to the officer, "The precious blood of Christ." He corrected himself in a moment, but he had said it, and it passed along the passage and reached the ear for which God meant it. The man found peace and spent his life in the fear of God, being in later years the means of completing one of our excellent translations of the word of God into the Hindu language.—11.178

1 Peter 2:3 *"Ye have tasted that the Lord is gracious."*

2242 When a man is ill, he often loses his taste. The most delicious food is nauseous to him. His "soul abhorreth all manner of meat" (Ps. 107:18). But such is the flavor of the truth that the Lord is gracious, that it is more pleasant to us when we are sick than at any other time. The love of Christ is a delicious refreshment for a sufferer.—36.561, 562

1 Peter 2:7 *"Unto you therefore which believe he is precious."*

2243 This text calls to my recollection the opening of my ministry. As a lad of sixteen I stood up for the first time in my life to preach the gospel in a cottage to a handful of poor people who had come together for worship. I felt my own inability to preach, but I ventured to take this text: "Unto you therefore which believe he is precious." I do not think I could have said anything upon any other text. Christ was precious to my soul, and I was in the flush of my youthful love, and I could not be silent when a precious Jesus was the subject.—5.137

Note: As CHS and a friend were walking to this cottage in the village of Teversham, CHS told him he was praying that God would bless the friend's sermon. It was then that both boys discovered they each assumed the other would be the preacher! Neither had delivered a sermon before or felt qualified to do so. But when the time came, CHS reluctantly stepped forward. Thus began the ministry of the Prince of Preachers!

2244 Do you inquire, "Do I believe on the Son of God?" Then answer this: Is Christ precious to you? For "unto you who believe he is precious."—36.236

2245 This is a text on which I think I could preach in my sleep. And I believe that if I were dying and were graciously led into the old track, I could with my last breath pour out a heartful of utterance on this delightful verse. I am sure it contains the marrow of what I have always taught in the pulpit.—52.553

1 Peter 3:1 *"Wives, be in subjection to your own husbands; that . . . they . . . may . . . be won."*

2246 A husband was a very loose, depraved man of the world, but he had a wife who for many years bore with his ridicule and unkindness, praying for him night and day. One night, being at a drunken feast with a number of his companions, he boasted that his wife would do anything he wished; she was as submissive as a lamb. "Now," he said, "she has gone to bed hours ago, but if I take you all to my house at once, she will get up and entertain you and make no complaint." The matter ended in a bet, and away they went.

In a few minutes she was up and remarked that she was glad that she had two chickens ready, and if they would wait she would soon have a supper spread for them. The table was spread, and she took her place at it, acting the part of hostess with cheerfulness. One of the company exclaimed, "Madam, I am at a loss to understand how it is you receive us so cheerfully, for being a religious person you cannot approve of our conduct."

Her reply was, "I and my husband were both formerly unconverted, but by the grace of God I am now a believer in the Lord Jesus. I have daily prayed for my husband and done all I can to bring him to a better mind. But as I see no change in him, I fear he will be lost forever. And I have

359

made up my mind to make him as happy as I can while he is here."

They went away, and her husband said, "Do you really think I shall be unhappy forever?"

"I fear so," said she. "I would to God you would repent and seek forgiveness." That night patience accomplished her desire. He was soon found with her on the way to heaven.—20.465, 466

1 Peter 3:18 *"Christ . . . suffered for sins."*

2247 One thing I know: Christ thinks more of our sins than he does of our righteousness, for he gave himself for our sins. I never heard that he gave himself for our righteousness.—44.377

1 Peter 3:18 *"Christ . . . suffered . . . the just for the unjust, that he might bring us to God."*

2248 No soul ever ate a morsel more dainty than this one—*substitution.* I do think that this is the grandest truth in heaven and earth—Jesus Christ the just one died for the unjust, that he might bring us to God. It is meat to my soul. I can feed on it every day, and all the day.—16.322

2249 "The just for the unjust" I can understand. But the "just dying for the just" would be a double injustice—an injustice that the just should be punished at all, and another injustice that the just should be punished for them. Oh, no! If Christ died, it must be because there was a penalty to be paid for sin committed. Hence he must have died for those who had committed the sin.—20.496

1 Peter 4:11 *"If any man speak, let him speak as the oracles of God."*

2250 Reckon that every sermon is a wasted sermon which is not Christ's Word. Believe that all theology is rotten rubbish which is not the Word of the Lord. Do not be satisfied with going to a place of worship and hearing an eloquent discourse, unless the sum and substance of it is the Word of the Lord. My brothers and sisters, whether you teach children or their parents, do not think you have done any good unless you have taught the Word of the Lord. For saving purposes we must have the Lord's Word, and nothing else.—33.440

1 Peter 5:7 *"Casting all your care upon him; for he careth for you."*

2251 There is nothing Christ dislikes more than for his people to make show of him and not to use him. He loves to be worked. He is a great laborer. He always was for his Father, and now he loves to be a great laborer for his brethren. The more burdens you put on his shoulders, the better he will love you. Cast your burden on him.—2.398, 399

2252 I heard of a man who was walking along the high road with a pack on his back. He was growing weary and was therefore glad when a gentleman came along in a carriage and asked him to take a seat with him. The gentleman noticed that he kept his pack strapped to his shoulders, and so he said, "Why do you not put your pack down?"

"Why, sir," said the traveler, "I did not venture to impose. It was very kind of you to take me up, and I could not expect you to carry my pack as well."

"Why," said his friend, "do you not see that whether your pack is on your back or off your back, I have to carry it?"

My hearer, it is so with your trouble. Whether you worry or do not worry, it is the Lord who must care for you.—59.129

2 Peter 1:10 *"Make your calling and election sure."*

²²⁵³ When Mr. Whitefield was once asked to use his influence at a general election, he returned answer to his lordship who requested him that he knew very little about general elections, but that if his lordship took his advice, he would make his own particular "calling and election sure." It was a very proper remark.—3.129

²²⁵⁴ I beseech you, give no sleep to your eyes till you have read your title clear to mansions in the skies. Shall your eternal destiny be a matter of uncertainty to you? What! Is heaven or hell involved in this matter, and will you rest until you know which of these shall be your everlasting portion? Are you content while it is a question whether God loves you or is angry with you?—6.46

2 Peter 1:19 *"We have also a more sure word of prophecy."*

²²⁵⁵ Peter was with Christ on the Mount of Transfiguration, and nothing could shake Peter's conviction that he had been there in the midst of that heavenly glory. And yet for all that, Peter says concerning the inspired word, "We have a more sure word of prophecy." He felt that even the memory of that vision, which he had assuredly seen, did not always yield to him so much assurance as did the abidingly inspired Word of God. You ought to feel the same.—37.16

2 Peter 1:21 *"Holy men of God spake as they were moved by the Holy Ghost."*

²²⁵⁶ The best interpreter of a book is generally the man who wrote it. The Holy Ghost wrote the Scriptures. Go to him to get their meaning, and you will not be misled.—18.616

2 Peter 2:7 *"And delivered just Lot, vexed with the filthy conversation of the wicked."*

²²⁵⁷ If Lot had not escaped, he would have perished with the men of Sodom. He could not endure them. He was vexed with their filthy conversation. How

horrible, then, would it have been for him to perish with them! I cannot bear to think that some of you upright, moral people may yet be lost. You were never drunkards, and yet you will perish with the drunkards unless you repent and trust in Jesus. You were never swearers, but you will be as surely damned as the blasphemers will be unless you come to Christ. You cannot bear unchastity or filthiness of language. There is much about you that is most amiable and excellent. But even to you the Savior says, "Ye must be born again" (John 3:7). And if you are not born again, if you have no faith in Christ, you will as surely perish as will the worst of men.— 41.78

2 Peter 2:21 *"It had been better for them not to have known the way of righteousness. . . ."*

2258 If you go down to destruction from the borders of salvation, it will be sevenfold destruction. If you die with Jesus weeping over you, as he did over Jerusalem, you will die horribly. If you sink down to hell with that word in your ears, "How often would I have gathered you, as a hen gathereth her chickens under her wings, and ye would not" (Matt. 23:37), your sinking will be like that of a millstone in the sea. If you perish under a gospel ministry, it were better for you that you had never been born.—33.365, 366

2 Peter 3:3, 4 *"There shall come . . . scoffers . . . saying, Where is the promise of his coming?"*

2259 Every time a blasphemer opens his mouth to deny the truth of revelation, he will help to confirm us in our conviction of the very truth which he denies. The Holy Ghost told us by the pen of Peter that it would be so.— 43.421

2 Peter 3:9 *"The Lord is . . . not willing that any should perish."*

2260 While I have prayed, "Come quickly," I have often felt inclined to contradict myself and cry, "Yet tarry for a while, good Lord. Let mercy's day be lengthened. Let the heathen yet receive the Savior." We may desire the coming of the Lord, but we ought also to be in sympathy with the tarrying of the Most High, to which his loving heart inclines him.—19.438

1 John 1:4 *"These things write we unto you, that your joy may be full."*

2261 I infer from this that everything which is revealed to us in Scripture has for its intention the filling up of the Christian's joy.— 60.232

1 John 1:7 *"The blood of Jesus Christ his Son cleanseth us from all sin."*

2262 If you have perpetrated all the sins that ever were committed by men or devils, if you have defiled yourself with all the blackness that could be raked out of the lowermost kennels of hell, if you have spoken the most damnable blasphemies and followed the most outrageous vices, yet Jesus Christ is an infinite Savior, and nothing can exceed the merit of his precious blood.—16.213

2263 The sin-offering under the law was only for sins of ignorance. But we have a far better sacrifice for sin than that, for "the blood of Jesus Christ his Son cleanseth us from *all* sin." Not from sins of ignorance only, but from all sin.—18.246

2264 Do you remember the story of Martin Luther when Satan came to him, as he thought, with a long black roll of his sins, which truly might make a swaddling band for the world? To the archenemy Luther said, "Yes, I must own to them all. Have you any more?" So the foul fiend went his way and brought another longer roll, and Martin Luther said, "Yes, yes, I must own to them all. Have you any more?" The accuser of the brethren, being expert at the business, soon supplied him with a further length of charges, till there seemed to be no end to it. Martin waited till no more were forthcoming, and then he cried, "Write at the bottom of the whole account, 'The blood of Jesus Christ cleanseth us from all sin.' "—25.466

1 John 2:1 *"If any man sin, we have an advocate with the Father, Jesus Christ."*

2265 Jesus is a *sinner's* Savior. It is not written, "If any man be holy, he has an advocate."—13.136

1 John 3:9 *"Whosoever is born of God doth not commit sin."*

2266 "What," say you, "does a Christian never sin?"

Not with the new nature. The new nature never sins; the old nature sins. It is the darkness which is dark; the light is not darkness. It is not possible that the Christ who dwells in us could sin. What sin there is in a believer comes from the remnants of corruption. The spirit which is implanted never can sin and never can have communion with sin, any more than light can have communion with darkness.—11.644

1 John 4:7 *"Love is of God."*

2267 The efficient cause of our love is the Holy Spirit of God. We would never have had a spark of love for Jesus if it had not been bestowed on us by the divine worker. Well said John, "Love is of God." Our love to Christ is one beam from himself, the Sun. Certainly a man can no more naturally love Christ than a horse can fly.—11.350

1 John 4:19 *"We love him, because he first loved us."*

²²⁶⁸ Think how much he must have loved you when you were going on in sin. You used to call his ministers hypocrites, his people fools. His Sabbaths were idle days with you. His precious book was unread. You never sought his grace. Perhaps you used to curse him, perhaps persecute him in his children, and yet he loved you. And when his Spirit came after you, you tried to quench him. You would not attend the place where the arrow had first stuck in your conscience. You went to the theater. You tried to quench the Spirit, but his love would not be mastered by you. He had resolved to have you, and the bridegroom would win your heart.—6.313

1 John 5:19 *"The whole world lieth in wickedness."*

²²⁶⁹ Some think that the old gospel cannot be right because everybody says it is out of date and wrong. That is one reason for being the more sure that it is right, for the world lies in the wicked one, and its judgment is under his sway. What are multitudes when they are all under the influence of the father of lies? The grandest majority in the world is a minority of one when that man is on God's side.—25.28

Jude 13 *"To whom is reserved the blackness of darkness for ever."*

²²⁷⁰ "Reserved" seats in hell! Did you ever think of that?—12.342

Jude 20 *"Praying in the Holy Ghost."*

²²⁷¹ That prayer which is not in the Holy Ghost is in the flesh. Only the prayer which comes from God can go to God.—12.614, 615

Jude 24 *"Now unto him that is able to keep you from falling. . . ."*

²²⁷² It strikes me just now—the author's name is Jude—Judas. Did he recollect Judas, his namesake that was called Iscariot, as he penned these words?—11.329

²²⁷³ He who can keep the saint from stumbling can bring the sinner into the right way. The same grace that can preserve the child of God from falling into sin can bring you out of sin. And as we have to look wholly to Christ, certainly you must do so.—39.93

²²⁷⁴ There is no doxology in Scripture which I enjoy more than that one at the end of the Epistle of Jude.—50.463

Revelation 1:7 *"Every eye shall see him . . . and all . . . shall wail because of him."*

²²⁷⁵ There is no true mourning for sin until the eye has seen

Christ. It is a beautiful remark of an old divine, that eyes are made for two things at least. First, to look with, and next, to weep with. The eye which looks to the pierced One is the eye which weeps for him.—33.521

Revelation 2:4 *"Thou hast left thy first love."*

2276 I was reading only the other day of an account of my ceasing to be popular. It was said my chapel was now nearly empty, that nobody went to it. I was exceedingly amused and interested. "Well, if it comes to that," I said, "I shall not grieve or cry very much. But if it is said the church has left its zeal and first love, that is enough to break any honest pastor's heart."—4.423

Revelation 2:7 *"He that hath an ear, let him hear what the Spirit saith unto the churches."*

2277 I have heard of a man who once went to chapel to hear the singing, and as soon as the minister began to preach, he put his fingers in his ears and would not listen. But some tiny insect settled on his face, so that he was obliged to take one finger out of his ear to brush it away. Just then the minister said, "He that hath ears to hear, let him hear." The man listened, and God met with him at that moment to his soul's conversion. He went out a new man, a changed character.—1.304

Revelation 3:16 *"Because thou art lukewarm . . . I will spue thee out of my mouth."*

2278 Five thousand members of a church all lukewarm will be five thousand impediments. But a dozen earnest, passionate spirits determined that Christ shall be glorified and souls won must be more than conquerors. In their very weakness and fewness will reside capacities for being the more largely blessed of God. Better nothing than lukewarmness.—20.424

Revelation 3:17 *"Thou sayest, I am rich . . . and knowest not that thou art wretched . . . and poor."*

2279 This church, which was so rich in its own esteem, was utterly bankrupt in the sight of the Lord. It had no real joy in the Lord; it had mistaken its joy in itself for that. It had no real beauty of holiness on it; it had mistaken its formal worship and fine building and harmonious singing for that. It had no deep understanding of the truth and no wealth of vital godliness; it had mistaken carnal wisdom and outward profession for those precious things. It was poor in secret prayer, which is the strength of any church. It was destitute of communion with Christ, which is the very lifeblood of religion. But it had the outward semblance of these blessings, and walked in a vain show.—20.425

Revelation 3:20 *"Behold, I stand at the door, and knock."*

²²⁸⁰ You remember what our Lord Jesus said of the Laodicean church—that he would spew it out of his mouth (Rev. 3:16). But what does he say afterward? "Behold, I stand at the door and knock." He says to the same church, "If any man opens the door, I will enter in"—enter into the same church which had so disgusted him—"and will sup with him"—sup with that church of which just now he was so sick. Come, then, you lukewarm ones, and in coming to Jesus you will cease to be disgusting to him.—31.492

Revelation 3:20 *"I will come in to him, and will sup with him, and he with me."*

²²⁸¹ There is no cure for lukewarmness like a good supper with Christ. If he enters in and sups with you, and you with him, your lukewarmness will disappear at once.—44.320

Revelation 4:1 *"A door was opened in heaven."*

²²⁸² Christ is that door. If you come to Christ you have come to God. If you trust in Jesus you are saved. The door to the ark was wide enough to admit the hugest beasts as well as the tiniest animals, and the door into God's mercy is wide enough to let in the greatest sinner as well as the more refined moralist. He that comes to Christ comes to heaven. He is sure of heaven who is sure of Christ.—15.472

Revelation 7:9 *"Lo, a great multitude, which no man could number."*

²²⁸³ John was a great mathematician, and he managed to count up to one hundred and forty-four thousand of all the tribes of the children of Israel. But that was only a representative number for the Jewish church. As for the church of God, comprehending the Gentile nations, he gave up all idea of computation and confessed that it is a number which no man can number.—25.318

Revelation 12:11 *"They overcame him by the blood of the Lamb."*

²²⁸⁴ The blood of Jesus is the life of faith and the death of sin. All the saints overcome through the blood of the Lamb.—23.227

Revelation 19:15 *"Out of his mouth goeth a sharp sword."*

²²⁸⁵ He bears a sword. But where? It is in his mouth! Strange place! Yet this is the only sword my Lord and Master wields. Muhammad subdued men with the scimitar, but Christ subdues men with the gospel. We have but to tell out the glad tidings of the love of God, for this is the sword of Christ with which he smites the nations. Be his mouths, my brethren.—25.23

Revelation 20:12 *"I saw the dead, small and great, stand before God."*

²²⁸⁶ Pharaoh! You must see a greater than Moses. Herod! You must see the young Child on his throne. Judas! You hanged yourself to escape the judgment of your conscience, but by no means can you escape the judgment of your God. Though four thousand years have elapsed since men died, yet when the trumpet rings out, their bodies shall live again, and they must all come forth, each one, to answer for himself before the Judge of all the earth.—27.312

Revelation 20:14 *"The lake of fire."*

²²⁸⁷ "Ah," says one, "that is a metaphor."

Yes, I know it is, and a metaphor is but a shadow of the reality. Then, if the shadow be a lake of fire, what must the reality be? If we can hardly bear to think of a "worm that never dieth" and a "fire that never shall be quenched" (Mark 9:44) and of a lake whose seething waves of fire dash over undying and hopeless souls, what must hell be in very deed? The descriptions of Scripture are, after all, but condescensions to our ignorance, partial revealings of fathomless mysteries. But if these are so dreadful, what must the full reality be?—16.132

Revelation 21:4 *"God shall wipe away all tears from their eyes."*

²²⁸⁸ If God would take me to heaven this morning, if he did not come in and for a special act of his omnipotence dry up that fountain of tears, I would almost forget the glories of paradise in the midst of my own shame that I have not preached more earnestly, prayed more fervently, and labored more abundantly for Christ.—11.441

Revelation 21:5 *"Behold, I make all things new."*

²²⁸⁹ Has he made *you* new? The gates of heaven are shut against the old creation. The floods destroyed it at the first; the floods of fire shall destroy it yet again. If you are not created new, you shall not outlive the general blaze.—11.648

Revelation 22:17 *"Whosoever will, let him take the water of life freely."*

²²⁹⁰ Are you willing to be saved? Are you willing to forsake sin, willing to take Christ to be your Master? Are you willing to be made happy, willing to escape hell? Strange that it should be necessary to ask such questions, but still it is. Are you willing? Then remember that whatever may be against you—whatever may have defiled you—however black, however filthy, however worthless you may be, you are invited this day to take of the fountain of the water of life freely,

for you are willing, and it is said, "Whosoever will, let him come."

Says one, "God knows I am willing, but still I do not think I am worthy."

No, I know you are not, but what has that to do with it? It is not "Whosoever is *worthy*," but "whosoever *will*."—5.437

2291 Nature's gospel is "make." Just change the letter and you have the gospel of grace, which is "take."—23.9

2292 The solemnity of this invitation lies partly in the fact that it is placed at the very end of the Bible, and placed there because it is the sum and substance, the aim and object of the whole Bible. It is like the point of the arrow, and all the rest of the Bible is like the shaft and the feathers on either side of it.—46.350

Subject Index

Scripture Index

Biblical Names Index

Nonbiblical Names Index